Teaching as *Jesus* Taught

Books by Roy B. Zuck

A Biblical Theology of the New Testament (editor)
A Biblical Theology of the Old Testament (editor)
Adult Education in the Church (coeditor)
Basic Bible Interpretation
Barb, Please Wake Up!
The Bib Sac Reader (coeditor)
The Bible Knowledge Commentary (coeditor)
Biblical Archaeology Leader's Guide
Childhood Education in the Church (coeditor)
Christian Youth: An In-Depth Survey (coauthor)
Church History Leader's Guide
Creation: Evidence from Scripture and Science
Communism and Christianity Leader's Guide
Devotions for Kindred Spirits (editor)
How to Be a Youth Sponsor
*Integrity of Heart, Skillfulness of Hands: Biblical and Leadership
    Studies in Honor of Donald K. Campbell* (coeditor)
Job
Learning from the Sages: Selected Studies on the Book of Proverbs
    (editor)
Reflecting with Solomon: Selected Studies on the Book of Ecclesiastes
    (editor)
Sitting with Job: Selected Studies on the Book of Job (editor)
Teaching as Jesus Taught
Teaching with Spiritual Power
The Life of Christ Commentary (coeditor)
Vital Biblical Issues (editor)
Vital Contemporary Issues (editor)
Vital Ministry Issues (editor)
Vital Theological Issues (editor)
Youth and the Church (coeditor)
Youth Education in the Church (coeditor)

Teaching as *Jesus* Taught

Roy B. Zuck

Wipf and Stock Publishers
150 West Broadway • Eugene OR 97401

Wipf and Stock Publishers
150 West Broadway
Eugene, Oregon 97401

Teaching As Jesus Taught
By Zuck, Roy B.
©1995 Zuck, Roy B.
ISBN: 1-57910-862-8
Publication date: January, 2002
Previously published by Baker Book House, 1995.

To **Howard G. Hendricks**
my teacher, mentor, and colleague
at Dallas Theological Seminary
who first stimulated my interest
in seeking to teach as Jesus taught

Contents

List of Tables

1

Is It Possible to Teach as Jesus Taught?

Do you remember a favorite teacher, someone whose classroom sessions were interesting, stimulating, exciting? Someone who in some way made a lasting impression on your life?

I well recall Mr. Dewey Fellars, teacher of the Junior Boys Sunday school class. I and about eight other active boys sat in two wooden pews in the front right side of the church. A curtain behind the second pew was one of several drapes separating six classes that met in the small auditorium of that Baptist church. The uncomfortable homemade pews, the distracting din of six teachers and classes all talking at once, the absence of visuals to help focus and sustain our interest—this was hardly the ideal classroom setting! A "Sunday School of the Year" award was never forthcoming.

And yet Mr. Fellars displayed excellent characteristics as a teacher of us nine-, ten-, and eleven-year-olds. We didn't mind sitting on uncomfortable pews for about forty minutes each Sunday because we knew he was interested in us. We knew he loved the Lord and the Bible, and wanted us to do the same. He didn't have a lot of variety in his teaching, but he did ask us questions from time to time, questions that made us think about the Bible passage we were studying. As this auto mechanic, fingers blackened with grease that never seemed to wash off, taught us

9

the Bible and how to live it, we sensed he was genuine. He lived what he taught. He modeled Christ-like love and concern.

Is it any wonder he made an indelible impression on us? Though un-schooled in higher levels of education, he knew, loved, and lived the Bible.

Perhaps as you reflect on your school days—whether in Sunday school as a child, or in high school or college—you remember someone whose teaching and personality attracted you and indelibly marked you. What was it about that person or his or her teaching that contrib-uted to that impact?

On the other hand, do you remember a teacher with the opposite kind of effect? A teacher who was boring, who seemed as anxious for the class to end as you did? Someone whose teaching you endured be-cause you had no choice?

I remember such a teacher. He read his notes in a lulling-to-sleep monotone; he seemed to resent questions from the class; the class ses-sions held no variety—always the droning, visual-less lectures, result-ing in the students figuratively if not actually yawning while thinking to themselves, "So what?"

What made the difference between these two teachers? Why did the man with a sixth-grade education make an impact on my life that has lasted for years, whereas the other teacher, with more than twice as many years of education as Mr. Fellars, leave the opposite impression? Why do I think of one as an effective teacher (though lacking in some respects educationally) and the other as ineffective? I believe it is be-cause one was following, perhaps unknowingly, some of the ways Jesus taught, whereas the other, also perhaps unknowingly, seemed to violate some of those principles.

Read through the Gospels, and you quickly conclude that Jesus was a dynamic, remarkably effective teacher. Never boring, always stimu-lating. Never obtuse, always clear. Never pompous or distant, always personal and lovingly concerned. No wonder people who heard him teach often addressed him as "Teacher"!

The Gospels stand as a ready resource of ideas and examples on how to teach. Studying how Jesus taught can prompt us to improve our own teaching, to enhance our own effectiveness in communicating the Bible to others.

Why Study How Jesus Taught?

Addressing Jesus' teaching procedures and analyzing his educational strategy can help us in two ways.

First, it can help trigger our thinking about our own teaching. Studying how Jesus taught can prompt us to ask several questions:

What is teaching?
What should teaching accomplish?
How should we teach?
What results should we work toward and pray for?
How can we improve?
What steps can we take to be more effective teachers?

As you trace Jesus' teaching in the Gospels, ask yourself these questions:

Why did people call him a teacher?
What qualities made him a teacher?
Whom did he teach—and when and where?
How did he teach?
How did he model what he taught?
How did he stimulate his learners to think?
How did he capture and hold his students' attention?
How did he react to various kinds of students?
How did he illustrate what he taught?
How did he vary what he taught?
How did he relate his teaching to individuals' needs?
How did he involve his learners in the teaching process?
Why were people amazed at his teaching?
How did his teaching content and style differ from the teaching of his contemporaries?
How were people's lives changed as a result of his teaching?

Second, examining Jesus' teaching can help us transfer ideas from his teaching to ours. Because Jesus was such an effective teacher, we should be open to seeing how he taught so we can incorporate some of those principles and procedures in our own teaching. Ask yourself, What can I learn from him about the following?

Knowing my subject more thoroughly
Knowing my students more intimately
Beginning my lessons more interestingly
Attracting interest more immediately
Aiming my lessons more pointedly
Arousing curiosity more frequently
Motivating my students more actively

Asking questions more provocatively
Answering questions more thoughtfully
Lecturing truths more effectively
Telling stories more captivatingly
Presenting Scripture more enthusiastically
Giving facts more picturesquely
Varying lessons more frequently
Involving students more meaningfully
Quoting Scripture more knowledgeably
Illustrating truths more colorfully
Visualizing concepts more graphically
Applying truths more specifically
Relating truths more personally
Changing lives more deeply
Encouraging students more tenderly
Affirming students more lovingly
Giving counsel more carefully
Correcting students more firmly
Helping students more compassionately
Meeting student needs more definitely
Testing student learning more accurately
Modeling truth more consistently
Associating with students more informally

Certainly Jesus modeled all thirty of these elements of teaching. He knew his subject thoroughly, he knew his students intimately, he began his teaching sessions in interesting, captivating ways, and so forth. Do you want to be a more skillful teacher? Then why not look in the Gospels for the ways Jesus accomplished these thirty functions and see how you can do the same? Mirror your teaching against his, in the light of these thirty aspects—and become a better teacher. As his way of teaching is more consistently reflected in yours, you can teach as Jesus taught.

Is It Possible to Teach as Jesus Did?

Some readers may question whether it is possible to teach as Jesus taught. After all, he is unique in several ways: the unique Son of God with a unique mission. Is it proper, then, to think we can model our teaching after his?

True, Jesus Christ is the Son of God. He was God manifest in the flesh (John 1:14). In him "all the fullness of the Deity lives in bodily form"

(Col. 2:9). Existing from all eternity as the second Person of the Trinity, he possesses all the attributes of the Godhead. He is all-knowing, all-powerful, everywhere present, and is perfect and complete in his sovereignty, holiness, majesty, glory, purity, righteousness, grace, love, and mercy. He created, he forgives sins, he performs miracles, he receives our worship, love, and obedience. Because he was God, he was sinless. He "had no sin" (2 Cor. 5:21), he was "without sin" (Heb. 4:15), he "committed no sin" (1 Pet. 2:22), and "in him is no sin" (1 John 3:5). No wonder no one could prove him "guilty of sin" (John 8:46). How then can we copy him?

The answer lies in the fact that Jesus Christ is also human. He is the eternal God ("being in very nature God," Phil. 2:6) but he is also the incarnate Son, that is, God manifest in a fleshly, human body. Born of a virgin, he became one of us ("being made in human likeness," Phil. 2:7).

As a human being, Jesus grew (Luke 2:52), he became tired (John 4:6), he was hungry and thirsty (John 4:7–8), he was tempted (Matt. 4:1–10; Luke 4:1–12; Heb. 4:15), he grieved (John 11:35, 38), and he experienced anger (Mark 3:5), sorrow (Matt. 26:37–38), joy (John 15:11; 17:13), and death (John 19:30). And because of that humanity, he taught in ways we can emulate. But because he was God, we accept the fact that we cannot do everything he did. We have limitations that he as the Son of God did not have.

Other readers may question whether we can teach as Jesus taught because his teaching situations differed from ours. He had no formal classroom. He followed no set curriculum or class schedule. He gave no course credit to his students, and they were never formally graduated. He had no modern devices such as slides, films, overhead projectors, flipcharts, flannelboards, puppets, or chalkboards. He never required written assignments or gave written examinations. He often taught outdoors or as he was walking along—ways of teaching seldom used today.

But do these facts mean we cannot learn from how he taught? Although our teaching environment, instructional situations, educational tools, and social milieu differ, much can be gained from the way he taught. How he gained interest, how he stimulated thinking, involved students, told stories, applied truths, answered questions, dealt with individuals of varying personalities and differing attitudes toward him, motivated and corrected students—these are a few of the many areas where we can learn from his style.

As LeBar wrote,

Students of Scripture sometimes wonder how our teaching today can be compared with Christ's teaching when He never taught in a classroom and we seldom teach outside one. What difference do four walls make? Often they make the teaching atmosphere formal and mechanical, but not necessarily so. A teacher who realizes that only individuals can change and grow will act as informal and make as much use of personal conversation as Christ did.[1]

Still others argue against the idea that modern-day teachers can follow Jesus' teaching style by pointing out that he has supernatural knowledge. Yes, his wisdom is perfect, his knowledge complete. He knew the Scriptures thoroughly and he had "a perfect and intuitive knowledge of human nature."[2] Obviously he exceeds us here, for as God he is omniscient.

Balancing the truth of our limited knowledge, however, are the facts that believers have the mind of Christ (1 Cor. 2:16) and that the Holy Spirit is our Teacher (John 14:26; 16:12–19; 1 Cor. 2:10–16). We do not have perfect knowledge of the Scriptures, complete wisdom, or full insight into the human heart, but we can grow in spiritual wisdom. The Book of Proverbs repeatedly challenges believers to be wise. It stands replete with numerous statements about how to become wise in God's eyes and about the lasting benefits of growing in spiritual wisdom. As we obey Jesus, we, like Stephen, can be "full of the Spirit and wisdom" (Acts 6:3). The apostle Paul wrote that he was "admonishing and teaching everyone with all wisdom" (Col. 1:28). Therefore it is no surprise that he urged believers to "teach and admonish one another with all wisdom" (3:16).

Teach as Jesus taught? Not in *every* way. He is God; we are humans with finite limitations. His teaching environment differed from ours. And his knowledge and wisdom, being supernatural, are complete. "After excluding all the disparities, what is left for us to apply? A great deal, and all of it is in the four gospels. We cannot perform the supernatural, but we can still learn to teach as he taught."[3]

"If one wishes to teach, what better example is there than that of the greatest teacher, our Lord Jesus Christ."[4]

The methods Jesus used are as effective today as when he used them. The problems he confronted are "similar to those confronted by men in all ages when seeking to impart religious truths."[5] The truths he taught are to be communicated today as well, for we are to teach others "to obey everything [he has] commanded" (Matt. 28:20). The educational

1. Lois E. LeBar, *Education That Is Christian* (Westwood, N.J.: Revell, 1958), 50.
2. Robert G. Delnay, *Teach as He Taught* (Chicago: Moody, 1987), 10.
3. Ibid., 12.
4. Francis Herbert Roberts, "The Teaching Methods of Jesus Christ" (Th.M. thesis, Dallas Theological Seminary, 1955), 2.
5. Donald Guthrie, "Jesus," in *A History of Religious Educators*, ed. Elmer L. Towns (Grand Rapids: Baker, 1975), 16.

principles he followed are universally applicable, having been utilized by many teachers throughout church history. Dedicated Christian teachers who have followed his teaching style have seen the Holy Spirit work through them to foster spiritual growth in students of all ages.

The challenge stands: Teach as Jesus taught!

Your Turn . . .

Think of a favorite teacher from your school days. What qualities made that person effective?

Think of a boring teacher you've had. What made him or her uninteresting?

Complete this sentence, "It bores me when a teacher. . ."

Complete this sentence, "It excites me when a teacher. . ."

Look back at the phrases on pages 11–12. In which of those teaching functions do you feel especially strong? In which ones do you need to improve?

Which aspects of Jesus' teaching do you want to begin to follow now?

As was his custom,
he taught them.

Mark 10:1

2

Who Considered Jesus
a Master Teacher?

*J*esus was a master teacher: *the* master Teacher, the greatest Teacher of all times.

Many writers have acknowledged that fact. For example, the early church father Ignatius (ca. A.D. 35–107) referred to Jesus Christ as "our only Teacher." Clement of Alexandria (155–216) called Jesus "our Tutor," and added, "As Teacher, He explains and reveals through instruction, but as an Educator He is practical."[1]

In 1895 B. A. Hinsdale wrote that Jesus "was the greatest of the greatest oral teachers." And in 1901 another writer affirmed without qualification that "Jesus is the greatest religious and moral Teacher whom the world has seen." Clarence H. Benson, a well-known educator several decades ago, stated that "Jesus Christ was . . . not only the master teacher but the master of all teaching." The very opening sentence of Claude C. Jones's book announces boldly, "Jesus Christ was the Master Teacher." Others have designated our Lord as "the Master Teacher par excellence," "the supreme Teacher," "the perfect teacher," "the greatest teacher," "the quintessential Teacher . . . the paragon of pedagogy,"

---

1. Ignatius *To the Ephesians* 15.1; Clement *"The Instructor"* 1.7.55; 13.102.

"the Master Teacher," the "most wonderful teacher the world has ever known," and "the greatest teacher of all time."[2]

Several authors refer to the excellence of Jesus' teaching style. He "was the supreme exponent of the art of teaching," "He has no peer in loftiness of teaching," and he is "remembered as one of the world's masters of the technique of teaching."[3]

Enthralled with Jesus' superior command of the art of teaching and his unsurpassed role as Teacher-Communicator, writers over the years have been unable to resist the pull to use the superlatives "master," "perfect," and "great" in their writings about Jesus. Note these book titles:

Learning to Teach from the Master Teacher
The Master and His Method
The Message of the Master Teacher
The Master's Influence
The Great Teacher
Jesus—The Master Teacher
The Perfect Teacher
The Wonderful Teacher
Jesus the Master Teacher
Master Teacher.[4]

2. Hinsdale, *Jesus as a Teacher* (St. Louis: Christian Publishing, 1895), 12; James Robertson, *Our Lord's Teaching* (London: Black, 1901), 1; Benson, *The Christian Teacher* (Chicago: Moody, 1950), 257; Jones, *The Teaching Methods of the Master* (St. Louis: Bethany, 1957), 9; Lois E. LeBar, *Education That Is Christian* (Westwood, N.J.: Revell, 1958), 51; and Edward Kuhlman, *Master Teacher* (Old Tappan, N.J.: Revell, 1987), 181; Henry Barclay Swete, *Studies in the Teaching of Our Lord* (London: Hodder and Stoughton, 1903), 11; Regina M. Alfonso, *How Jesus Taught* (New York: Alba, 1986), vii; Lee Magness, "Teaching and Learning in the Gospels: The Biblical Basis of Christian Education," *Religious Education* 70 (November–December 1975): 629; and Kenneth O. Gangel and Warren S. Benson, *Christian Education: Its History and Philosophy* (Chicago: Moody, 1983), 72; Howard G. Hendricks, "Following the Master Teacher," in *The Christian Educator's Handbook on Teaching*, ed. Kenneth O. Gangel and Howard G. Hendricks (Wheaton, Ill.: Victor, 1989), 13; Ralph W. Sockman, *The Paradoxes of Jesus* (New York: Abingdon, 1936); and Ronald T. Habermas, "Learning to Teach Like the Master Teacher," *Fundamentalist Journal*, June 1985, 54; Herbert Lockyer, *Everything Jesus Taught*, 5 vols. (New York: Harper and Row, 1976), 2:20; and Lilas D. Rixon, *How Jesus Taught* (Croydon, N.S.W.: Sydney Missionary and Bible College, 1977), 8.

3. Donald Guthrie, "Jesus," in *A History of Religious Educators*, ed. Elmer L. Towns (Grand Rapids: Baker, 1975), 15; C. B. Eavey, *History of Christian Education* (Chicago: Moody, 1964), 77; and William Barclay, *The Mind of Jesus* (New York: Harper, 1960), 89.

4. J. A. Marquis (Philadelphia: Westminster, 1913); E. Griffith-Jones (London: Hodder and Stoughton, 1914); B. S. Winchester (Boston: Pilgrim, 1917); Charles Reynolds Brown (Nashville: Cokesbury, 1936); John Harris (London: Thomas Ward and Co., 1937; reprinted as *The Teaching Methods of Christ* [Minneapolis: Klock and Klock, 1984]); Her-

Chapter titles also convey the unqualified adulation writers have for Jesus as the paramount Pedagogue:

"The Master Teacher"
"Christ the Master Teacher"
"Following the Master Teacher"
"Fixing Our Eyes on Jesus: Teacher Par Excellence."[5]

Secular educators, too, have acclaimed Jesus as an outstanding teacher. Almost one hundred years ago, E. L. Kemp wrote, "Measured by the nature of the lessons he taught, by his method of presenting them, by the number of persons whom they reached, and by the results they have accomplished, he was the greatest teacher of all teachers." Frederick Eby and Charles Arrowood assert, "Jesus must be acknowledged as the greatest teacher of all time." Even Jewish writers acknowledge his superiority in this regard: "Jesus was the first and greatest teacher of the Christian Religion."[6]

Was Jesus Successful as a Teacher?

Though many people have extolled Jesus as the supreme Teacher of all ages, others may challenge this acclaim. Was he really successful as a Teacher? Many people who heard him lecture turned away "and no longer followed him" (John 6:65). Religious teachers in his day doggedly challenged his teaching, refused to accept his claims, and schemed repeatedly to capture him and have him put to death.

---

man Harrell Horne (Grand Rapids: Kregel, 1984; originally published as *Teaching Techniques of Jesus* [New York: Association, 1922]); Katherine Lever (New York: Seabury, 1964); D. J. Burrell (New York: Revell, 1902); Clifford A. Wilson (Grand Rapids: Baker, 1974); Kuhlman. Other book titles designate Jesus as "the Teacher": William A. Curtis, *Jesus Christ the Teacher* (New York: Oxford University Press, 1943); Joseph A. Grassi, *Jesus the Teacher* (Winona, Minn.: St. Mary's College, 1978); John P. Kealy, *Jesus, the Teacher* (Denville, N.J.: Dimension, 1978).

5. Clarence H. Benson, chapter 20 in *The Christian Teacher*, and Barclay, chapter 10 in *The Mind of Jesus*; Valerie A. Wilson, in *Introduction to Biblical Christian Education*, ed. Werner C. Graendorf (Chicago: Moody, 1981), and Warren S. Benson, in *Christian Education: Foundations for the Future*, ed. Robert E. Clark, Len Johnson, and Allyn K. Sloat (Chicago: Moody, 1991); Hendricks, in *The Christian Educator's Handbook on Teaching*; Matt Friedemann, in *The Master Plan of Teaching* (Wheaton, Ill.: Victor, 1990).

6. Kemp, *History of Education* (Philadelphia: Lippincott, 1901), 101; Eby and Arrowood, *The History and Philosophy of Education Ancient and Modern* (Englewood Cliffs, N.J.: Prentice-Hall, 1940), 54; *Universal Jewish Encyclopedia* (1942 ed.), s.v. "Education," by Max Salmon, 3:83.

Were other great teachers treated this way? Is rejection by a nation as a whole and execution evidence of a master teacher? How can Jesus be championed as the greatest Teacher of all times when, at the end of his life, so few defended his cause?

Even one of Jesus' carefully chosen learners, Judas Iscariot, who had been with him for three and a half years, betrayed him to the religious authorities (chief priests, officers of the temple guard, and elders, Luke 22:52), identifying him by a hypocritical kiss. A traitor among his closest followers!

And Peter, the spokesman of the group of twelve, a man who had vowed he would never renounce the Lord Jesus and would go with him to prison or death (Matt. 26:33, 34; Mark 14:29, 31; Luke 22:33; John 13:37), denied that he knew the Lord! Only a few years before, attracted by his personal invitation, the Twelve had forsaken everything—their families, occupations, homes, way of living—to become his followers and learners (Mark 1:18; Luke 5:11). Now all twelve deserted him when he was arrested (Matt. 26:56; Mark 14:50). Is that an indication of an effective teacher?

Old Testament predictions about Jesus' first advent say little about his coming as a Teacher, and, apart from the Gospels, the New Testament lays little emphasis on his teaching ministry.[7] He wrote no books, he never told others how to teach, he never discussed pedagogical principles, he had no access to mass media. No typists, stenographers, typesetters, computer operators, or printers recorded and printed his words. The task of communicating his words in writing was taken up by four individuals, only two of whom, Matthew and John, were among his twelve close associates. The other two, Mark and Luke, were traveling companions of the apostle Paul. Mark had no doubt also been associated with Peter.[8] Clearly, then, Jesus depended on others to record his words and deeds.

Jesus never attended a school of higher learning to train to become a rabbi. Aware of this fact, the Jews asked, "How did this man get such learning without having studied?" (John 7:15). Literally this question reads, "How does this man know letters *(grammata)*, not having learned?" *Grammata* refers to literature or writings in general, but here probably designates the Old Testament Scriptures,[9] with which he was

7. Curtis, *Jesus Christ the Teacher,* 11.

8. The early church father Papias (ca. A.D. 110) quoted John the elder, probably the apostle John, as indicating that Mark, though not an eyewitness follower of Jesus, accompanied the apostle Peter in his preaching, thereby learning from Peter about Jesus' words and works (Eusebius *Ecclesiastical History* 3.39.19).

9. F. Godet, *Commentary on the Gospel of St. John,* trans. M. D. Cusin and S. Taylor, 3d ed. (Edinburgh: Clark, 1892), 2:275. Also see Walter Bauer, William F. Arndt, and

so familiar. The words *not having learned* suggest that Jesus had never been a disciple of another rabbi in a rabbinical school.[10] Being omniscient, he knew all things and had no need to enroll in a Jewish school of higher learning.

Are we correct in viewing Jesus as an outstanding Teacher? Do these deficiencies detract from his standing? He was indeed the greatest Teacher the world has ever known. The fact that he was rejected by national leaders points to the uniqueness of his message, a message that opposed the sham of their perfunctory religiosity. The fact that he was deserted by his apprentices shows the frailty of the human heart when faced with what began to look like a lost cause. The fact that Jesus left the recording of his works and words to others does not detract from his teaching ability. Rather it demonstrates that his biographers could not forget what he did and said. His actions and teachings had a profound effect on his followers, an impact that changed their lives forever. Though they forsook him when he was arrested, their desertion was temporary. After they saw the resurrected Jesus, and after the Holy Spirit descended on them with spiritual power on the day of Pentecost, they became the leaders of a movement, Christianity, that has spread around the world and has acquired millions of converts.

Truly, without question, Jesus Christ was the Teacher par excellence!

To Think About . . .

Do you think of Jesus as a great Teacher? If so, why? What aspects of Jesus' ministry have earned him the accolade "Master Teacher"?

Has anyone called you a teacher? What aspects of your life or work would lead someone to think of you as a teacher?

F. Wilbur Gingrich, *A Greek-English Lexicon of the New Testament and Other Early Christian Literature*, 2d ed., rev. F. Wilbur Gingrich and Frederick W. Danker (Chicago: University of Chicago Press, 1979), 165.

10. Leon Morris, *The Gospel according to John* (Grand Rapids: Eerdmans, 1971), 405. "The surprise would be connected with the fact that Jesus could carry on a sustained discourse apparently in the manner of the Rabbis and perhaps also with the amount of Scripture Jesus could quote."

Have you had a "failure" in your class, a student who rejected what you taught or who dropped out because of lack of interest? How did you feel about that individual? What could you have done to encourage him or her? What can you do now?

"Rabbi, we know you are a teacher
who has come from God."

John 3:2

3

How Was Jesus Recognized as a Teacher?

*T*itles or names we give people show what we think of them.

When a husband calls his wife his sweetheart, he means she is sweet and precious to him. If you call someone an egghead, you mean he or she is stupid. When we refer to a person as the head of an organization, we mean he or she is in charge. When we address a man as "Sir," we show we respect him.

Some titles show our affection. Others express our disdain. Still others describe what an individual is or does. And other titles reveal our respect.

Titles used of Jesus express what he is and what we think of him. The Bible ascribes numerous names and titles to Jesus, some of which are Lord, God, Savior, Lord Jesus Christ, Son of God, Son of man, Son of David, Master, Emmanuel, Messiah, King, Ruler, Firstborn, Word, Lamb, Bread, Light, Shepherd, Vine, Prophet, and Servant.

William Barclay and Vincent Taylor each suggest Jesus had forty-two names and titles, and W. Graham Scroggie lists forty-three.[1]

1. Barclay, *Jesus as They Saw Him* (Grand Rapids: Eerdmans, 1962); Taylor, *The Names of Jesus* (London: St. Martin's, 1953); and Scroggie, *A Guide to the Gospels* (London: Pickering and Inglis, 1948), 519–20. However, some of the titles Scroggie lists may be questioned, such as "consolation" (Luke 2:25). Other writers have given even lengthier

Of the twenty-eight titles occurring in more than one Gospel, those translated "Teacher" rank fourth in frequency after "Jesus" (which occurs 615 times), "Lord" (used 191 times), and "Son of Man" (occurring 80 times).[2] The five words referring to Jesus as Teacher are *didaskalos,* occurring 45 times (11 of the occurrences being parallel passages)[3]; *rabbi,* which occurs 14 times (with 1 occurrence being a parallel passage); *rabboni,* used twice; *epistatēs,* occurring 7 times; and *kathēgētēs,* used once. This is a total of 70 occurrences. How remarkable that Jesus is spoken of this many times as a Teacher! Certainly teaching was a major component of his ministry on earth. And from his titles as Teacher we can learn much for our own teaching.

Table 1
The Most Common Titles of Jesus
in the Gospels by Frequency of Occurrence

	Matthew	Mark	Luke	John	Total
Jesus	170	97	97	251	615
Lord	47	11	53	40	151
Son of man	29	15	26	10	80
Teacher					
Didaskalos	12	12	15	7	46
Rabbi	2	4		8	14
Epistatēs			7		7
Rabboni		1		1	2
Kathēgētēs	1				1
Total	261	140	198	317	916

---

lists. Charles Spear discussed eighty titles (*Names and Titles of the Lord Jesus Christ* [Boston: Mussey and Tompkins, 1841]), and Benjamin B. Warfield listed ninety-five titles (*The Lord of Glory* [1907; reprint, Grand Rapids: Baker, 1974]).

2. Individuals usually addressed Jesus as "Lord," and seldom as "Jesus." In only 6 out of 615 references is the vocative "Jesus" used by people in addressing him directly: Mark 5:7; 10:47; Luke 8:28; 17:13; 18:38; John 6:42.

3. *Didaskalos* is also used of the teachers with whom Jesus was conversing in the temple at age twelve (Luke 2:46), of John the Baptist (Luke 3:12), and of Nicodemus (John 3:10). These three additional occurrences bring the total number of references to *didaskalos* in the Gospels to forty-nine. The word is used only ten times elsewhere in the New Testament—eight times denoting teachers of the church (Acts 13:1; 1 Cor. 12:28–29; Eph. 4:11; 1 Tim. 2:7; 2 Tim. 1:11; Heb. 5:12; James 3:1), once in reference to unsaved Jews (Rom. 2:20), and once in referring to false teachers (2 Tim. 4:3). Thus more than three-fourths (78 percent) of the New Testament occurrences of *didaskalos* (forty-six out of fifty-nine) refer to Jesus Christ.

Table 2 shows that Jesus' opponents and interested individuals called him *didaskalos* more often than did his close followers, and that the twelve disciples and other followers of Jesus most often called him *rabbi* or *rabboni*, a title never used of Jesus by his opponents. Jesus referred to himself as *didaskalos* nine times[4] and as *kathēgētēs* once.

What do these five titles mean? What is their significance? What do they suggest about Jesus' teaching role?

Table 2
The Five Greek Words Used of Jesus as a Teacher
by Frequency of Usage and by Speakers

	Opponents	Interested or Neutral Individuals	Disciples or Other Followers	Jews	Jesus	Total
Didaskalos	12 (+4 parallel passages)	8 (+4 parallel passages)	8	7 (+3 parallel passages)		35 (+11 parallel passages)
Rabbi		1	12 (+1 parallel passage)			13 (+1 parallel passage)
Rabboni		1	1			2
Epistatēs		1	6			7
Kathēgētēs					1	1
	12 (16)	11 (15)	27 (28)	7 (10)	1	58 (70)

Table 3
People Who Referred to Jesus as Teacher *(Didaskalos)*

Opponents

Pharisees	"Why does your *teacher* eat with tax collectors and 'sinners'?" (Matt. 9:11)
Pharisees and teachers of the law	"*Teacher,* we want to see a miraculous sign from you" (Matt. 12:38)
Tax collectors	"Doesn't your *teacher* pay the temple tax?" (Matt. 17:24)
Pharisees and Herodians	"*Teacher* . . . Is it right to pay taxes to Caesar or not?" (Matt. 22:16–17; cf. Mark 12:14; Luke 20:21–22)

4. These nine self-descriptions include three references of a proverbial nature (Matt. 10:24–25; Luke 6:40), spoken by the Lord, which probably refer by implication to himself.

Sadducees	*"Teacher* . . . at the resurrection, whose wife will she be of the seven, since all of them were married to her?" (Matt. 22:24, 28; cf. Mark 12:19, 23; Luke 20:28, 33)
Teachers of the law	"Well said, *teacher!*" (Luke 20:39)
A Pharisee, an expert in the law	*"Teacher,* which is the greatest commandment in the law?" (Matt. 22:36)
	"'Well said, *teacher,*' the man replied. 'You are right in saying that God is one and there is no other but him'" (Mark 12:32)
A Pharisee named Simon	"Jesus answered him, 'Simon, I have something to tell you.' 'Tell me, *teacher,*' he said" (Luke 7:40)
An expert in the law	*"Teacher,* when you say these things, you insult us also" (Luke 11:45)
Pharisees	*"Teacher,* rebuke your disciples!" (Luke 19:39)
Teachers of the law and Pharisees	*"Teacher,* this woman was caught in the act of adultery" (John 8:4)

Interested or Neutral Individuals

A teacher of the law	*"Teacher,* I will follow you wherever you go" (Matt. 8:19)
An expert in the law	"'*Teacher,*' he asked, 'what must I do to inherit eternal life?'" (Luke 10:25)
A rich young man	*"Teacher,* what good thing must I do to get eternal life?" (Matt. 19:16; cf. Mark 10:17; Luke 18:18)
	"'*Teacher,*' he declared, 'all these I have kept since I was a boy'" (Mark 10:20)
Jairus' servants	"Your daughter is dead. . . . Why bother the *teacher* any more?" (Mark 5:35; cf. Luke 8:49)
A father of a demon-possessed boy	*"Teacher,* I brought you my son, who is possessed by a spirit that has robbed him of speech" (Mark 9:17; cf. Luke 9:38)
Someone in the crowd	*"Teacher,* tell my brother to divide the inheritance with me" (Luke 12:13)
Nicodemus	"Rabbi, we know you are a *teacher* who has come from God" (John 3:2)

Followers of Jesus

Two disciples	"Rabbi (which means *Teacher*), where are you staying?" (John 1:38)
Disciples	*"Teacher,* don't you care if we drown?" (Mark 4:38). The parallel Matthean passage, 8:25, has *kyrie,* "Lord," instead of *didaskalos.*

John	"'*Teacher,*' said John, 'we saw a man driving out demons in your name and we told him to stop, because he was not one of us'" (Mark 9:38)
James and John	"'*Teacher,*' they said, 'we want you to do for us whatever we ask'" (Mark 10:35)
One of the Twelve	"As he was leaving the temple, one of his disciples said to him, 'Look, *Teacher!* What massive stones! What magnificent buildings!'" (Mark 13:1)
Disciples	"'*Teacher,*' they asked, 'when will these things happen? And what will be the sign that they are about to take place?'" (Luke 21:7)
Martha	"'The *Teacher* is here,' she said, 'and is asking for you'" (John 11:28)
Mary of Magdala	"She turned toward him and cried out in Aramaic, 'Rabboni!' (which means *Teacher*)" (John 20:16)

Jesus' References to Himself as *Didaskalos*

"A student is not above his *teacher*" (Matt. 10:24; Luke 6:40a)[*]

"It is enough for the student to be like his *teacher*" (Matt. 10:25)[*]

"Everyone who is fully trained will be like his *teacher*" (Luke 6:40b)[*]

"Go into the city to a certain man and tell him, 'The *Teacher* says, My appointed time is near. I am going to celebrate the Passover with my disciples at your house'" (Matt. 26:18; Mark 14:14; Luke 22:11)

"You call me '*Teacher*' and 'Lord,' and rightly so, for that is what I am. Now that I, your Lord and *Teacher,* have washed your feet, you also should wash one another's feet" (John 13:13–14)

[*] In these verses Jesus did not explicitly call himself a teacher, but the verses suggest that he was referring to himself.

Didaskalos

In classical Greek, from Homer on, the word *didaskalos* was widely used of those who

> regularly engaged in the systematic imparting of knowledge or technical skills: the elementary teacher, the tutor, the philosopher, also the chorus-master who has to conduct rehearsals of poetry for a public performance. Since the teacher's activity is confined to specific areas (reading, writing, the art of war,

a trade, etc.), the word *didaskalos* is often more closely defined by the subject he teaches.[5]

In the New Testament *didaskalos* occurs fifty-nine times, with forty-nine of those occurrences in the Gospels. In the forty-six references to Jesus (see tables 2 and 3) the word applies to individuals who publicly instructed others about the things of God. Two-thirds (thirty out of forty-six) of the references to Jesus are a direct form of address (Greek: *didaskale*), and both friend and foe addressed him in this way. Why did his adversaries—including Pharisees, teachers of the law, tax collectors, Herodians, and Sadducees—call him "Teacher"? Were they giving him respect as *their* Teacher? Were they honoring him as the One from whom they were willing to learn? Probably not. They were acknowledging his function in society, as One instructing others about spiritual truth. Possibly even a touch of irony is to be sensed in their referring to him as "Teacher" when they questioned his actions or his disciples' actions[6] or sought to trick him.[7]

Interested or committed followers of Jesus sometimes addressed him as Teacher because they wanted to be taught by him,[8] but at other times they wanted help from him.[9] Perhaps "Teacher," then, was a common title of respect, much as students today call a respected teacher "Prof." Readers of the King James Version will find that the word *didaskalos* is obscured in that version by the frequent translation "Master."[10] "Master" is an Old English term from the Latin *magister*, "schoolmaster," an outmoded term.

5. *New International Dictionary of New Testament Theology*, s.v. "Teach, Instruct, Tradition, Education, Discipline," by K. Wegenast, 3:766. Also see *Theological Dictionary of the New Testament*, s.v. "διδάσκω, διδάσκαλος, διάκονος," by K. H. Rengstorf, 2:148–50.

6. "Why does your teacher eat with tax collectors and 'sinners'?" (Matt. 9:11). "Doesn't your teacher pay the temple tax?" (Matt. 17:24). "Teacher, when you say these things you insult us also" (Luke 11:45). "Teacher, rebuke your disciples!" (Luke 19:39).

7. "Teacher . . . Is it right to pay taxes to Caesar or not?" (Matt. 22:16–17; Mark 12:14; Luke 20:21–22). "Teacher . . . at the resurrection, whose wife will she be of the seven, since all of them were married to her?" (Matt. 22:24, 27; cf. Mark 12:19, 23; Luke 20:28, 33). "Teacher, this woman was caught in the act of adultery" (John 8:4).

8. For example, an expert in the law asked Jesus, "Teacher . . . what must I do to inherit eternal life?" (Luke 10:25); Nicodemus said, "We know you are a teacher who has come from God" (John 3:2); and the disciples asked him, "Teacher . . . when will these things happen?" (Luke 21:7).

9. In a storm Jesus' disciples asked, "Teacher, don't you care if we drown?" (Mark 4:38). A father said to Jesus, "Teacher, I brought you my son, who is possessed by a spirit that has robbed him of speech" (Mark 9:17). James and John said to Jesus, "Teacher . . . we want you to do for us whatever we ask" (Mark 10:35).

10. This is not to be confused with the rendering of "Master" in the NIV which translates a different word, *epistatēs*, in its seven occurrences in the Gospel of Luke (see table 4).

Didaskalos is the Greek equivalent of the Hebrew and Aramaic *rabbi* (see pp. 34–42). The noun *didaskalos* comes from the verb *didaskō*, "to teach or instruct. " According to Wegenast, this word comes from the root *dek-*, "to accept or extend the hand to." The duplication at the beginning of the word (*di-das-kō*) conveys "the idea of repeatedly extending the hand for acceptance; the word therefore suggests the idea of causing someone to accept something."[11] In teaching, then, the idea is to cause someone to accept knowledge, a concept, or an idea, or to accept improvement in skill. The duplication of *di* and *das* suggests a continued activity for the purpose of assimilation.[12]

Of the ninety-five occurrences of the verb *didaskō* in the New Testament, more than half (fifty-seven) are in the Gospels, with forty-seven of them referring to Jesus' teaching. The Gospel writers thus reveal that teaching was one of Jesus' most prominent activities.[13] Clearly he was recognized as an eminent Teacher.

Table 4
Occurrences of "Teach," "Teaching," and "Taught" in the Gospels in Reference to Jesus

Matthew 4:23	Jesus went throughout Galilee, *teaching* in their synagogues.
5:1–2	Now when he saw the crowds, he went up on a mountainside and sat down. His disciples came to him, and he began to *teach* them.
7:28–29	The crowds were amazed at his *teaching*, * because he taught as one who had authority.
9:35	Jesus went through all the towns and villages, *teaching* in their synagogues.
11:1	He went from there to *teach* and preach in the towns of Galilee.
13:54	Coming to his home town, he began *teaching* the people in their synagogue, and they were amazed.
19:11	"Not everyone can accept this *teaching* [*logon*, literally, word]."
21:23	Jesus entered the temple courts, and while he was *teaching*, the chief priests and the elders of the people came to him.

11. *New International Dictionary of New Testament Theology*, s.v. "Teach, Instruct, Tradition, Education, Discipline," by K. Wegenast, 3:759.

12. *Theological Dictionary of the New Testament*, s.v. "διδάσκω, διδασκαλος, διάκονος," by K. H. Rengstorf, 2:135.

13. Forty-six times the Gospels refer to Jesus' healing ministry, and eighteen times to his preaching ministry.

22:15–16	Then the Pharisees . . . [and] the Herodians . . . [said], "*Teacher* . . . we know you are a man of integrity and that you teach the way of God in accordance with the truth."
22:33	When the crowds heard this, they were astonished at his *teaching.**
26:55	"Every day I sat in the temple courts *teaching*."
Mark 1:21–22	They went to Capernaum, and when the Sabbath came, Jesus went into the synagogue and began to *teach*. The people were amazed at his *teaching,** because he *taught* them as one who had authority, not as the teachers of the law.
1:27	The people were all so amazed that they asked each other, "What is this? A new *teaching**—and with authority!"
2:13	A large crowd came to him, and he began to *teach* them.
4:1–2	Again Jesus began to *teach* by the lake. . . . He *taught* them many things by parables, and in his *teaching** said. . . .
6:2	When the Sabbath came, he began to *teach* in the synagogue. . . .
6:6	Then Jesus went around *teaching* from village to village.
6:34	When Jesus landed and saw a large crowd, he had compassion on them, because they were like sheep without a shepherd. So he began *teaching* them many things.
8:31	He then began to *teach* them that the Son of Man must suffer many things. . . .
9:30–31	They left that place and passed through Galilee. Jesus did not want anyone to know where they were, because he was *teaching* his disciples.
10:1	Jesus then left that place and went into the region of Judea and across the Jordan. Again crowds of people came to him, and as was his custom, he *taught* them.
11:15, 17	Jesus entered the temple area. . . . And as he *taught* them, he said, "Is it not written: 'My house will be called a house of prayer for all nations'? But you have made it 'a den of robbers.'"
11:18	The whole crowd was amazed at his *teaching.**
12:13–14	The Pharisees and Herodians . . . came to him and said, "*Teacher*, we know you are a man of integrity . . . you *teach* the way of God in accordance with the truth."
12:35	While Jesus was *teaching* in the temple courts, he asked, "How is it that the teachers of the law say that the Christ is the son of David?"

12:38	As he taught [literally, in his *teaching*,*] Jesus said, "Watch out for the teachers of the law."
14:49	"Every day I was with you, *teaching* in the temple courts. . . ."
Luke 4:15	He *taught* in their synagogues, and everyone praised him.
4:31–32	Then he went down to Capernaum, a town in Galilee, and on the Sabbath began to *teach* the people. They were amazed at his *teaching*,* because his message had authority.
4:36	All the people were amazed and said to each other, "What is this *teaching* [*logos*, literally, word]?"
5:3	Then he sat down and *taught* the people from the boat.
5:17	One day as he was *teaching*, Pharisees and teachers of the law . . . were sitting there.
6:6	On another Sabbath he went into the synagogue and was *teaching*, and a man was there whose right hand was shriveled.
11:1	"Lord, *teach* us to pray."
13:10–11	On a Sabbath Jesus was *teaching* in one of the synagogues, and a woman was there who had been crippled by a spirit for eighteen years.
13:22	Then Jesus went through the towns and villages, *teaching* as he made his way to Jerusalem.
13:26	"Then you will say, 'We ate and drank with you, and you *taught* in our streets.'"
19:47	Every day he was *teaching* at the temple.
20:1	One day as he was *teaching* the people in the temple courts and preaching the gospel, the chief priests and the teachers of the law, together with the elders, came up to him.
20:21	So the spies questioned him: "Teacher, we know that you speak and *teach* what is right, and that you do not show partiality but *teach* the way of God in accordance with the truth."
21:37–38	Each day Jesus was *teaching* at the temple . . . and all the people came early in the morning to hear him at the temple.
23:4–5	The chief priests and the crowd . . . insisted, "He stirs up the people all over Judea by his *teaching*. He started in Galilee and has come all the way here."
John 6:59–60	He said this while *teaching* in the synagogue in Capernaum. On hearing it, many of his disciples said, "This is a hard *teaching* [*logos*, literally, word]. Who can accept it?"

7:14–17	Not until halfway through the Feast did Jesus go up to the temple courts and begin to *teach*. The Jews were amazed and asked, "How did this man get such learning without having studied?" Jesus answered, "My *teaching** is not my own. It comes from him who sent me. If anyone chooses to do God's will he will find out whether my *teaching** comes from God or whether I speak on my own."
7:28	Then Jesus, still *teaching* in the temple courts, cried out, "Yes, you know me, and you know where I am from."
7:35	The Jews said to one another . . . "Will he go where our people live scattered among the Greeks, and *teach* the Greeks?"
8:2	At dawn he appeared again in the temple courts, where all the people gathered around him, and he sat down to *teach* them.
8:20	He spoke these words while *teaching* in the temple area near the place where the offerings were put.
8:28	"I do nothing on my own but speak just what the Father has *taught* me."
8:31	To the Jews who had believed him, Jesus said, "If you hold to my *teaching* [*logō*, literally, *word*], you are really my disciples."
14:23	Jesus replied, "If anyone loves me, he will obey my *teaching* [*logous*, literally, *words*]."
14:24	"He who does not love me will not obey my *teaching* [*logos*, literally, *word*]."
15:20	"If they obeyed my *teaching* [*logon*, literally, *word*], they will obey yours also."
18:19	Meanwhile, the high priest questioned Jesus about his disciples and his *teaching.** "I have spoken openly to the world," Jesus replied. "I always *taught* in synagogues or at the temple, where all the Jews come together. I said nothing in secret."

*The noun *teaching* translates *didachē*, "what is taught," a word that is used eleven times of Jesus in the Gospels (Matt. 7:28; 22:33; Mark 1:22, 27; 4:2; 11:18; 12:38; Luke 4:32; John 7:16–17; 18:19). Also, as noted, seven times the NIV renders the Greek *logos* (word) by the noun *teaching*.

   In both classical Greek and the New Testament *didaskō* is often used with the accusative of the person(s) taught and/or the accusative of the subjects(s) taught. Almost without exception, when *didaskō* is followed by the accusative of the person taught, it refers to Jesus' teaching of groups.[14] Note the groups he is said to have taught.

   14. Roy B. Zuck, "Greek Words for Teach," *Bibliotheca Sacra* 122 (April–June 1965): 159–60.

Crowds (Matt. 5:1–2; Mark 2:13; 4:2; 6:34; 10:1; 11:18; 12:37–38)
The people (Matt. 13:54; Mark 1:22; Luke 4:31; 5:3; 20:1; 21:37–38;
    John 8:2)
His disciples (Matt. 5:2; Mark 8:31; 9:31; Luke 11:1)

Of course he taught on many other occasions, though the word *di-dasko* is not used. Interestingly *didasko* is never used of his teaching his opponents.

Other times *didasko* is used with a prepositional phrase indicating where Jesus taught. Note these places:

In a synagogue (Matt. 4:23; 9:35; 13:54; Mark 1:21; 6:2; Luke 4:15;
    6:6; 13:10; John 6:59; 18:20)
In the temple courts in Jerusalem (Matt. 21:23; 26:55; Mark 11:15,
    17; 12:35; 14:49; Luke 19:47; 20:1; 21:37; John 7:14, 28; 8:2, 20;
    18:20)
In houses (Luke 5:17–18; 7:36–50)
In towns and villages (Matt. 11:1; Mark 6:6; Luke 13:22)
Outdoors
    On a mountainside (Matt. 5:1–2)
    By a lakeshore in a boat (Mark 4:1; Luke 5:3)
    In the streets (Luke 13:26)

Other outdoor places where he taught (where the word *teach* is not used) include dinner tables (Luke 5:29–31; 7:36; 11:37; 22:14), a tomb (John 11:38–44), a garden (Matt. 26:36–45), and a road (Luke 24:32).

Towns and areas where Jesus taught include Capernaum (Mark 1:21; Luke 4:31; John 6:59), Galilee (Mark 9:30), Transjordan (Mark 10:1), Judea and Galilee (Luke 23:4–5), and Jerusalem (the temple courts). He is also said to have taught in a number of towns, without any reference to what he taught (Matt. 21:23; Mark 1:21–22; 4:1; 6:2, 6; 12:38; Luke 5:17).

Several times the verb *didasko* is used with reference to what Jesus taught. He taught "many things" to crowds (Mark 4:2; 6:34), he taught his disciples about his forthcoming crucifixion and resurrection (Mark 8:31). The Pharisees and Herodians admitted to him that he taught "the way of God" (Matt. 22:16; Mark 12:14) and "what is right" and "the way of God in accordance with the truth" (Luke 20:21).

The content of Jesus' teaching is summarized in the noun *didache*, related to the verb *didasko*. Eleven times this noun refers to his subject matter. (See the note at the end of table 4.) These uses occur in the Sermon on the Mount (Matt. 7:28), in his response to the Sadducees about the resurrection (Matt. 22:33), in his teaching in the synagogue at Capernaum (Mark 1:22; Luke 4:32), in his command to a demon-possessed man in that synagogue (Mark 1:27), in his teaching of the parables of the kingdom (Mark 4:1), in his teaching in the temple after he expelled the money changers (Mark 11:18), in his warning to beware of the pompous actions of the teachers of the law (Mark 12:38), and in his teaching in the temple on the Feast of Tabernacles (John 7:16–17).

Three other verbs used of Jesus' instructional ministry are *paratithēmi*, "to place before," used when he "told" two parables (Matt. 13:24, 31); *dianoigō*, "to open," used of Jesus' explaining the Scriptures to the two on the road to Emmaus (Luke 24:32) and of Jesus' opening the minds of the eleven disciples so they could understand the Scriptures (Luke 24:45); and *diermēneuō*, "to explain or interpret," used in the Gospels only in Luke 24:27, which states that Jesus "explained to them [the two from Emmaus] what was said in all the Scriptures concerning himself."

Rabbi and Rabboni

The Gospels use four other Greek words that refer to Jesus as a Teacher. Two of these words are "Rabbi" and "Rabboni." As table 5 shows, Rabbi is used only by Jesus' followers, with one exception (by a crowd).

Table 5
Four Greek Words Used of Jesus as a Teacher

Rabbi

Used by two disciples of Jesus
> They said, *"Rabbi"* (which means Teacher), "where are you staying?" (John 1:38)

Used by the disciples three times
> 1. Meanwhile his disciples urged him, *"Rabbi*, eat something" (John 4:31)
> 2. His disciples asked him, *"Rabbi*, who sinned, this man or his parents, that he was born blind?" (John 9:2)
> 3. "But *Rabbi*," they said, "a short while ago the Jews tried to stone you, and yet you are going back there?" (John 11:8)

Used by Nathaniel
> Then Nathaniel declared, *"Rabbi*, you are the son of God; you are the king of Israel" (John 1:49)

Used by Peter twice
> 1. Peter said to Jesus, *"Rabbi*, it is good for us to be here" (Mark 9:5). In parallel passages Matthew used "Lord" (Matt. 17:4) and Luke used "Master" (*epistatēs*, Luke 9:33).

2. Peter . . . said to Jesus, "*Rabbi*, look! The fig tree you cursed has withered" (Mark 11:21). In the Matthean parallel passage (21:20) "Rabbi" is not included.

Used by the crowd
"*Rabbi*, when did you get here?" (John 6:25)

Used by Nicodemus, an interested Pharisee
"*Rabbi*, we know you are a teacher who has come from God" (John 3:2)

Used by Judas twice
1. Then Judas, the one who would betray him, said, "Surely not I, *Rabbi?*" (Matt. 26:25)
2. Going at once to Jesus, Judas said, "Greetings, *Rabbi*," and kissed him (Matt. 26:49; cf. Mark 14:45)

Rabboni

Used by blind Bartimaeus
The blind man said, "*Rabbi* [literally, *Rabboni*], I want to see" (Mark 10:51)

Used by Mary of Magdala
She turned toward him and cried out in Aramaic, "*Rabboni!*" (which means Teacher) (John 20:16)

Epistatēs

Used by Jesus' disciples six times
1. Simon answered, "*Master*, we've worked all night and haven't caught anything" (Luke 5:5)
2, 3. "*Master, Master*, we're going to drown!" (Luke 8:24). In parallel passages Matthew used the word *Lord* (8:25), and Mark used the word *Teacher* (4:38).
4. Peter said, "*Master*, the people are crowding and pressing against you" (Luke 8:45)
5. Peter said to him, "*Master*, it is good for us to be here" (Luke 9:33). In parallel passages Matthew used the word *Lord* (17:4), and Mark used the word *Rabbi* (9:5).
6. "*Master*," said John, "we saw a man driving out demons in your name" (Luke 9:49)

Used by ten men who had leprosy
They called out in a loud voice, "Jesus, *Master*, have pity on us!" (Luke 17:13)

Kathēgētēs

Used by Jesus of himself
"Nor are you to be called 'teacher,' for you have one *Teacher*, the Christ" (Matt. 23:10)

"Rabbi," the Greek transliteration of the Hebrew and Aramaic *rabbi*, means "my great one" (from the Hebrew *rab*, great). It was a term of respect addressed primarily to teachers (though it also pointed to the exalted relationship of a master to his slave or of a craftsman to his apprentice or associate). Matthew 23:8 and John 1:38 show that *rabbi* is the equivalent of *didaskalos*. Luke did not use the word *rabbi* of Jesus, undoubtedly because it would have been a meaningless term to his non-Jewish audience.[15] In each of the other three Gospels, Jesus is addressed as Rabbi.[16] Jesus told his disciples not to allow others to call them Rabbi; only he qualifies for such a title (Matt. 23:8).

The disciples (and Nicodemus and a crowd) addressed Jesus by the title *Rabbi* in a variety of ways: with *questions* about his habitat (John 1:38), his time of arrival (asked by a crowd, John 6:25), the reason for a man's congenital blindness (John 9:2), the reason he would endanger his life again by going to Jerusalem (John 11:8), and denial of the intention to betray him (Matt. 26:25); with a *suggestion*, born out of concern for his physical well-being, that he eat (John 4:31); with *exclamations* about Jesus' identity (John 1:49), the marvel of the Transfiguration (Mark 9:5),[17] and the withered fig tree (Mark 11:21); with two *statements* about his identity, one by Nathaniel (John 1:49), and one by Nicodemus (John 3:2); and in a *greeting* by Judas to identify Jesus to the authorities who came to arrest him (Matt. 26:49; Mark 14:45). Not surprisingly, Jesus' opponents never addressed him as Rabbi. They recognized his teaching ministry by calling him "Teacher" (*didaskalos*), but they refused to give him the respect indicated by the word *Rabbi*.

Jewish rabbis were held in high respect as men who were distinguished for their learning and their authority as teachers of the law. Most scribes, because of their devotion to and acquaintance with the law, interpreted and taught the law, and therefore were respectfully called teachers[18] and rabbis. In fact, they and the Pharisees, as Jesus noted, loved to be called "Rabbi" (Matt. 23:7) and to be greeted as such publicly in marketplaces. They also loved being treated as honored guests at banquets and having the front benches in synagogues (Matt. 23:6; Mark 12:39; Luke 11:43; 20:46), and being praised by the public (John 5:44; 12:43). The scribes were also lawyers, administering justice

15. F. W. Farrar points out that the Gospel of Matthew is "the Gospel for the Jews," Mark is "the Gospel for the Romans" and Luke is "the Gospel for the Greeks" (*The Gospel according to St Luke*, Cambridge Greek Testament for Schools and Colleges [Cambridge: Cambridge University Press, 1884], xxiv). On Luke's non-Jewish audience, see also Scroggie, *A Guide to the Gospels*, 334, 337–39.

16. In the New Testament the only others referred to as Rabbi are John the Baptist (John 3:26) and the teachers of the law and Pharisees who, Jesus said, "love to be greeted in the marketplaces and to have men call them 'Rabbi'" (Matt. 23:7; cf. 23:8).

17. Since Mark recorded that Peter said "Rabbi" (Mark 9:5) and Matthew wrote that Peter said "Lord" (Matt. 17:4), it may be that Peter addressed him by both titles.

18. In fact the NIV consistently translates *grammateus* (literally "a person of letters," that is, writer or scholar) as "teacher of the law," whereas the KJV and the NASB render it "scribe."

in accord with the law. The scribe was thus "a combination of theologian and lawyer."[19] The Pharisees, often associated with the scribes (teachers of the law) in the Gospels, were a religious group devoted to keeping the law and Jewish traditions as taught by the scribes. Many scribes were also Pharisees.[20]

"The honor paid to the Rabbis exceeded even that due to parents. The 'elder in knowledge' was revered even more than the 'elder in years' (Kid. 32b)."[21] If a person's father and teacher are each carrying burdens, one must first help the teacher, or if both one's father and one's teacher are in captivity one must first ransom the teacher.[22] This respect bordered on honor given to God. "Let the honor of thy friend border on the honor of thy teacher, and the honor of thy teacher on the fear of God" (Mishnah, *Abōth* 4:12).[23] "To dispute with a rabbi, or to murmur against him, was as sinful as to murmur against God. The Jew gave preference to his teacher over his father [because] the one gave him temporal life, the other eternal life."[24] The rabbi was highly regarded not only by his pupils but also by the public in general.[25]

Though obviously Jesus was not a professional scribe, he was a rabbi, a respected teacher. His manner of teaching resembled that of the rabbis in a number of ways.

Jesus had a small group of learners (Matt. 4:18–22; Mark 1:16–20; 3:13–19; Luke 6:12–16; John 1:35–51). Every Jewish rabbi had a small band of disciples or pupils whom he trained. Even John the Baptist, called a rabbi (John 3:26), had a number of followers called disciples (Matt. 9:14; 11:7; 14:12; Mark 2:18; 6:29; Luke 5:33; 7:18; John 3:25).

Jesus respected the law (Matt. 5:18), as did the rabbis.

The rabbis frequently quoted the Old Testament, and so did Jesus (e.g., Mark 7:6–7; 11:17; 12:10–11; 12:28–33, 36; 13:24–25; 14:27).

Like the rabbis, Jesus taught in synagogues (Matt. 4:23; 9:35; 13:54; Mark 1:21; 6:2; Luke 4:15; 6:6; 13:10; John 6:59; 18:20).

19. *The New Encyclopedia Britannica, Macropaedia,* 1986 ed., s.v. "Jesus," 22:363.

20. Anthony J. Saldarini, *Pharisees, Scribes, and Sadducees in Palestinian Society: A Sociological Approach* (Wilmington, Del.: Michael Glazier, 1988), 266–67, 273. The Greek of the first part of Luke 5:30 reads literally, "the Pharisees and *their* scribes," suggesting some teachers of the law belonged to the Pharisaical group.

21. *Jewish Encyclopedia,* 1895 ed., s.v. "Rabbi," 10:295.

22. Emil Schürer, *The History of the Jewish People in the Age of Jesus Christ (175 B.C.– A.D. 135),* rev. and ed. Geza Vermes, Fergus Mullar, and Matthew Black, 3 vols. (Edinburgh: Clark, 1973–1979), 2:327.

23. Cited in Joachim Jeremias, *Jerusalem in the Time of Jesus* (Philadelphia: Fortress, 1969), 235.

24. Clarence H. Benson, *History of Christian Education* (Chicago: Moody, 1943), 25.

25. *Theological Dictionary of the New Testament,* s.v. "ῥαββί, ῥαββουνί," by Eduard Lohse, 6:962.

Jesus often sat while teaching, as did the rabbis.[26] He sat to teach in the temple courts (Luke 2:46; John 8:2; Matt. 26:55), by a well (John 4:6), in the synagogue at Nazareth (Luke 4:20–21), on a mountainside (Matt. 5:1), in a boat (Matt. 13:2; Mark 4:1; 5:2), in a house in Capernaum (Mark 9:33–35), in Mary's and Martha's home (Luke 10:39), and on the Mount of Olives (Matt. 24:3; Mark 13:3). Presumably he was seated in a house when he looked at listeners who were "seated in a circle around him" (Mark 3:34).[27] Twice we read of his teaching in the temple courts daily (Matt. 26:55; Luke 21:37). Of course his teaching in the synagogues was on the Sabbath (Mark 1:21; 6:2; Luke 4:31–32; 6:6; 13:10).

Jesus taught, as did the rabbis,[28] in parables. (See chapter 16 on Jesus' frequent use of parables.)

Jesus taught by means of aphorisms, pithy, easy-to-remember sayings. The rabbis did the same.[29]

Like the rabbis, Jesus supported his teachings and actions from Scripture (Matt. 10:35–36; 11:10; 12:7; 15:4, 8–9; 18:16; 19:4–5; 21:13, 16; 21:42; 22:32; 24:29; 26:31; Mark 2:25–26; 4:12; 7:10; 10:6–8, 19; 11:17; 12:10–11, 26; 13:14, 25; etc.).

The rabbis debated with each other over religious matters. Jesus disputed with them and other religious leaders over various interpretations of Scripture and their unwritten traditions. Note these examples of issues he debated with them:

Whether it is acceptable to gather food and to heal on the Sabbath (Matt. 12:1–3)

Whether it is acceptable to eat without ritual cleansing of the hands (Matt. 15:1–11)

Whether it is legal for a man to divorce his wife (Matt. 19:3–9)

26. *Universal Jewish Encyclopedia*, 1942 ed., s.v. "Education," by Max Salmon, 3:84.

27. Only in three instances did the Gospel writers refer to Jesus standing as he taught. One was in the synagogue at Nazareth when he stood to read from Isaiah (Luke 4:16), another was when he was standing by the Sea of Galilee with people "listening to the Word of God" (Luke 5:1), and the third was when he stood in the temple courts on the last day of the Feast of Tabernacles and in a loud voice invited people who were spiritually thirsty to come to him (John 7:37). No doubt on other occasions he was standing as well.

28. Parables were "a form of homiletic teaching commonly used by rabbinic preachers" (Geza Vermes, *Jesus the Jew* [New York: Macmillan, 1973], 27). Rabbi Hillel (who died around A.D. 10) taught by means of parables, picturesque language, and brief, memorable sayings (James L. Blevins, "First-Century Rabbis," *Biblical Illustrator* 9 [winter 1993]: 22).

29. G. K. A. Bell and D. Adolf Deissmann, *Mysterium Christi: Christological Studies by British and German Theologians* (New York: Longmans, Green, 1930), 53.

Whether Jesus had a legitimate basis of authority (Matt. 21:23–37)
Whether the Jews should pay taxes to Caesar (Matt. 22:15–22)[30]
Whether a woman with seven husbands would have one of them as
   her husband in the resurrection (Matt. 22:23–32)
Whether Jesus is God (Matt. 22:41–45)
Whether the Jews were enslaved to sin (John 8:33–47)
Whether Jesus was demon-possessed (John 8:48–59)
Whether Jesus is the Messiah (John 8:24–38)

The rabbis, being authorities on the law, were consulted by their pupils and by the populace on matters of conduct and doctrine. Jesus too
was consulted for authoritative answers on several matters. The Sadducees asked him about marriage after the resurrection (Mark 12:18–27);
a teacher of the law (a scribe) asked him which is the most important
of all the Old Testament commandments (Mark 12:28–34); his disciples
questioned who can be saved (Matt. 19:25–26) and inquired about the
reason for a man's blindness (John 9:1–5).

Rabbis, being lawyers, were also asked to settle legal disputes. Jesus
was asked to do the same when a man asked him to settle a dispute
about an inheritance (Luke 12:13–15) and when the teachers of the law
and the Pharisees asked him if a woman they caught in the act of adultery should be stoned (John 8:2–11).

After addressing the public Jesus often explained his teachings to his
disciples privately. Mark 7:17–23 follows the public teaching recorded
in Mark 7:1–15, and in Mark 4:10–12 Jesus privately told the disciples
more about what he had said in the open to the crowd (Mark 4:1–9).
This pattern of public teaching followed by private explanation was
also occasionally followed by the rabbis.[31]

Since Jesus shared many characteristics with the rabbis, can there be
any question that Jesus was an honored rabbi? As Bultmann put it, "we
cannot doubt that the characteristics of a rabbi appeared plainly in
Jesus' ministry and way of teaching."[32]

However, was Jesus a rabbi in the fullest sense? How could he be,
when he had not trained in the rabbinical schools (located either in
the synagogues or in priests' homes)?[33] As the issue was stated in John

30. This is a remarkable question in view of the fact that rabbis had "the privilege of
exemption of taxes" (*Jewish Encyclopedia*, 1895 ed., s.v. "Rabbi," 10:295). Apparently they
wanted to see if Jesus took advantage of this exemption or if he, unlike them, would support paying taxes to the oppressive Roman government.

31. *Interpreter's Dictionary of the Bible*, s.v. "Teaching of Jesus," by K. Grayston, 4:524.

32. Rudolf Bultmann, *Jesus and the Word*, trans. Louise Pettibone Smith and Erminie
Huntress Lantero (New York: Scribner, 1938), 61.

33. Schürer, *History of the Jewish People in the Age of Jesus Christ*, 2:333–34.

7:15, "How does this man know letters, not having learned?" (author's translation). His teaching was strikingly different from that of the teachers of the law ("He taught as one who had authority, and not as their teachers of the law," Matt. 7:29; cf. Mark 1:22). No wonder people in Nazareth asked, "Where did this man get this wisdom?" (Matt. 13:54).

Jesus disassociated himself from the scribes, many of whom were honored as rabbis, by publicly pointing out their hypocrisy, their burdening of others with numerous obligations difficult to fulfill, their haughty display of wealth, their pomposity at banquets and in the synagogues, their penchant for being recognized by the populace as accomplished rabbis, their heartless taking advantage of helpless widows, and their ostentatious pretense of piety by their lengthy prayers (Matt. 23:1–7; Mark 12:38–40; also see Matt. 23:13–36 for Jesus' seven scathing denunciations of their blatant hypocrisy). He differed from the rabbis not only in his lack of any of these undesirable characteristics, but also in several other ways (see table 6).

Table 6
Differences between the Rabbis and Jesus

The rabbis quoted other rabbinical authorities in their teaching.[a]	Jesus was his own authority.[b]
Pupils chose the rabbi under whom they wished to study.	Jesus reversed this process, selecting his disciples himself (Matt. 4:18–21; John 15:16).
Pupils were disciples of the traditions of the teacher.	Jesus' twelve pupils were disciples of *him*.
The rabbis continually repeated their teaching so their pupils, also by repetition, could memorize them verbatim.[c]	Jesus did not teach in this way. However, his sayings were so memorable that his disciples remembered them.[d]
The rabbi often taught in a fixed, indoor location.[e]	Jesus taught in many locations, often outdoors while walking.
Disciples of the rabbis were obligated to serve him in various ways.[f]	Jesus did not permit his disciples to give him special deference; he called them friends (John 15:14).
The rabbis were concerned with teaching the details of ceremony.	Jesus presented broad principles, applicable in many situations.[g]
The rabbis seldom if ever associated with tax collectors or prostitutes, or with women or children.	Jesus often associated with these people (Matt. 9:10–11; 11:19; 21:31; Luke 7:34; 15:1).

The rabbis' disciples became rabbis themselves when they completed their training.[h]	Jesus told his disciples they were not to be called "Rabbi" because only he was their teacher and they were equal as brothers (Matt. 23:8).
The rabbis followed the traditions of previous teachers, traditions that went beyond the demands of Scripture (Matt. 15:2–3, 6–9; Mark 7:3–9, 13).	Jesus refused to follow such traditions and even opposed them as leading to hypocrisy (Matt. 15:7; Mark 7:6).

a. A statement commonly attributed to the rabbis is, "Nor have I ever in my life said a thing which I did not hear from my teachers" (John P. Kealy, *Jesus, the Teacher* [Denville, N.J.: Dimension, 1978], 11).

b. Jesus' repeated words, "But I say to you," "cannot have its equivalent in the literature of the rabbis" (Günther Bornkamm, *Jesus of Nazareth*, trans. Irene and Fraser McLusky and James M. Robinson [New York: Harper and Brothers, 1960], 99).

c. A primary responsibility of the student was to memorize his rabbi's teachings and to express himself in his teacher's words (Josephus *The Antiquities of the Jews* 4.8.12). "Whoever forgets one word of his instruction in the Torah, he is reckoned as though he had forfeited his life" (Mishnah, *ʾAbôth* 3.8). "The highest praise of a student was to liken him to 'a plastered cistern which loses not one drop'" (Mishnah, *ʾAbôth* 2.8). Both Mishnah quotations are cited in Schürer, *History of the Jewish People in the Age of Jesus Christ*, 2:333.

Cicero's saying was applied to its fullest extent in Rabbinic Judaism: *repetitio est mater studoprium.* "Knowledge is gained by repetition, passed on by repetition, kept alive by repetition" (Berger Gerhardsson, *Memory and Manuscript* [Lund: Gleerup, 1961], 168).

d. Of course Jesus may have repeated some of his sayings and parables on different occasions, but not with the same sentence being repeated over and over by him and his followers. The Holy Spirit reminded the New Testament writers who had been with Jesus of his words so that their writings were inspired, that is, God-breathed (2 Tim. 3:16; 2 Pet. 1:21).

e. *Dictionary of Jesus and the Gospels*, 1992 ed., s.v. "Teacher," by R. Riesner, 808. However, on occasion the rabbis would teach in the open air (A. Büchler, "Learning and Teaching in the Open Air in Palestine," *Jewish Quarterly Review* 4 [1913–1914]: 485–91). Apparently Jesus taught in the open air more frequently than did most rabbis in his day.

f. "Disciples customarily opened a way before their teacher going through a crowd, or helped him put on his sandals. Jesus permitted nothing of this kind" (Joseph A. Grassi, *Jesus the Teacher* [Winona, Minn.: St. Mary's College, 1978], 28). See *Theological Dictionary of the New Testament*, s.v. "διδάσκω, διδάσκαλος, διάκονος," by K. H. Rengstorf, 2:154; and s.v. ἀκολουθεῖν, by Gerhard Kittel, 1:213.

g. Anthony C. Deane, *Rabboni: A Study of Jesus Christ the Teacher* (New York: Hodder and Stoughton, 1921), 86–87.

h. *Theological Dictionary of the New Testament*, s.v. "ῥαββί, ῥάββουνί," by Eduard Lohse, 6:965.

Called a rabbi fourteen times in the Gospels, Jesus shared a number of characteristics with the rabbis of his day. However, his departure from their practices in several highly significant ways reveals his uniqueness as a Teacher.

Rabboni, a heightened form of *rabbi,* is the Greek transliteration of the Hebrew word for "My very great one" or "my very highly exalted one."[34] Like *rabbi,* it is the equivalent of "Teacher," as John explained (20:16). The blind man, Bartimaeus, apparently had heard of Jesus because he addressed him as "Jesus" and "Son of David" and then as "Rabboni" (Mark 10:47, 51). In using the word *Rabboni,* the blind man was acknowledging his own lowly position before Jesus, the highly exalted One. When Mary of Magdala saw the risen Savior, she was so overjoyed she exclaimed "Rabboni" (John 20:16), perhaps acknowledging, like Bartimaeus, her lowly position in the presence of the highly exalted One. Interestingly, the Gospels record only these two needy individuals addressing Jesus in this way.

Epistatēs

Only Luke used the title *epistatēs* of Jesus (see table 5). This is not surprising in light of Luke's literary versality. In Luke and Acts he used about eight hundred words that occur nowhere else in the New Testament; he had a larger vocabulary than that of any other New Testament writer.[35] The New International Version's translation of *epistatēs* by "Master" accurately conveys the meaning. In classical Greek the word is used of one who watched over herds or was the driver of an elephant, an inspector of public works, a leader of an athletic society, a leader of a musical competition, a high official, or a city governor.[36] Perhaps "leader" is a good contemporary translation.

In two parallel passages Matthew used "Lord" (*kyrie*)—8:25 (cf. Luke 8:24) and 17:4 (cf. Luke 9:33). Mark used "Teacher" (*didaskalos*) in 4:38 (cf. Luke 8:24) and "Rabbi" in 9:5 (cf. Luke 9:33). Luke never used the Hebrew *rabbi* because of his Hellenistic readership.

Six times the word *epistatēs* was on the lips of Peter, or John, or the disciples, and one time it was used by a leper. The term always suggests Jesus' authority,[37] and yet in every case it is used when the speaker ex-

34. The honor suggested in the Hebrew spelling of *rabbōn* (very great one) seems to be superior to that given to a person addressed as *rab* (great one) (*Jewish Encyclopedia,* s.v. "Rabbi," 10:294).

35. Norval Geldenhuys, *Commentary on the Gospel of Luke* (Grand Rapids: Eerdmans, 1951), 38. See also Farrar, *The Gospel according to St Luke,* xlvi.

36. *Theological Dictionary of the New Testament,* s.v. "ἐπιστάτης," by Albrecht Oepke, 2:623.

37. I. Howard Marshall, *The Gospel of Luke,* New International Greek Testament Commentary (Grand Rapids: Eerdmans, 1978), 385.

pressed a note of urgency or need (e.g., "we're going to drown," Luke 8:24; "the people are crowding and pressing against you," 8:45; "have pity on us," 17:13). "It is always followed by the user being rebuked for his action or conclusion, or the user experiencing something that causes him to grow in his understanding of who Jesus is."[38]

We too can acknowledge Jesus our Teacher as our Master or Leader, the One who can deepen our knowledge of himself in our times of need or misunderstanding.

Kathēgētēs

Twice in one verse Jesus used *kathēgētēs*, a word that occurs only here in the New Testament. "Nor are you to be called 'teacher,' for you have one Teacher, the Christ" (Matt. 23:10). Since the word is formed from the verb *agō*, "to lead," it suggests that Jesus is our Guide who leads us into the truth and into right conduct. Since the disciples were not qualified to do this on their own, they were not to have this title.

Give It Some Thought . . .

Do people think of you as a teacher? If so, why do you suppose they do?

How can you keep yourself on a level with your students, so they do not think they have to defer to you?

How can you minister to individuals whom others might reject or neglect? Think of someone who is shunned by others. Ask yourself how you can help that individual in tangible ways.

Can you teach in various locations as Jesus did? Can you sometimes take your class outside? If you cannot leave your classroom, can you

38. Elmer L. Towns, *The Names of Jesus* (Denver: Accent, 1987), 87.

teach occasionally from a different position in the room, or walk around the room as you teach? Or can you rearrange the chairs? What about taking your class to your home, or meeting with some of your students in your office or at a coffeeshop? What about arranging a field trip for your students?

The crowds were amazed at his teaching,
because he taught as one who had authority,
and not as their teachers of the law.

Matthew 7:28-29

What Made Jesus
an Authoritative Teacher?

Think of people you know who are in positions of authority. Presidents, governors, mayors, local judges, city board members, county commissioners, pastors—these have authority by being elected. When their terms expire, they no longer hold the authority that goes with those positions.

Others are appointed, such as policemen (appointed by city or county officials), presidents of schools (appointed by school boards of trustees), directors of organizations (appointed by boards of directors), and Supreme Court justices and ambassadors (appointed by the president).

Kings and queens, on the other hand, usually have their positions by virtue of family lineage. They are born into a royal family and maintain regal authority throughout their lives. Husbands are heads of their families by virtue of marriage.

Authorities who are elected or appointed have *derived* authority, given them by others. Others such as kings, queens, and husbands have *inherent* authority. Their authority is based on who they are.

Jesus had authority as a Teacher—not because someone appointed or elected him to that role, but because of who he is. His authority is inherent in his Person, as the eternal Son of God.

45

Amazement at Jesus' Teaching

Is it surprising, then, that people were amazed when Jesus taught? When he read from the Book of Isaiah in the synagogue at Nazareth and explained that he was the fulfillment of the prophecy in Isaiah 61:1–2a (Luke 4:16–21), the people "were amazed at the gracious words that came from his lips" (4:22). Soon after that, when he taught in the synagogue at Capernaum, the people there too "were amazed at his teaching" (Mark 1:22; Luke 4:32). There was something startling about his teaching, something different. This Teacher was unique!

Immediately after the people expressed their amazement, Jesus demanded that an evil spirit leave a demon-possessed man who was in the synagogue. This too amazed the people, so that "they asked each other, 'What is this? A new teaching!'" (Mark 1:27), or as Luke put it, "All the people were amazed and said to each other, 'What is this teaching?'" (4:36).[1]

When Jesus completed the lengthy discourse we call the Sermon on the Mount—it could more properly be titled the Lecture on the Mount—on a mountainside near the Sea of Galilee, "the crowds were amazed at his teaching *[didachē]*" (Matt. 7:28).

Still later that same year Jesus returned to Nazareth, where he again taught in the synagogue. Once more the people "were amazed" (Matt. 13:54; Mark 6:2).

Those incidents happened in Jesus' second year of ministry. Then in his third year, on his visit to Jerusalem for the Feast of Tabernacles, he taught in the temple courts, and "the Jews were amazed" (John 7:15) because they knew he had not studied in a rabbinical school.

Later that year Jesus was in Perea, on the east side of the Jordan River. On his final journey to Jerusalem, the twelve "disciples were amazed at his words" (Mark 10:24) when he said, after talking with a rich young man, "How hard it is for the rich to enter the kingdom of God" (10:23). Sensing their amazement, Jesus made an interesting contrast, stating that "it is easier for a camel to go through the eye of a needle than for a rich man to enter the kingdom of God" (10:25). At this, they "were even more amazed" (10:26; cf. Matt. 19:25).

In his final week before the crucifixion, people were still astounded by Jesus' teaching. In the temple, he taught the people that they had made the temple "a den of robbers" (Mark 11:17), undoubtedly referring to the dishonest dealings of the money changers. "The whole crowd

---

1. In Mark 1:27 the word *teaching* translates *didachē*, the content of what is taught, and in Luke 4:36 the word rendered "teaching" is *logos*, the truth conveyed what he said.

was amazed at his teaching *[didachē]*" (11:18), and "all the people hung on his words" (Luke 19:48).

Seeking to trap Jesus in his words, the Pharisees and Herodians asked his opinion on the question of paying taxes to the Roman government. "They were amazed" at his answer (Matt. 22:22; Mark 12:17; Luke 20:26) and were silenced (Luke 20:26) and left (Matt. 22:22).

That same day, when Jesus answered the Sadducees' question about the resurrection (Matt. 22:23–32; Mark 12:18–27; Luke 20:27–38), "the crowds . . . were astonished at his teaching *[didachē]*" (Matt. 22:33). Some of the teachers of the law—scribes who believed in the resurrection and therefore disagreed with the Sadducees, who denied a physical resurrection—were delighted with his reply to the Sadducees, and so they remarked, "Well said, teacher!" (Luke 20:39).

The response of the crowds on the Lord's last week before the cross contrasted with that of the religious authorities. While the leaders wanted to trap him in his words by their questions and thereby find a basis for accusing him and having him put to death, the populace was thrilled with his teaching. Teaching in the temple he engaged the Pharisees in a discussion on his identity. They were silenced by his challenging questions (Matt. 22:41–46), but "the large crowd listened to him with delight" (Mark 12:37).

Even before the Lord began his public ministry, he astonished the people in the temple when at the age of twelve he sat talking with the teachers. "Everyone who heard him was amazed at his understanding and his answers" (Luke 2:47).

So on at least ten occasions people were amazed at what and how Jesus taught. It is interesting to note the words used by the Gospel writers in recording the people's wonderment. Those who heard the boy Jesus in the temple were beside themselves *(existēmi)* with amazement (Luke 2:47). When Jesus told of his fulfilling Isaiah's prophecy, the people "marveled" or "admired" *(thaumazō,* Luke 4:22); and when he answered the Pharisees and the Herodians about taxes, they too marveled at his response (Matt. 22:22; Mark 12:17; Luke 20:26). "Surprise" seems to be the idea in the word *thambeō* that expresses the disciples' response to Jesus' teaching about rich people and the kingdom of God (Mark 10:24, 32).[2] This same word is used in Mark 1:27 to describe the people's astonishment at his healing the demon-possessed man. In reporting the same scene Luke used the noun *thambos* in writing that surprise or astonishment came on all (Luke 4:36).

2. Walter Bauer, William F. Arndt, and F. Wilbur Gingrich, *A Greek-English Lexicon of the New Testament and Other Early Christian Literature,* 2d ed., rev. F. Wilbur Gingrich and Frederick W. Danker (Chicago: University of Chicago Press, 1979), 350.

The most common word used for amazement at Jesus' teaching is *ek-plēssō*, which conveys the idea of being astounded or overwhelmed.[3] "The word expresses more sudden and vehement astonishment than the more deeply-seated 'amaze' *[thambos]* of vs. 36."[4] It is used only in the three synoptic Gospels and Acts.[5] Twelve times it is used of the response of groups to Jesus' teaching (Matt. 7:28; 13:54; 19:25; 22:33; Mark 1:22; 6:2; 7:37; 10:26; 11:18; Luke 2:48; 4:32; 9:43).

Why Such Amazement at Jesus' Teaching?

On one occasion when the people were overwhelmed by Jesus' teaching, they responded with a question, "Where did this man get this wisdom?" (Matt. 13:54). Mark's Gospel words this response in two questions: "Where did this man get these things?" and "What's this wisdom that has been given him?" (Mark 6:2).

Why were the people who heard Jesus teach so astonished? Four verses in the Gospels give the answer: "He taught as one who had authority" (Matt. 7:29; Mark 1:22). "What is this? A new teaching—and with authority!" (Mark 1:27). There was an absoluteness about his teaching, a sense of finality, "a unique freshness"[6] and confidence about this Teacher's words.

But why should this quality so startle and surprise the people? Had they not heard this kind of teaching? Matthew and Mark tell us: He taught "as one who had authority, and not as their teachers of the law" (Matt. 7:29; Mark 1:22). How did his teaching differ from that of the teachers of the law? Jesus *was* like the teachers of the law (many of whom were called rabbis) in some ways (see chap. 3). But he differed from them in many ways. The teachers of the law quoted Scripture, tradition, or other teachers to support their own instructions. Their teaching was second-hand repetition of the views and decisions of previous rabbis. They dared not be independent in their views. One rabbi would

3. Ibid., 244.

4. F. W. Farrar, *The Gospel according to St Luke*, Cambridge Greek Testament for Schools and Colleges (Cambridge: Cambridge University Press, 1884), 155.

5. In classical Greek the related verb *plēssō* meant "to strike or blow" (James Hope Moulton and George Milligan, *The Vocabulary of the Greek Testament* [London: Hodder and Stoughton, 1930; reprint, Grand Rapids: Eerdmans, 1972], 520). Hence *ekplēssō* suggests being struck out of their senses with astonishment (cf. John D. Grassmick, "Mark," in *The Bible Knowledge Commentary, New Testament*, ed. John F. Walvoord and Roy B. Zuck [Wheaton, Ill.: Victor, 1983], 109).

6. Norval Geldenhuys, *Commentary on the Gospel of Luke*, New International Commentary on the New Testament (Grand Rapids: Eerdmans, 1951), 169.

present a precept on the basis of another illustrious rabbi, who in turn had spoken on the authority of a previous rabbi. "For example, R[abbi] Eliazer piously disavowed novelty: 'nor have I ever in my life said a thing which I did not hear from my teachers' (*Sukkah* 28a; a similar statement is made about R[abbi] Johanan b[en] Zakkai. . . ."[7] It is reported that on one occasion the Rabbi Hillel (?B.C. 70–? A.D. 10) spoke on "the matter all the day, but they did not receive his teaching until he said, Thus I heard from Shemaiah and Abtalion."[8]

Jesus Christ, of course, made no such appeal to older authorities. He was his own authority. "The authority which held the audience spell-bound was not the magic of a great reputation, but the irresistible force of a Divine message, delivered under the sense of a Divine mission."[9] Nor was he quibbling over minute details of religious function, as the teachers of the law so often did.

The differences were clear. They argued; he announced. They deliberated about the truth; he delivered the truth. While they pondered, he proclaimed. They taught what their fathers had said, but Jesus taught what God the Father said. Their burdens were heavy (Luke 11:46), but his "burden" is light (Matt. 11:30).

Mark wrote that the people in the synagogue at Capernaum referred to Jesus' teaching as "new," as well as "with authority" (Mark 1:27). It was new *(kainos)* in the sense of being "fresh," and not previously known.[10] So his new content, taught in an attitude of certainty and finality, surprised and dumbfounded his listeners. His words today, recorded in the Gospels, still bring amazement to many.

Jesus' authoritative teaching astounded the multitudes but disturbed the religious leaders. During his last few days, the chief priests, teachers of the law, and elders challenged the source of his authority, asking, "Who gave you this authority?" (Matt. 21:23; Mark 11:28; Luke 20:2). Because of their belligerence, he refused to answer them (Matt. 21:27; Mark 11:33; Luke 20:8). Of course, his authority was granted by God the Father (Matt. 28:18; John 5:27; 17:2)—another fact that clearly distinguished him from other religious teachers of his day.

7. Leon Morris, *The Gospel according to St. Luke,* Tyndale New Testament Commentaries (Grand Rapids: Eerdmans, 1974), 109.

8. W. D. Davies and D. C. Allison, *A Critical and Exegetical Commentary on the Gospel according to Saint Matthew,* International Critical Commentary, 2 vols. (Edinburgh: Clark, 1988), 1:726.

9. Henry Barclay Swete, *Studies in the Teaching of Our Lord* (London: Hodder and Stoughton, 1903), 19.

10. Alfred Plummer, *The Gospel according to St. Mark,* Thornapple Commentaries (1914; reprint, Grand Rapids: Baker, 1982), 69; and Bauer, Arndt, and Gingrich, *Greek-English Lexicon,* 394.

No wonder the temple guards who were sent by the chief priests and Pharisees to arrest Jesus (John 7:32) returned empty handed! Hearing Jesus invite spiritually thirsty people in the temple to come to him, the guards were impressed. They reported, "No one ever spoke the way this man does" (John 7:46). Even they, perhaps calloused militiamen, were so impressed with this unusual Instructor that they did not attempt to apprehend him.

Why Was Jesus' Teaching Authoritative?

The Gospels reveal at least four reasons why the Savior's teaching possessed the ring of authority.

The Identity of His Words

The teachers of the law tutored people on previous teachers' opinions. Jesus' words, however, were from a different source—God the Father. He stated it this way:

> "For the one whom God has sent speaks the words of God" (John 3:34)
>
> "My teaching is not my own. It comes from him who sent me" (John 7:16)
>
> "But he who sent me is reliable, and what I have heard from him I tell the world" (John 8:26)
>
> "I do nothing on my own but speak just what the Father has taught me" (John 8:28)
>
> "For I did not speak of my own accord, but the Father who sent me commanded me what to say and how to say it. . . . So whatever I say is just what the Father has told me to say" (John 12:49–50)
>
> "The words I say to you are not just my own. Rather, it is the Father, living in me, who is doing his work" (John 14:10)
>
> "These words you hear are not my own; they belong to the Father who sent me" (John 14:24)
>
> "For I gave them the words you gave me and they accepted them" (John 17:8)

No rabbi or teacher of the law, with his quibbling and dependence on ancestral authorities, could ever say his words were what God the Father had given him to communicate.

Jesus' words were from God the Father because he himself was sent by God. Forty-two times the Gospel of John mentions that Jesus was "sent" by the Father. These references occur in seventeen of the twenty-one chapters in John (all except chapters 1, 2, 19, 21). Nine times Jesus said he came down from heaven (John 3:13, 31; 6:33, 38, 41–42, 50–51, 58), and six times mention is made of the fact that he was "from God" (John 3:2; 13:3; 16:27–28, 30; 17:8). Therefore he and his words are the source of spiritual life, as is stated thirty-two times in John (3:15, 19, 36; 4:14; 5:21 [twice], 24 [twice], 39; 6:27, 33, 35, 40, 47–48, 51, 53–54, 57–58, 68; 8:12; 10:10, 28; 11:25; 12:25, 50; 14:6, 19; 17:2–3; 20:31).

As the authoritative Teacher whose words were from God, Jesus affirmed the eternal, lasting nature of his words: "My words will never pass away" (Matt. 24:35; Mark 13:31; Luke 21:33).

The Certainty of His Knowledge

Another reason Jesus' teaching exhibited such heaven-sent authority is that his words reveal his innate knowledge of human nature. Because of his deity, he is omniscient; therefore, as John wrote, "he knew all men" and "knew what is in a man" (2:24–25). No human teacher in his day, no matter how well schooled in the traditions of the rabbis, and no teacher today, no matter how well trained in education or psychology, can claim to know the thoughts or intentions of his or her pupils. Jesus' insight into what others were thinking was evidence of his unique position.

Jesus knew the minds of three groups: inquirers, his disciples, and his enemies.

Regarding *inquirers,* "When Jesus saw Nathaniel approaching, he said of him, 'Here is a true Israelite, in whom there is nothing false [*dolos,* literally, no deceit].'" Surprised, Nathaniel asked, "How do you know me?" (John 1:47–48). Sensing Jesus' remarkable foreknowledge of him, Nathaniel made a notable statement about Jesus' identity: "Rabbi, you are the Son of God; you are the King of Israel" (v. 49).

When Jesus talked with the Samaritan woman about "living water" (John 4:10), he startled her by observing, "You have had five husbands, and the man you now have is not your husband" (v. 18). Leaving her water jar at the well so she could return quickly to town,[11] she urged the townspeople to go "see a man who told me everything I ever did" (v. 29). As a result, many Samaritans "believed in him because of the woman's testimony, 'He told me everything I ever did'" (v. 39). She was so im-

---

11. Her leaving her water jar was "a pledge of her speedy return, the proof that she goes to seek someone. . . . What a contrast between the vivacity of this woman and the silent and contemplative departure of Nicodemus!" (F. Godet, *Commentary on the Gospel of John,* 3 vols. [Edinburgh: Clark, 1892], 2:120–21).

pressed with his knowledge of her that she and others believed in the Savior. His words were unquestionably the words of a Teacher whose authority was from heaven.

Jesus also knew that the crowd he fed near the Sea of Galilee wanted to "make him king by force" (John 6:15). After Jesus fed the five thousand and walked on water, he was discussing with the crowds his claim to be the bread of life (John 6:32–59). Many of those who heard him commented, "This is a hard teaching. Who can accept it?" (v. 60). Jesus, "knowing in himself" (as the Greek in v. 61 reads) that they "were grumbling," asked, "Does this offend you?" (v. 64). Then "many of his disciples turned back and no longer followed him" (v. 66). From this it is obvious that the word *disciples* does not always mean believers. Here it refers to interested listeners, those who were following him in the sense of listening and learning. (Those disciples were distinguished from the Twelve, whom Jesus addressed in verse 67.) John explained that Jesus knew "from the beginning which of them did not believe" (v. 64).

Jesus knew the thinking of his *disciples*. He knew who would betray him (John 6:64, 70–71). He knew of their discussion about his comment on the yeast of the Pharisees and Sadducees (Matt. 16:5–8). When they argued "which one of them would be the greatest," he knew "their thoughts" (Luke 9:46–47). The word *thoughts* is the plural of *dialogismos* (a derivative is "dialogue"), the same word rendered "argument" in verse 46. So Luke conveyed the idea that Jesus was fully aware of their argument or dispute. When a woman poured expensive perfume on Jesus' head while he was seated at dinner, the disciples were indignant about what they called a waste (Matt. 26:6–9). Jesus knew what they were saying (v. 10). When Jesus was washing the disciples' feet in the upper room, he commented, "You are clean, though not every one of you" (John 13:10). Then the apostle John added an explanation (a common feature in John's Gospel) that Jesus made the comment because "he knew who was going to betray him" (v. 11; cf. v. 21).

Jesus also knew the thinking of his *enemies*. The Gospels reveal six instances in which this fact is revealed about our Lord. In Capernaum he told a paralyzed man, who had been lowered on his mat through the roof, "Your sins are forgiven." Pharisees and teachers of the law, who had come from throughout Galilee and Judea to hear Jesus, "began thinking to themselves" that his pronouncement of forgiveness bordered on blasphemy. They correctly understood that only God can forgive sins, but they failed to recognize that Jesus possesses deity as God the incarnate Son. Immediately Jesus knew "in his spirit that they were reasoning that way" (Mark 2:8 NASB) in their hearts. "Were reasoning" translates the verb *dialogizomai* (related to the noun *dialogismos*, used in the parallel passage in Luke 5:22).

When Simon the Pharisee invited Jesus to dinner, a sinful woman poured a jar of perfume on Jesus' feet. Seeing this, the Pharisee "said to himself" that if Jesus were a prophet, he should know the woman's character (Luke 7:39). Jesus then told him a story about two debtors and a creditor (Luke 7:40–47). The Lord's response shows he knew what Simon the Pharisee was thinking.

As we have seen in Luke 9:47–48, *dialogismos* means a debate or a dispute. In Mark 2:8 the noun conveys the idea of thinking or reasoning, though perhaps the word here too suggests a dispute in one's mind, turning over a question in one's thinking. Matthew, recording the same incident, used *enthymēsis*, "reflection or thinking" (Matt. 9:4).[12]

On another occasion when Jesus was teaching in a synagogue, the Pharisees and the teachers of the law were watching Jesus closely to see if he would heal a man's shriveled right hand on the Sabbath. They wanted, of course, to accuse him of breaking the Sabbath, thereby violating the law. "Jesus knew what they were thinking" (Luke 6:8).[13] Here again, *dialogismos*, "thoughts or disputes," is used.

A fourth time the Lord knew the thinking of his enemies was when the Pharisees, having seen him heal a demon-possessed man who was blind and mute, felt Jesus was driving out demons by the power of Beelzebub, the prince of demons (Matt. 12:22–24). Without having heard their words, "Jesus knew their thoughts" (v. 25, *enthymēsis*, the same word Matthew used in 9:4) and he readily pointed out the falseness of their accusation. Luke wrote that Jesus knew their minds (11:17, *dianoēmata*, a word used only here in the New Testament).

In a fifth incident tax collectors had asked Peter if Jesus paid the temple tax. When Peter entered a house to ask Jesus about it, Jesus spoke first, raising the issue of tax payments. The fact that Jesus spoke first shows that he knew of the question being asked by the collectors (Matt. 17:24–27).

The sixth time Jesus was aware of his enemies' thoughts was when the Pharisees and Herodians asked him about payment of taxes to Caesar in an effort "to trap him in his words" (Matt. 22:15). Jesus knew "their evil intent," as Matthew put it (v. 18), "their hypocrisy," as Mark wrote (12:15), and "their duplicity," as Luke stated (20:23). The Greek word

12. Matthew also wrote *enthymēsis* in Matthew 12:25. The word is used elsewhere in the New Testament only twice (Acts 17:29, where the NIV translates it "design," and Heb. 4:12). Marshall observes that Matthew may have associated the word *enthymēsis* in Matthew 9:4 and 12:25 (and the verb *enthysmeomai* in 1:20 and 9:4) with evil or incorrect thoughts (I. Howard Marshall, *The Gospel of Luke*, New International Greek Testament Commentary [Grand Rapids: Eerdmans, 1978], 473).

13. In recording this incident, Matthew and Mark did not mention that Jesus knew the thoughts of his enemies.

Luke used is *panourgia*, which always conveys the idea of craftiness or trickery (1 Cor. 3:19; 2 Cor. 4:2; 11:3; Eph. 4:14). Literally the word means "readiness to do anything."[14] In the upper room, the eleven disciples admitted, "Now we can see that you know all things" (John 16:30).

Jesus' knowledge of what people were thinking demonstrates his authority over all others. Such authoritative knowledge resulted in amazement, belief, praise, rejection, humility, anger, and silence.

The Finality of His Claims

The source of Jesus' words was unique (from God the Father); the knowledge Jesus had was also unique, for it was complete. In addition his claims were unique because they had a note of finality to them. What he claimed to be true matched reality. What he promised came to pass. What he asserted was fact, what he affirmed was correct. Even his religious rivals had to admit this. "Teacher," they said, "we know you are a man of integrity and that you teach the way of God in accordance with the truth" (Matt. 22:16).

In his assertions Jesus made no apologies. His claims left no room for debate or further investigations.[15] What he said was certain, simply because he said it. He was sure of what he proclaimed. As Robertson noted, "He always speaks as if His word were enough."[16] This becomes patent in his frequent references to "my word(s)" and the Gospel writers' references to his "word(s)."

Table 7
References to Jesus' Words as Authoritative

"Everyone who hears *these words of mine* . . . " (Matt. 7:24, 26; Luke 7:47, 49)
"*My words* will never pass away" (Matt. 24:35; Mark 13:31; Luke 21:33)
Then Peter remembered *the word* Jesus had spoken (Matt. 26:75; Mark 14:72; Luke 22:61)
With many similar parables Jesus spoke *the word* to them (Mark 4:33)
"If anyone is ashamed of me and *my words* . . . " (Mark 8:38; Luke 9:26)
The disciples were amazed at *his words* (Mark 10:24)
All . . . were amazed at *the gracious words* that came from his lips (Luke 4:22)
When they heard *Jesus' words*, [they] acknowledged that God's way was right (Luke 7:29)
All the people hung on *his words* (Luke 19:48)
Then they remembered *his words* (Luke 24:8)

14. Bauer, Arndt, and Gingrich, *Greek-English Lexicon*, 608.
15. G. Campbell Morgan, *The Teaching of Christ* (Old Tappan, N.J.: Revell, 1913), 4.
16. James Robertson, *Our Lord's Teaching* (London: Black, 1901), 3.

He was a prophet, *powerful in word* and deed (Luke 24:19)

Then they believed the Scriptures and *the words* that Jesus had spoken (John 2:22)

The one whom God has sent speaks *the words* of God (John 3:34)

And because of *his words* many more became believers (John 4:41)

"Whoever hears *my word* and believes him who sent me has eternal life" (John 5:24)

"*The words I have spoken* to you are spirit and they are life" (John 6:63)

"You have *the words* of eternal life" (John 6:68)

On hearing *his words,* some of the people said, "Surely this man is the Prophet" (John 7:40)

He spoke *these words* while teaching in the temple area (John 8:20)

"Yet you are ready to kill me, because you have no room for *my word*" (John 8:37)

"If a man keeps *my word,* he will never see death" (John 8:51)

At *these words* the Jews were again divided (John 10:19)

"As for the person who hears *my words* but does not keep them, I do not judge him" (John 12:47)

"There is a judge for the one who rejects me and does not accept *my words; that very word* which I spoke will condemn him at the last day" (John 12:48)

"*The words* I say to you are not just my own" (John 14:10)

"*These words* you hear are not my own" (John 14:24)

"You are already clean because of *the word* I have spoken to you" (John 15:3)

"If you remain in me and *my words* remain in you . . . it will be given you" (John 15:7)

"Remember *the words* I spoke to you" (John 15:20)

"For I gave them *the words* you gave me" (John 17:8)

This happened so that *the words* Jesus had spoken would be fulfilled (John 18:32)

Morgan commented on the significance of these verses in this way.

> My own conviction is that there is not a single one of these passages that we can believe to be true if we deny the Deity of our Lord. And if the statement be questioned, then take any of these claims, and put them into the lips of any other teacher, and it must at once be seen how entirely and absolutely they are out of place. They are words which claim a full and final authority for the One who uttered them.[17]

Another indication of the finality of Jesus' claims is his frequent use of the clause, "I tell you the truth," with which he began numerous statements, thereby adding a note of solemnity to his words. (The King James Version renders these words, "Verily I say unto you.")[18] The

17. Morgan, *The Teaching of Christ,* 8.
18. "Verily" or "truth" translates the same Greek word *amēn.*

clause occurs in each of the four Gospels for a total of seventy-five times[19] (thirty in Matthew, thirteen in Mark, six in Luke, and twenty-six in John).[20]

Another clause that points up Jesus' authoritative teaching is "I tell you." Occurring sixty-six times in the Gospels,[21] this clause too is unlike any used by the teachers of the law, who depended on the views of their predecessors rather than making their own assertions.

Our Lord's authority beyond the mere human level also shows up in his "I am" claims, especially in the Gospel of John. He declared, "I am the bread of life" (John 6:35, 41, 48, 51), "I am the light of the world" (8:12; 9:5), "I am the gate" (10:7, 9), "I am the good shepherd" (10:11, 14), "I am the resurrection and the life" (11:25), "I am the way and the truth and the life" (14:6), and "I am the vine" (15:1, 5). Again such bold claims are without precedent!

To these claims can be added Jesus' many promises and numerous prophecies, all of which he faithfully has fulfilled or will fulfill. Those to whom he addressed these directives felt the compulsion of his words; they sensed the authority by which he spoke, and they responded accordingly (see the Appendix). Jesus gave commands to individual disciples, to the Twelve as a group, to demons, to individuals he healed, to John's disciples, to servants at a wedding, to Zacchaeus, to the Pharisees, to Mary of Magdala, to Thomas, to the crowds, to Satan, and even to dead people!

In addition to the direct quotations of Jesus' many commands, the Gospel writers recorded a number of occasions when Jesus commanded or ordered people regarding certain facts. He ordered evil spirits to depart (Mark 1:25; 9:25; Luke 4:36; 8:29), he commanded people not to tell of his miracles of healing (Mark 3:12; 5:43; 7:36; Luke 5:14;

19. Six other times the NIV has the clause "I tell you the truth." However, the Greek wording differs slightly. Three times Luke has, literally, "I say to you truly" (9:2; 12:44; 21:3), and three times John wrote, literally, "I say truth" (8:46) or "I am the truth" (8:45; 16:7).

20. Matt. 5:18, 26; 6:2, 5, 16; 8:10; 10:15, 23, 42; 11:11; 13:17; 16:28; 17:20; 18:3, 13, 18; 19:23, 28; 21:21, 31; 23:36; 24:2, 34, 47; 25:12, 40, 45; 26:13, 21, 34; Mark 3:28; 8:12; 9:1, 41; 10:15, 29; 11:23; 12:43; 13:30; 14:9, 18, 25, 30; Luke 4:24; 12:37; 18:17, 29; 21:32; 23:43; John 1:51; 3:3, 5, 11; 5:19, 24, 25; 6:26, 32, 47, 53; 8:34, 51, 58; 10:1, 7; 12:24; 13:16, 20, 21, 38; 14:12; 16:7, 20, 23; 21:18. Of interest is the fact that when John recorded these words by Jesus, the Greek word *amēn* is repeated. That is why the King James Version has the double "Verily, verily." (The NIV does not make that distinction.) This doubling occurs only in John, and is for emphasis.

21. Matt. 5:20, 22, 28, 32, 34, 39, 44; 6:25, 29; 11:9, 22, 24; 12:6, 31, 36; 16:18; 17:12; 18:10, 19, 22; 19:9, 24; 21:43; 23:39; 26:29, 64; Mark 2:11; 5:41; 9:13; 11:24; Luke 5:24; 6:27; 7:14, 26, 28, 47; 10:12; 11:8, 9, 51; 12:4, 5, 8, 22, 27, 51, 59; 13:3, 5, 24, 35; 14:24; 15:7, 10; 16:9; 17:34; 18:8, 14; 19:26, 40; 22:16, 18, 34, 37; John 4:35; 13:33.

8:56), he ordered the disciples to cross to the other side of the lake (Matt. 8:18), he ordered the winds and waves to be calm (Luke 8:25), he ordered the disciples to say nothing about his identity as the Son of God (Luke 9:21), he ordered people to bring the blind beggar to him (Luke 18:40), he commanded Peter to put away his sword (John 18:11), and he commanded the disciples to love each other (John 13:34; 14:15, 21; 15:10, 12, 14, 17).

Can there be any question about Jesus' towering level of unmatched authority in his teaching? No wonder God the Father told Peter, James, and John on the Mount of Transfiguration, "This is my Son, whom I have chosen; *listen to him*" (Luke 9:35)!

Can We Teach with Jesus' Authority?

Since only Jesus Christ is the Son of God, only he could teach with intrinsic authority from God the Father. Our authority, however, is derived. Therefore we cannot expect to duplicate Jesus in receiving words directly from the Father, in having innate, complete knowledge of what others were thinking, in the unparalleled absoluteness of his claims, and in exercising the sovereign authority of his commands.

Why then consider the subject of his authority? Because we can derive authority from Jesus through his words. Christ authoritatively revealed the word of God; we too can have teaching that is authoritative—that has the ring of divine authority about it—"to the extent to which it is faithful to God's . . . revelation."[22] The authority does not stem from within us; it is within the Scriptures, which we teach. God is the ultimate authority and the Bible, which reveals him to us, "is divinely authoritative, possessing divinely *delegated* authority."[23] Since the Bible, then, is our "absolute standard and test of truth,"[24] we can teach with authority as we are true to the Scriptures. It is not what we say that is authoritative; it is what God says in his written Word. Authoritative teaching lies in what we say *he* says!

We can summarize the similarities and differences between Jesus' authoritative teaching and ours in these ways.

1. Jesus' words were from God the Father; he taught only what the Father instructed him to teach.

---

22. Robert W. Pazmiño, *Principles and Practices of Christian Education* (Grand Rapids: Baker, 1992), 125.

23. Roy B. Zuck, *Teaching with Spiritual Power* (1963; reprint, Grand Rapids: Kregel, 1993), 118 (italics added).

24. Ibid.

As we faithfully study and then teach the Scriptures, we are communicating those words of our Lord to others. We are part of a divine chain of communication from God the Father, to God the Son, to us (by revealed truths in the Bible), to our students. "We can use our minds to master our subject, and just as Jesus taught with absolute expertise, we can achieve a relative expertise based on study."[25]

2. Jesus possessed innate knowledge of what others were thinking.

We can study our students, seeking to know the characteristics of the age group we teach, and seeking to know them individually—their backgrounds, characteristics, interests, problems, strengths, weaknesses.

3. Jesus made unique claims about himself and his teaching, referring to his imperishable and efficacious words and asserting, "I tell you the truth," "I say to you," and "I am."

We can point others to this One whose claims are demanding and absolute, and to the Scriptures where these claims are faithfully recorded.

4. Jesus voiced scores of commands to individuals and groups—imperatives to follow him, his example, and his teachings.

We can urge our students to know these commands revealed in Scripture and to respond to them in obedience to Christ.

In these ways our teaching can take on a new flavor, a significant dynamic. Though our authority is derived, not inherent, we can teach as he taught.

You Can Do It . . .

As you get ready to teach, prepare thoroughly, knowing that the better prepared you are, the better the Lord can use you. Begin early in the week in order to give yourself adequate time to read, study, meditate, think, and pray.

As you prepare, ask the Lord to give you a sense of confidence, knowing that you are teaching his Word which is "living and active" (Heb. 4:12).

Read about the common characteristics of the age group you are teaching. Note how these traits are evident in the individuals in your group or class.

25. Robert E. Delnay, *Teach as He Taught* (Chicago: Moody, 1987), 31.

On three-by-five cards write facts you know about your students' backgrounds, problems, and interests. If you do not know these facts, spend time with the students. Invite them to your home, visit them in their homes, talk with them before and after class, converse with them by telephone, take part in social events together.

Encourage your pupils to know—and obey—God's commands to them in the Bible. Point out that his revelation requires a response.

"Take my yoke upon you
and learn from me."

Matthew 11:29

5

What Qualities Marked Jesus as an Outstanding Teacher?

Think back on your teachers. A few have no doubt been outstanding; others may have been average or passable. Still others may have seemed incapable in the classroom—people who did not quite have the skill to communicate well or to make the lessons interesting, and in whose classes you therefore felt uncomfortable or bored.

What is it about this third category of teachers that contributes to their ineffectiveness? Perhaps you have heard students make remarks about a teacher. Or perhaps you have made these remarks yourself. The following fourteen remarks point up common areas of weakness. Note how they relate to various deficiencies.

Typical Student Remarks about Inept Teachers	Deficiencies Revealed by These Remarks
1. "He (or she) doesn't really seem to know and love the Lord deeply, nor to have a balanced personality."	1. Maturity
2. "He doesn't seem well prepared and doesn't seem to know his subject."	2. Mastery

3. "He seems unsure of what he says, as if he   3. Certainty
   hasn't made up his mind."

4. "He seems arrogant and proud that he is a   4. Humility
   teacher."

5. "He doesn't always live what he teaches.   5. Consistency
   Sometimes he does the opposite of what he
   tells us to do."

6. "He never wants us to get on some other   6. Spontaneity
   subject; he wants to follow his material
   without being interrupted or diverted."

7. "I seldom know what he is talking about;   7. Clarity
   he is often unclear and speaks over our
   heads."

8. "He doesn't seem excited about what he's   8. Urgency
   teaching."

9. "Each lesson is always the same. There's no   9. Variety
   variety, and he never involves us in the lessons or asks us questions or uses visuals."

10. "He often runs out of material before the   10. Quantity
    classtime is ended."

11. "I don't sense that he really knows us, is in- 11. Empathy
    terested in us, or is concerned about our
    needs."

12. "He never spends any time with us outside   12. Intimacy
    class to get to know us better and teach in-
    formally."

13. "Sometimes he makes remarks in class that   13. Sensitivity
    denigrate some of the students. At times he
    seems insensitive to us."

14. "He seldom relates the lessons to our lives. 14. Relevancy
    He doesn't help us see how to apply what
    he taught."

As you describe effective teachers under whom you have studied, no doubt you would include several of the fourteen qualities listed in the right-hand column. Skillful teachers have personal and spiritual maturity, mastery of their subjects, consistency of life, and certainty of what they are teaching. They are humble, spontaneous, and flexible, clear in what they are communicating. They portray enthusiasm and a sense of urgency in their teaching. Variety is a keynote of their pedagogy. They often seem to have more to share than time allows. They love their students and show compassion and empathy for them. Being sensitive, they are careful not to hurt the feelings of their pupils. And they always help students see how to apply truth to their lives.

Jesus demonstrated these fourteen qualities superbly! And he did so consistently. Besides teaching with unique, absolute authority (see chap. 4), Jesus modeled the teaching process ideally by exhibiting these qualities, eight of which are discussed in this chapter and six in the next. Seeing how the model Teacher displayed these virtues can help each of us to become better teachers.

Maturity

From a human standpoint Jesus was a balanced, mature person. And of course, as the Son of God, possessing full deity, he was spiritually mature. In his childhood days he "grew and became strong; he was filled with wisdom, and the grace of God was upon him" (Luke 2:40). This account suggests growth physically, mentally, and spiritually. In his teen years he matured "in wisdom and stature, and in favor with God and men" (2:52), a reference that points to his maturing in four ways: mentally ("in wisdom"), physically ("stature"), spiritually ("in favor with God"), and socially ("in favor with . . . men"). The word *grew (prokaptō)* in verse 52 means "to progress or advance." It "has lost its original sense 'to make one's way forward by chopping away obstacles.'"[1] This word, used elsewhere in the New Testament only in Romans 13:12; Galatians 1:1; and 2 Timothy 3:9, "is derived from pioneers *cutting down* trees in the path of an advancing army."[2] The word conveys progress. *Hēlikia* (stature) often means age, though here (as in Luke 19:3) it means physical height.

The picture in Luke 2:40, 52 is one of perfect and complete development. Jesus was indeed mature. As a result, "He was more and more highly esteemed and loved by his fellow-men" and "enjoyed the highest respect and affection of people who knew Him."[3]

Leading others to accept the things of God calls for teachers today to have balanced personalities—to be growing mentally, spiritually, and socially.

1. I. Howard Marshall, *The Gospel of Luke*, New International Greek Testament Commentary (Grand Rapids: Eerdmans, 1978), 130.

2. F. W. Farrar, *The Gospel according to St Luke*, Cambridge Greek Testament for Schools and Colleges (Cambridge: Cambridge University Press, 1884), 125 (italics his).

3. Norval Geldenhuys, *Commentary on the Gospel of Luke*, New International Commentary on the New Testament (Grand Rapids: Eerdmans, 1951), 130.

Mastery

Jesus certainly knew his subject. Having come to earth to reveal God (John 1:18; 17:26) and his words (John 3:34; 14:10, 24; 17:8), he displayed full mastery of what he taught. He was never dependent on notes, never at a loss for what to say, never unprepared, never taken aback or confused by a question from friend or foe, never unsure of what to communicate. He had something to say—and people listened, hanging on to every word (Luke 19:48).

Because of the time when and the place where Jesus lived, he undoubtedly knew three languages. Aramaic, a Semitic language related to Hebrew, may have been his mother tongue since "it is generally accepted that Aramaic was the native tongue of Palestine in the first century."[4] Support for this is seen in a quotation from the Aramaic (Acts 1:19, *Akeldama*, Field of Blood), which Luke said was the language of the people of Jerusalem. The Gospel writers, writing in Greek, recorded a number of Aramaic words Jesus spoke.[5]

Abba (Father, Mark 14:36)

Bar (son, Matt. 16:17)

Boanērges (sons of thunder, Mark 3:17)

Cephas (Peter, John 1:42)

Eloi, Eloi, lama sabachthani (My God, My God, why have you forsaken me? Matt. 27:46; Mark 15:34)

Ephphatha (Be opened, Mark 7:34)

Gehenna (hell, Matt. 5:22, 29, 30; 10:28; 18:9; 23:15, 33; Mark 9:43, 45, 47; Luke 12:5; 16:23)

Mamōnas (money, Matt. 6:24; Luke 16:9, 11, 13)

Pascha (Passover, Matt. 26:2, 18; Mark 14:14; Luke 22:8, 11, 15)

Rabbi (teacher, Matt. 23:7–8)

Raca (you fool, Matt. 5:22)

Sabbata (Sabbath, Matt. 12:5, 11; Mark 3:4)

Sata (measures, Matt. 13:33)

Satanas (Satan, Matt. 4:10; 12:26; 16:23; Mark 3:23, 26; 4:15; 8:33; Luke 10:18; 11:18; 13:16; 22:31)

Talitha koum (Little girl, I say to you, arise, Mark 5:41).

4. Robert H. Stein, *The Method and Message of Jesus' Teachings* (Philadelphia: Westminster, 1978), 5.

5. Cf. ibid.

Also certain expressions in the Gospels are Aramaisms, Greek translations of sayings that were originally Aramaic.[6]

No doubt Jesus also spoke and read Hebrew. He referred to the "jot and tittle" (Matt. 5:18 KJV) of the Hebrew alphabet, the jot being the Hebrew letter *yod* and the *tittle* being a small portion of a Hebrew letter. He also frequently quoted the Old Testament. Beginning at age six, Jesus may well have studied Hebrew in a Jewish school as a child.[7] Schools for children were normally held in the local synagogues. Before entering primary school, however, children in Jesus' day were given instruction in the home, in which they memorized Scripture and learned to read Hebrew. At five years of age they began at home to study the Old Testament, beginning with the Book of Leviticus.[8] At age twelve Jesus may have conversed in Hebrew with the teachers in the temple courts (Luke 2:46–47).

Jesus no doubt spoke Greek, for that was the language of Sepphoris, Caesarea, and Tiberias, towns not too far from his hometown of Nazareth.[9] No doubt he spoke Greek when he was in the Decapolis (Mark 5:20; 7:31), an area east of the Jordan River with ten cities established by the Greek Empire. When he talked with the centurion's friends about the centurion's servant in Capernaum (Luke 7:1–10), they may have relayed his message in Greek. The soldier was not a Jew (vv. 5–9).

Jesus' visit northward to the region near Tyre and Sidon would have involved his speaking in Greek to a Canaanite woman (Matt. 15:22), "a Greek born in Syrian Phoenicia" (Mark 7:26), whose daughter he healed of demon possession (Matt. 15:22–28; Mark 7:25–30). And his brief conversation with Pilate (Matt. 27:11; Mark 15:1–5; Luke 23:1–3; John 18:33–37; 19:8–11) would have required a knowledge of Greek.

Thorough mastery of his subject and competence in the languages of the people with whom he communicated helped make Jesus a dynamic teacher. This fact challenges teachers today to know their subjects well, to prepare thoroughly, and to adapt their subjects to the students' level of comprehension. Adequate preparation of each lesson may call for hours of study (unlike our Lord who, as the eternal Son of God, knew what he was teaching without preparation). Is the time and effort worth it? Certainly, because thorough preparation results in more effective communication.

6. Ibid., and Joachim Jeremias, *New Testament Theology,* trans. John Bowden (New York: Scribner's Sons, 1971), 6–7.

7. Alfred Edersheim, *Sketches of Jewish Social Life in the Days of Christ* (1876; reprint, Grand Rapids: Eerdmans, 1976), 133.

8. Ibid., 130.

9. Frederick W. Farrar, *The Life of Christ* (New York: Doran, 1876), 42.

Certainty

Because of Jesus' mastery of his subject matter, he spoke with certainty. He never sensed or expressed doubt about what he taught; he never once said "maybe," "perhaps," or "possibly" in making his assertions of truth.

The Gospels give no hint that Jesus ever was unsure of his words. Not once did he say, "I think so," "Perhaps you should," "This might be true," "I hope this is right," or "I don't know." He never stumbled or fumbled over his words. "He never spoke tentatively, timidly, or apologetically. He knew His message and never stuttered in declaring it."[10]

To the extent they are well prepared, teachers today can also teach with a note of certainty and confidence. Teachers who are unsure of what they say do not engender confidence on the part of the students in what they are teaching. Uncertainty breeds uncertainty.

Of course sometimes a teacher does need to say, "I don't know," and at other times he or she may need to express tentativeness about a suggested interpretation of a Bible passage. But even so, the teacher can assure the students that he or she will seek an answer or admit that some spiritual matters are unclear to our finite minds.

Humility

Writing about Jesus' incarnation, Paul stated that our Lord "humbled himself" (Phil. 2:8). Jesus' coming to earth was an act of humiliation, in which he took on himself the very form of a servant (2:7). This explains why Jesus said that he, the Son of Man, "did not come to be served, but to serve" (Matt. 20:28; Mark 10:45) and "I am among you as one who serves" (Luke 22:27).

Such statements about humility stand in sharp contrast to the proud attitude of Jesus' adversaries, the Pharisees and the teachers of the law (Luke 18:9; Matt. 23:5–7). After speaking of the pride of the Pharisaical hypocrites, Jesus addressed the disciples: "The greatest among you will be your servant. For whoever exalts himself will be humbled, and whoever humbles himself will be exalted" (Matt. 23:11–12).[11] What a shocking statement to say that to be a servant is to be the greatest!

10. Howard G. Hendricks, "Following the Master Teacher," in *The Christian Educator's Handbook on Teaching*, ed. Kenneth O. Gangel and Howard G. Hendricks (Wheaton, Ill.: Victor, 1989), 20.

11. Luke recorded Jesus' having made this same statement on two earlier occasions. One was at the home of a prominent Pharisee when the guests all picked the places of honor at the table (Luke 14:1–11), and the other was after he told the parables of the Phar-

"To serve" translates *diakoneō*, which refers to carrying out "undone activities, such as waiting on tables or caring for household needs—activities without apparent dignity."[12] To the Greeks such submission and dependence was dishonoring. "In Greek eyes, service is not very dignified. Ruling and not service is proper to a man. . . . For the Greek in his wisdom and freedom there can certainly be no question of existing to serve others."[13] Apparently the Jews took on this same attitude toward serving.[14]

Rather than proudly seeking acclaim and praise from people, as did the teachers of the law, Jesus demonstrated humility and urged his followers to do the same. This is demonstrated in a clarion way when Jesus took the position of a lowly household slave and washed the disciples' feet (John 13:1–17).

Teaching is an art of serving, a process of humbly guiding others not to oneself but to the Lord and his Word. Therefore pride is totally inappropriate in a teacher. Paul put it bluntly, using two related phrases to underscore his point: "Do not be proud. . . . Do not be conceited" (Rom. 12:16). The first exhortation is a participle that literally reads, "Do not become wise concerning yourselves."

Respect from our students comes not from exalting ourselves, but from humbling ourselves and taking the attitude of a servant. Pride is repulsive; humble service is appreciated. Pride repels, humility attracts. Do you want your pupils to respond to the truths you are teaching? Then do not let pride (and the refusal to serve) stand as an obstacle to learning. Effectiveness in teaching calls for humility in attitude. Effective teachers follow the example of the Lord Jesus, who said, "I am gentle and humble in heart" (Matt. 11:29).

Consistency

One of the quickest ways to discourage learners from living out the Word of God is inconsistency. Instructing students in the way to live, but not living that way ourselves, bottlenecks learning. When students

---

isee and the tax collector who prayed in the temple (Luke 18:9–14). The Lord also spoke to the disciples about self-humbling like that of a little child (Matt. 18:4).

12. J. Gary Inrig, "Called to Serve: Toward a Philosophy of Ministry," *Bibliotheca Sacra* 140 (October–December 1983): 336.

13. *Theological Dictionary of the New Testament*, s.v. "διακονέω, διακονία, διάκονος," by H. W. Beyer, 2:82–83.

14. *The New International Dictionary of New Testament Theology*, s.v. "Serve, Deacon, Worship," by K. Hess, 3:545.

see that we are "not practicing what we preach" (as Jesus accused the Pharisees, Matt. 23:3), they lose confidence in us, in the Bible, and in the Lord. When we lead lives of integrity in modeling the truths we teach, our students are encouraged to develop similar qualities in themselves. Exemplifying the truth reinforces what we teach, adding to the impact of our words.

Jesus demonstrated full harmony between his life and his lessons.[15] He told his disciples to love their enemies (Matt. 5:43–48)—and he did (Luke 23:34). He taught them to pray (Matt. 6:5–15; 7:7–12; 9:38; Mark 11:22–26; Luke 6:28; 11:1–13; 18:1)—and he did (Matt. 14:23; Mark 1:35; 6:46; Luke 5:16; 6:12; 9:28; 22:41, 44; John 17:1, 9, 20). He urged them to trust in him and not worry (Matt. 6:25–33; Luke 12:4–7, 22–34; John 14:1)—and he trusted in the Father (Matt. 26:39, 42; Mark 14:36). He challenged them to love each other (John 15:12a, 17)—and he loved them (John 15:9, 12b).

How Jesus lived never once contradicted what he taught. His manner of life matched his mode of teaching. His character was consistent with his content. He declared, "I am the truth" (John 14:6), and he lived it!

No wonder he could ask the Jewish leaders, "Can any of you prove me guilty of sin?" (John 8:46). No wonder Pilate "announced to the chief priests and the crowd, 'I find no basis for a charge against this man'" (Luke 23:4) and "What crime has this man committed? I have found in him no grounds for the death penalty" (23:22). No wonder one of the two criminals crucified with Jesus said, "This man has done nothing wrong" (23:41). No wonder a centurion, after seeing Jesus die on the cross, said, "Surely this was a righteous man" (23:47).

One of the ways Jesus modeled what he taught was by associating with his disciples daily for several years. They could see how he lived, how he reacted, how he answered opponents, how he expressed compassion for the needy, how he handled interruptions, how he prayed, how he was patient, how he forgave. "Not only could He better teach them what He said by constant contact, but also, and possibly more important, the disciples were able to see their master at work twenty-four hours a day. . . . The twelve saw Christ as He really was, every hour of every day."[16]

Jesus invited the Twelve to follow him (Matt. 4:19; 8:22; 9:9; 19:21; Mark 1:17; 2:14; 10:21; Luke 5:27; 9:59; 18:22; John 1:43; 21:19, 22). Fol-

15. William Gorden Blaikie, *The Public Ministry of Christ* (London: Nisbet, 1883; reprint, Minneapolis: Klock and Klock, 1984), 151.

16. Dennis Neil Cramer, "A Study of the Teaching Ministry of Christ in the Light of Developing Leadership in the Local Church" (Th.M. thesis, Dallas Theological Seminary, 1969), 26.

lowing him meant being with him, observing him, and imitating him. It also meant personal sacrifice and a willingness to identify with Jesus (Mark 8:34) and to become like him. Jesus expressed this goal in the statement, "Everyone who is fully trained will be like his teacher" (Luke 6:40).

Educators have long recognized the importance of teachers establishing personal relationships with their students so that the teachers' modeling by their character further encourages learning. "It is a pedagogical truism that we teach more by what we are than by what we say. . . . We learn by association with persons."[17] "Proximity between tutor and apprentice is a potent force for all learning."[18] Writing about the lack of impact by today's Christian teachers on their pupils' lives, Kirsch noted, "A personal relationship with the student is the only thing that will allow the Christian teacher to have any influence beyond the cognitive level. Students will never treasure and obey the truths of Scripture unless they are taught by people whose opinions they value."[19]

The Lord's example of consistency and integrity suggests three things for teachers. First, it suggests that they model Christian character and biblical qualities, consistently seeking with the help of the Holy Spirit to "be doers of the Word and not hearers only" (James 1:22 KJV). Second, the Lord's example shows the importance of teachers seeking opportunities to be with their students outside the classroom. This helps a teacher to understand his or her learners better and to see what they are doing with what has been taught.[20] It also can enhance the students' appreciation of the teacher and his or her views and values, and it can help pupils see that God's truth does work, that it is relevant and practical.

Third, the Lord's integrity suggests that teachers (in contrast to the Lord's knowledge and perfection) may occasionally need to "admit a lack of knowledge, acknowledge mistakes, and ask for forgiveness."[21]

Spontaneity

Jesus did not follow a set curriculum that required him to sit down with his learners for a designated amount of time each day. Though he obvi-

17. Herman Harrell Horne, *Jesus the Master Teacher* (reprint, Grand Rapids: Kregel, 1964), 143.

18. Edward Kuhlman, *Master Teacher* (Old Tappan, N.J.: Revell, 1987), 78.

19. Phillip L. Kirsch, "Personal Interaction: The Missing Ingredient in Christian Education," *Journal of Christian Education* 3 (1982): 50.

20. Ibid., 49.

21. Robert W. Pazmiño, *Principles and Practices of Christian Education* (Grand Rapids: Baker, 1992), 128.

ously had subjects he was determined to communicate, and though he
did deliver a number of lengthy discourses, many times his lessons
came as "teachable moments," as unplanned, spontaneous occasions
when the teaching was determined by situations that arose.

LeBar observes that "just about half the teaching incidents in the
gospels were initiated by the learners themselves. . . . How much easier
it is to teach when our pupils begin a lesson! When they begin, we may
be assured of their interest, attention, and personal involvement."[22]

A list of such occasions recorded in Matthew appears in table 8.
Many of these teachable moments stemmed from questions. (For more
on questions addressed to Jesus, see chapter 15.) For an interesting
study, make a similar chart of spontaneous teaching occasions in the
Gospels of Mark, Luke, and John.

Table 8
Occasions Enabling Jesus to Teach Spontaneously
as Recorded in Matthew

The Occasion	The Teaching
Healing of the centurion's servant (8:5–13)	Subjects of the kingdom (8:11–12)
Calming of a storm (8:23–27)	Needless nature of fear (8:26)
Healing of a paralyzed man (9:1–8)	Jesus' authority to forgive sins (9:5–6)
Question by the Pharisees about Jesus eating with tax collectors and sinners (9:9–13)	Jesus' purpose in coming to earth (9:12–13)
Question by John the Baptist's disciples about Jesus' disciples not fasting (9:14–17)	Difference between the old and new (9:15–17)[a]
Question by John the Baptist about Jesus' identity (11:2–3)	Commendation of John the Baptist as a great prophet (11:7–19)
Accusation by the Pharisees of Jesus' breaking the Sabbath (12:1–2)	Jesus' relationship to the Sabbath (12:3–8)
Accusation by the Pharisees of Jesus' casting out demons by Beelzebub (12:24)	Blasphemy against the Holy Spirit and the fact that words reflect one's heart (12:25–37)
Request by the Pharisees for a miraculous sign (12:38)	Comparison of Jesus to Jonah and Solomon (12:39–45)
Mention of Jesus' mother and brothers (12:46)	Doing the will of God (12:48–50)

22. Lois E. LeBar, *Education That Is Christian* (Westwood, N.J.: Revell, 1958), 81.

Question by the Pharisees about ceremonial washing (15:1–7)	Traditions of men versus God's commandments, and unclean hearts (15:3–20)
Request by the Pharisees and Sadducees for a sign (16:1)	Condemnation of that generation as wicked (16:2–4)
Disciples' confusion about Jesus' words on yeast (16:5–7)	Explanation of the yeast (16:8–12)
Question by Peter, James, and John about Elijah (17:10)	Prediction of Jesus' suffering (17:11–13)
Question by the disciples on their inability to drive out a demon (17:19)	Faith like a mustard seed (17:20–21)
Question by the disciples on who is the greatest in the kingdom of heaven (18:1)	Need for humility, and the seriousness of causing others to sin (18:2–14)
Question by Peter on the extent of forgiveness (18:21)	Parable of the unforgiving servant (the need to forgive, 18:22–35)
Question by a rich young man on eternal life (19:16)	Reward for following Jesus (19:28–30)
Request by the mother of James and John (20:20–21)	Challenge to humility and service (20:24–28)
Question by the disciples about the withering of the fig tree (21:20)	Challenge to faith in prayer (21:21–22)
Question by the Sadducees about the resurrection (22:23–28)	Information about the resurrection and marriage (22:29–32)
Question by the disciples on the end of the age (24:3)	Discourse on the end of the age (24:4–25:46)

[a] Jesus' teaching about not mixing new cloth with an old garment or new wine into an old wineskin meant that John the Baptist "belonged to the old age [and] Jesus was the One who was bringing in a new dispensation" and that the two were not confused (Stanley D. Toussaint, *Behold the King: A Study of Matthew* [Portland, Ore.: Multnomah, 1980], 131).

As Jesus was flexible, open to questions and interruptions and spontaneous in his teaching, so teachers today can learn to be more flexible. While having a lesson plan to follow and being well prepared, teachers need to be open to questions and issues that arise in class. Out-of-class contacts can be helpful in providing informal teaching settings. Some issues students raise in class may need to be answered then. With other inquiries the teacher may need to suggest they be discussed in a later class session or after class with the individual.

Clarity

"I don't know what the teacher was talking about."

"She used so many words I didn't understand."

"He never clearly stated what he was trying to get across."

"The lesson was confusing; I didn't understand it."

Comments like these by students are unfortunately all too common in describing their teachers, whether in Sunday school or university.

However, not one of these remarks could ever have been made about the master Teacher! Jesus always spoke with clarity, he always taught so his hearers could follow him and comprehend his words.

True, a number of times the disciples failed to understand Jesus, but that was their fault, not his.[23] Since he never muffled his words, his listeners were never befuddled. He was always clear, never confusing. He always spoke to communicate, never to impress others with his knowledge or spiritual depth. He always taught so the people would comprehend the material; he never taught merely to cover the material.

Jesus' vocabulary was always simple and easy to follow. Scan the Gospel of John and you will see how simple were his words. Profound? Yes. But still short words, easy to understand. Or read the Sermon on the Mount. "There is scarcely a word in it which a ten-year-old boy cannot pronounce and spell and measurably understand."[24]

Do you want to teach with clarity? Then think carefully of your vocabulary. If there are technical words or biblical terms your pupils may not understand, are you careful to explain them? Ask yourself if you are teaching over the heads of your students. Are you sharing concepts they may not be ready to comprehend? By thoroughly preparing your lessons, thinking through what you will say and the vocabulary you will use, you can enhance your communication skills—and teach more as the Master taught.

23. The disciples did not understand what Jesus said about the yeast of the Pharisees and the Sadducees until he explained it to them (Matt. 16:5–12). Nor did the disciples understand his miracle of the feeding of the five thousand because their hearts were hardened (Mark 6:52). They could not comprehend what he was telling them about his forthcoming betrayal, crucifixion, and resurrection (Mark 9:32; Luke 9:45; 18:34), because this was totally foreign to their thinking about the Messiah and the kingdom. His triumphal entry (John 12:16), his footwashing (13:12), and his statement about his returning after "a little while" (16:16) were also issues they could not comprehend, again probably because of their own dullness. The spiritually blind Pharisees could not understand Jesus' teaching about God the Father (8:27) or his comments about sheep and sheep thieves (10:6).

24. Charles Reynolds Brown, *The Master's Influence* (Nashville: Cokesbury, 1936), 2.

Urgency

Jesus taught and ministered with a sense of urgency, compelled by a mission he had to fulfill. As you read the Gospels, you get the distinct impression that the Savior was determined, that he was pulled along by a firm commitment to accomplish his work in the short time allotted him. He knew he had only three and a half years in which to communicate his message and his purpose and in which to train a small band of followers who would carry on his work after he left.

Each day brought Jesus closer to the cross. Each day the darkness of that hour before him increased like the growing shadow of an ominous cloud on his path. Knowing his mission had to be completed in the allotted time, he was compelled to carry on the work God the Father sent him to do. He told his disciples, "As long as it is day, we must do the work of him who sent me. Night is coming, when no one can work" (John 9:4).

Yet never once did Jesus hurry. He never ran,[25] he never seemed behind schedule. He never canceled a meeting because he lacked time. He always had time to minister to the needy, to answer his opponents, to instruct his disciples.

His sense of timing contributed to Jesus' calm, unhurried approach, while at the same time driving him ahead with determination and eagerness. "I am with you for only a short time," he told the temple guards who came to arrest him, "and then I go to the one who sent me. You will look for me but you will not find me; and where I am, you cannot come" (John 7:33–34).

Well aware of how long he had in which to minister, several times Jesus told others that his "time," the time for his crucifixion, had not yet come (John 2:4; 7:6, 8, 30; 8:20). In the upper room, "Jesus knew that the time had come for him to leave this world and go to the Father" (John 13:1). And as he began his high-priestly prayer to God the Father, he said, "Father, the time has come" (John 17:1). He often spoke of his crucifixion and resurrection as the time when he would be "glorified,"

---

25. On several occasions, however, people ran to him. Shepherds, hearing of his birth, ran to Bethlehem to see the infant (Luke 2:16). The demoniac from Gerasa ran to him (Mark 5:6), and the people who saw Jesus heal him ran to their town to tell others (Luke 8:34). People ran to be with Jesus (Mark 6:33) and they ran bringing the sick for him to heal (Mark 6:55). A crowd ran to Jesus when he came down from the Mount of Transfiguration (Mark 9:15, 25). Two men ran to him—a rich young man (Mark 10:17) and Zacchaeus (Luke 19:4). After Jesus was raised from death, the women, seeing the empty tomb, ran to tell the disciples (Matt. 28:8; John 20:2), and Peter (Luke 24:12) and John (John 20:4) both ran to the tomb.

that is, when his attributes would be seen by the world and his mission would be finished (John 7:39; 12:16, 23, 28; 13:31).

With the cross only hours away, Jesus told his eleven disciples, after Judas had left the upper room, "My children, I will be with you only a little longer" (John 13:33). He added, "Before long, the world will not see me anymore" (14:19), and "In a little while you will see me no more" (16:16).

To do the will of the Father and "to finish his work," Jesus said, was his "food" (John 4:32, 34). That is, his sustenance was spiritual. As Godet observed, "Since the beginning of His ministry, Jesus had probably not experienced such joy as that which He had just felt. It had revived Him even physically."[26] Then Godet suggested this paraphrase of what Jesus meant in verses 32, 34: "You say to me: Eat! But I am satisfied; in your absence I have had a feast of which you have no conception."[27]

Jesus then conveyed to his disciples that his work was urgent, calling for immediate attention to spiritual needs, like those of the Samaritan woman. A common proverb in farming areas in Palestine was "Four more months and then the harvest" (John 4:35). Harvesting began in April, four months after the planting of seeds was completed toward the end of November.[28] The people knew the time of harvesting could not be hurried; they had to wait (James 5:7). But Jesus did not share this view regarding spiritual things.[29] He had an urgent mission, requiring reaping of fields already ripened for harvest. The sowing of the "seed" in the heart of the Samaritan woman resulted in an immediate "harvest" of many other Samaritans coming to Christ. When Jesus told his disciples to open their eyes "and look at the fields" because "they are ripe for harvest" (4:35),[30] he may have had in mind the Samaritans in their white garments coming from the village (4:30). With their belief

26. F. Godet, *Commentary on the Gospel of St. John*, 3d ed., 3 vols. (Edinburgh: Clark, 1892), 2:121.

27. Ibid.

28. The agricultural year was divided into six periods of two months each: Seedtime (October–November), winter (December–January), spring (February–March), harvest (April–May), summer (June–July), and the time of extreme heat (August–September) (Leon Morris, *The Gospel according to John*, New International Commentary on the New Testament [Grand Rapids: Eerdmans, 1971], 278–79).

29. Ibid., 279.

30. "Ripe" translates *leukos*, "white." Since time-ripened barley and wheat are gold-colored, not white, Jesus may have referred to the Samaritans in their white clothing. Morris reports a similar incident mentioned by H. V. Morton: "As I sat by Jacob's Well a crowd of Arabs came along the road from the direction in which Jesus was looking, and I saw their white garments shining in the sun. Surely Jesus was speaking not of the earthly but of the heavenly harvest, and as He spoke I think it likely that He pointed along the road where the Samaritans in their white robes were assembling to hear His words"

(4:39, 41), he was harvesting a "crop for eternal life" (4:36). The disciples too were commissioned to reap a spiritual harvest (4:38) by introducing others to the Savior.

Jesus' prayer to God the Father soon before the cross includes his report that he completed what he had set out to do: "I have brought you glory on earth by completing the work you gave me to do" (John 17:4). The word *completing* is an accurate rendering of the verb *teleioō*, "to bring to a complete end," in this case to finish a task or reach a goal. The same word is rendered "finished" in John 5:36, "For the very work that the Father has given me to finish, and which I am doing, testifies that the Father has sent me." Since he came "to give his life a ransom for many" (Matt. 20:28), the cross climaxed his mission. For this reason, after hanging on the cross for six hours and "knowing that all was now completed" (from *teleō*, "to come to an end," John 19:28), he said he was thirsty. Someone gave him a drink, and then he said, "It is finished" (from *teleō*) and died (19:30). His work was done, his mission accomplished.

Do we teach in such a way that others sense our commitment to our task, our burden to teach the Word of God?

Do we look forward to each lesson with anticipation and eagerness? Do our students sense our excitement?

Do we realize that our time is limited, that we must make the best of each class session?

Do time limitations help compel us to excellence in our teaching?

Are we driven by a strong sense of commitment, determined to complete the work God has given us to do?

Affirmative answers to these questions can help us become better teachers, teaching as Jesus taught.

To Ask Yourself . . .

What can you do that you are not doing now to help yourself grow mentally, socially, and spiritually?

Are you spending adequate time in lesson preparation? If not, how can you rearrange your schedule to give yourself more preparation time?

(*In the Steps of the Master* [New York: Dodd, Mead, 1934], 154, cited in Morris, *The Gospel according to John*, 279 n. 85).

Do you usually feel confident about what you are teaching?

If pride is a problem you face, ask the Lord for grace to be more humble and thus more Christ-like.

Do you seek with the Lord's help to live what you teach? If you have difficulty being consistent in some area, face up to that fact and seek the Lord's help.

Are you flexible in your teaching, being open to questions or issues that may arise spontaneously?

Is your teaching on the level of your students' understanding? Sometime after class ask some students to tell you frankly if your vocabulary and concepts are understandable.

Are you excited about and committed to teaching God's Word?

*All spoke well of him
and were amazed
at the gracious words
that came from his lips.*

Luke 4:22

6

What Other Qualities Marked Jesus as an Outstanding Teacher?

We have considered eight qualities that marked Jesus' teaching, and yet to be discussed (chap. 11) are the many methods Jesus used, including lecture-discourses, discussions, dialogues, disputations, problem solving, assignments, field trips, visuals, demonstrations, challenges, rebukes, commands, riddles, arguments, maxims, questions, and stories. First, however, we will look at six other qualities that demonstrate Jesus' outstanding effectiveness in teaching.

Variety

Teaching every lesson in the same way can lead to boredom. Since students know what to expect, they are not stimulated or challenged. The great amount of variety in the way Jesus taught kept his learners enthralled and excited. When he taught, no one was ever bored! He varied the way he began his lessons, the way he captured attention, the way he involved his learners, the way he challenged them, the way he prodded them to think, the way he deepened their values and developed their skills.

Since "the variety of His methods brought unparalleled freshness to His teaching,"[1] teachers today would do well to follow his example by incorporating a variety of methods in their own lessons. In preparing each class session, teachers could ask themselves, How can I vary this lesson from other sessions? How can I involve the students? What methods will best communicate what I want to teach? What means can I use to stimulate the students to think, to get them to interact, to challenge them to apply the Scriptures?

Quantity

Another striking feature of Jesus' instructional ministry is the extensive amount of material he taught. He never ran out of something to say or teach. He was never at a loss for something to communicate.

The percentage of Jesus' words in each of the Gospels demonstrates this fact (see table 9). More than half the verses in the four Gospels include words Jesus spoke. And one-fourth (exactly 25 percent) of the 7,800 verses in the New Testament record Jesus' words.[2]

Table 9
Portions of the Four Gospels Recording Jesus' Words

Gospel	Number of Verses	Number of Verses Recording Jesus' Words	Percentage of the Total
Matthew	1,071	646	60
Mark	564	288	51
Luke	1,151	584	51
John	843	432	51
Total	3,629	1,950	54

1. Donald Guthrie, "Jesus," in *A History of Religious Educators*, ed. Elmer L. Towns (Grand Rapids: Baker, 1979), 19.
2. If Jesus' words in Revelation 1:17–3:22 are included, the percentage increases to 25.7, and the total number of verses with Jesus' words is 2,005.

Many of Jesus' teachings were given in discourses, as a list of fifty such speeches shows (table 10).[3] The topics on which he lectured cover a wide range. Some of the better-known discourses, longer than most of the others, include the Sermon on the Mount (Matt. 5–7), the parables of the "secrets" of the kingdom (Matt. 13), the pronouncements of woes on the teachers of the law and the Pharisees (Matt. 23), the Olivet Discourse on the tribulation and Jesus' second advent (Matt. 24–25), and the Upper Room Discourse (John 13–16).

Table 10
Jesus' Discourses*

1.	Sowing and reaping	John 4:31–38
2.	Jesus as the source of life	John 5:19–47
3.	Commissioning instructions to the Twelve	Matthew 10:5–42; Luke 9:3–5
4.	The Sermon on the Mount	Matthew 5:2–7:27; Luke 6:20–49
5.	Ministry of John the Baptist	Matthew 11:7–19; Luke 7:24–35
6.	Announcement of judgment on cities	Matthew 11:20–24
7.	Answer regarding blasphemy	Matthew 12:25–45; Mark 3:23–29; Luke 11:17–36
8.	Parables about the kingdom	Matthew 13:3–52
9.	The Bread of life	John 6:26–59
10.	Traditions of the elders	Matthew 15:3–20; Mark 7:6–23
11.	Gaining and losing life	Mark 8:34–38; Luke 9:23–27
12.	Jesus' messiahship, coming death, and the reward for discipleship	Matthew 16:13–28

*The discourses included in this table are those in which Jesus presented information, including some parables, but the table excludes dialogues (with Nicodemus, John 3:1–21; the Samaritan woman, John 4:7–26; the rich young man, Matt. 19:16–30; Mark 10:17–22; Luke 18:18–25); the two disciples on the road to Emmaus (Luke 24:13–31); Simon the Pharisee (Luke 7:36–47); and various conversations with Peter and others.

The discourses are listed in chronological order, based on the harmony of the Gospels in *The Ryrie Study Bible* (Chicago: Moody, 1978), 1925–32, which in turn is based on A. R. Fausset, *Bible Encyclopedia Critical and Expository* [Hartford, Conn.: Scranton, n.d.], 359–77).

3. Bible students disagree on the number of discourses Jesus gave. Some lists include dialogues of Jesus with an individual; others include all or some of his parables. W. Graham Scroggie lists forty discourses (*A Guide to the Gospels* [London: Pickering and Inglis, 1948], 556–57). Horne presents sixty-two (Herman Harrell Horne, *Jesus the Master Teacher* [reprint, Grand Rapids: Kregel, 1964], 66–69), and Delnay lists twenty-six, including only those discourses of six verses or more (Robert G. Delnay, *Teach as He Taught* [Chicago: Moody, 1987], 26–27). Chapter 16 in this book discusses Jesus' use of parables.

13.	Humility and forgiveness	Matthew 18:3–35; Mark 9:35–50
14.	The source of Jesus' message	John 7:14–24
15.	The Light of the world	John 8:12–20
16.	Jesus' relationship to God the Father	John 8:21–30
17.	Spiritual freedom and Jesus' preexistence	John 8:31–58
18.	The Gate and the Shepherd	John 10:1–18
19.	Commissioning instructions to the seventy-two	Luke 10:2–20
20.	True neighborliness and the parable of the good Samaritan	Luke 10:29–37
21.	Effectiveness of prayer	Luke 11:5–13
22.	Hypocrisy of the Pharisees and teachers of the law	Luke 11:37–52
23.	Hypocrisy and fear	Luke 12:1–12
24.	Greed and worry	Luke 12:14–34
25.	Watchfulness	Luke 12:35–48
26.	Family divisions	Luke 12:49–53
27.	Discernment of the times	Luke 12:54–59
28.	Judgment for failure to repent	Luke 13:6–9
29.	Exclusion from the kingdom	Luke 13:22–30
30.	Jesus' oneness with the Father	John 10:25–38
31.	Feasting in the kingdom	Luke 14:15–24
32.	The cost of discipleship	Luke 14:26–35
33.	The Father's love	Luke 15:3–32
34.	Love of money	Luke 16:1–13, 15–31
35.	Offenses, forgiveness, faith, and service	Luke 17:1–10
36.	The coming kingdom	Luke 17:20–37
37.	Persistence and prayer	Luke 18:1–8
38.	Marriage and divorce	Matthew 19:4–12; Mark 10:2–12
39.	Reward in the kingdom	Matthew 19:28–20:16; Mark 10:29–31
40.	False ambition and servanthood	Matthew 20:23–28; Mark 10:39–45
41.	Investing in the kingdom	Luke 19:11–27
42.	Faith and prayer	Matthew 21:21–22; Mark 11:22–26

43. Entrance in the kingdom	Matthew 21:28–22:14; Mark 12:1–11; Luke 20:9–18
44. Marriage and the resurrection	Matthew 22:29–32; Mark 12:24–27; Luke 20:34–38
45. Denunciation of the teachers of the law and the Pharisees	Matthew 23:1–39; Mark 12:38–40; Luke 20:45–47
46. Prediction of Jesus' death	John 12:23–36
47. The tribulation and Jesus' second coming	Matthew 24:4–25:46; Mark 13:2–37; Luke 17:20–37; 21:5–36
48. True greatness	Luke 22:24–30
49. Jesus' departure, the coming and work of the Holy Spirit, abiding in Christ, and hatred of the world	John 13:31–16:16
50. The disciples' grief and suffering	John 16:19–33

Several observations may be made about these lecture-discourses. First, Jesus was always careful to present the material when the groups or individuals addressed were interested. He did not present the contents of all these lectures all at once, with no regard for whether his listeners were ready and able to receive it. Second, he varied the length of the lectures; some were extensive, whereas others were quite brief. He knew how to make his point, depending on the spiritual condition of his hearers. Third, he addressed some subjects more than once, but always with variation. These repeated subjects include humility; forgiveness; fear; money; worry; prayer; false ambition; sin and judgment; God's kingdom and how to enter it; watchfulness; hypocrisy and legalistic traditions; his own identity; his death, departure, and return; and the ministry of the Holy Spirit. These subjects deal with one's spiritual relationship to God, relationships with others, and God's plans. Fourth, Jesus accompanied his lectures with other teaching methods. A study of the contents of these discourses reveals a number of other teaching means Jesus used to convey the content.

Teachers today can be encouraged to follow these same principles in their teaching. First, help students get ready for and interested in the material to be lectured, being careful to communicate only as much as they are ready to comprehend and appropriate. Second, vary the length of your lectures, depending on the spiritual condition of your students. Third, repeat certain concepts in various lectures. Consider the topics Jesus repeated. What do their themes suggest for our own teaching? Fourth, use other teaching methods along with lectures, such as visuals, discussions, questions, assignments, or panels.

Empathy

Tenderness, compassion, and empathy always characterized Jesus' ministry. He loved his students and responded to each one with care and concern. He spent hours with them each day for several years. He lived for *them*, not for himself. His concern was to develop them, not to make a name for himself.

Near the beginning of his ministry, when the Lord read from Isaiah in the synagogue at Nazareth and explained that the words were fulfilled in him, he obviously spoke tenderly and graciously, for all who heard him "spoke well of him and were amazed at the gracious words that came from his lips" (Luke 4:22).

Even when some of his hearers turned against him, Jesus still loved them as a shepherd loves his sheep (John 10:11–18). And when his disciples/learners did not understand what he said, he patiently explained his point to them. He never begrudged their dullness or their interruptions or questions. When they selfishly expressed the desire to have exalted positions, he taught them about humility and service without chiding them (Matt. 18:3–9; 20:20–28; Mark 9:35–37; 10:35–45; Luke 22:24–30).

Jesus "loved all his pupils, not merely the loveable or the bright ones, but even the unlovable."[4] When the disciples criticized a woman for pouring expensive perfume on Jesus' head instead of selling it and giving the money to the poor, Jesus responded with kindness and love in correcting them and commending her (Matt. 26:6–13; Mark 14:3–9). Interestingly, Peter, who denied the Lord three times, was commanded by Jesus to feed his sheep, that is, to care for and nurture believers (John 21:15–19). When Thomas doubted that Jesus was resurrected from the dead, the Savior did not berate him for unbelief. Instead, he encouraged Thomas to examine the evidence (John 20:24–29).

Much of Jesus' teaching was directed toward encouraging his followers not to be afraid (Matt. 10:26–31; 14:27; 17:7; Mark 5:36; 6:50; Luke 5:10; 8:50; 12:4, 7, 32; 21:9; John 14:27) and not to worry (Matt. 6:25, 28, 31, 34; 10:19; Mark 13:11; Luke 12:11, 22, 26, 29; 21:14). His loving concern for them is evident in these frequent words of consolation and comfort.

As Jesus prepared his disciples for his departure, an event that would bring sadness to their hearts, he lovingly consoled them by presenting reassuring facts: He would return (John 14:2–3, 18; 16:16b), he would

4. Clarence H. Benson, *The Christian Teacher* (Chicago: Moody, 1950), 205.

send the Holy Spirit, another comforter (14:16–17, 26; 16:7–15), and his presence would be with them (Matt. 28:20). In times of persecution (John 15:18–21; 16:2–4, 32) and grief (16:20), they would know his peace (14:27; 16:33) and joy (16:20–22).

Jesus' love for the Twelve is seen in his addressing them as "children" (Mark 10:24). The word *teknon*, literally, "a born one," is a form of familiar address, as in a parent-child relationship.[5] In addition, he demonstrated his love by washing their feet (John 13:1, 5) and by telling them directly that he loved them (15:9, 12).

Jesus' miracles were occasions for teaching, either by word or act. They revealed his love and compassion for people in need, many of whom were ostracized socially or religiously from the community. These included the sick, the mentally ill, the blind, dumb, and deaf, tax collectors, Gentiles, and women.[6] He had compassion on a leper (Matt. 8:2–3; Mark 1:41) whom he touched[7] and healed. Seeing the crowds of people coming to him, "he had compassion[8] on them because they were harassed and helpless,[9] like sheep without a shepherd" (Matt. 9:36; Mark 6:34). Many sick people were brought to Jesus by a large crowd and "he had compassion on them and healed their sick" (Matt. 14:14). Two blind men near Jericho were healed by Jesus: he "had compassion on them and touched their eyes" (Matt. 20:34). Jesus' miracles of feeding the five thousand stemmed from his compassionate heart (Matt. 15:32; Mark 8:2). He healed the demon-possessed man of the Gerasene region because he had "mercy"[10] on him (Mark 5:19).

Jesus raised three people from the dead, and in two of the cases the Gospel writers referred to his compassion or love for the dead persons

5. Walter Bauer, William F. Arndt, and F. Wilbur Gingrich, *A Greek-English Lexicon of the New Testament and Other Early Christian Literature*, 2d ed., rev. F. Wilbur Gingrich and Frederick W. Danker (Chicago: University of Chicago Press, 1979), 808.

6. Joseph A. Grassi, *Jesus the Teacher* (Winona, Minn.: St. Mary's College, 1978), 33–37.

7. His touching a leper was an alarming act because leprosy was considered contagious, lepers were social and religious outcasts, and they were required to warn others of their presence by calling out, "Unclean! Unclean!"

8. "Compassion," which translates *splanchnizomai*, "to have pity or feel compassion" (from *splanchna*, the entrails), is used only of Jesus or by Jesus in his parables. (In the parables the word occurs in Matthew 18:27, 33; and Luke 19:20.) Because people of the ancient world thought the viscera were the seat of emotions, this word connotes Jesus' deep-seated emotional feelings of sympathy and empathy. "What we are to see here is not purely human pity, but divine compassion for troubled people" (Leon Morris, *The Gospel according to Matthew* [Grand Rapids: Eerdmans, 1992], 239).

9. "Harassed," from *skyllō*, originally meant "to skin or flay" and this is used metaphorically for serious trouble. "Helpless" renders *kriptō*, "to throw or hurl," suggesting that the people were downcast (ibid., 239 n. 87).

10. Here the Greek has the verb *eleeō*, "to have pity."

or their grieving relatives. He raised back to life the son of the widow of Nain, for he "felt compassion for her" (Luke 7:13 NASB; "his heart went out to her," NIV). At the death of Lazarus, "Jesus was deeply moved in spirit and troubled" (John 11:33) and he wept (11:35). Going to Lazarus' tomb, Jesus was again "deeply moved" (11:38). No wonder the Jews said, "See how he loved him" (11:36). Mary and Martha, Lazarus' sisters, knew of his love for all three of them (11:3, 5).

Two other individuals the Gospels refer to as being loved by Jesus are the rich young man ("Jesus looked at him and loved him," Mark 10:21) and John, "the disciple whom Jesus loved" (John 13:23; 19:26; 20:2; 21:7, 20).

No substitute exists for a teacher's love for his or her students. Sympathy for and empathy with them in their times of distress is an essential quality for teachers. Teaching is far more than getting across content; it also calls for communicating a genuine personal interest in and love for each student—the belligerent, the boisterous, and the bullheaded, as well as the compliant, the conscientious, and the committed. In discussing teaching skills, Granrose suggests that the first essential skill is love and respect for the students.[11]

A teacher's impatience, resentment, and disinterest must be replaced by patience, respect, and concern if he or she is to teach as the master Teacher taught.

Intimacy

The quality of intimacy also marked our Lord's teaching ministry. He was close to his disciples, spending extended periods of time with them alone and sometimes with individuals in the groups. In fact one of his purposes in calling them to follow him was "that they might be with him" (Mark 3:14). For this reason, after Jesus had ascended to heaven and his small band began their ministry as apostles, the Jewish leaders marveled at the courage of Peter and John, realizing "that these men had been with Jesus" (Acts 4:13).

Study the ways Jesus developed the disciples as an intimate group as recorded in these twenty-two passages in Matthew and note the effects these incidents had on them.

11. John T. Granrose, "Conscious Teaching: Helping Graduate Assistants Develop Teaching Styles," in *New Directions for Teaching and Learning: Improving Teaching Styles*, ed. Kenneth E. Eble (San Francisco: Jossey-Bass, 1980), 29, cited in Robert W. Pazmiño, *Principles and Practice of Christian Education* (Grand Rapids: Baker, 1992), 129.

Reference	What Jesus Did with the Disciple(s)	Effect on the Disciples
Matthew 8:23–27		
9:10–13		
10		
12:1–2		
14:22–28		
15:15		
16:5–6		
16:13–38		
17:1–13		
19:13–15		
19:25–29		
20:17–19		
20:20–23		
21:1–7		
21:18–22		
24:3–8		
26:1–2		
26:6–13		
26:17–30		
26:31–35		
26:36–46		
28:16–20		

How do these various incidents illustrate Jesus' development of the disciples? How do the incidents demonstrate his intimate care for them?

For an additional exercise, look through the other three Gospels and chart Jesus' moments alone with the disciples and the effect those occasions had on them.

Writing about effective teaching in undergraduate colleges, Chickering and Garmson suggest seven principles of good practice, the first of which is contact between students and teachers. "Frequent student-faculty contact in and out of classes is the most important factor in student motivation and involvement."[12] This sounds as if these two writers

12. Arthur W. Chickering and Zelda F. Garmson, "Seven Principles for Good Practice in Undergraduate Education," *AAHE* [American Association of Higher Education] *Bulletin*, March 1987, 4.

had read the Gospels! Another writer has pointed out that "repeatedly, one of the overriding differences found between faculty and students who engage in effective teaching and learning and those who do not was *the amount of interaction*—both inside and outside the classroom—that students and teachers have with one another."[13]

This principle, so well exemplified by our Lord, is true of all teaching—whether you are teaching two- or three-year olds, junior-age boys, teen-age girls, college-age youth, single adults, or young or older couples.

Sensitivity

Related to the characteristic of empathy is sensitivity. And being sensitive to students' needs comes as we get to know them in intimate moments outside the classroom. Jesus paced his teaching to his learners' ability to assimilate what they were hearing, as suggested in two verses. "With many similar parables Jesus spoke the word to them, as much as they could understand" (Mark 4:33). "I have much more to say to you, more than you can now bear" (John 16:12).

Sensitive to his students' pace of learning, Jesus "did not resort to a storage-tank approach to education,"[14] seeking to pour material from his teaching jug to their learning mug. There was a tenderness about his approach, a gentleness that fostered rather than blocked learning. He said of himself, "I am gentle" (Matt. 11:29). The word for "gentle" is *praus*, occurring only in Matthew 5:5; 11:29; 21:5; and 1 Peter 3:4. It speaks of being mild and considerate, not overbearing, harsh, or vengeful.

Because of this admirable quality, Jesus never lost his temper; he never yelled at his students. Being sensitive and gentle, his attitude toward his learners was flawless.

Also of interest is Jesus' gentle attitude toward and concern for women and children. Jewish rabbis did not teach women,[15] for they considered women to be of lower social status than men. But Jesus taught them and ministered to them, treating them as of equal standing with men.[16] Note the numerous occasions (in chronological order)

13. Robert C. Wilson et al., *College Professors and Their Impact on Students* (New York: Wiley and Sons, 1975), 167 (italics theirs).

14. Howard G. Hendricks, "Following the Master Teacher," in *The Christian Educator's Handbook on Teaching*, ed. Kenneth O. Gangel and Howard G. Hendricks (Wheaton, Ill: Victor, 1989), 26.

15. K. N. Giles, *Women and Their Ministry* (Melbourne: Done Communications, 1977), 19.

16. K. N. Giles, "Teachers and Teaching in the Church: Part I," *Journal of Christian Education* [Australia] 70 (April 1981): 12.

when Jesus ministered to women or when they ministered to him, and how he was sensitive to their needs (see table 11).

Table 11
Jesus' Ministry to Women

1.	Jesus' mother, Mary	John 2:1–5
2.	A Samaritan woman	John 4:5–26
3.	Peter's mother-in-law	Luke 4:38–39
4.	A widow of Nain	Luke 7:11–15
5.	Women who had been healed/exorcised	Luke 8:1–3
6.	Women traveling with and supporting Jesus	Luke 8:1–3 (cf. Matt. 27:55–56)
7.	A woman with a hemorrhage for twelve years	Mark 5:25–34
8.	A Canaanite woman from Syrophoenicia	Matthew 15:21–28; Mark 7:24–30
9.	A woman caught in adultery	John 8:2–11
10.	Mary and Martha	Luke 10:38–42
11.	A woman crippled for eighteen years	Luke 13:10–16
12.	Mother of James and John	Matthew 20:20–28; Mark 10:35–45
13.	Mary and Martha after their brother died	John 11:17–44
14.	A widow at the temple	Mark 12:41–44; Luke 21:1–4
15.	Mary, who anointed Jesus' head with perfume	Matthew 26:6–13; Mark 14:1–9; John 12:1–8
16.	Women at the cross	John 19:25–27
17.	Women at the empty tomb	Matthew 28:1–10; Mark 16:1–8; Luke 24:1–10; John 20:1–2

Some of these women were sick, others were grieving, and still others were helping, sinning, loving, sacrificing, or rejoicing. Nowhere in the Gospels do we read of women who were hostile to Jesus. They came to receive help from him and to express their devotion to him.[17] Being sensitive to each of them and their needs, Jesus helped, forgave, comforted, healed, encouraged, commended, defended, and taught them.

17. Norval Geldenhuys, *Commentary on the Gospel of Luke,* New International Commentary on the New Testament (Grand Rapids: Eerdmans, 1951), 239.

He accepted women, regardless of their status in life. Some were sinful, others were godly. Some were strangers to him, others were his friends. Some had substantial material means, others were poor. Some were presumptuous, others were humble. With all of them he was respectful and thoughtful—truly an ideal model for men today.[18]

Jesus' healing of two children shows his sensitivity to and love for them: the official's son (John 4:43–52) and the demon-possessed epileptic boy (Matt. 17:14–18; Mark 9:14–27). In addition, he brought two dead children back to life—Jairus' daughter (Matt. 9:18–25; Mark 5:21–24, 35–42) and the son of a widow of Nain (Luke 7:11–15).

Jesus' tender, loving interest in children is seen in two other instances in the Gospels. When the disciples were arguing which of them was the greatest, the Lord stood a little child among them and then took the infant[19] boy in his arms and encouraged the disciples to welcome little children (Mark 9:33–37). Surely they realized that rather than clamoring for honored positions they were to be as unassuming and unpretentious as young children. Imagine their chagrin at being rebuked by this gentle act! Imagine too the delight of the small boy being held in Jesus' arms!

On his last trip to Jerusalem, Jesus was in Perea, east of the Jordan River, when "people were bringing little children[20] to Jesus to have him touch them" (Mark 10:13) "and place his hands on them and pray for them" (Matt. 19:13). The disciples rebuked the parents for bothering Jesus in this way. Being indignant,[21] he responded to the disciples by rebuking *them!* "He was indignant that His disciples should put such a limit on His love and His work as to exclude children. In a smaller degree it was a repetition of the error of Peter (viii. 32). Peter wished to keep Him from future suffering and death; the disciples now wish to keep Him from present trouble and fatigue."[22]

Jesus commanded the disciples to allow the children to come to him (a positive word) and to stop hindering them (a negative directive). He

18. For more on Jesus' ministry to and relationship with women, see Webb Garrison, *Women in the Life of Jesus* (New York: Bobbs-Merrill, 1962); Michael Wiley Perry, "Jesus' Relationship to Women in His Earthly Ministry" (Th.M. thesis, Dallas Theological Seminary, 1976); and Charles C. Ryrie, *The Role of Women in the Church* (Chicago: Moody, 1978).

19. The word *paidion* often means a young child or sometimes an infant (though in Mark 5:39 it is used of Jairus' twelve-year-old daughter, perhaps as an affectionate term).

20. This is the same word *paidion* for small child used in Mark 9:36. Luke 18:15 states that people were bringing babies (*brephē*) to him.

21. The verb *aganakteō* is used only in the synoptic Gospels (six times) and only this one time of Jesus. It speaks of strong displeasure or scorn over something considered unjust.

22. Alfred Plummer, *The Gospel according to Mark*, Thornapple Commentaries (1914; reprint, Grand Rapids: Baker, 1982), 235.

added that the kingdom of God belongs to and can be entered only by those who, like children, know they are "helpless and small, without claim or merit" and who "take openly and confidently what is given."[23] Jesus then embraced the children in his arms, and blessed them (Mark 10:16). The Greek word for "blessed" (*kateulogeō*), occurring nowhere else in the New Testament, is made intensive in form by the prefixed preposition, thus suggesting fervency,[24] and the imperfect verb tense suggests he blessed them repeatedly. "Instead of the mere touch for which the friends had asked, He laid his hands on them . . . with the words of blessing."[25]

From Jesus' sensitivity to his disciples' slow pace of learning, and from his gentle concern for women and children, individuals considered socially lower than men, teachers observe the need to be sensitive to students of varying abilities and to be gentle toward women, children, and individuals in minority groups.

Relevancy

Without question our Lord's lessons were relevant to his hearers. He never taught something that had no pertinence to life or to reality. Like an arrow hitting its target with flawless precision, his teaching hit its mark, and penetrated his hearers' souls. After all, this was his goal—to see individuals turn to him as their personal Savior and to grow in spiritual maturity. (The goals of his ministry are discussed more fully in chapters 7 and 8.)

Conclusion

In light of these fourteen aspects of our Lord's instructional activity it is no surprise to read repeatedly in the Gospels that large crowds followed him. Throughout his entire teaching career, he was popular. Eighty-two times we read of a crowd following Jesus—either to hear him teach or to see him heal—with twenty of those references adding the adjective *large* before the word *crowd*. And twenty-two times the Gospel writers referred to "crowds" (plural), four times adding the ad-

23. William L. Lane, *The Gospel according to Mark*, New International Commentary on the New Testament (Grand Rapids: Eerdmans, 1974), 361.

24. Henry Barclay Swete, *The Gospel according to St Peter* (London: Macmillan, 1913), 222.

25. Ibid.

jective *large*. Three times in John "a great crowd" is referred to (6:2, 5; 12:12 NIV). Luke 6:17 refers to "a great number of people" going from Judea, Jerusalem, and Tyre and Sidon to see Jesus. The Pharisees were concerned that, as they saw it, "the whole world" was following him (John 12:19).[26] People were "crowding" around him, as recorded in Mark 3:9; 5:31; Luke 5:1; and 8:45. On one occasion the people who heard him were so numerous that Luke wrote that "a crowd of many thousands. . . were trampling on one another" (12:1).

The world's most masterful Teacher was the world's most popular Teacher! Why? Because he taught with maturity, mastery, certainty, humility, consistency, spontaneity, clarity, urgency, variety, quantity, empathy, intimacy, sensitivity, and relevancy.

Look at Your Teaching . . .

As you prepare each lesson, do you consciously ask yourself, How can I vary this lesson? What methods will best communicate the material?

Do you vary the length of your lectures, based on the spiritual condition and needs of your learners?

Do you think your pupils sense your interest in them? Have you ever lost your patience with your class? If so, what resulted?

How much contact do you have with your students outside of class? How can you increase that time?

Would you rate your level of sensitivity to women, children, and individuals in minority groups in your class as high, average, or low?

Do you make a special effort to relate each lesson to your students' lives?

Are you excited about and committed to teaching God's Word?

---

26. Similar statements speak of "all the people" (Matt. 12:23; Mark 9:15; Luke 7:29; 8:47; 18:43; 19:48; John 8:2).

He was . . . powerful in word.

Luke 24:19

7

What Goals Did Jesus Have in His Teaching?

*E*very meaningful activity we engage in has some purpose. We eat to satisfy our hunger. We work in order to receive money. We go to school to acquire learning. We watch televised news to see what is happening in the world. We discipline our children to help them be self-controlled. We serve the Lord in order to experience joy in helping others and in pleasing him. We teach a Sunday school class or we teach in a formal educational setting to help others learn.

Yes, our activities focus on goals.

Why then did Jesus come to the earth? What was he seeking to accomplish? And why did he teach—and preach, heal, disciple, and train? Why did he teach so extensively on so many subjects? Why did he spend so much time with the twelve disciples? From his teaching goals what can we learn about the objectives we should have before us as we teach?

The overarching objective of Jesus' ministry on earth was to do the work God the Father had assigned him, thereby accomplishing his will. As Jesus told the disciples early in his ministry, his "food" was "to do the will of him who sent me and to finish his work" (John 4:34). That is, spiritual sustenance was his priority; helping the Samaritan woman find "living water" for her soul was more important than his finding food for his stomach.

Did he accomplish his goal, finishing the "work" God the Father had given him, doing the will of the Father (John 6:38–40)? At the end of his ministry, before the cross, he reported in his prayer to the Father, "I have brought you glory on earth by completing the work you gave me to do" (John 17:4).

Was Jesus' Purpose to Teach or to Preach?

Jesus was extensively involved in teaching (see chap. 3). He was widely known as a teacher, and much of what he did was to teach. A number of verses, however, point to his involvement in preaching. Are we wrong then in presenting him as a Teacher? Is there a difference between preaching and teaching, or are these referring to the same activities?

Actually the Lord engaged in three major functions in his ministry on earth: preaching, teaching, and healing. These are summarized in Matthew 4:23: "Jesus went throughout Galilee, teaching in their synagogues, preaching the good news of the kingdom, and healing every disease and sickness among the people."

Preaching the good news of God and the need for repentance (Matt. 4:17; Mark 1:15; Luke 5:32; cf. 13:3, 5; 15:7) constituted one of Jesus' stated goals. Early in his ministry he told the disciples, "Let us go somewhere else—to the nearby villages—so I can preach there also. That is why I have come" (Mark 1:38). And as Luke recorded it, "He said, 'I must preach the good news of the kingdom of God to other towns also, because that is why I was sent'" (Luke 4:43).

These verses, along with the many verses on his teaching role, show that Jesus was involved in both preaching and teaching.[1] The Greek word for "preaching" is *kēryssō*, which means "to announce or proclaim as a herald."[2] This verb is related to the noun *kēryx*, "herald."

Matthew 9:35 mentions the same three activities of Jesus: "Jesus went through all the towns and villages [presumably in Galilee], teaching in their synagogues, preaching the good news of the kingdom and healing every disease and sickness." And Matthew 11:1 reports his carrying on two of these: "He went on from there to teach and preach in the towns of Galilee." These two verses also use the verb *kēryssō* in reference to Jesus' ministry as a herald. He announced "the good news [*eu-*

---

1. Of course teaching was Jesus' primary activity, judging by the frequent occurrences of the verb *didaskō* (to teach) in the Gospels in relation to Jesus (forty-seven times), compared to eighteen references to his preaching and forty-six references to his healing.

2. Walter Bauer, William F. Arndt, and F. Wilbur Gingrich, *A Greek-English Lexicon of the New Testament and Other Early Christian Literature*, 2d ed., rev. F. Wilbur Gingrich and Frederick W. Danker (Chicago: University of Chicago Press, 1979), 431; cf. Leon Morris, *The Gospel according to Matthew* (Grand Rapids: Eerdmans, 1992), 51.

angelion] of the kingdom,"[3] that is, he proclaimed the fact that he had come to present himself to Israel as her King and to establish his kingdom on earth. This would certainly have been welcomed as good news by his Jewish audiences, for they had long anticipated the coming of the Messiah and his establishing God's sovereign rule on earth.[4]

Luke 20:1 is a fourth verse (along with Matt. 4:23; 9:35; 11:1) that mentions Jesus' teaching and preaching ministries together: "One day as he was teaching the people in the temple courts and preaching the gospel, the chief priests and the teachers of the law, together with the elders, came up to him." Here, however, the words *preaching the gospel* translate one word, *euangelizomai,* literally, "to announce good news." Luke seemed fond of this word, for he used it eleven times in his Gospel and sixteen times in Acts, whereas Matthew used it only once (11:5) and Mark never used it.[5] When Luke referred to Jesus' preaching, he usually used the verb *euangelizomai.* Matthew and Mark, however, preferred the verb *kēryssō* (see table 12).

John the Baptist, like Jesus, was involved in preaching,[6] and some tax collectors addressed him as a teacher (Luke 3:12).

3. Only Matthew used this expression (4:23; 9:35; 11:1).

4. The millennial kingdom, however, was not established at Jesus' first advent because the nation Israel rejected him as her Messiah. Without the King they could have no kingdom. This rejection was evident when the Pharisees blasphemously accused Jesus of driving out demons by the power of Satan (Matt. 12:24). They thereby "rejected God's purpose for themselves" (Luke 7:30).

Therefore, because the "builders" (Jewish leaders) rejected the "stone" (Jesus Christ), he said, "the kingdom of God will be taken away from you and given to a people who will produce its fruit" (Matt. 21:43). Some writers say this "people" to whom the kingdom was given refers to the church (e.g., Stanley D. Toussaint, *Behold the King: A Study of Matthew* [Portland, Ore.: Multnomah, 1980], 250–52; and Morris, *The Gospel according to Matthew,* 544), whereas others hold that it refers to a future generation of Israel, a generation that will respond in saving faith to the Messiah when he returns (e.g., A. C. Gaebelein, *The Gospel of Matthew: An Exposition,* 2 vols. in 1 [Neptune, N.J.: Loizeaux, 1910], 2:138; and Louis A. Barbieri, "Matthew," in *The Bible Knowledge Commentary, New Testament,* ed. John F. Walvoord and Roy B. Zuck [Wheaton, Ill.: Victor, 1983], 70–71).

Weeping over Jerusalem after his triumphal entry, the Lord bemoaned the fact that the nation "did not recognize the time of God's coming to you" (Luke 19:44), another indication of the nation's rejection. As Jesus told his disciples, he "must suffer many things and be rejected by this generation" (Luke 17:25). The millennial kingdom, then, was not established; it is yet future. "Because of the Jewish rejection of the Messiah, the promised kingdom is now held in abeyance" (Toussaint, *Behold the King,* 176).

5. However, Matthew and Mark used the noun *euangelion* (good news) frequently (Matthew, seven times, and Mark, eight times).

6. John was preaching *(kēryssō)* in the desert of Judea (Matt. 3:1) and in all the country around the Jordan River (Luke 3:3), and he preached the good news *(euangelizomai,* Mark 1:4; Luke 3:18). The message he communicated was that people should repent (Matt. 3:2; Mark 1:4; Luke 3:3, 8).

Table 12
References to Jesus' Preaching

References to Jesus' Teaching and Preaching in Which Two Words Are Used Together

Matthew 4:23	(*didaskō* and *kēryssō*)
Matthew 9:35	(*didaskō* and *kēryssō*)
Matthew 11:1	(*didaskō* and *kēryssō*)
Luke 20:1	(*didaskō* and *euangelizomai*)

References to Jesus' Preaching, Using the Word *Kēryssō*

Matthew 4:17	From that time on Jesus began to preach *[kēryssō]*.
Mark 1:14	Jesus went into Galilee, proclaiming *[kēryssō]* the good news *[euangelion]* of God.
Mark 1:38	Jesus replied, "Let us go somewhere else—to the nearby villages—so I can preach *[kēryssō]* there also. That is why I have come."
Mark 1:39	So he traveled throughout Galilee, preaching *[kēryssō]* in their synagogues and driving out demons.
Luke 4:18	"He has set me to proclaim *[kēryssō]* freedom for the prisoners . . . to proclaim *[kēryssō]* the year of the Lord's favor."
Luke 4:44	And he kept on preaching *[kēryssō]* in the synagogues of Judea.

References to Jesus' Preaching, Using the Word *Euangelizomai*

Matthew 11:5	"Good news is preached *[euangelizomai]* to the poor."
Luke 4:18	"The Spirit of the Lord is on me, because he has anointed me to preach good news *[euangelizomai]* to the poor."
Luke 4:43	"I must preach the good news *[euangelizomai]* of the kingdom of God."
Luke 7:22	"the good news is preached *[euangelizomai]* to the poor."
Luke 16:16	"the good news of the kingdom of God is being preached *[euangelizomai]*."

One Reference Including Both *Kēryssō* and *Euangelizomai*

Luke 8:1	And it came about afterwards, that he began going about from one city and village to another, proclaiming *[kēryssō]* and preaching *[euangelizomai]* the kingdom of God (NASB; the NIV does not bring out the use of the two words).

Jesus also commissioned his disciples to preach *(kēryssō)* the kingdom (Matt. 10:7; Mark 3:14; Luke 9:2), proclaiming the message that people should repent (Mark 6:12). After his resurrection he commanded the disciples to teach (Matt. 28:20).[7]

Was There a Difference between Jesus' Teaching and Preaching?

At times the Savior's teaching and preaching ministries seemed to overlap. As table 12 shows, four verses refer to both ministries together (Matt. 4:23; 9:35; 11:1; Luke 20:1). And where Matthew referred to Jesus' teaching in the temple courts (21:23), Luke wrote of the Lord's preaching in the temple courts (20:1). Is there no difference? Do these verses indicate that "the gospel writers did not distinguish sharply between the functions of teaching and preaching"?[8] The fact that several verses mention Jesus carrying out both ministries in the same places seems insufficient evidence for making his teaching and preaching identical. We never read, for example, of Jesus' *teaching* the good news. That is what he preached.

References to his preaching and evangelizing occur more often in the earlier part of Jesus' work on earth (see table 12), whereas teaching occurred throughout his ministry[9] (see the references in table 4 in chapter 3). The five titles used of Jesus Christ as a Teacher occur a total of seventy times in the Gospels (see table 2 in chapter 3), and yet, though he preached, he is never given the title of Preacher or Herald.

What then are the differences? In his preaching Jesus proclaimed the message of salvation, available through repentance from sin and faith in him.[10] In his teaching, however, he communicated numerous subjects (see the list of fifty discourses, table 10 in chapter 6).

Preaching was for evangelization, to bring sinners to Christ. Teaching was for edification, to instruct believers in Christ. In preaching,

7. On teaching and preaching in Mark's Gospel, see Robert P. Meye, *Jesus and the Twelve: Discipleship and Revelation in Mark's Gospel* (Grand Rapids: Eerdmans, 1968), 52–60.

8. Charles M. Laymon, *The Life and Teachings of Jesus*, rev. ed. (Nashville: Abingdon, 1962), 121.

9. Lewis Joseph Sherrill, *The Rise of Christian Education* (New York: Macmillan, 1944), 87.

10. "To repent" *(metanoeō)* means to change one's thinking and therefore to alter one's direction. Faith is the act of trusting. Repentance and faith occur together. When persons believe (place their faith) in Jesus Christ, they thereby change the direction of their life. These are not two separate actions; they occur simultaneously (Mark 1:15; Acts 20:21; cf. 1 Thess. 1:9).

Jesus announced; in teaching, he instructed. One was proclaiming; the other was explaining. In his preaching, he called for repentance; in his teaching, he called for discipleship. One was a summons to become a believer; the other was a summons to live the life of a believer.

If Jesus evangelized but did not also instruct, people may have formed "distorted ideas of what the coming Kingdom would be, reading into it all their previous notions. The nature of his mission as Messiah required that he should teach what the Kingdom of God was, and that teaching was a constant accompaniment of preaching and evangelizing."[11] The good news he preached was accompanied by teaching. "Without teaching, his Gospel in every probability would have been so grossly misunderstood as to defeat his mission altogether."[12]

Because Jesus proclaimed good news and the need for repentance and faith, many people thought of him as a prophet. These included the following individuals and groups:

The Samaritan woman (John 4:19)
People in the funeral procession of the widow's son (Luke 7:16)
The five thousand who were fed (John 6:14)
People (Mark 5:15; Matt. 16:13–14)
People in Jerusalem at the Feast of Tabernacles (John 7:40)
A man born blind (John 9:17)
Crowds in Jerusalem at the triumphal entry (Matt. 21:11)
People in Jerusalem a few days after the triumphal entry (Matt. 21:46)
Two believers on the road to Emmaus (Luke 24:19)

Jesus referred to himself as a prophet (Mark 6:4; Luke 4:24; 13:33; John 4:44). Why did people think of him as a prophet? Like Old Testament prophets, he claimed to be sent by God the Father as his representative, to be in communion with God, to receive, proclaim, and interpret divine revelation, to work miracles, to be anointed by God, to warn the people of impending divine judgment, and to predict coming events.[13]

11. Sherrill, *The Rise of Christian Education*, 87–88.
12. Ibid., 89.
13. See G. K. A. Bell and D. Adolf Deissmann, *Mysterium Christi: Christological Studies by British and German Theologians* (London: Longmans, Green, 1930), 56–66; Robert H. Stein, *The Method and Message of Jesus' Teachings* (Philadelphia: Westminster, 1978), 3–4; A. J. B. Higgins, "Jesus as Prophet," *Expository Times* 57 (1945–1946): 292–94; R. E. Davies, "Jesus and the Role of the Prophet," *Journal of Biblical Literature* 64 (1945): 241–54; and F. W. Young, "Jesus the Prophet," *Journal of Biblical Literature* 68 (1949): 285–99.

Jesus' Goal of Providing Salvation

Related to Jesus' goal of preaching good news was his objective of providing salvation. He said he "came to seek and to save what was lost" (Luke 19:10), "to save the world" (John 3:17), and "to give his life as a ransom for many" (Matt. 20:28; Mark 10:45). An angel told Joseph that Mary's son was to be named Jesus, "because he will save his people from their sins" (Matt. 1:21), and at Jesus' birth angels announced to shepherds, "Today in the town of David a Savior has been born to you" (Luke 2:11). The Samaritans who believed in Jesus realized that he is "the Savior of the world" (John 4:42).

John the Baptist said that Jesus, as the Lamb of God, "takes away the sin of the world" (John 1:29). And as a shepherd, Jesus gave his life for the sheep (10:11, 15, 17–18). He came to give eternal life (3:16, 36; 5:24; 6:54; 10:10, 28; 11:25; 14:6) and in spiritual darkness he provides light (1:4, 9; 3:19–21; 8:12; 9:5; 12:46). Jesus also said he came to satisfy spiritual thirst (4:10, 14; 6:35; 7:37) and hunger (6:35, 41, 48, 50–51, 58), to give freedom (8:36) and grace and truth (1:17b). His goal was to encourage people "to believe" in himself, "the one he [God the Father] has sent" (John 6:29), for those who do believe in him become God's children (John 1:12) and are saved (note the word *saved* in Luke 8:12; 13:23; 18:26; John 10:9).

Jesus' Other Teaching-Related Goals

The Lord Jesus stated several other goals in his becoming the incarnate Son of God. One was "to fulfill the Law and the Prophets" (Matt. 5:17). The idea in this statement is that he came "to reveal the full depth of meaning"[14] of the Mosaic law and to have realized in himself the predictions about him in the writings of the Old Testament prophets. "The prophetic teachings point forward (principally) to the actions of Christ and have been realized in them in an incomparably greater way. The Mosaic laws point forward (principally) to the teachings of Christ and have also been realized in them in a more profound manner."[15] To fulfill the Law and the Prophets means "starting with it [the Law] as it stands, and bringing it on to completeness; working out the spirit of it;

14. Alan Hugh McNeile, *The Gospel according to Matthew,* Thornapple Commentaries (London: Macmillan, 1915; reprint, Grand Rapids: Baker, 1980), 58.
15. Robert Banks, "Matthew's Understanding of the Law: Authenticity and Interpretation in Matthew 5:17–20," *Journal of Biblical Literature* 93 (1974): 231.

getting at the comprehensive principles which underlie the narrowness of the letter."[16] This stands in contrast to the traditional misinterpretations of the teachers of the law and the Pharisees. Jesus' ministry was to carry out the true intent of the Old Testament Scriptures, to abolish not the Scriptures but the oppressive rulers and burdensome trappings added to them by the religious leaders of his day.[17] Many of his frequent confrontations with the teachers of the law and the Pharisees related to this purpose—to point them to the true spiritual concerns of the Old Testament Scriptures (with their emphasis on godly living and their focus on Christ) and away from the perfunctory legalistic requirements the leaders had added to the Old Testament. Much of what he taught related to this goal.

Another stated goal of our Lord was to reveal God the Father (John 1:18). As the Word (John 1:1), Jesus communicates God to man, just as a person's "word is the means whereby he reveals what he is thinking."[18] In addressing the Father, Jesus said that it was God's "good pleasure" to reveal truths to some but not others (Matt. 11:25–26). In the upper room he told Philip, "Anyone who has seen me has seen the Father" (John 14:9). And to the disciples Jesus explained, "Everything that I learned from my Father I have made known to you" (15:15). And he prayed to God the Father, "I have revealed you to those whom you gave me out of the world" (17:6), and "I have made you known to them" (v. 26a).

Related to this purpose of revealing the Father is Jesus' revealing the Father's words. "I gave them the words you gave me and they accepted them" (v. 8a), and "I have given them your word" (v. 14a). What God the Father wanted communicated by the Son is exactly what Jesus revealed.

Another purpose the Savior said he had was to testify to the truth—and in "fulfilling" the Old Testament Law and Prophets, and in revealing God and his words—he was committed to developing spiritually those who followed him. To bring individuals to repentance and faith in Christ, to save the lost by granting forgiveness of sins, to preach good news so that those who believe would receive eternal life—these objectives were only the beginning. They related to his preaching. Once a person came to Christ, the Savior's goal in his teaching ministry was *to foster spiritual growth and maturity.*

16. Alfred Plummer, *An Exegetical Commentary on the Gospel according to St. Matthew,* Thornapple Commentaries (1915; reprint, Grand Rapids: Baker, 1982), 76.
17. Ibid., 77.
18. Leon Morris, *The Gospel according to John,* New International Commentary on the New Testament (Grand Rapids: Eerdmans, 1971), 74.

Jesus emphasized ten points in his teaching as ways his followers can grow spiritually. Teachers today should seek to foster these same activities in their learners.

Grow by loving the Lord. As Jesus told an expert in the law, "Love the Lord your God with all your heart and with all your soul and with all your mind" (Matt. 22:37).[19] And to his disciples he said, "Remain in my love" (John 15:9–10). He emphasized the priority of loving him when he asked Peter three times, "Do you love me?" (John 21:15–17).

Grow by loving others. In the Sermon on the Mount, Jesus presented a difficult command, "Love your enemies" (Matt. 5:44). And to the expert in the law, the Lord quoted Leviticus 19:18 as conveying what he considered the second greatest commandment: "Love your neighbor as yourself" (Matt. 22:39; Mark 12:31; Luke 10:27). To the disciples he gave what he called "a new commandment": "Love one another" (John 13:34; cf. 15:17). "Love each other as I have loved you" (15:12).

Grow by obeying God's Word. Obedience to Christ is a hallmark of followers of Christ. He spoke of "practicing" the commands of Scripture (Matt. 5:19) and "these words of mine" (7:24; cf. Luke 6:47). Those who put God's Word into practice, he said, are like his mother and brothers (Luke 8:21), that is, they are ones most deeply related to him for they are affiliated with him spiritually, not just physically. In the upper room Jesus emphasized to his disciples the importance of their obeying him as evidence of their loving him. "Whoever has my commands and obeys, he is the one who loves me" (John 14:21). "If anyone loves me, he will obey my teaching" (v. 23). "If you obey my commands, you will remain in my love" (15:10). "You are my friends if you do what I command" (v. 14).

Grow by doing good deeds. Jesus urged his learners to so live that others "may see your good deeds and praise your Father in heaven" (Matt. 5:16). He chose them, he said, for the purpose of bearing "fruit—fruit that will last" (John 15:16), and they can bear spiritual fruit, that is, be spiritually productive, as they abide in him (vv. 4–5). Bearing "much fruit," he explained, brings glory to God and demonstrates to others that they are his disciples (v. 8). "A good tree," he explained, "cannot bear bad fruit" (Matt. 7:18).

Grow by putting spiritual priorities first. This includes laying up treasures in heaven (Matt. 6:19–21; Luke 12:33–34; cf. Matt. 19:21), and pursuing God's kingdom and his righteousness (Matt. 6:33).

Grow by fellowshiping with God in prayer. Jesus frequently spoke of the value of prayer. Twice he discussed it in the Sermon on the Mount

19. The parallel passages, Mark 12:30 and Luke 10:27, add "and with all your strength."

(Matt. 6:5–13; 7:7–11; cf. Luke 11:1–13), and he encouraged his disciples always to pray and not give up (Luke 18:1).[20] Prayer was explained a number of times in the Upper Room Discourse, a not-so-surprising fact in light of Jesus' imminent departure. Note these several verses:

"I will do whatever you ask in my name, so that the Son may bring glory to the Father" (John 14:13)
"You may ask me for anything in my name, and I will do it" (v. 14)
"If you remain in me and my words remain in you, ask whatever you wish, and it will be given you" (15:7)
"I tell you the truth, my Father will give you whatever you ask in my name" (16:23)
"Ask and you will receive, and your joy will be complete" (16:24b)

Grow by exercising faith in the Lord. Those who exercised faith in the Lord were commended by him, including the centurion (Matt. 8:10) and the Canaanite woman of Syrophoenicia (16:28). The faith of these two non-Israelites stands in contrast to that of the disciples, whose limited faith Jesus reproved on several occasions (8:26; 14:31; 16:8; 17:20). One of his most comforting words of encouragement is recorded in John 14:1, "Do not let your heart be troubled. Trust in God; trust also in me."

Grow by resisting temptation. When faced with his own trial in the garden of Gethsemane, Jesus urged Peter, "Watch and pray, so that you will not fall into temptation" (Matt. 26:41; Mark 14:38; Luke 22:40, 46). The model prayer the Lord gave his disciples includes the petition, "Lead us not into temptation" (Matt. 6:13; Luke 11:4). Why is it necessary to pray such a prayer when God does not want people to sin and since he tempts no one (James 1:13)? The point of the request is to ask the Lord to decrease the attractiveness of sin, thereby keeping believers from circumstances that would encourage them to sin.[21]

Grow by serving the Lord. In calling Peter and Andrew to leave their fishing and to follow him, Jesus added that he would make them "fishers of men" (Matt. 4:19; Mark 1:17), that is, to draw others to the Lord. Jesus engaged these two disciples and the other ten he chose in serving him by preaching (Mark 3:14; 6:12) and healing. They could testify to others about the Lord because they had been with him (John 15:27; cf. Mark 3:14; John 3:22). Strengthening others spiritually was a signifi-

20. The verb *enkakeō* means "to become weary, to lose heart, to despair" (A. T. Robertson, *Word Pictures in the New Testament*, 6 vols. [Nashville: Broadman, 1930), 2:231.
21. Norval Geldenhuys, *Commentary on the Gospel of Luke*, New International Commentary on the New Testament (Grand Rapids: Eerdmans, 1951), 321.

cant responsibility Jesus specifically assigned to Peter ("strengthen your brothers," Luke 22:32; "Feed my lambs," "Take care of my sheep," "Feed my sheep," John 21:15–17). Before he ascended to heaven, he informed the Eleven that they would be witnesses for him to others (Acts 1:8).

Grow by manifesting spiritual virtues. In his teaching Jesus highlighted numerous qualities of significance for growth. For an interesting study, read the many verses listed with each trait (listed in the order in which they occur in the Gospels).

> Humility (Matt. 5:3–5; 6:11; 18:2–5; 23:5–12; Luke 6:20; 9:47–48; 14:8–11; 17:10; 18:14, 17; 20:46–47; 22:24–27; John 13:5, 14–15)
> Mercy (Matt. 5:7, 9; 9:13; 12:7; Luke 6:36)
> Purity (Matt. 5:8, 27–32)
> Joy (Matt. 5:12; Luke 6:23; 10:20; John 15:11; 16:22; 17:13)
> Honesty (Matt. 5:33–37)
> Sacrifice and nonretaliation (Matt. 5:10–11, 38–42; 10:37–39; 16:24–25; 19:29–30; 20:25–28; Mark 12:41–44; Luke 6:22, 27–30; 9:57–62; 14:26–33; 18:28–29; John 12:25; 15:20; 16:2–4, 22)
> Forgiveness (Matt. 5:21–26; 6:12, 14–15; 18:15, 21–35; Luke 17:3–4)
> Righteousness (Matt. 5:6; 6:1–18, 33)
> Faithfulness (Matt. 6:24; 23:23b; 25:21, 23; Luke 12:42; 16:8–13)
> Trust, without worry or fear (Matt. 6:25, 28, 31, 34; 10:26–31; 13:22; Mark 4:19; 5:36; Luke 8:14, 50; 10:41; 12:4–7, 22, 25–26, 29; John 6:20; 14:27)
> Noncritical spirit (Matt. 7:1–5; Luke 6:37; John 7:24)
> Concern for the poor (Matt. 6:2; Luke 6:20; 12:33–34; 14:12–14; 18:22; 19:8)
> Gratitude (Luke 17:11–19)
> Peace (Matt. 5:9; Mark 9:50b; John 14:27; 16:33)
> Generosity (Matt. 5:42; 7:2; 10:8; Mark 4:24; Luke 6:30, 38)

What's Your Answer?

Do you know if everyone in your class has received Jesus Christ as his or her Savior? What steps can you take to be sure each one is a believer?

To what extent do you feel each of your students is growing spiritually? What evidence do you see in their lives of the ten means of spiritual growth discussed in this chapter?

What specific steps can you take in your class to help encourage your pupils to grow spiritually?

How often do you mention one or more of the fifteen desirable characteristics (p. 101) in your teaching? Can you stress these more? How?

"Everyone who is fully trained will be like his teacher."

Luke 6:40b

8

Were Jesus' Teaching Goals Limited to Knowing the Truth?

$\mathcal{A}$s we have seen, Jesus presented a vast array of content to his audience. Does this mean he was satisfied with people knowing the material, grasping mentally the truths he taught? A number of verses specify that he did desire his listeners to know and understand what he taught. However, he did not limit his ministry objectives to the acquiring of knowledge. And yet that knowledge formed a foundational beginning, a framework within which he shared other concerns. Jesus wanted people to learn in the fullest sense, as we will see later in this chapter. Truth to be lived must first be known and understood. Comprehending God's truth provides the stepping stone for experiencing God's truth.

Knowing and Understanding

The Gospels often refer to the need for knowing, understanding, and learning. For example, Jesus spoke of his disciples knowing "these things" (John 13:17), that is, the humble place a servant maintains. By holding to God's truth, individuals become his disciples, and thereby "know the truth" (8:32). Several times Jesus spoke of the disciples knowing him or the Father (John 14:7, 17; 17:3), and knowing that Jesus came from God the Father (17:7–8). The Lord wanted them to know ("keep in mind," NIV) that any hatred the unregenerate may express toward them as believers would result from the unsaved having already hated him (15:18).

The Gospels use several Greek words in speaking of Jesus' desire that others understand what he was teaching. In giving the parables of the kingdom in Matthew 13, Jesus explained to his disciples that for two reasons he was communicating "the knowledge of the secrets of the kingdom of heaven" (v. 11) in parables. One reason was to reveal truth to his followers and the other was to conceal truth from those who rejected him, "those on the outside" (Mark 4:11). Having revealed their rejection of Jesus (3:22), the teachers of the law were unable, because of their hardened hearts, to comprehend the meaning of his parables. Conversely, the disciples, open to him and his truths, would understand the parables because of insight from God. "The word of God is always effective: it brings enlightenment or judgment—enlightenment to the disciples, judgment to those who rejected Jesus."[1] Then Jesus quoted Isaiah 6:9–10 to support his statement that his adversaries would not understand (Matt. 13:14–15; cf. Mark 4:12; Luke 8:10). Three times in Matthew 13:13–15 the Lord used the word *syniēmi*, "to comprehend, gain insight into, understand,"[2] in underscoring the inability of people with "calloused" hearts (v. 15) to understand the truth, even though they heard it. After twice associating *syniēmi* with hearing (vv. 13–14), Jesus used it a third time in connection with "hearts" ("understood with their hearts," v. 15). This demonstrates that genuine comprehension of spiritual realities involves more than hearing; it is a matter of the heart.[3] To hear is not enough. One's ears must be opened, but so must one's heart.

1. Leon Morris, *The Gospel according to Matthew* (Grand Rapids: Eerdmans, 1992), 34. Jesus' purpose in parabolic teaching was "educational to disciples, and disciplinary to those who refused to become disciples" (Alfred Plummer, *An Exegetical Commentary on the Gospel according to St. Matthew*, Thornapple Commentaries [1915; reprint, Grand Rapids: Baker, 1982], 189).

2. Verse 13, however, has *syniō*, a shortened form of the verb *syniēmi* (Walter Bauer, William F. Arndt, and F. Wilbur Gingrich, *A Greek-English Lexicon of the New Testament and Other Early Christian Literature*, 2d ed., rev. F. Wilbur Gingrich and Frederick W. Danker [Chicago: University of Chicago Press, 1979], 790; cf. *Theological Dictionary of the New Testament*, s.v. "συνίημι, σύνεσις, συνετος, ἀσύνετος," by Hans Conzelmann, 7:888–96).

3. Plummer, *An Exegetical Commentary on the Gospel according to St. Matthew*, 190.

Jesus' foes also failed to comprehend other aspects of his teaching. When he spoke of the One who sent him (John 8:26), the Pharisees "did not understand that he was telling them about his Father" (v. 27). In verse 27 "understand" translates *ginōskō*, "to know." Continuing his discussion with the Jewish leaders, he asked, "Why is my language not clear to you?" (v. 43, literally, "Why do you not know *[ginōskō]* my word?").

When Jesus told the Pharisees (9:40) about sheep knowing their shepherd but not a stranger, "they did not understand *[ginōskō]* what he was telling them" (10:6). Again their rejection of Christ's person led to their blindness to Christ's teaching. However, if they believed in his miracles, Jesus said, they could come "to understand *[ginōskō]* that the Father is in me, and I in the Father" (10:38).

Crowds too misunderstood. A few days after Jesus' triumphal entry many people "still would not believe in him" (12:37). The apostle John then quoted Isaiah 6:9–10 (in John 12:40) about their lack of understanding, to support his statement that "they could not believe" (v. 39).[4]

When Jesus talked with a crowd and said that what comes out of a person's mouth is what makes him unclean (because words reflect the heart), Jesus began his remark by saying, "Listen and understand" (*syniēmi*, Matt. 15:10, 18; Mark 7:14–15).

Jesus' enemies and the crowds that heard him lacked spiritual insight. However, even his disciples often failed to grasp the meaning of his teachings. For example, the disciples asked him what he meant by his comments to the crowd about what makes a person "unclean" (Matt. 15:15; Mark 7:17). Jesus asked, "Are you still so dull?" (Matt. 15:16; Mark 7:18).[5] He was apparently taken aback that with their having been with him for some time they did not have more understanding of his meaning.

On several other occasions the disciples did not understand the Lord. They did not understand *(syniēmi)* about the loaves for their hearts were hardened (Mark 6:52). This means they had failed to grasp that the feeding of the five thousand "pointed beyond itself to the secret of Jesus' person," missing its significance and seeing "only 'a marvel.'"[6]

When Jesus told his disciples that he would be betrayed, killed, and

---

4. The rejectors *could* not believe (v. 39) because they *would* not believe (v. 37). Being unwilling to believe led to their being unable to believe. God sealed their fate because of their willful rejection.

5. The word *dull*, which translates *asynetos*, "without comprehension," is related to the verb *syniēmi* and is used only here in the Gospels.

6. William L. Lane, *The Gospel according to Mark*, New International Commentary on the New Testament (Grand Rapids: Eerdmans, 1974), 237–38.

raised to life (Mark 9:32; Luke 9:45),[7] they did not know (*agnoeō*, to be ignorant).

When Jesus told them about the yeast of the Pharisees and Sadducees, they thought he meant not to buy yeast for bread from his enemies (Matt. 16:6–7). Surprised, he asked, "Do you still not understand?" and "How is it you don't understand that I was not talking to you about bread?" (vv. 9, 11). In these two questions he used yet another word for understand. This verb, *noeō*, "to perceive with the mind," is related to the noun *nous*, "mind or intellect." After he explained he was referring not to bread but to the religious leaders' false teaching, "they understood" (*syniēmi*, v. 12).

When again Jesus told the Twelve about his being killed and raised, along with his being mocked, insulted, spit on, and flogged, they "did not understand [*syniēmi*] any of this" and "they did not know [*ginōskō*] what he was talking about" (Luke 18:34).[8]

By the question, "Do you understand what I have done for you?" (John 13:12), which Jesus asked the disciples after he had washed their feet, Jesus expressed his desire that they know the significance of that symbolic act.

Thomas failed to comprehend what Jesus meant by his words about his going away (John 14:1–5).

After Jesus said he would be gone for a little while the puzzled disciples admitted they did not "understand [*oida*, to know inherently] what he [was] saying" (16:18).

John wrote that even after Peter and John saw the empty tomb, "they still did not understand [*oida*] from Scripture" the truth of Jesus' resurrection (20:9).

On other occasions, however, the disciples did understand his teaching. After telling his seven parables of the kingdom, Jesus asked his disciples, "Have you understood [*syniēmi*] all these things?" and they replied, "Yes" (Matt. 13:51). This was because he spoke to them "as much as they could understand"[9] and "he explained everything" to them when they were alone (Mark 4:33). They also understood *(syniēmi)* the Scriptures when the risen Savior opened their minds *(nous)*, explaining to them what was written about him in the Old Testament.

---

7. Matthew wrote that they were "filled with grief" (Matt. 17:23). When Luke added that they "did not grasp it," he used the verb *aisthanomai*, a word that occurs only here in the New Testament.

8. Matthew and Mark did not mention the disciples' lack of understanding (Matt. 20:17–19; Mark 10:33–34).

9. Here the Greek word is *akouō*, "to hear" in the sense of apprehending. Literally the phrase "as they were able to hear it" means that Jesus adapted his teaching to their level of understanding (Lane, *The Gospel according to Mark*, 172).

Certainly then Jesus wanted his audiences to understand what he taught, to perceive the meaning of his words. That was one of the goals of his teaching. Some people, however, could not grasp their significance because of spiritual dullness.

Is Understanding Enough?

Knowing spiritual facts and comprehending their meaning is basic to learning. But does that comprise the essence of learning? Was Jesus satisfied with the people comprehending truths he taught, or was he concerned that his audiences go beyond recognition and perception? To answer that question, we need to look at the word *manthanō* (to learn), which occurs twenty-five times in the New Testament including six times in Matthew, Mark, and John.

Manthanō carries a wide range of meaning. It can involve coming to know facts intellectually (Acts 23:27; 1 Cor. 14:31, 35; Phil. 4:9; 2 Tim. 3:7, 14); gaining insight into facts or sensing their significance (Matt. 9:13; 24:32; Mark 13:28;[10] John 6:45;[11] 1 Cor 4:6; Col. 1:7; Heb. 5:11); studying or seeking instruction from another (John 7:15; Rom. 16:17; 1 Tim. 2:1); becoming accustomed to or gaining experience in (Phil. 4:11; 1 Tim. 5:4; Tit. 3:14; Heb. 5:8); acquiring skill (1 Tim. 5:13; Rev. 14:3); or being committed to something or someone (Matt. 11:29; Eph. 5:20).

When Jesus said, "Take my yoke upon you and learn of me" (Matt. 11:29), which meaning of *manthanō* did he have in mind? He was probably referring to more than acquiring facts about himself. He doubtless had in mind the challenge of being committed to him, of being his follower.[12] This seems evident because of his words, "Take my yoke upon you," with which verse 29 begins. In Jewish literature the yoke spoke

10. In Matthew 9:13 Jesus challenged his Pharisaical assailants to learn (see the significance of) God's words in Hosea 6:6. In Matthew 24:32 (also Mark 13:28) he challenged the Twelve to know the significance of his lesson about the fig tree.

11. To hear and learn from God the Father (i.e., to gain insight into what one hears from God) results in his accepting Jesus. "All those who are taught in this way, who hear God, and learn what they hear, do come to Him" (Leon Morris, *The Gospel according to John*, New International Commentary on the New Testament [Grand Rapids: Eerdmans, 1971], 372). "The 'hearing' brings out the external communication, the learning the internal understanding of it" (B. F. Westcott, *The Gospel according to St John* [London: John Muray, 1890], 105).

12. *Theological Dictionary of the New Testament*, s. v. "μανθάνω et al." by K. H. Rengstorf, 4:408.

metaphorically of obligation, submission, or commitment.[13] The *Didache* (an early-church manual of instruction) mentions "the yoke of the Lord" (*Didache* 6.2).

Learning, then, in this sense is spiritual as well as intellectual, moral as well as mental. It involves a commitment to a Person, the Lord Jesus—being identified with him, spending time with him, and acquiring his outlook, attitudes, and values. "For the disciples, learning was living, living with and like Jesus."[14]

The range of ideas in *manthanō* is also seen in the breadth of meaning for *ginōskō* and *oida* (to know). As Richards explains, *ginōskō*

> involves knowing or coming to know about (truth, John 8:32; God's will, Luke 12:47; a tree by its fruit, Matt. 12:33). It also is used of finding out (Mark 5:43; Luke 24:18), comprehending (Luke 18:34; Heb. 3:10) or realizing (Luke 8:46), and recognizing or acknowledging (Matt. 7:23). Another basic Greek word, οἶδα *[oida]*, includes knowing a person or about him (Mark 1:34; John 1:26, 31, 33; 6:42; 7:28; Acts 3:16; 7:18; Gal. 4:8; 1 Thess. 4:5; Heb. 10:30), being intimately acquainted (Matt. 26:72, 74; Mark 14:71; Luke 22:57; 2 Cor. 5:16), and of knowing how, or being able (Matt. 7:11; Luke 11:13; cf. 1 Thess. 4:4; 1 Tim. 3:5; James 4:17). In addition it is used of knowing God in a relational, not theoretical way (Matt. 25:12; John 7:28; 8:19; 2 Thess. 1:8; Titus 1:16). A third, ἐπιγινώσκω *[epiginōskō]*, emphasizes the completeness of knowledge, but can have the same range of usages as the other two.[15]

This shows unmistakably that "the terms for knowing fail to exalt the intellectual as an end in itself."[16]

Jesus revealed his deep concern for living the truth that is known mentally. The person who hears his words "and puts them into practice" is wise, for he is like a man building a house on a rock and not sand. Failing to put into practice Jesus' words, even though one hears them, is foolishness (Matt. 7:24–27; Luke 6:47–49). A person who "does not do what I say," Jesus said (Luke 6:46), is not doing "the will of my Father in heaven" (Matt. 7:21).

To "hear God's word and put it into practice" is to be Jesus'

13. The Mishnah, ʾAbōth 3.8, refers to the yoke of the law. Acts 15:10 refers to that same yoke, and Galatians 5:1 calls the Mosaic law "a yoke of slavery." Also see Sirach 51:23–27; the Apocalypse of Baruch 41:3; and the Psalms of Solomon 7:8; 17:32 in the apocryphal literature.

14. Lee Magnen, "Teaching and Learning in the Gospels: The Biblical Basis of Christian Education," *Religious Education* 70 (November–December 1975): 631.

15. Lawrence O. Richards, *A Theology of Christian Education* (Grand Rapids: Zondervan, 1975), 33.

16. Ibid., 34.

mother and brothers, he said (Luke 8:20–21). That is, those who obey him enjoy a closer relationship to him than even his closest family members.[17]

On one occasion when the Lord was teaching, a woman shouted a note of praise about his mother: "Blessed is the mother who gave you birth and nursed you" (Luke 11:27). Without denying her commendation, he pointed out that an even greater blessing than being Mary, his mother, comes from hearing the Word of God and obeying it (v. 28).

The one who "practices the truth" (John 3:21 NASB) manifests his commitment by living in the light and not in the darkness of evil (v. 20). After Jesus washed the disciples' feet, a remarkable display of humility, he focused their need for humility by saying, "No servant is greater than his master" (John 13:16). Then he added, "Now that you know these things, you will be blessed if you do them" (v. 17).

Clearly, then, to hear God's truth, recognizing it cognitively, falls short of Jesus' desire that his followers put into practice or obediently live out what they know. We are to act on what is known.

Numerous times Jesus invited others to "follow me" (Matt. 4:19; 8:22; 9:9; 10:38; 19:21; Mark 1:18; 2:14; 8:34; 10:21; Luke 5:27; 9:23, 59; 18:22; John 1:40; 12:20; 21:19, 22; cf. Matt. 16:24; 19:27; Mark 10:28; Luke 5:11; 18:28; John 10:4, 27). By this he challenged them to abandon self-interest (Luke 14:26–27), to be with him (Mark 3:14), to accept his authority, to learn from and be trained by him (Luke 6:40), to be committed to him, to work with him (Luke 15:10), to work for him (Matt. 10:1; Mark 3:14–15; 6:14; Luke 10:1), to obey him (John 14:15, 21, 23–24; 15:10), to trust him (John 14:1, 11–12), to love him (John 14:15, 21, 23; 21:15–17), and even to suffer for him (Matt. 10:22; Mark 8:34–35; Luke 14:2; 21:12; John 15:20; 16:32–33; 21:18–19).[18] This invitation carried no whimsical idea of merely listening to Jesus for a few hours or days. He wanted committed, obedient learners! "This call clearly points to a long association; Jesus is not inviting them to a pleasant stroll along the seashore but inviting them to discipleship; there is the thought of

17. Again Matthew in the parallel passage spoke of doing "the will of my Father in heaven" (12:50; cf. 7:21; Mark 3:35), whereas Luke twice referred to putting into practice the Lord's words (6:46; 8:21).

18. In the Roman Empire a criminal condemned to die by crucifixion was compelled to carry his cross beam to the place of execution. To take up the cross meant he was going to die. In associating with Jesus as a disciple, a person must be characterized, like Jesus, with a willingness to die. Jesus "heads the procession going out to die, and all who follow Him must face death to self" and even the possibility of physical death (D. Edmond Hiebert, *Mark: A Portrait of the Servant* [Chicago: Moody, 1974], 209). Also see Michael P. Green, "The Meaning of Cross-Bearing," *Bibliotheca Sacra* 140 (April–June 1983): 117–33.

personal attachment."[19] In fact, this call "clearly meant separation from the kind of life they had been living hitherto. . . ."[20]

In this way the Lord's followers would become like him, for as he said in Luke 6:40, "everyone who is fully trained[21] will be like his teacher." The student will not be superior to his teacher, but by being prepared or equipped by his teacher, he behaves like him, not differently from him. Such a person comes to understand what Jesus teaches, but more importantly, comes to share in Jesus' likeness. These followers "would only be properly trained when they exhibited in their life something of the life of the master."[22] Imitating the Lord's values and virtues, obeying his instructions and injunctions, results in greater Christ-likeness of character.

"Jesus called his disciples to *be with* him because they needed to see enfleshed the concepts which he taught. They needed to see the Word incarnated if they were to truly understand and be moved to respond, and thus become like their teacher!"[23]

What Is a Disciple?

Mathētēs, Greek for "disciple," carries this same concept. This word, used only in the Gospels (234 times) and Acts (28 times) for a total of 262 occurrences, suggests far more than a student sitting and listening to a teacher lecture.

In classical Greek the word meant a learner who had a personal relationship with his teacher, as Rengstorf explains:

> The emphasis is not so much on the incompleteness or even deficiency of education as on the fact that the one thus designated is engaged in learning, that his education consists in the appropriation or adoption of specific knowledge or content, and that it proceeds deliberately and according to a set plan. Thus there is no μαθητής without a διδάσκαλος [teacher]. The process involves a corresponding personal relation.[24]

19. Morris, *The Gospel according to Matthew*, 85.

20. Ibid.

21. "Fully trained" translates *katērtismenos*, a passive participle, from *katartizō*, meaning "to put in order, prepare, complete, or equip." Matthew 4:21 and Mark 1:19 use the verb in reference to mending nets, that is, getting them ready for use. It carries the notion of restoring in Galatians 5:1 and 1 Peter 5:10, and of equipping in Ephesians 4:12. Preparation is the thought in Hebrews 10:5 and 11:3 ("formed").

22. K. N. Giles, "Teachers and Teaching in the Church: Part 5," *Journal of Christian Education* [Australia] 70 (April 1981): 12.

23. Richards, *Theology of Christian Education*, 34–35.

24. *Theological Dictionary of the New Testament*, s.v. "μανθάνω et al.," by K. H. Rengstorf, 4:416.

He added that the word "implies a direct dependence of the one under instruction upon an authority superior in knowledge."[25] *Mathētēs* "implies that the person not only accepts the views of his teacher, but that he is also in practice an adherent."[26]

In the New Testament "disciple" is used primarily of Jesus' followers, though at times it refers to followers of John the Baptist (Matt. 9:14; 11:2; 14:2; Mark 2:18; 6:29; Luke 5:33; 11:1; John 1:35, 37; 3:25; 4:1), of Pharisees (Matt. 22:15–16; Mark 2:18; Luke 5:33), and of Moses (John 9:28). However, *mathētēs* does not always bear the same meaning. It is used of large crowds of people who followed Jesus, including "a large crowd of his disciples" (Luke 6:17) who followed him and listened to his Sermon on the Mount, and "the whole crowd of disciples" (19:37; the Pharisees called them "your disciples," v. 39), who praised him as he entered Jerusalem in his triumphal entry. From John 6:60–61, 64, 66 it is plain that some who were called his disciples did not believe him ("many of his disciples turned back and no longer followed him," literally, they "no longer walked with him," v. 66). Why then were they called disciples? The answer lies in the fact that *mathētēs* here refers to people who had been following and listening to Jesus. They were curious but not convinced.[27] Having heard what Jesus said (John 6), they decided that discipleship differed from what they had expected. "His rejecting their desire to make him their political king; his demand for personal faith; his teaching on atonement; his stress on total human inability and on salvation as a work of God—all these proved to be unpalatable for many people."[28]

Many times the word *disciple* designates Jesus' twelve men, whom he chose to be closely associated with him. Examples of the many verses referring to them include Matthew 5:1; 10:1; 11:1; 20:17; 26:20; Mark 3:7, 9; 4:34–35; Luke 6:13; 8:1, 9; 9:12, 14; John 6:67, 70–71; 20:24. Sometimes three of the Twelve are called disciples (Matt. 17:6, 10, 13; Luke 9:36) and sometimes two of the Twelve (Matt. 21:1, 6). Individuals, such as John (John 13:23; 19:26; 21:7) and Joseph of Arimathea (19:38), are called disciples.[29] The twelve disciples, Jesus' inner circle of follower-learners, are also called apostles (Matt. 10:2; Mark 3:14; 6:30;

25. Ibid.

26. *International Standard Bible Encyclopedia*, 1924 ed., s.v. "Disciples," by G. H. Trever, 2:851.

27. J. Dwight Pentecost, *Design for Discipleship* (Grand Rapids: Zondervan, 1971), 14–17.

28. Edwin A. Blum, "John," in *The Bible Knowledge Commentary, New Testament*, ed. John F. Walvoord and Roy B. Zuck (Wheaton, Ill.: Victor, 1983), 298.

29. In the Book of Acts the term *disciple* describes the community of believers in Christ (Acts 6:1–2, 7; 9:36; 11:26).

Luke 6:13; 9:10; 11:49; 17:5; 22:14; 24:10; Acts 1:2).[30] After Judas betrayed the Lord, the close circle became known as "the eleven disciples" (Matt. 28:16), "the Eleven" (Mark 16:14; Luke 24:9, 33), or "the eleven apostles" (Acts 1:26).

The verb *mathēteuō*, related to *mathētēs*, occurs only four times in the New Testament, with the meaning "to become a disciple" (Matt. 27:57) or "to make a disciple" (Matt. 13:52;[31] 28:19; Acts 14:21). Most frequently a *mathētēs*, "disciple," suggests someone who accepts the teachings of an instructor or model and becomes a loyal follower, supporter, and subject. The word implies "a personal attachment which shapes the whole life" of the adherent;[32] it calls for a commitment[33] and obedience.[34]

So a committed disciple—not just a curious inquirer—is noted for learning from the Savior, loyalty to the Savior, and love for the Savior. Abandonment and allegiance, service and suffering characterize committed disciples. They know the beliefs taught by the Lord, but more than that, they practice the behavior modeled by the Lord. Not only do they understand God's will, they also undertake it (Matt. 12:49–50)!

Implications for Teachers

What does all this say to teachers? One point stands out distinctively: Jesus' model of teaching challenges teachers to hear and heed three things:

Like Jesus, we are to model the truth by exemplary living.
Like Jesus, we are to communicate truth clearly and cogently so that it is understood.
Like Jesus, we are to challenge students to practice in their hearts and lives what they know in their minds.

Was Jesus' goal to help people know the truth? Certainly. But he did not stop there. Building on that foundation, he urged his listeners to become loyal learners, committed to be with him and to become like him.

---

30. In the Book of Acts the common term for this small circle, "apostles," is used twenty-eight times.

31. The NIV renders this word in Matthew 13:52, "who has been instructed," whereas the NASB translates it, "who has become a disciple."

32. *Theological Dictionary of the New Testament*, s.v. "μανθάνω et al.," by K. H. Rengstorf, 4:441.

33. Ibid., 442.

34. Ibid., 448.

Now What?

Are there times when you sense that some of your students do not understand what you are teaching? What is the reason? Do you need to be clearer? Or have they failed to grasp the significance of what is being taught? How can you find out? What can you do to improve their level of understanding?

What specific actions can you take to encourage your students to become more Christ-like?

Examine your lesson goals. Are you aiming to help your students go beyond the comprehension of facts? Can you write each lesson aim so it relates to both knowing and doing? Try using this formula in writing one of your lesson aims: "That my students, by knowing _____ [fill in the fact(s) you want them to know] will _____ [fill in an action or attitude you want them to do or develop]."

How can you follow Jesus' example and develop a closer relationship with your students? List some specific things you can do this week or this month to let them get to know you better as a person.

Think of ways you can show your love to your students, communicating your care for and interest in them.

"This is my Son, whom I love;
with him I am well pleased.
Listen to him!"

Matthew 17:5

9

What Impact Did Jesus Have on the Crowds and on His Disciples?

*E*very class has them. The quiet students, the noisy ones; the shy, the talkative. Some students are disciplined while others are unruly and boisterous. Some take life seriously; others are carefree. The aloof, and the warm and friendly; the conscientious and the careless; slow learners and fast learners—it seems that every class, no matter how large or how small, has students with vastly different personalities.

Think of the class you are presently teaching, or one you have taught. Did it include some of those kinds of individuals? Doubtless it did, for few if any classes ever seem to have individuals with the same backgrounds or traits.

How do you meet the needs of students whose characteristics are so diverse? How do you respond to the belligerent student who challenges much of what you say, while at the same time encouraging the reticent, reserved student? This is a challenge all teachers face to one degree or another.

Jesus, too, ministered to diverse groups, to "classes" with individuals of varied interests, needs, concerns, and outlooks on life. He dealt with individuals, small groups, and large crowds. Some were curious, others were committed; some were hospitable, others hostile. Seeing how he taught these people can help teachers today gain insight in how to minister effectively to student diversity. Noting how he related to students and how they responded to him can enlighten us on how better to relate to our students and how to have a greater spiritual impact on their lives.

Whom Did Jesus Teach?

Jesus' amazing teaching ability comes to light when one considers the varied audiences and individuals he taught. He debated with religious leaders and talked about spiritual things with simple villagers. He taught large crowds and trained a small group of disciples.[1] He dealt with an inquiring Nicodemus, a weeping prostitute in a Pharisee's house, and a believing Roman centurion. "He could speak with gentle forgiveness to self-confessed sinners, and with stern denunciation to religious hypocrites."[2] The wide diversity of Jesus' listeners and learners can be seen from the lists in tables 13 and 14.

Table 13
People Whom Jesus Taught*

Disciples	Matthew 5:1–2; Mark 8:31; 9:31; Luke 11:1; John 14:23–24; 15:20
Crowd(s)	Matthew 7:28; 22:33; Mark 2:13; 4:1; 6:34; 10:1; 11:18
People	Luke 5:3; 23:5
People in villages and towns	Matthew 11:1; Mark 6:6; Luke 13:22, 26
People in synagogues	Mark 1:21–22, 27; 6:2; Luke 4:15; 6:6; 13:10; John 6:59; 18:20
People in the temple	Mark 12:35, 38; Luke 19:47; 20:1; 21:37–38; John 7:14, 28; 8:2

*The references in this chart include the word *teach, teaching,* or *taught.* Of course Jesus instructed many others, though a form of the word *teach* is not used. These are listed in table 14.

1. Norman Anderson, *The Teaching of Jesus* (Downers Grove, Ill.: InterVarsity, 1983), 10.
2. Ibid.

Table 14
Groups Whom Jesus Taught*

Religious Leaders

A teacher of the law	Matthew 8:19–22; Luke 9:57–62
Pharisees	Matthew 12:1–8; 19:3–9; 22:41–46; Mark 2:24–28; 10:2–9; Luke 6:1–7; 16:14–31; 17:20–22; 18:9–14; 19:34–40
Pharisees and teachers of the law	Matthew 12:9–14; 15:1–20; Mark 3:1–6; Luke 6:6–11; 15:1–32
Pharisees and Sadducees	Matthew 16:1
Pharisees and Herodians	Matthew 22:15–22; Mark 12:13–17
Chief priests and elders	Matthew 21:23–46; Mark 11:27–12:12; Luke 20:1–8
Sadducees	Matthew 22:23–32; Mark 12:18–27; Luke 20:27–44
A Pharisee who was an expert in the law	Matthew 22:34–40; Mark 12:28–34
Caiaphas, the high priest	Matthew 26:62–63; Mark 14:61–62
Teachers of the law	Mark 2:6–10
A Pharisee named Simon	Luke 7:39–47
An expert in the law	Luke 10:25–37
A Pharisee with whom Jesus ate	Luke 11:37–44
Another expert in the law	Luke 11:45–53
A Pharisee and an expert in the law	Luke 14:1–6
Guests at the home of a prominent Pharisee	Luke 14:7–11
A prominent Pharisee	Luke 14:12–14
A guest at the home of the prominent Pharisee	Luke 14:15–24

John the Baptist's Disciples and Jesus' Disciples

John the Baptist's disciples	Matthew 9:16; 11:2–6
Peter	Matthew 16:16–17, 23; 18:21–35; Luke 12:41–53
Nine of Jesus' twelve disciples	Matthew 17:19–20; Mark 9:14–29; Luke 9:41

John	Mark 9:38–50
James and John	Luke 9:54–55
The seventy–two	Luke 10:1–20

Others

A rich young man	Matthew 19:16–22 (= Mark 10:17–22; Luke 18:18–30)
Mary and Martha	Luke 10:38–42
An unnamed woman	Luke 11:27–28
A man with a brother	Luke 12:13–21
Some in the crowd	Luke 13:1–9
A synagogue ruler	Luke 13:14–17
An unidentified person	Luke 13:23–30
Women at the tomb	Matthew 28:10
Two on the road to Emmaus	Luke 24:13–35

*Though the word *teach, teaching,* or *taught* is not used of Jesus' relationship to these individuals and groups, he did talk to them. This list does not include those individuals whom Jesus healed.

Jesus and the Crowds

Jesus taught numerous groups of individuals, people referred to as "crowds" (see table 13). These included the crowds who heard his Sermon on the Mount (Matt. 7:28; 8:1), given outdoors on a mountainside in Galilee (5:1); crowds who heard Jesus' response to the Sadducees (22:33); a crowd beside the Sea of Galilee (Mark 2:13); a crowd on the shore of the Sea of Galilee when he taught parables in a boat (4:1); a large crowd that followed him around the lake when he sailed to "a solitary place" (6:32–34); a crowd that he taught and then fed (6:35–44); a crowd that was amazed at his teaching when he cleansed the temple (11:17); and a crowd of people who followed him into Transjordan (Luke 10:1).

Other references to crowds following him (to learn from him or have their sick healed by him) recorded in the Gospel of Matthew include 4:25 (large crowds from all the regions of Palestine who followed him); 8:18 (a crowd that was around him after he healed many people); 9:8 (a crowd who saw Jesus heal a paralytic); 9:23, 25 (a "noisy crowd" outside the home of Jairus, whose daughter Jesus healed; Luke 8:42 says, "the crowds almost crushed him"); 9:33 (an amazed crowd that saw a demon exorcized by Jesus); 9:36 (crowds on whom he had compassion because they were like sheep without a shepherd); 11:7 (a crowd to whom Jesus spoke about John the Baptist); 12:46 (a crowd outside a home where Jesus addressed the Pharisees); 13:34 (the crowd to whom Jesus gave the parables of the "secrets" of the kingdom of heaven); 15:10 (a crowd that was with Jesus when he answered the Pharisees about ceremonial handwashing); 15:33, 35, 39 (a crowd of four thousand, whom he fed); 17:14 (a crowd of people with a man and his epileptic, demon-possessed boy); 19:2 (large crowds who followed him to the Transjordan); 20:29 (a large crowd that followed Jesus from Jericho to Jerusalem); 21:8 (a "very large crowd" that spread their cloaks and branches on the road as Jesus entered Jerusalem and shouted praise to him); 21:46 (a crowd in Jerusalem that believed Jesus was a prophet); and 23:1 (crowds that heard Jesus denounce the Pharisees' hypocrisy; Luke 12:1 says this crowd included many thousands). In addition a large crowd was involved in Jesus' arrest (26:47, 55) and was present at Jesus' trial before Pilate (27:15, 17, 20, 24).

Other references to crowds that were with Jesus include these: Mark 7:33 (a crowd around him when in Decapolis he healed a deaf and dumb man); 8:34 (a crowd to whom he spoke about the cost of discipleship); 12:37 (a large crowd in the temple courts that was delighted with Jesus' teaching when he discussed his lordship and his relationship to David); Luke 4:30 (a crowd in the synagogue of Nazareth when he taught there); 5:15 (crowds that heard of his healing power); 5:29 (a large crowd of tax collectors and others who were eating with Jesus in Levi's house); 7:12 (a large crowd with the widow of Nain in her son's funeral procession); 11:29 (crowds that increased as Jesus spoke about the Pharisees' request for a miraculous sign); 19:3 (a crowd in Jericho that prevented Zacchaeus, a short man, from seeing Jesus); John 5:13 (a crowd in Jerusalem near the Pool of Bethesda); 6:22, 24 (a crowd that sailed in boats to Capernaum to see Jesus); 7:12, 20, 31–32 (a crowd in Jerusalem at the Feast of Tabernacles, some of whom accused him of being demon-possessed and others of whom believed); 12:9 (a crowd who went to Lazarus' house in Bethany); and 12:29, 34 (a crowd at the Passover Feast who heard God the Father's voice from heaven glorifying Jesus' name).

It is impossible to know how many people were in these crowds, but the five thousand men besides women and children whom Jesus fed (Matt. 14:21) give some indication of the large numbers. Luke's reference to "a crowd of many thousands" (12:1) who heard Jesus denounce the Pharisees' hypocrisy provides another indicator of the huge following he had. The attraction of his message, his healing power, and his Person were indeed powerful! Few other teachers could claim such magnetism over so many people in so many cities, towns, and villages.

The crowds reacted to Jesus and his ministry in interesting ways. Many were amazed at his words and works (see chap. 4). Matthew 22:33; Mark 1:22, 27; 11:18; and Luke 4:22, 32 refer to the amazement of the people or the crowds.

Another reaction of the crowds was belief in Jesus. Many people in Jerusalem at the Passover Feast, seeing his miraculous signs, believed (John 2:23). Hearing the testimony of the Samaritan woman who came to Christ, many Samaritans believed on him (4:39), and because of his own words to them many more believed (4:41–42). As the Lord told the people he is the light of the world, "many put their faith in him" (8:30). And in the Transjordan "many believed in Jesus" (10:42). Seeing Jesus raise Lazarus from the dead, many Jews believed on him (11:45). Many leaders believed in Christ (12:42).

Praise was another response of the crowds to Jesus. The crowd that saw Jesus heal the paralytic who was let down through a roof was filled with awe and praised God (Matt. 9:8; Mark 2:12; Luke 5:26). Amazed at Jesus' power to heal dumb, lame, and blind people, people in Galilee praised God (Matt. 15:31). And when people in Galilee heard Jesus' teaching in the synagogues, "everyone praised him" (Luke 4:15). The crowd on the way to bury the son of the widow of Nain praised God when they saw Jesus restore the boy to life (7:16). A similar reaction was experienced by those in Jericho who saw Jesus restore the sight of the blind beggar (18:43). A crowd joyfully praised God in loud voices as Jesus entered Jerusalem in his triumphal entry (19:37).

An unusual response of a crowd is recorded only once in the Gospels. A large crowd with nine of Jesus' disciples, who were unable to heal a demon-possessed boy, "ran to greet" Jesus (Mark 9:15, 25).

In the temple courts a large crowd expressed delight at hearing Jesus' words (Mark 12:37). People "hung on his words" (Luke 19:48). Even the chief priests, trying to find a basis for killing Jesus, told Pilate that he was stirring up the populace "all over Judea by his teaching" (23:5). Everyone recognized that here was a powerful Teacher, one whose words led people to be in awe, to think, to respond, to believe, and to worship—One whose words were penetratingly disturbing to some and pleasingly delightful to others.

Jesus and the Twelve

What impact did Jesus have on the twelve disciples? And how did they respond to his teaching and training? We may note several things Jesus did for and with the Twelve.

Jesus selected and trained the Twelve. They shared a number of traits that helped make them a compatible team. All were Jews, all were from the same geographical area, all spoke the same language. Each lacked formal education, each one was teachable, each was an adult male, and each could relate to common people.[3] They were ordinary people.

Yet these disciples were a diverse group. "Their diversity of backgrounds, vocations and outlooks added to His team-building challenge. . . . Certainly, they were a far cry from the conformity that leads to cohesion in team-building."[4] Their personalities differed; and though the occupations of most of the Twelve are not known, we do know that four of them were fishermen (Peter, Andrew, James, and John) and that Matthew was a tax collector. One of them, Simon (not Peter), had been a Zealot, a party that advocated the overthrow of the Roman government and the reestablishment of the independent Jewish state.

The remarkable fact is that Jesus chose these twelve men to be with him, to be trained by him, and to be sent out to serve him. Seeing him pray, they were inspired to ask him to teach them to pray (Luke 11:1), and listening to him teach, they asked him to increase their faith (Luke 17:5).

Jesus trained them by example, by verbal instruction,[5] by his miracles, by personal association, and by involvement. As a result, they were changed individuals, men who, because they believed him and were committed to him, were transformed by him. "Having time to walk the roads and sit at lunch daily with the King of kings has to be the most enviable privilege imaginable."[6]

Jesus loved the Twelve. More than a formal teacher-student relationship, Jesus' relationship to the Twelve was one of love, evidenced by his concern for their best interests. John, the apostle of love, wrote that Jesus, "having loved his own who were in the world . . . showed them the full extent of his love" (John 13:1) by washing their feet. Soon thereafter Jesus said he compared his love for them to that of God the Father's love for him (15:9). He then commanded them to love each other

3. Ronald Lee Rushing, "A Comparison of the Discipleship Principles and Methods of Christ and Paul" (Th.M. thesis, Dallas Theological Seminary, 1981), 33–34.

4. David L. McKenna, *Power to Follow, Grace to Lead* (Dallas, Tex.: Word, 1989), 124.

5. Only a few times do the Gospels specifically refer to Jesus' "teaching" the disciples verbally (Matt. 5:2; Mark 8:31; 9:31; Luke 11:1). However, being with the crowds who followed Jesus and were taught by him, the Twelve heard his many discourses and dialogues.

6. Warren S. Benson, "Christ the Master Teacher," in *Christian Education: Foundation for the Future*, ed. Robert E. Clark, Len Johnson, and Allyn K. Sloat (Chicago: Moody, 1991), 98.

"as I have loved you" (v. 12). His love for them, he said, was also evidenced by his giving his life for them (v. 13).

In this reciprocal mentor-disciple relationship, three times Jesus challenged his disciples to love him and to show that love by obedience to him (14:15, 21, 23). Jesus' love for Peter was revealed by calling him blessed (Matt. 16:17), and by his not criticizing or rejecting him even though Peter denied him.

Even though he knew Peter would deny him (Luke 22:34), Jesus told the apostle he prayed for him (v. 32). This love for the disciples also shows in Jesus' confidence in them. Confident they could find success in ministering on his behalf, he commissioned them to preach and heal (Matt. 10:1, 7–8; Mark 3:14–15). He assured them that anyone who received them was thereby receiving him (Matt. 10:40). Jesus told them that after he returned to heaven they would do "greater things" than what he did (John 14:12).[7] In their ministry after his ascension, they would testify of him (15:27), they would make disciples (Matt. 28:19), and they would be his witnesses (Acts 1:8). In commissioning them to make disciples of all nations, he assured them of the backing of his authority and the blessing of his presence. "What more could they ask for?"[8] The intimacy of his love is also seen in his calling them his friends, not his servants (John 15:13–15).

Jesus believed in his prayerfully chosen disciples and relayed that confidence to them. His "attitudes and opinions about the disciples were aimed at positively imparting their self-esteem and performance."[9]

Still another evidence of Jesus' love is his defense of the disciples when they were criticized unjustly. When the Pharisees saw the disciples picking and eating some heads of grain on the Sabbath, he defended that action by referring to David's eating consecrated bread from the tabernacle, and by quoting Hosea 6:6 (Matt. 12:1–8).

---

7. This does not mean apostles would do more outstanding miracles than those Jesus performed. From a human standpoint their miracles (recorded in Acts) were less spectacular than his (what miracle could have been greater than the raising of Lazarus, who was already dead and buried?) and were certainly fewer in number. The "greater things" suggests that their outreach would be greater. "On the day of Pentecost alone more believers were added to the little band of believers than throughout Christ's entire earthly life" (Leon Morris, *The Gospel according to John,* New International Commentary on the New Testament [Grand Rapids: Eerdmans, 1971], 646). In addition Jesus' ministry was confined to Palestine and nearby regions, whereas the apostles traveled extensively. Also conversion of the soul far exceeds the healing of the body.

8. Howard G. Hendricks, "Following the Master Teacher," in *The Christian Educator's Handbook on Teaching,* ed. Kenneth O. Gangel and Howard G. Hendricks (Wheaton, Ill.: Victor, 1989), 24.

9. Matt Friedeman, *The Master Plan of Teaching* (Wheaton, Ill.: Victor, 1990), 125.

Again the Pharisees criticized the disciples; this time the criticism pertained to the disciples' failure to follow the tradition of ceremonial handwashing. Turning the accusation around on them, Jesus told the Pharisees they were the ones who were breaking, not tradition, but the very command of Scripture, therefore nullifying its effectiveness and showing themselves to be hypocrites (Matt. 15:1–9). Again this rebuke is from the Old Testament, namely, Isaiah 29:13.

When some people accused the disciples of not fasting, Jesus once again defended his followers (Luke 5:33–35). A fourth defense occurred when the Pharisees at Jesus' triumphal entry wanted him to rebuke his disciples for joyfully praising him by calling him king. He simply replied somewhat enigmatically, "If they keep quiet, the stones will cry out" (Luke 19:37–40). In other words, praise was inevitable.

Because of his love for and commitment to the Twelve, Jesus did not let unfair criticism go unanswered. Hearing these remarks the Lord made to his critics must have greatly encouraged the disciples, and led them to reciprocate his love.

Jesus rebuked and corrected the Twelve. The Savior's love for his own "was no sentimental slush; it was tough love."[10] He did not hesitate to correct them when necessary; that was part of his teaching and training. On fifteen occasions Jesus corrected, reprimanded, rebuked, or chided the Twelve for some deficiency, failure, or false concept on their part (see table 15).

To correct or rebuke the disciples showed Jesus' concern for their maturation. The actions and/or statements that revealed deficiencies on their part gave Jesus excellent opportunities to teach them. Failure was never reason for rejection. "Regardless of His demanding statements regarding the cost of discipleship, He never demanded a fully developed faith at the beginning of one's spiritual pilgrimage. He never rejected anyone because of his incomplete, faltering faith or failure to live up to God's laws."[11] (Peter is singled out in four of the incidents, though of course he was involved with several or all of the other disciples in seven other incidents.)

Jesus selected and trained the Twelve. He loved them, and he corrected them. How did they respond to his ministry to them? What impact did Jesus have on them?

The Gospel writers mention several things in relation to these questions. Like the populace, the disciples too "were amazed at his words" (Mark 10:24; cf. v. 26) and astonished (v. 32). Though at times they questioned what he was doing (e.g., John 11:8), sought to inform him

10. Hendricks, "Following the Master Teacher," 21.
11. Ibid., 22.

Table 15
Jesus' Corrections of the Disciples' Deficiencies

Category[a]	Incident	Jesus' Reply	Scripture
Lack of faith	1. The disciples were afraid they would drown in a storm on the lake.	Jesus asked, "You of little faith, why are you so afraid?"	Matthew 8:23–26; Mark 4:40
	2. Nine disciples were unable to heal an epileptic boy.	Jesus asked, "O unbelieving and perverse generation, how long shall I stay with you? How long shall I put up with you?"	Matthew 17:17; Mark 9:19; Luke 9:41
Lack of understanding about his death and resurrection	3. Jesus predicted his death and resurrection and Peter's denial of them.	Jesus rebuked Peter, saying, "Get behind me, Satan! You are a stumbling block to me."	Matthew 16:22–23; Mark 8:32–33
	4. Peter, James, and John slept while Jesus was praying in Gethsemane.	Jesus asked, "Could you men not keep watch with me for one hour?"	Matthew 26:40, 45; Mark 14:37, 41; Luke 22:46
	5. Peter cut off the right ear of the high priest's servant.	Jesus responded, "No more of this!" "Put your sword away!"	Luke 22:49–51; John 18:10–11
Lack of understanding about the nature of his kingdom	6. James and John suggested that they call down fire from heaven on an unbelieving Samaritan village.	Jesus turned and rebuked[b] them.	Luke 9:54–55

a. These categories are adapted from James Jones Steward, "The Causes for Which Christ Corrected His Disciples" (Th.M. thesis, Dallas Theological Seminary, 1979), though he has five categories and ten incidents of Jesus' corrections.

b. The word *epitimaō* means a stern rebuke. Jesus' plans did not call for executing judgment on cities in his first advent. This word is used not only of Jesus' rebuking the disciples but also of his rebuking demons on several occasions (Matt. 17:18; Mark 9:25; Luke 4:41; 9:42), rebuking a storm (Matt. 8:26; Mark 4:39; Luke 8:24), and rebuking a fever (Luke 4:39). Jesus never rebuked his enemies.

Category	Incident	Jesus' Reply	Scripture
	7. The disciples rebuked parents[c] who brought young children to Jesus for him to touch them and pray for them.	Jesus was indignant[d] with the disciples, and explained that young children in their humility and trust characterize those who will be in God's kingdom.	Mark 19:13–14; 10:13–16; Luke 18:15–17
Lack of humility	8. John told a man who was exorcising a demon to stop.[e]	Jesus told John, "Do not stop him."	Mark 9:38–39
	9. James and John asked to sit on Jesus' right and left, positions of authority.	Jesus said, "You don't know what you are asking."	Mark 10:35–40
	10. The ten disciples were indignant at James and John for their bold, proud request.	Jesus said a servant is greatest.	Mark 10:41–42; Luke 22:24–30
	11. Peter proudly announced he would never renounce the Lord.	Jesus said Peter would deny him.	Matthew 26:33–34; Mark 14:29–30; Luke 22:33–34; John 13:37–38

c. Apparently the disciples thought Jesus would be wasting his time on supposedly unimportant people like children. To them, such demands on his time and energy seemed unreasonable, spending time on children was beneath his dignity, and they wanted more uninterrupted time with him (Alfred Plummer, *An Exegetical Commentary on the Gospel according to St. Matthew*, Thornapple Commentaries [1915; reprint, Grand Rapids: Baker, 1982], 261–62).

d. The Greek word for indignant, *aganakteō*, occurs only in the Gospels (three times each in Matthew and Mark, and once in Luke). Only one time (Mark 10:14) is it used of Jesus. It suggests intense annoyance, deep displeasure, or angered resentment. The disciples too were indignant on several occasions (Matt. 20:24; 26:8; Mark 10:41; 14:4).

e. This may have been an effort on John's part to change the subject from Jesus' rebuke of their pride. (Knowing the disciples were arguing about which of them was greatest, Jesus spoke about being humble like a child, Mark 9:33–37). Perhaps John also jealously wanted to win praise from the Lord for his zeal (James W. Shepherd, *The Christ of the Gospels* [Grand Rapids: Eerdmans, 1947], 331).

Category	Incident	Jesus' Reply	Scripture
	12. Peter asked about John's future.	Jesus told him not to be concerned about John.	John 21:21–22
Lack of appreciation for honor due Christ	13. The disciples sharply rebuked[f] Mary for anointing Jesus' feet with expensive perfume.	Jesus replied, "Leave her alone. . . . She did [it] to prepare for my burial."	Matthew 26:6–13; Mark 14:3–9; John 12:4–8
Lack of appreciation of the testimony of others	14. The Eleven refused to believe the words of those who saw him after he had risen.	Jesus rebuked them for their distrust.	Mark 16:14
	15. Thomas refused to believe Jesus was resurrected unless he could touch him.	Jesus said that those who have not seen him and have believed are blessed.	John 20:27–29

f. The word *embrimaomai*, rendered in the NIV "rebuked sharply," means "to charge with vehement threats" or "to be strongly or sternly indignant." Classical Greek usages relate it to the roaring of a lion or the snorting of a horse (G. F. MacLear, *The Gospel according to Mark*, Cambridge Greek Testament for Schools and Colleges [Cambridge: Cambridge University Press, 1889], 61). The word is also used in Matthew 9:30; Mark 1:43; and John 11:33, 38 to speak of being moved with deep emotions.

(Matt. 15:12), or were surprised at what he did (John 4:27), they believed him (John 2:22; 17:8), acknowledged that he is the Messiah (Matt. 16:16; Mark 8:29; Luke 4:20), and worshiped him (Matt. 14:33; 28:17; Luke 24:52–53).

Unquestionably this small band of men was profoundly affected by the Lord Jesus. Because of the Master, their lives were changed, their hearts transformed. And, as we see in the Book of Acts, they became powerful witnesses for Jesus Christ. Having been touched by the Savior they in turn became his agents in touching the lives of many hundreds of others by leading them to faith in Christ. Judging only by his impact on the disciples, Jesus was truly a supremely effective Teacher.

Check Yourself . . .

How well are you following Jesus' example in the way he taught his disciples?

Are you, like Jesus, personally interested in each of your students? How well do you know them?

Do you let your students know you love them and are concerned about them and their spiritual needs? In what specific ways can you communicate your love and concern this week?

How can you encourage your students to think?

Have you had to correct your students' ideas or conduct? If so, did you do it carefully and lovingly? And did you, like Jesus, use the corrections as opportunities for further teaching?

What specific steps can you take to show your students you have confidence in them, and to help build their self-esteem?

What assignments, responsibilities, or challenges can you give those you teach whereby they may learn and grow?

*"No one ever spoke
the way this man does."*

John 7:46

10

What Impact
Did Jesus Have
on His Opponents?

*H*ow do you react when a student disagrees with what you say? How should you respond if a student becomes openly belligerent or defiant? How do you handle a student who tries to trap you, thereby seeking to discredit you?

Jesus faced this kind of opposition to his teaching from several religious and political groups who heard him. And the groups were numerous: Pharisees, Sadducees, teachers of the law, Herodians, chief priests, elders. The masterful way in which he responded to their combative spirit and the brilliant way in which he sometimes took the initiative in confronting these groups gives us insights in how to deal with troublesome or implacable students.

Who Were the Pharisees and the Sadducees?

Who were these groups and what did they believe? Why did they oppose Jesus' teaching, even to the point of wanting to murder him?

129

Names and Origins

The Pharisees, who are mentioned almost one hundred times in the New Testament (eighty–eight times in the Gospels, nine times in Acts,[1] and once in Philippians 3:5), originated in the second century before Christ. In 175 B.C. Antiochus Epiphanes became the ruler of Palestine. His efforts to force Greek culture and pagan practices on the Jews led to rebellion. The Hasidim (loyal ones), who continued Ezra's work of studying and meticulously carrying out the law, joined the Hasmoneans (also known as the Maccabees) in revolting against foreign domination. Possibly the Pharisees were one of several groups spawned by the Hasidim.[2]

The word *Pharisee* derives from the Hebrew word *p^erushim*, which means "the separated ones."[3] But from what or whom were they separated? Some suggest their name refers to the fact that they withdrew support from John Hyrcanus (134–104 B.C.) and the Hasmonean Dynasty, turning their attention to more religious matters and away from political concerns.[4] Others say the Pharisees were separating themselves as lay leaders from the priests. According to the most common view they voluntarily separated themselves from the common people in an effort to be ritually clean.[5]

In Jesus' day there were "more than six thousand" Pharisees in full membership,[6] though many others may have been associated with them. They became the "leading sect,"[7] having gained the support of the

1. Acts 5:34; 15:5; 23:6 (three times), 7–9; 26:5.

2. R. Travers Herford, *Pharisaism: Its Aim and Method* (London: Williams and Norgate, 1912), 19.

3. Some scholars have argued that the Hebrew verb *pārash*, from which stems the plural noun *p^erushim*, means "to make distinct, to declare," and therefore refers to the Pharisees as interpreters of the Law (W. O. E. Oesterley, and G. H. Box, *Religion and Worship of the Synagogue* [London: Pitman and Sons, 1907]). Suggesting a different view, Manson says the word originally meant "Persian," a nickname given the group by their opponents because of Persian-like beliefs in the resurrection, angels, and spirits (T. W. Manson, "Sadducee and Pharisee: The Original Significance of the Names," *Bulletin of the John Rylands Library* 22 [1938]: 153–58). Another explanation is that the Hebrew noun means "those who specify" (A. I. Baumgarten, "The Name of the Pharisees," *Journal of Biblical Literature* 102 [1983]: 420, 426–28). None of these views, however, has won much favor among the majority of scholars.

4. Eduard Lohse, *The New Testament Environment*, trans. John E. Steeley (Nashville: Abingdon, 1976), 77.

5. Ibid. Cf. *International Standard Bible Encyclopedia*, 1986 ed., s.v. "Pharisees," by R. J. Wyatt, 2:822.

6. Josephus *The Antiquities of the Jews* 17.2.4.

7. Josephus *The Jewish Wars* 2.8.14.

populace. A few of them were teachers of the law,[8] though most of them were lay craftsmen, farmers, and merchants. The Pharisees dominated Jewish public life[9] and had a great impact on the ordinary people.[10] They stood as "the nucleus of the nation, distinguished from the rest only by their greater strictness and consistency."[11]

The Sadducees, by contrast, were from wealthy, influential families, many of whose members were priests and temple officials. They "had accommodated themselves to a certain degree to the Hellenistic influence."[12] The name *Sadducee* may be derived from Zadok, the high priest in David's day (2 Sam. 8:17; 20:25; 1 Kings 1:8, 26, 32–33) and in Solomon's time (1 Kings 2:35; 4:4).[13] They supposedly arose around the time of the Hasmoneans, for the first mention of the Sadducees is by Josephus, who associated them with the time of Jonathan, brother of Judas Maccabeus (160–143 B.C.).[14]

The seventy-member Sanhedrin, the Jewish Supreme Court, consisted largely of Sadducees, though some Pharisees were members as well. The Sadducees had little control or influence over the people. "Even in the Sanhedrin they were obliged to accept the presence . . . of the Pharisees."[15] The Sadducees "were conservatives in politics as well as in religion."[16]

The word *Sadducees* occurs only fourteen times in the New Testament. Nine occurrences are in the Gospels (Matt. 3:7; 16:1, 6, 11–12; 22:23, 34; Mark 12:18; Luke 20:27) and five in the Book of Acts (4:1; 5:17; 23:6–8).

8. Joachim Jeremias, *Jerusalem in the Time of Jesus,* trans. F. A. Cave and C. H. Cave (Philadelphia: Fortress, 1969), 246–51.

9. Josephus *The Antiquities of the Jews* 13.6.2.

10. Ibid. 13.10.6.

11. Emil Schürer, *The History of the Jewish People in the Age of Jesus Christ (175 B.C.– A.D. 135),* rev. and ed. Geza Vermes, Fergus Millar, and Matthew Black, 2 vols. (Edinburgh: Clark, 1973, 1979), 2:389.

12. R. Alan Culpepper, "Pharisees and Sadducees in the First Century," *Biblical Illustrator* 8 (fall 1981): 51.

13. Again scholars have suggested other views on the origin of the term *Sadducee.* T. W. Manson suggests, for example, that "Sadducee" transliterates the Greek *syndikoi,* meaning "syndics" or judges ("Sadducee and Pharisee: The Original Significance of the Names," 144–59). Others have said the word means "righteous ones" (Alfred Edersheim, *The Life and Times of Jesus the Messiah,* 2 vols. [reprint, Grand Rapids: Eerdmans, 1962], 1:323–24).

14. Josephus *The Antiquities of the Jews* 13.5.9.

15. Marcel Simon, *Jewish Sects at the Time of Jesus,* trans. James H. Farley (Philadelphia: Fortress, 1967), 24.

16. Ibid.

Beliefs and Practices

What the Pharisees and Sadducees believed and how they practiced those beliefs show why they clashed with Jesus and his teachings. The major beliefs of these two groups may be summarized as in table 16.

Table 16
Beliefs of the Pharisees and the Sadducees

Pharisees	Sadducees
Oral tradition is equal in authority to the Old Testament.[a]	Only the Old Testament is authoritative; oral tradition has no authority.[b]
God determines some events; man determines others.[c]	Man has unrestricted free will.
The soul survives death.[d]	The soul perishes along with the body.[e]
The body will be resurrected.[f]	Physical resurrection of the dead will not occur.
Yahweh is the God of the universe and anyone could join the Jewish faith and worship him.[g]	Yahweh is the God of the Jews only.
Angels and demons exist in a hierarchical system.	Angels and demons do not exist.

a. "The Pharisees had passed on to the people certain regulations handed down by the traditions of the fathers and they were not written in the Laws of Moses" (Josephus *The Antiquities of the Jews* 13.10.6; cf. 13.6.2).

b. "Only those laws should be considered valid which were written down, and that those which came down by tradition of the fathers need not be observed" (ibid.).

c. "As for the Pharisees, they say that certain events are the work of fate, but not all; as to other events, it depends upon ourselves whether they shall take place or not. . . . But the Sadducees do away with fate, holding that . . . all things lie within our own power" (ibid. 13.5.9).

d. "Souls have an unmortal vigor in them, and . . . under the earth there will be rewards and punishments, according as they have lived virtuously or viciously in this life" (ibid. 18.1.3).

e. "As for the persistence of the soul after death, penalties in the underworld, and rewards, they will have none of them" (ibid. 18.1.4). "They also take away belief in the immortality of the soul, and in punishment or rewards in Hades" (Josephus *The Jewish Wars* 2.8.14).

f. Josephus *The Antiquities of the Jews* 18.1.3. Cf. Solomon Zeitlin, "The Pharisees: A Historical Study," *Jewish Quarterly Review* 52 (October 1961): 115.

g. Zeitlin, "The Pharisees," 115–16.

Since the Pentateuch did not make provision for every aspect of daily life and every possible situation, the Pharisees felt obligated to develop details of instruction. These intricate regulations were passed down orally from generation to generation, and since they were interpretations of what Moses wrote, the Pharisaic party believed they were of equal authority with Moses.

Oral traditions became like "a fence around the law" (Mishnah, *ʾAbôth* 1.1), as a guard against violating the law unintentionally. This resulted in directives that were "overly meticulous and hairsplitting in the extreme."[17] And yet, because of this zeal for the law and their intense piety and austerity, the Pharisees held the respect and support of the masses.[18]

What comes to mind when you hear the word *Pharisee* or *pharisaical?* Many people no doubt think of these terms: hypocrisy, legalism, self-righteousness, traditions, separatism and intolerance, pride, scrupulous attention to details of worship, religious pretense, ritual purification, and ostentatious display of religious acts. These terms accurately describe the Pharisees of Jesus' day, as revealed in the New Testament. However, did Jesus and the Pharisees have nothing in common? They shared a number of beliefs, including God's attributes of sovereignty, creative power, justice, love, omniscience, and omnipresence; revelation; man made in God's image; sin; forgiveness; prayer; immortality; resurrection; rewards; and angels and spirits.[19]

Pharisees' Commendable Qualities

In addition the Pharisees had a number of commendable qualities.

First, they took separation, holiness, and purity seriously. They sincerely sought to follow the Old Testament injunction, "Be holy because I, the LORD your God, am holy" (Lev. 19:2; cf. 11:44–45). They were committed to holy living, because God had said, "I am the LORD your God, who has set you apart from the nations" (20:24), and "I have set you apart from the nations to be my own" (20:26). The frequent references in Leviticus to being "clean" or "cleansed" (sixty-one times) and to being "holy" (seventy times) impelled the Pharisees to be unusually meticulous about ritual cleansing.

Second, the Pharisees took religious obligations seriously. Keeping the Sabbath, tithing, fasting, praying, almsgiving, observing religious festivals, and being morally upright occupied the attention of the Pharisees. They rigorously gave themselves to the study of the law.

17. Simon, *Jewish Sects at the Time of Jesus,* 32.
18. Josephus *The Antiquities of the Jews* 13.10.6.
19. For more on the beliefs the Pharisees and Jesus shared, see R. Travers Herford, *The Pharisees* (1924; reprint, Boston: Beacon, 1952), 147–75.

Third, they were concerned about the religious welfare of the people. As Collins wrote, "Because they considered the laws of God just as binding on the common folk as upon the priests, they took seriously their role of teaching the populace."[20] Religion was more than temple worship by the priests; it was to be a central focus of life for all the people.

Fourth, the Pharisees sought to relate God's Word to everyday life. As new circumstances arose, they showed the people how the Scriptures could be interpreted to answer those needs.

ℋow Did Jesus and the Pharisees Respond to Each Other?

Jesus' Criticism of the Pharisees

Why then did Jesus criticize the Pharisees? In view of their devotion and zeal, why did he vehemently oppose them? The Gospels reveal a number of facts about the Pharisees that led to Jesus' condemnation of them.

They ostentatiously displayed their religious devotion. This was evident in their dress, their almsgiving, their praying, and their fasting. So Jesus said: "Everything they do is done for men to see: They make their phylacteries wide and the tassels on their garments long" (Matt. 23:5). In his Sermon on the Mount Jesus challenged the people not to follow the attention-getting actions of the Pharisees. "So when you give to the needy, do not announce it with trumpets, as the hypocrites do in the synagogues and on the streets, to be honored by men" (6:2).[21] "And when you pray, do not be like the hypocrites, for they love to pray standing in the synagogues and on the street corners to be seen by men" (6:5). "When you fast, do not look somber as the hypocrites do, for they disfigure their faces to show men they are fasting" (6:16). The supposed outward righteous acts of the Pharisees did not result in salvation, for Jesus said that to enter the kingdom of heaven a person's righteousness must exceed that of the Pharisees (5:20). Later he told the Pharisees, "On the outside you appear to people as righteous" (23:28).

20. A. O. Collins, "The Pharisees," *Biblical Illustrator* 11 (winter 1985): 33.
21. "These hypocrites were people who acted a concern for the poor whereas their real concern was to establish a reputation for piety" (Leon Morris, *The Gospel according to Matthew* [Grand Rapids: Eerdmans, 1992], 137). Jesus did not specify the hypocrites in Matthew 6:4, 5, 16 as Pharisees, but they undoubtedly were included since he called the Pharisees hypocrites numerous times in Matthew, once in Mark, and three times in Luke.

They were noted for pride and for seeking the attention of others. The verses cited also suggest the motivation for the Pharisees' deeds: "done for men to see" (Matt. 23:5), "to be honored by men" (6:3), "to be seen by men" (6:5), "to show men they are fasting" (6:16). In addition Jesus said they "love the place of honor at banquets and the most important seats in the synagogues" (23:6) and "they love to be greeted in the marketplaces and to have men call them 'Rabbi'" (23:7; cf. Luke 11:43). He told them, "On the outside you appear to people as righteous" (Matt. 23:28); "You are the ones who justify yourselves in the eyes of men" (Luke 16:15).

They followed traditions handed down from earlier generations, traditions that neglected and violated the Scriptures. "Why do you break the command of God for the sake of your tradition?" (Matt. 15:3). "Thus you nullify the word of God for the sake of your tradition" (15:6). "The Pharisees . . . [are] holding to the tradition of the elders" (Mark 7:3). "And they observe many other traditions" (7:4). "You have let go of the commands of God and are holding on to the traditions of men" (7:8). "You have a fine way of setting aside the commands of God in order to observe your own traditions" (7:9). "Thus you nullify the word of God by your tradition that you have handed down. And you do many things like that" (7:13).

They disassociated themselves from people they considered spiritually ignorant or unclean, feeling they were superior. "Some . . . were confident of their own righteousness and looked down on everybody else" (Luke 18:9). This is seen in the Pharisees' questioning why Jesus ate with tax collectors and sinners (Mark 2:16). This is also seen in the Pharisees' questioning of the woman who kissed Jesus' feet and poured perfume on them (Luke 7:39). They became narrowminded and intolerant of anyone who disagreed with them.

They gave attention to punctilious, scrupulous observance of rituals to the neglect of moral issues. "You give a tenth of your spices—mint, dill and cummin. But you have neglected the more important matters of the law—justice, mercy and faithfulness" (Matt. 23:23). "You give God a tenth of your mint, rue and all other kinds of garden herbs, but you neglect justice and the love of God" (Luke 11:42).[22] Their perverting spiritual priorities were comparable to straining out a gnat but swallowing

---

22. God had ordered the Israelites to tithe "everything from the land, whether grain from the soil or fruit from the trees" (Lev. 27:30) and "all that your fields produce each year" (Deut. 14:22). The Pharisees understood this to include the smallest herbs. Perhaps this was going further than the Old Testament required, but it was not wrong to do so. As Jesus said, "You should have practiced the latter, without neglecting the former" (Matt. 23:23; cf. Luke 11:42). Jesus did not fault them "for what they did, but for what they left undone" (ibid., 583). The Pharisee in Jesus' parable also boasted that he gave "a tenth of all I get" (Luke 18:12).

a camel (Matt. 23:24).[23] However, what they "highly valued . . . is detestable in God's sight" (Luke 16:15).

Considering themselves superior to others, they developed an attitude of greed and self-indulgence. "The Pharisees," Luke wrote, "loved money" (Luke 16:14), and Jesus told them, "You are full of greed and wickedness" (11:39) and "full of greed and self-indulgence" (Matt. 23:25).

They occupied themselves unduly with details of ceremonial cleanliness. Concerned for maintaining ritual purity, they emphasized the proper washing of hands (Matt. 15:2; Mark 7:2–4a; Luke 11:38), lest they ceremonially contaminate their food by something they touched, including even touching the outside of a cup with defiled hands.[24] They also insisted on the cleaning of eating utensils (Matt. 23:25; Mark 7:4b; Luke 11:39); the avoidance of work on the Sabbath[25] (Matt. 12:1–2; Mark 2:24; 3:1–2; Luke 6:1–2, 6–7; 13:14; 14:1–3; and frequent fasting (Matt. 9:14; Mark 2:19; Luke 5:33; 18:12).[26]

They made distinctions in their regulations that erroneously circumvented God's commands. For example, Jesus stated in Matthew 23:16–22 that the Pharisees said taking an oath by the temple was not obligatory whereas an oath taken by the gold of the temple was to be kept. Swearing by the altar meant nothing, but swearing by a gift on the altar was binding. Jesus explained that such quibbling was illogical, since God would not be concerned with the precise wording of an oath to the point of disregarding one but considering the other valid.

In addition, the Pharisees sought to sidestep the command to honor their parents by allowing a person to tell them that he was giving as an offering to God what he might have otherwise given to his parents (Matt. 15:3–6; Mark 7:9–13). Mark used the word *Corban* in referring to the gift given to God (7:11), a word that transliterates a Hebrew term used in Leviticus 2:1, 4, 12–13; 7:13, 38; 9:7, 15 to refer to offerings to the Lord. Such twistings of God's Word for man's benefit were numerous; as Jesus said, the Pharisees "do many things like that" (Mark 7:13).

They hindered people from entering God's kingdom. While proselytiz-

23. This referred to straining a liquid through gauze to remove the smallest source of defilement (a gnat) while gulping down a camel (the largest of the beasts normally found in Palestine, and an unclean animal, Lev. 11:4).

24. Asher Finkel, *The Pharisees and the Teacher of Nazareth* (Leiden: Brill, 1974), 50–55, 141.

25. The Pharisees listed thirty-nine major categories of work that were forbidden on the Sabbath (Mishnah, *Shabbath* 7.2), such as sowing, plowing, reaping, threshing, winnowing, slaughtering, writing, tilling (Werner Förster, *Palestinean Judaism in New Testament Times* [Edinburgh: Oliver and Boyd, 1964], 172).

26. The Pharisees fasted twice a week, on Mondays and Thursdays (Lohse, *The New Testament Environment*, 79).

ing to acquire converts to Pharisaic Judaism (Matt. 23:15), the Pharisees actually hindered individuals from coming to salvation. "You shut the kingdom of heaven in men's faces. You yourselves do not enter, nor will you let those enter who are trying to" (23:14; cf. Luke 11:52). "You make him [the proselyte] twice as much a son of hell as you are" (Matt. 23:15). In their inconsistency they claimed to help people into God's kingdom whereas they actually prevented them from doing so. People who heard Jesus and were interested in his teaching were dissuaded from following him by the Pharisees who discredited Jesus. The Pharisees, having "the key to knowledge" (Luke 11:52) of God in the Scriptures, were blind to its truths. By rejecting Jesus, who came to fulfill the Law and the Prophets (Matt. 5:17), they kept people from coming to salvation through the Lord Jesus.

They added burdens to the populace, without helping them. Jesus said, "They tie up heavy loads and put them on men's shoulders, but they themselves are not willing to lift a finger to move them" (Matt. 23:4). To the experts in the law, many of whom were Pharisees, he said, "You load people down with burdens they can hardly carry, and you yourselves will not lift one finger to help them" (Luke 11:46). The Pharisees' extensive regulations for ritual purity became burdensome to the people. Yet the Pharisees put forth no effort to assist others in carrying out those obligations or to lighten the restrictions.

They claimed spiritual superiority but were hypocritical. Sitting "in Moses' seat" (Matt. 23:2) means the Pharisees assumed for themselves the authority of Moses as his successors. However, they were spiritually barren, for as Jesus plainly stated, "they do not practice what they preach" (23:3). Repeatedly Jesus addressed them as hypocrites, as those whose lives fell short of what they professed to believe and what they taught others to believe. The "hypocrites . . . in the synagogues" (6:2) were probably Pharisees, for the Pharisees were much involved in synagogue worship (the Sadducees, most of whom were priests, were engaged in temple services). Possibly the hypocrites standing and praying in the synagogues and on street corners (6:5) where they would readily be seen by others were Pharisees, as were the somber-looking hypocrites who fasted (6:16). Jesus also addressed the Pharisees as hypocrites when he accused them of nullifying the word of God for their tradition (15:7). When the Pharisees and Herodians tried to trap Jesus by their question about paying taxes, he responded by first calling them hypocrites (22:18; cf. Mark 12:15, "Jesus knew their hypocrisy").

Seven times in Matthew 23 Jesus pronounced "woe" on the teachers of the law and the Pharisees, and in six of the woes he called them hypocrites (vv. 13, 15, 23, 25, 27, 29). In Luke 11:42–53 he denounced the Pharisees with six woes (vv. 42–44, 46–47, 52). The word *woe* expresses displeasure or reproof,[27] for Jesus' pronouncements carried a strong note of coming judgment on their hypocritical living.

Another way Jesus pictured the Pharisees' hypocrisy was by likening them to "whitewashed tombs." Like graves painted white, the Pharisees were attractive outwardly but were spiritually unclean inwardly (Matt. 23:27–28). If a person stepped on a grave, he became ceremonially unclean (Num. 19:16). Therefore graves were whitewashed to make them easily visible. In a contrasting statement in Luke 11:44, Jesus compared the Pharisees to "unmarked graves," which people "walk over without knowing it." The thought here seems to be that associating with the Pharisees would adversely affect a person spiritually, just as touching an unmarked grave would make the individual ceremonially unclean.

Though the Pharisees paid homage to great men of the past by building tombs for the prophets, they lacked the spirit of the prophets (Matt. 23:29–30; Luke 11:47–51).

What did Jesus mean when he compared the Pharisees' hypocrisy to yeast (Matt. 16:6, 11–12; Mark 8:15; Luke 12:1)? The thought seems to be that yeast may exist without being detected, or that it is pervasive, or that it is swelling. Hypocrisy too may not be readily seen, can pervade all of one's attitudes, and can lead to pride.[28] In Matthew 16:6, 12, Jesus spoke of the *teaching* of the Pharisees and Sadducees being like yeast. In other words, the error of their doctrines may not be readily detected (hence the command to "be on your guard against the yeast of the Pharisees and Sadducees," v. 6), may be pervasively influential, and may result in pride.

Not surprisingly, then, Jesus twice called the Pharisees a "brood of vipers" (12:34; 23:33) whose condemnation was certain. Like snakes (23:33) the Pharisees were filled with evil intentions.[29] Their spiritual deadness is seen in that they "rejected God's purpose for themselves" (Luke 7:30).

Because of their hypocrisy—their outer religious pretense without

---

27. Some writers, however, say the word *woe* expresses sorrow or regret (e.g., Morris, *The Gospel according to Matthew*, 462; R. V. G. Tasker, *The Gospel according to Matthew*, Tyndale New Testament Commentaries [Grand Rapids: Eerdmans, 1961], 217). But reproof more than compassion seems to mark Jesus' statements. "These seven Woes are like thunder in their unanswerable severity, and like lightning in their unsparing exposure" (Alfred Plummer, *An Exegetical Commentary on the Gospel according to St. Matthew*, Thornapple Commentaries [1915; reprint, Grand Rapids: Baker, 1982], 316). These woes "serve as a counterbalance to the Beatitudes. The yoke of Jesus, which is easy . . . is contrasted with that of the Pharisees" (W. D. Davies, *The Setting of the Sermon on the Mount* [Cambridge: Cambridge University Press, 1964], 106).

28. Albert Barnes, *Barnes' Notes on the New Testament* (reprint, Grand Rapids: Kregel, 1962), 218.

29. John the Baptist too called the Pharisees a "brood of vipers" (Matt. 3:7).

inner spiritual reality—the Pharisees, the Lord said, were spiritually blind. Several times he cited their lack of true knowledge of God by calling them "blind guides" (Matt. 15:14; 23:16, 24), "blind fools" (23:17), "blind men" (23:19), and "blind" (23:26). Obviously Jesus could see through their pretense, recognizing the true condition of their hearts ("God knows your hearts," Luke 16:15). Why then did Jesus say to his disciples, "You must obey them [the Pharisees] and do everything they tell you. But do not do what they do" (Matt. 23:3)? According to some commentators, Jesus spoke these words sarcastically.[30] More likely, however, he was encouraging obedience to those teachings of the Pharisees that corresponded to what Moses taught.[31]

The Pharisees' Responses to Jesus

Reasons for their opposition. Why did the Pharisees oppose Jesus and his ministry? The Gospels reveal several reasons for their antagonism.

First, Jesus opposed their empty religiosity. He repeatedly pointed out their shortcomings. He did this frequently no doubt because they had such an influence and hold on the people.

Second, Jesus violated their strongly held traditions. Anyone who so publicly and persistently confronted their practices was certain to receive the brunt of their opposition. They were angered by his associating with "sinners" and tax collectors (Matt. 9:10–11; Mark 2:16; Luke 5:30; 7:39; 15:11; 19:7); his not fasting (Mark 2:18; Luke 5:33); his healing on the Sabbath (Mark 3:1–3; Luke 13:14; 14:1–4; John 5:8–10; 9:13–14),[32] which they considered unlawful labor; and his failure on two occasions to keep their rituals regarding handwashing (Matt. 15:2; Mark 7:1–5; Luke 11:37–41). In the Gospels of Matthew and Mark the Pharisees and teachers of the law asked Jesus why his disciples did not observe the ritual of handwashing; and in the passage from Luke Jesus himself did not observe the practice when in a Pharisee's house.[33] In

30. For example, D. A. Carson, "Matthew," in *The Expositor's Bible Commentary*, 12 vols. (Grand Rapids: Zondervan), 8:473.

31. Morris, *The Gospel according to Matthew*, 573.

32. On five occasions Jesus healed on the Sabbath, and in *each* instance the religious leaders challenged him. All five individuals had serious maladies: a man with a shriveled hand (Mark 3:1), a woman crippled for eighteen years (Luke 13:11), a man with dropsy (Luke 14:2), a man who had been an invalid for thirty-eight years (John 5:5), and a man born blind (John 9:1).

33. "The dispute was inevitable because of the large and important place such practices held in Judaism. Of the six Books of the Mishnah, the largest, called 'Purifications' ... containing twelve treatises, is devoted to this subject. The object aimed at was not physical cleanliness, but ceremonial purity ..." (J. W. Lightley, *Jewish Sects and Parties in the Time of Jesus* [London: Epworth, 1925], 122).

addition Jesus condoned the action of his disciples in picking and eating heads of grain on the Sabbath (Matt. 12:1–8; Mark 2:23–28; Luke 6:1–5), an action that troubled and angered the Pharisees. To the Pharisees, these actions on Jesus' part clearly meant he was a transgressor of the law.

Third, the Pharisees opposed Jesus because he was a threat to their religious system and their leadership status. His teaching, preaching, and healing attracted the attention of many people throughout Judea, Galilee, and other parts of Palestine. As a prominent public figure who confronted the Pharisees on a number of their basic teachings and practices, Jesus "threatened to destroy what to them was of life and death importance."[34] Therefore they felt compelled to resist him; otherwise they would be false to their convictions and would have to admit that their predecessors of several previous centuries were wrong.

Fourth, the Pharisees were enraged because Jesus forgave the sins of a paralytic (Luke 5:20–21)[35] and of a sinful woman (7:47–48). The Pharisees viewed this as blasphemy because they believed only God can forgive sins (Matt. 9:3; Mark 2:7; Luke 5:21). But that was Jesus' point— only God can forgive sins, and since Jesus did so, he is God. His direct claim of equality with God the Father (John 10:30) stirred the Jews (probably Jewish religious leaders) to pick up stones to stone him "for blasphemy, because you, a mere man, claim to be God" (10:33).

Fifth, the Pharisees were disturbed because Jesus challenged their limited view of the Scriptures. Jesus was concerned about the impact of the Old Testament on people's inner attitudes, not just their outer obedience to its commands. Anger is as serious as murder, a lustful look is condemned along with adultery, God intends marriage to be a lifelong union, oaths should not be needed to back up one's words, revenge is to be replaced with helpfulness, love of enemies should accompany love of one's friends (Matt. 5:21–48).

Reactions to Jesus. How did the Pharisees express their hostility to Jesus? To counteract his repeated assaults on their religious system, they utilized a number of various tactics and responded with varying emotions. Their responses included wonderment, suspicion, accusations, criticism, anger, sneering, and murderous plots (see table 17 for a chronological listing of these many responses to Jesus).

The Pharisees' most-often-used tactic was questioning. Points 2, 3, 4, 10, 11, 13, 15, 18, 20, 30, 31, 35, and 37 record occasions when they

34. Herford, *The Pharisees*, 208.
35. The parallel passages (Matt. 9:3; Mark 2:5–7) mention only teachers of the law, whereas Luke referred to both teachers of the law and Pharisees.

Table 17
Responses of the Pharisees to Jesus

1. Wondered to themselves who Jesus is because he forgave sins — Luke 5:21

2. Questioned Jesus' disciples about his eating with tax collectors and sinners — Matthew 9:11; Mark 2:16; Luke 5:30

3. Questioned Jesus about fasting — Matthew 9:14; Mark 2:18; Luke 5:33

4. Questioned Jesus about picking grain on the Sabbath — Matthew 12:2; Mark 2:24; Luke 6:2

5. Watched for a reason to accuse Jesus — Matthew 12:10; Mark 3:2; Luke 6:7

6. Plotted to kill Jesus — Matthew 12:14; Mark 3:6; Luke 6:11[a]

7. Wondered whether Jesus was a prophet — Luke 7:39

8. Charged Jesus with casting out demons by the prince of demons — Matthew 9:34

9. Accused Jesus of casting out demons by the power of Beelzebub — Matthew 12:24

10. Questioned Jesus by asking him for a sign from heaven — Matthew 12:38; Luke 11:16

11. Questioned Jesus about his disciples not washing their hands ceremonially before they ate — Matthew 15:1-2; Mark 7:1-2, 5

12. Were offended at Jesus' answer to their question — Matthew 15:12

13. Asked Jesus a second time for a sign from heaven — Matthew 16:1; Mark 8:11

14. Sent temple guards to arrest him — John 7:32

15. Questioned Jesus on whether the woman caught in adultery should be stoned — John 8:3-6

16. Accused Jesus of appearing as his own witness — John 8:13

17. Exclaimed that Jesus could not be from God because he violated the Sabbath — John 9:16

18. Asked Jesus if they too were blind[b] — John 9:40

a. Luke added the observation that seeing Jesus heal a man with a shriveled hand on the Sabbath made the Pharisees furious. The Greek states they were "filled with mad fury (or unreasonableness)." This anger was a furious "loss of reason which is caused by extreme excitement" (Fritz Ridenour and Cleon L. Rogers Jr., *A Linguistic Key to the Greek New Testament* [Grand Rapids: Zondervan, 1980], 154). They became senselessly fanatical in their desire to get rid of Jesus.

b. The Pharisees' question implied a negative response. It may be paraphrased, "Surely we are not blind too, are we?" The answer to their question is that they *were* blind! But they were spiritually blind, though seeing physically, whereas the man who was physically blind now had spiritual sight.

19. Were surprised that Jesus did not ceremonially Luke 11:38
    wash his hands before eating
20. Besieged Jesus with questions to try to trap him Luke 11:53–54
    in his words
21. Started to stone Jesus because he claimed to be John 10:31, 33
    God
22. Tried to seize him   John 10:39
23. Encouraged him to leave Herod's territory   Luke 13:31
    (Galilee and Perea) and go to Judea^c
24. Watched Jesus when he was the dinner guest of   Luke 14:1
    a prominent Pharisee
25. Refused to answer when Jesus asked them if it   Luke 14:3–4, 6
    is lawful to heal on the Sabbath
26. Complained among themselves that Jesus wel-   Luke 15:2
    comed and ate with sinners
27. Sneered at Jesus after he told a parable about a Luke 16:14
    shrewd manager
28. Expressed concern that Jesus' increasing popu-   John 11:47–48
    larity would jeopardize their power
29. Plotted to take his life   John 11:53
30. Questioned Jesus about when the kingdom   Luke 17:20
    would come
31. Questioned Jesus about causes for divorce   Matthew 19:3; Mark 10:2
32. Ordered the people to report where Jesus was   John 11:57
    so they could arrest him
33. Ordered Jesus to rebuke his disciples when   Luke 19:39
    they were praising God at the triumphal entry
34. Looked for a way to arrest Jesus   Matthew 21:46
35. Questioned Jesus about paying taxes to Caesar   Matthew 22:15, 17;
                                                     Mark 12:13, 15
36. Responded with amazement at Jesus   Mark 12:17
37. Asked Jesus which commandment is greatest   Matthew 22:34–36
38. Were silenced by his remarks on Psalm 110:1   Matthew 22:46
39. Went to Gethsemane with soldiers and priests   John 18:3
    to arrest Jesus

c. Some scholars see this as the Pharisees' friendly attempt to warn Jesus of danger but more likely it was their effort to persuade him to leave their territory, where he was popular, and go to Judea, where he would be more exposed to the Sanhedrin (e.g., Jacob Neusner, *From Palestine to Piety: The Emergence of Judaism* [Englewood Cliffs, N.J.: Prentice-Hall, 1973], 71).

questioned him—one out of three of the points of contact with Jesus![36] Some of the earlier questions expressed suspicion and/or honest inquiry about him, but the later questions clearly became efforts to trap him in giving wrong answers, answers that would have violated the law and therefore would have been just cause for having him executed.

The Pharisees also accused or charged Jesus (points 8, 9, 16), and plotted against him (points 6, 14, 21, 22, 29, 34, 39). Their plotting began early, about halfway through his ministry (Mark 3:6). And yet on three occasions Jesus' words silenced them (points 25, 36, 38). Clearly their concerns intensified to the point of open rejection and flagrant hostility.

Not all Pharisees, however, rejected Jesus. Nicodemus, who secretly visited Jesus at night (John 3:1–2), may have been a believer; he later challenged his fellow Pharisees who wanted to condemn Jesus without giving him a full hearing (7:50–51) and provided the myrrh and aloes for Jesus' burial (19:39).

On three occasions, recorded only in Luke, a Pharisee invited Jesus to dine with him (Luke 7:36; 11:37; 14:1),[37] but the Scriptures do not indicate if they were true followers of Jesus.[38] Apparently some Pharisees were impressed with his miracle-working, for they wondered how he could perform miracles such as restoring sight to the blind if he were a sinner and not a man of God (John 9:16).

Jesus' Responses to the Pharisees

Jesus responded to most of the strategies by using them as occasions for teaching. Many times his reactions included questions. (For an interesting study, look up the references in table 17 and read the verses that follow them to see how Jesus replied. Note the many questions and the numerous subjects he taught in his answers.) After Jesus' replies, the Pharisees seldom said anything further in response.

How Did the Sadducees Respond to Jesus?

The Gospel writers referred to the Sadducees, the wealthy, priestly aristocracy, only nine times—seven times in Matthew, once in Mark, and

36. See chapter 15 on how Jesus responded to these and many other questions.

37. The Gospels record six occasions when Jesus was invited to dinner. Besides the three Pharisees, the other dinner hosts were Matthew (Matt. 9:10; Mark 2:15), Zacchaeus (Luke 19:1–10), and Mary, Martha, and Lazarus (John 12:2).

38. Joseph of Arimathea, mentioned in all four Gospels (Matt. 27:57; Mark 15:43; Luke 23:51; John 19:38), was a secret disciple of Jesus (as John reported). Some suggest he was a Pharisee, but the Gospels say only that he was a member of the Council or Sanhedrin. Since the Sanhedrin included both Pharisees and Sadducees, Joseph may have been either.

once in Luke.[39] Five of the seven verses in Matthew mention the Pharisees and Sadducees together (Matt. 3:7; 16:1, 6, 11–12). The other two verses in Matthew pertain only to the Sadducees (22:23, 34), references in Mark (12:18) and Luke (20:27) being parallel to Matthew 22:23.

In light of the profound differences between the Pharisees and the Sadducees (see table 16) it is remarkable that they went together to see John the Baptist (Matt. 3:7). They went to the place near the Jordan River where John was baptizing, either for baptism or out of curiosity and concern. The latter seems possible since John denounced them as a "brood of vipers," whose lives did not evidence genuine repentance (v. 8) and who were concerned only about escaping divine judgment (vv. 10–12).

Together the Sadducees and the Pharisees tested Jesus by asking him for a sign from heaven (16:1). (Earlier, in 12:38, the Pharisees and teachers of the law joined in their request that Jesus perform a miraculous sign.) By "testing" him they apparently felt he would fail to produce a miracle, and a failure would discredit him before the people. Refusing to comply with their evil-intentioned request, Jesus responded by telling them they were incapable of interpreting "the signs of the times" (v. 3), they were "a wicked and adulterous generation" (v. 4), and the only "sign" they would have is that of Jonah (v. 4). He had already explained the significance of Jonah's experience in his earlier reply to their request for a sign (12:39–41).

Then Jesus spoke of the two groups together when he warned the disciples, "Be on your guard against the yeast of the Pharisees and Sadducees" (16:5). This comment, he said (v. 12), referred to their teaching, which was not easy to detect and was corrupting and pervasive.[40]

One of the major differences between the Pharisees and the Sadducees was that the former believed in a future resurrection whereas the latter denied it. In an attempt to trap Jesus, the Sadducees asked for his opinion about a woman widowed by seven husbands who were brothers (the law of levirate marriage, Deut. 25:5). Their question, "At the resurrection whose wife will she be?" (Matt. 22:28; Mark 12:23; Luke 20:33), was designed to show the supposed absurdity of a physical resurrection. Since she could not have seven husbands at the same time in heaven, they reasoned that this disproved a resurrection life. Jesus easily outwitted them. First, he pointed out their ignorance, for there will

---

39. Outside the Gospels, only the Book of Acts mentions the Sadducees. These five occurrences (4:1; 5:17; 23:6–8) bring the total references to fourteen.

40. In the parallel passage Mark mentioned the yeast of the Pharisees and of Herod (8:15), "probably meaning the Herodians, who were comparable to the Sadducees in their political opportunism" (*International Standard Bible Encyclopedia*, 1988 ed., s.v. "Sadducees," by William J. Moulder, 4:280). The Lucan parallel mentions only the yeast of the Pharisees (12:1).

be no marriage in the resurrected life (Matt. 22:30; Mark 12:25; Luke 20:35–36). Second, he reminded them that the Torah (which the Sadducees accepted as authoritative) *does* speak of the resurrection (Matt. 22:31–32; Mark 12:26–27; Luke 20:37–38). Exodus 3:6 refers, he said, to the Lord's words, "I am . . . the God of Abraham, the God of Isaac, and the God of Jacob." Jesus' point was that the verb *am* is in the present tense (not the past tense, "I was"), which implies that the patriarchs are alive. While this text does not specify the resurrection, "Jesus, as a Jew, regards it as axiomatic that immortality implies the resurrection of the body."[41]

In this teaching-response, Jesus used logic, as his contenders had done, and he quoted from the Old Testament. Remarkably the Sadducees were silenced (Matt. 22:34). Hearing this conversation, some of the teachers of the law, who with the Pharisees believed in the resurrection, were so pleased with Jesus' defense of that doctrine and his challenge to their opponents that they responded, "Well said, teacher!" (Luke 20:39).

How Did the Teachers of the Law React to Jesus?

"Teacher of the law" is the translation used in the New International Version for the Greek *grammateus* (literally, a person of letters), that is, a writer or a scholar. Other Bible versions translate the Greek word as "scribe." Another term used of the same group is "lawyer" or "expert in the law." *Grammateus* occurs alone sixteen times in the Gospels; in an additional nineteen times in the Gospels the teachers of the law are associated with the Pharisees.[42] (The translation *expert[s] in the law* occurs eight times: once in Matthew and seven times in Luke.) Twenty-two other times "teachers of the law" occurs (with the chief priests eleven times, the elders once, and chief priests and elders ten times), for a total of fifty-seven occurrences in the Gospels. References to other combinations of groups also occur: Pharisees and Sadducees (five times), Pharisees and Herodians (four times),[43] and Pharisees and chief

---

41. Tasker, *The Gospel according to St. Matthew*, 211.

42. In Luke 5:17 "teachers of the law" (NIV) renders the Greek synonym *nomodidaskoloi*, used elsewhere in the New Testament only in Acts 5:34 (of Gamaliel) and in 1 Timothy 1:7.

43. The Herodians were officials in Herod's court, family members of the Herodian Dynasty, or other supporters of Herod Antipas (H. W. Rowley, "The Herodians in the Gospels," *Journal of Theological Study* 41 [1941]: 14–27). The Pharisees, who were nationalists, joined with the hated Herodians, who favored friendship with the Romans, in their plot to kill Jesus (Mark 3:6) and later in their effort to trap Jesus with their question about paying taxes to Caesar (12:13; Matt. 22:16). If Jesus said taxes need not be paid to Caesar,

Table 18
References in the Gospels to Jesus' Various Opponents*

	Matthew	Mark	Luke	John	Totals
Sadducees (mentioned alone)	22:23, 34	12:18	20:27		4
Sadducees and Pharisees	3:7; 16:1, 6, 11–12				5
Teachers of the law (mentioned alone)	7:29; 8:19; 9:3; 13:52; 17:10; 23:34	1:22; 2:6, 16;+ 9:11, 14; 12:28, 35, 38	20:39, 46		16
Teachers of the law and Pharisees	5:20; 12:38; 15:1; 23:2, 13, 15, 23, 25, 27, 29	7:1, 5	5:17, 21, 30; 6:7; 7:30; 11:53; 14:3; 15:2	8:3	19
Experts in the law (mentioned alone)	22:35		10:25, 37; 11:45, 46, 52		6
Pharisees and experts in the law			7:30; 14:3		2
Pharisees and Herodians	22:16	3:6; 8:15; 12:13			4
Pharisees and chief priests	21:45; 27:62			7:32, 45; 11:47, 57; 18:3	7
Chief priests and elders	21:23; 26:3, 47; 27:1, 3, 12, 20; 28:12	15:1	22:52		10
Chief priests and teachers of the law	2:4; 20:18; 21:15	10:33; 11:18; 14:1; 15:31	19:47; 20:19; 22:2; 23:10		11
Teachers of the law and elders	26:57				1
Chief priests, teachers of the law, and elders	16:21; 27:41	8:31; 11:27; 14:43; 53; 15:1	9:22; 20:1; 22:66		10
					95

*This chart excludes references to the Pharisees alone since those references are so numerous in the Gospels.
+Mark 2:16 has literally "teachers of the law of the Pharisees."

priests (seven times). Details about the references are summarized in table 18.

Who were these teachers of the law (or scribes)? They were devoted to studying, interpreting, and teaching the law of Moses (see chap. 3). They were a professional and not a political group. Because of their thorough knowledge of the law, they were respected, and because of their teaching of the law they were often called rabbis.

In the Gospels they are often (twenty-one times) associated with the Pharisees because many teachers of the law were also Pharisees. The Pharisees, because of their interest in keeping the law scrupulously, became closely aligned with the teachers of the law. "A Pharisee was usually a layman without a scribal education, whereas a scribe was trained in rabbinic law and had official status."[44] As some Pharisees themselves became experts in the law, they often became scribes.[45] However, the Pharisees and the teachers of the law were not identical. Most Pharisees were not scribes, and a number of scribes were not Pharisees.[46] From the fact that Mark 2:16 refers to "teachers of the law who were Pharisees" and Luke 5:30 speaks literally of "the Pharisees and their teachers of the law," one may infer that some teachers of the law were Sadducees.[47] Most teachers of the law, then, were Pharisees, some were Sadducees, and some were neither.[48] This relationship could be illustrated in this way (though no effort is made to depict numerical relationships among the groups):

Teachers of the Law

"the Herodians would report him to the Roman governor and he would be executed for treason. If he said 'Yes,' the Pharisees would denounce him to the people as disloyal to his nation" (*The NIV Study Bible* [Grand Rapids: Zondervan, 1985], 1474).

44. *International Standard Bible Encyclopedia*, 1986 ed., s.v. "Pharisees," by R. J. Wyatt, 3:823.

45. Ch. Guignebert, *The Jewish World in the Time of Jesus*, trans. S. H. Hooke (New York: Dutton, 1939), 168–69.

46. Ibid., 71.

47. Schürer, *History of the Jewish People*, 1:320.

48. G. H. Box, "Scribes and Sadducees in the New Testament," *Expositor* 15 (June 1918): 402, 408, 411; and 15 (July 1918): 55–56.

These points may be stated in summary:

1. Most teachers of the law were Pharisees.
2. Some teachers of the law were Sadducees.
3. Some teachers of the law were neither Pharisees nor Sadducees.
4. Most Pharisees were not teachers of the law.
5. Most Pharisees were laymen and most Sadducees were priests.

The teachers of the law were linked with the chief priests twenty-one times in the Gospel accounts. Perhaps the teachers were viewed as associates of the priests in enforcing Jewish law and tradition. The opposition of the Jewish religious establishment to Jesus was strong but not surprising. When Jesus, another teacher, came teaching with superior authority (Matt. 7:29; Mark 1:27) and a new message—and yet had no formal training as did the rabbis—"a clash was inevitable."[49] Early in Jesus' ministry the teachers of the law became hostile to him. Many of their concerns pertained to the law and Jesus' authority. They were troubled by his forgiving sins, which they felt was blasphemy (Mark 2:6–7; Luke 5:17, 21), and by his eating with "sinners" and tax collectors, which to them indicated he was not a separatist (Mark 2:16; Luke 5:30).[50] They accused him of being demon-possessed (Mark 3:22).[51] Again demon possession was the concern of the teachers of the law when they argued with Jesus' nine disciples about a demon-possessed boy (Mark 9:14).[52]

An expert in the law asked Jesus a question that stemmed from Old Testament interpretation: "What must I do to inherit eternal life?" (Luke 10:25). In answering this question Jesus told the parable of the good Samaritan.

When Jesus pronounced woes on the Pharisees for their hypocrisy, their eternal adherence to the law to the neglect of spiritual matters, and their pride (Luke 11:39–44), the experts in the law said they were insulted too (11:45). This is not surprising: the two groups held so many beliefs in common, and many of the teachers of the law were also Pharisees.

Rather than apologizing for insulting the teachers of the law, Jesus directed three woes specifically against them (11:46–52). These are sim-

---

49. *International Standard Bible Encyclopedia*, 1988 ed., s.v. "Scribes," by Donald A. Hagner, 4:361.

50. In both these instances Luke included the Pharisees with the teachers of the law.

51. Matthew wrote that the Pharisees made this accusation (12:24), and Luke simply referred to some of the crowd (11:15).

52. What they argued about is not stated, but apparently the teachers of the law were seeking to discredit Jesus because of the disciples' inability to exorcise the demon.

ilar to three of the seven woes later addressed to both the teachers of the law and the Pharisees (Matt. 23:4, 14, 29–32). Jesus' response so angered these religious leaders that they "began to oppose him fiercely and to besiege him with questions" (Luke 11:53), an effort to trap him in his words in some specific violation of the law.

Once more taking the initiative against his antagonists, Jesus asked the Pharisees and the teachers of the law if it was lawful to heal on the Sabbath (Luke 14:3)—again a question of the interpretation of the law.

Since the Pharisees believed in the resurrection and the Sadducees did not, the Pharisees were naturally pleased with Jesus' defense of that doctrine in answering the Sadducees' question. The fact that "the teacher of the law" commended him by saying, "Well said, teacher!" (Luke 20:39) shows that he may have been a member of the Pharisaical party.

One of the teachers of the law, pleased with Jesus' answer to the Sadducees, asked him which Old Testament commandment is the most important (Matt. 22:35; Mark 12:28). This too was another issue in relation to the Torah.

Jesus raised a question pertaining to the interpretation of Psalm 110:1 in relation to himself (Mark 12:35–37). Then he urged the people to beware of the teachers of the law because of their ostentatious dress, their love of attention and seats of recognition, their taking advantage of widows, and their pretentious praying (12:38–40; Luke 20:46–47).

When the Pharisees were with the teachers of the law, the two groups were agitated about Jesus' lack of ritual purity and his association with sinners (Matt. 15:1; Mark 7:1, 5; Luke 15:2). Other shared concerns included their desire for a miraculous sign (Matt. 12:38), their accusations of blaspheming (Luke 5:21), and their questioning of Jesus' right to heal on the Sabbath (Luke 6:7; cf. 14:3). But as is already noted, when the teachers of the law are seen apart from the Pharisees, the concerns they addressed to Jesus pertained more to Old Testament teachings and interpretations (Mark 1:22; 2:6; 9:11; 12:28, 32, 35; Luke 10:25, 37; 11:45).[53]

The teachers of the law, along with the chief priests, elders, and Pharisees,[54] sought to put Jesus to death. They never acted alone to instigate his execution; they always acted with other groups, probably because as religious teachers they had little or no political power.

53. Elizabeth Struthers Malbon, "The Jewish Leaders in the Gospel of Mark: A Literary Study of Marcan Characterization," *Journal of Biblical Literature* 108 (summer 1989): 266.
54. See the following section on Jesus' relationship to the chief priests and elders.

One law teacher, however, expressed willingness to follow Jesus (Matt. 8:19), but Jesus' reply about his not having a home (v. 20) may suggest that the teacher had not thought of the sacrifice involved in following him. Another teacher, who was pleased with Jesus' response to the Sadducees and who asked him which commandment is the most important (Mark 12:28), answered the Lord "wisely" and was "not far," Jesus said, "from the kingdom of God" (v. 34). Whether the man became a follower of Jesus is not stated.

Jesus' impact on the teachers of the law was obviously limited. None of the religious authorities (except possibly one) became a convert of the Lord. They were too ingrained in their ways to abandon their long-standing traditions and accept Jesus' revolutionary teachings. This suggests that teachers today need not be discouraged when people with differing viewpoints reject our beliefs, for even Jesus faced rejection and even animosity.

How Did the Chief Priests and Elders React to Jesus?

Who were the chief priests? How could there be more than one, since the high priest held that office for life? Who were the elders? How did they respond to Jesus' ministry? The answer to the first two questions lies in the fact that the Roman rulers in Jesus' day sometimes deposed the high priest, and so the chief priests included those who had formerly held the office as well as the newly appointed priest,[55] along with some members of important priestly families. They were Sadducees, leaders who were conservative both religiously and politically. The high priest was the moderator or president of the Sanhedrin, the seventy-member Jewish tribunal consisting of Sadducees and some Pharisees, teachers of the law, and elders.[56] Thus at Jesus' trial before the Sanhedrin, Caiaphas, the high priest, was the president (Matt. 26:57–59; John 18:13).

The elders were lay leaders, senior members of prominent families "who like the priestly aristocracy were also of Saducean sympa-

55. The term *chief priests* may also include priestly officials such as the captain of the temple, the priestly financial officer, and others (Jeremias, *Jerusalem in the Time of Jesus*, 160–81).

56. For more on the Sanhedrin see *Zondervan Pictorial Encyclopedia of the Bible*, s.v. "Sanhedrin," by Donald A. Hagner, 5:268–73; *International Standard Bible Encyclopedia*, 1988 ed., s.v. "Sanhedrin," by William J. Moulder, 4:331–34; and Schürer, *History of the Jewish People*, 2:163–95. Acts 23:6 clearly states that both Pharisees and Sadducees sat as members of the Sanhedrin.

thies."[57] The synagogues' congregations were governed by elders, called rulers of the synagogue (Mark 5:22; Luke 13:14; Acts 18:8).[58]

Three times Jesus predicted his death and resurrection to his disciples (Matt. 16:21; 17:22–23; 20:18–19; the parallel passages are Mark 8:31; 9:31; 10:33–34; Luke 9:22, 44; 18:31–33). In his first prediction all three passages (Matt. 16:21; Mark 8:31; Luke 9:22) report that Jesus said the elders, chief priests, and teachers of the law would instigate his death. The lay aristocracy, the temple priestly leaders (mostly Sadducees), and the scholars (many of them Pharisees) all were to be involved. In the three parallel passages that record Jesus' second prediction, he referred simply to "men" (Matt. 17:22, Mark 9:31; Luke 9:44). In the third prediction, Matthew and Mark stated that Jesus referred to chief priests and teachers of the law (Matt. 20:18; Mark 10:33), and in Luke's Gospel Jesus included Gentiles (18:32), probably a reference to the Roman governor, Pilate, and his soldiers.

Just as Jesus predicted, the chief priests actively sought to arrest and kill him, for his teachings and actions threatened their powerful status as the nation's religious leaders. Sometimes they acted alone in prompting Jesus' death, but more often they functioned with the teachers of the law and the elders, and occasionally with the Pharisees. The Gospel writers sometimes varied in the groups they listed in opposition to Jesus. Perhaps the three—the chief priests, teachers of the law, and elders—acted together in most cases, and the Synoptic writers chose, under the Holy Spirit's inspiration, to emphasize at some times one or two groups and at other times all three.

The Gospel of John does not mention the elders, mentions the teachers of the law only once (8:3), and mentions the chief priests by themselves only five times (12:10; 18:35; 19:6, 15, 21) and in association with the Pharisees five times (7:32, 45; 11:47, 57; 18:3). The Gospel of John also refers sixty-three times to "the Jews," usually indicating the religious authorities who opposed Jesus.[59] These "Jews" may have included chief priests and elders. This seems consistent with the fact that

57. *Zondervan Pictorial Encyclopedia of the Bible,* s.v. "Sanhedrin," by Donald A. Hagner, 5:271.

58. *The Illustrated Bible Dictionary,* s.v. "Synagogue," by Charles L. Feinberg, 3:1502. For more on synagogue leaders and the synagogue order of service, see Brian Breffny, *The Synagogue* (New York: Macmillan, 1978); Alfred Edersheim, *The Life and Times of Jesus the Messiah,* 2 vols. in 1 (1906; reprint, Grand Rapids: Eerdmans, 1986), 1:430–50; Lohse, *The New Testament Environment,* 158–67; and Schürer, *History of the Jewish People,* 2:415–54.

59. Urban C. von Wahlde, "The Terms for Religious Authorities in the Fourth Gospel: A Key to Literary Strata," *Journal of Biblical Literature* 98 (1979): 233–34; and B. F. Westcott, *The Gospel according to St John* (London: John Murray, 1890), ix–x.

Table 19
Involvement of Religious Leaders in Jesus' Arrest, Trial, and Death

	Action	Matthew	Mark	Luke	John
1.	Arrested Jesus	26:47, chief priests and elders	14:43, chief priests, teachers of the law, and elders	22:2, 47, chief priests, temple guard officers, and elders	18:3, chief priests and Pharisees
2.	Took Jesus to Caiaphas, the high priest	26:57, chief priests, teachers of the law, and elders	14:53, chief priests, elders, and teachers of the law	22:66, council of the elders (Sanhedrin), chief priests, and teachers of the law	
3.	Looked for evidence to put Jesus to death	26:59, chief priests and the whole Sanhedrin	14:55, chief priests and the whole Sanhedrin		
4.	Took Jesus to Pilate	27:1–2, chief priests and elders	15:1, chief priests, elders, teachers of the law, and the whole Sanhedrin	23:1, whole assembly	18:28, the Jews
5.	Accused Jesus before Pilate	27:12, chief priests and elders	15:3, chief priests		
6.	Accused Jesus before Herod			23:8–10, chief priests and teachers of the law	
7.	Persuaded Pilate to release Barabbas and crucify Jesus	27:20, chief priests and elders	15:11, chief priests	23:18, "they" (chief priests and teachers of the law, v. 10)	19:6, chief priests and officials

Action	Matthew	Mark	Luke	John
8. Protested to Pilate about the inscription on the cross				19:21, chief priests of the Jews
9. Mocked Jesus on the cross	27:41, chief priests, elders, and teachers of the law	15:31, chief priests and teachers of the law	23:35, rulers	
10. Asked Pilate to seal the tomb and provide guards	27:62–64, chief priests and Pharisees			
11. Paid guards to lie about Jesus' body	28:11–14, chief priests and elders			

after Jesus healed an invalid at the Pool of Bethesda, they tried to kill him because he broke the Sabbath and made himself equal with God (John 5:16, 18). This latter claim would have particularly incensed the chief priests and elders. Then the chief priests and Pharisees failed in their attempt to have temple guards arrest Jesus (John 7:32, 45). After Jesus raised Lazarus from the dead, the chief priests and Pharisees called a meeting of the Sanhedrin in an unsuccessful effort to arrest Jesus (11:47, 57).

Soon after Jesus' triumphal entry the chief priests and teachers of the law were angered that Jesus cleansed the temple and that children were praising him (Matt. 21:12–15). They began looking for a way to kill him, for they feared that his popularity would jeopardize their positions (Mark 11:18). This led the chief priests and elders to question him directly about his authority (Matt. 21:23). (Mark 11:27–28 and Luke 20:1 say that all three groups, the chief priests, teachers of the law, and elders, challenged his authority.)

The rift intensified when Jesus told the religious leaders that because they were rejecting him, the "Stone," the kingdom of God would be taken from them (Matt. 21:43). So again they plotted to arrest him, though they were afraid of opposition from the crowd (v. 46). Matthew 26:3 states that these leaders were the chief priests and elders, and Mark 14:11 and Luke 22:2 specify chief priests and teachers of the law.

The opposition of the religious leaders reached its climax in their active involvement in Jesus' arrest, trial, and crucifixion, as the Gospel writers record (see table 19). In each of the ten actions, the chief priests were involved.

Jesus' response to the chief priests and other leaders is interesting. When they expressed concern that children were praising him, he replied by quoting Psalm 8:2 (Matt. 21:16). When the chief priests and elders challenged Jesus' authority, he silenced them with a provocative question about John the Baptist's origin (21:24–25). Knowing his death was God's plan for him, Jesus did not resist arrest. And since his accusers were inexorably set in their ways, he refused to answer them (Mark 15:3–5). Nor did he answer Herod's many questions (Luke 23:8–9) or those who mocked him as he hung on the cross.

What Can We Learn from Jesus' Relationships to His Adversaries?

A number of observations may be made about Jesus' interactions with his assailants. First, he did not hesitate to differ with his opponents, pointing out their wrong views and practices. He was deeply disturbed by false beliefs and improper conduct. Second, Jesus often answered his antagonists' accusations with questions, challenging them to think. His interchange was provocative. Third, he sought to win his foes to his point of view, even though they relentlessly clutched their tenets of belief. Fourth, Jesus did not hesitate to criticize his foes when he sensed they were entrenched in their ways. Fifth, he held firmly to correct doctrine and behavior even though it cost him his life. He championed the truth uncompromisingly; he did not hedge on divine certainties for the sake of personal convenience. Sixth, Jesus often used his foes' questions or challenges as occasions for teaching additional truth. Those tense incidents became "teachable moments."

These six practices suggest how teachers today may respond to those who disagree with them, openly oppose them, or persist in holding erroneous views. First, point out views that conflict with Scripture. Firmly but lovingly help people to see where their conduct diverges from biblical standards. Second, consider responding to opponents' verbal assaults by using thought-arousing questions. Third, rather than engaging in forays that further provoke those who differ with us, we should seek to win them to the truth in loving, prudent ways. Fourth, criticize only when all other approaches have failed to awaken them to the dangers of their errors in belief and/or behavior. Fifth, do not compromise God's Word for the sake of personal convenience. Sixth, if a student defies the truth or challenges the authority of God's Word, seek to use the occasion as an opportunity for further instruction, rather than engaging in extended debate.

Mulling It Over . . .

Are you disturbed by a contentious student in class? Does someone persist in challenging your teaching? Examine the six suggestions in the preceding paragraph and seek to put them into practice. Pray that God will help you lovingly win over unmanageable pupils to his ways.

Think of a time when you talked with someone who insisted on continuing in his or her false views. What did you do or say? Could you have handled the situation better? If so, how?

"You call me 'Teacher' and 'Lord,' and rightly so, for that is what I am."

John 13:13

11

How Did Jesus Interest Students in Learning?

You read a book. A mystery. A western. Or a biography. Why? Because you are interested.

You go to a game. Football. Baseball. Basketball. Or hockey. Why? Because of your interest in that sport.

You vacuum your house or apartment. You buy a dress or a suit. You enroll in a course. You attend church. You teach a Bible study group. You support your church and other Christian organizations financially. You study a foreign language.

You engage in these and scores of other activities. Why?

Because of your interest.

Without interest, you do not act. But add interest and you carry out the activity.

Most activities, however, have a cost. It takes time to read a book. It takes money to buy clothes. It takes effort to vacuum or to teach a Bible study. But in spite of the cost, your interest motivates you. Interest spells the difference between what you do and do not do. It is the boundary line separating activity from nonactivity.

This principle also holds true in education. People learn what they are interested in learning. Interest therefore becomes an important ingredient for teachers—a key to unlock the door to enjoyment in learning.

Jesus succeeded as a masterful Teacher, and one of the reasons was his remarkable ability to capture the interest of his audiences, to arouse their desire to learn what he was teaching.

The Son of God did not come to earth to present information to people before they were ready to receive it. He did not deliver lectures while people yawned through his sessions. He first led people to *want* to hear what he had to say and to want him to meet their needs. Much of his teaching was spontaneous in response to problems, needs, or questions posed by his hearers.

Jesus used a number of teaching tools to make people eager for the truth, desirous to learn, hungry for his teaching. Four elements in his ministry—motivation, variation, participation, and visualization—enabled him to interest his students in what he taught. Jesus found ways to motivate his followers, whether crowds, small groups, or individuals, to learn. Jesus utilized great variety in the way he taught. He never bored students with the same method. Jesus involved his students in mental and physical activities—activities that held their interest and contributed to their learning. Jesus enabled his learners to see what he talked about. This too captured their attention and contributed to their comprehension.

Motivation: How Did Jesus Use Motivation?

Why is a person interested in a subject or an activity? Because he or she is motivated. Motivation lies behind and leads to interest, because a motive moves us to undertake an activity.[1] It is the basis of all our actions. And as we motivate students, they become interested, and then learning takes place.

Educators have long recognized the significant, essential role of motivation in teaching and learning, as the following statements demonstrate. "Motivation is regarded as crucial in learning." "Motivation is the key to learning." "Where there is no motivation to learn, there is no learning." "There must be some degree of motivation to formally learn anything. . . ." As I have written elsewhere, "motivating learning simply means making learning desirable or desired. It is causing people to *want* to learn."[2]

How then can we get students to want to learn? How can we turn the faucet of motivation, so the tap water of interest flows? When Jesus

1. Herman Harrell Horne, *Jesus—The Master Teacher* (reprint, Grand Rapids: Baker, 1964), 149.
2. B. R. Bugelski, *The Psychology of Learning* (New York: Holt, 1956), 220; Edward Kuhlman, *Master Teacher* (Old Tappan, N.J.: Revell, 1987), 88; Raymond J. Wlodkowski,

taught, people learned. Why? Because he motivated them and interested them. He used at least five ways—five steps we too can follow in creating a desire to learn, in developing a thirst for learning, so that our students, like a horse, go to the water *and* drink.

Jesus Captured People's Attention

As Barlow wrote, to motivate, "be sure you capture the student's attention at the very outset."[3] Jesus did this effectively in several ways.

First, he asked for attention. He challenged his audiences to "hear" (Matt. 11:15; 13:9, 43; Mark 4:9, 23; Luke 8:18; 14:35), "listen" (Matt. 13:18; 15:10; 21:33; Mark 4:3; 7:14; Luke 9:44; 18:6), and "behold" (usually not translated in the NIV, as it is in the KJV in Matt. 10:16; 11:10; 12:41, 42, 49; 13:3; 20:18; 22:4; 23:34, 38; 24:25; Mark 3:34; 10:33; 14:41; Luke 7:25, 27, 34; 10:3, 19; 11:31, 32, 44; 13:7, 30, 32, 35; 18:31; 21:29; 22:10, 31; John 4:35; 5:14; 16:32).

Second, Jesus made startling statements. For example, as he began his Sermon on the Mount, he no doubt captured the attention of his hearers immediately by his assertions that the poor in spirit, the mourners, and the meek are blessed (Matt. 5:3–5). Usually those individuals would not have a sense of being blessed. His authoritative word to the paralytic, "Son, your sins are forgiven" (Mark 2:5) no doubt startled those who heard him.

Third, Jesus engaged people's attention by telling stories (see chap. 16), asking questions (see chap. 14), using visuals (see a later section in this chapter), and by his many miracles.

Fourth, he captured attention by requests, such as his word to the Samaritan woman, "Will you give me a drink?" (John 4:7).

Fifth, he gained attention by addressing individuals by name. Examples are his references to Martha (Luke 10:41), Zacchaeus (19:5), and Peter (22:31; John 1:42).

Jesus Aroused People's Curiosity and Perplexity

As people become curious, their interest is piqued. Wondering about the answer to a question or the solution to a problem engages attention.

Enhancing Adult Motivation to Learn (San Francisco: Jossey-Bass, 1985), 3, 13; also see H. J. Wahlberg and M. Uguroglu, "Motivation and Educational Productivity: Theories, Results, and Implications," in *Achievement Motivation: Recent Trends in Theory and Research*, ed. L. J. Fyans Jr. (New York: Plenum, 1980); Roy B. Zuck, *Teaching with Spiritual Power* (1963; reprint, Grand Rapids: Kregel, 1993), 156 (italics mine).

3. David Lenox Barlow, *Educational Psychology: The Teaching-Learning Process* (Chicago: Moody, 1985), 366.

Perplexity or confusion also motivates learners to seek answers. "A number of modern educators believe that creating 'perplexity,' 'unrest,' and 'doubt' in the students is essential as a prelude to learning."[4]

Wlodkowski expands on this thought. "Learning involvement is at its best when learner perplexity is just short of frustration. When people feel a positive sense of dissatisfaction, they will think harder to reflect more deeply."[5]

Jesus often used this motivational tool. His parable of the weeds in the field awakened the curiosity of the disciples, resulting in their request, "Explain to us the parable of the weeds in the field" (Matt. 13:36). His words about what enters a person's mouth and what comes out of one's mouth stimulated Peter's curiosity so that he requested, "Explain the parable to us" (Matt. 15:15).

When Jesus spoke of the difficulty of rich people entering the kingdom, the disciples were amazed. Their puzzlement contributed to their learning, for they asked, "Who then can be saved?" (Mark 10:26).

The Savior's words to the Samaritan woman about living water aroused her curiosity, leading her to inquire where he got such water (John 4:10–11).

Curiosity caused Peter to ask Jesus, "Lord, where are you going?" (John 13:36), and when Jesus answered, Peter asked again, "Lord, why can't I follow you now?" (13:37). Perplexity led Thomas to ask for an answer to where Jesus was going (14:5). Being puzzled over Jesus' words about his being gone "a little while," they admitted, "We don't understand what he is saying" (16:18). This admission of their curiosity and perplexity led Jesus to add further teaching in 16:19–33.

In introducing the parable of two sons, Jesus asked the disciples, "What do you think?" (Matt. 21:28), thus making them curious about the parable's meaning.

Puzzled by his remark about the temple being destroyed, the disciples were curious as to when that would happen and how they would know (Mark 13:3–4). In response to their aroused interest, Jesus presented his Olivet Discourse (13:5–37).

It is interesting to note that in each of these instances, Jesus did not dispense certain information until the disciples were either curious for an answer or perplexed to the point of wanting a solution. This tactic motivated them to learn more effectively than they might otherwise have learned.

---

4. William A. Reinsmith, "Education for Change: A Teacher Has Second Thoughts," *College Teaching* 35 (summer 1987): 83.
5. Wlodkowski, *Enhancing Adult Motivation to Learn*, 168.

Jesus Addressed People's Needs and Problems

Help people become aware of their needs, and they are apt to want solutions. As Hendricks put it, one of the best ways to motivate is to "help the learner become aware of his need."[6] The Gospel of Mark records many needs people brought to him—their own or those of others (table 20).

Table 20
Needs People Brought to Jesus as Recorded in Mark

Needs	References	Jesus' Solutions
1. Demon possession	1:23–26	
2. Physical illness	1:30–34	
3. Leprosy	1:40–45	
4. Forgiveness of sins and healing from paralysis	2:1–12	
5. Acceptance with God	2:17	
6. Shriveled hand	3:1–6	
7. Danger in a lake storm	4:35–41	
8. Insanity and demon possession	5:1–20	
9. Death of a daughter	5:21, 35–43	
10. Continued hemorrhaging	5:25–34	
11. Food for five thousand	6:30–44	
12. Demon-possessed daughter	7:24–30	
13. Deafness and dumbness	7:31–37	
14. Food for four thousand	8:1–13	
15. Blindness	8:22–26	
16. Disciples' inability to heal	9:14–19, 28–29	
17. Demon-possessed boy with seizures	9:17–27	
18. Blindness	10:46–52	

For an intriguing study, look up the references noting how Jesus met those needs. Chart these and other needs recorded in the Gospels of Matthew, Luke, and John. Look for these and other needs in the other Gospels:

6. Howard G. Hendricks, *Teaching to Change Lives* (Portland, Ore.: Multnomah, 1987), 129.

how to have release from fear
how to resolve doubt
how to react to persecution
how to receive God's Word
how to respond to rejection
how to be effective in ministry
how to help others
how to have guidance on how to pray
how to have relief from worry
how to be ready when Jesus returns
how to become Jesus' disciple
how to be welcomed by God
how to avoid hell
how to have greater faith
how to persist in prayer
how to invest in God's kingdom
how to avoid life's anxieties
how to be born again
how to overcome spiritual thirst
how to be led by Jesus our Shepherd
how to have resurrection life
how to express humility
how to have answers to prayer
how to be led by the Holy Spirit
how to express love to God
how to rejoice in grief

Other people approached Jesus with problems (table 21). What is the difference between a need and a problem? A need is a condition of lack or deficiency (e.g., lack of health, food, forgiveness, life, sight, peace), whereas a problem is a question raised for inquiry. A need represents a deficiency; a problem voices a perplexity. One is the inability to perform and the other is the inability to understand. Look up the references and write down Jesus' answers.

Note that Jesus did not give answers before the questions were raised. He waited for people to recognize their problems and then he responded.

Jesus Expressed Appreciation

Another way to motivate people is to express appreciation for them. Criticize students for their shortcomings and you squelch their interest in learning. But commend him or her for what was done well, and you

Table 21
Problems People Voiced to Jesus as Recorded in Mark

Problems	References	Jesus' Solutions
1. Why was Jesus working on the Sabbath?	2:23–28	
2. Why was Jesus healing on the Sabbath?	3:1–6	
3. What was the source of Jesus' power?	3:20–30	
4. What was the source of Jesus' wisdom?	6:1–6	
5. Why did Jesus not follow purification laws?	7:1–23	
6. Who will be the greatest in the kingdom?	9:33–37	
7. Should someone be allowed to cast out demons?	9:38–51	
8. Is it lawful for a man to divorce his wife?	10:1–12	
9. What is the way to receive eternal life?	10:17–22	
10. How can rich people be saved?	10:23–27	
11. Who will be allowed positions of authority in the kingdom?	10:35–45	
12. Who gave Jesus authority?	11:12–33	
13. Should taxes be paid to Caesar?	12:13–17	
14. Will marriage be in heaven?	12:18–27	
15. Which is the most important commandment?	12:28–34	
16. When will the temple be destroyed and what sign will point to this event?	13	
17. Why was money wasted by the woman at Simon's house?	14:1–11	
18. Is Jesus the Messiah?	14:61–62	

incite the individual to reach even greater heights of learning. "If a person's feelings of competence and self-determination are enhanced, his intrinsic motivation will increase," but if those feelings are diminished, his motivation will decrease.[7]

On several occasions, Jesus commended others, thus gaining their attention while boosting their self-confidence.

Jesus commended Nathaniel, apparently in the hearing of others, by saying of him, "Here is a true Israelite, in whom there is nothing false" (John 1:47). This motivated Nathaniel to want to know how Jesus knew of him (v. 48) and then to ascribe three titles to the Lord: "Rabbi, you are the Son of God; you are the King of Israel" (v. 49).

The Lord pointed out the significance of the disciples by telling them, "You are the salt of the earth" and "You are the light of the world" (Matt. 5:13, 14). When Peter declared Jesus' messiahship and deity ("You are the Christ, the Son of the living God," 16:16), Jesus responded with words of approbation, beginning, "Blessed are you, Simon son of Jonah" (16:17). On another occasion he honored the disciples with words of blessing: "Blessed are the eyes that see what you see" (Luke 10:23). In the upper room, Jesus repeatedly assured his disciples of his love for them. "As I have loved you, so you must love one another" (John 13:34). "Love each other as I have loved you" (15:12). Surely they were encouraged to hear him say, "You are my friends . . . I no longer call you servants . . . You did not choose me, but I chose you" (15:14–16).

Jesus commented with appreciation on the faith of two non-Israelites: a centurion, a commander of one hundred men in the Roman army, whose servant Jesus healed (Matt. 8:10; Luke 7:9) and a Greek woman of Phoenicia, whose daughter Jesus healed (Matt. 15:28; cf. Mark 7:29).

Jesus commended the answer given by a Pharisee ("You have judged correctly," Luke 7:43), and an expert in the law ("You have answered correctly," 10:28). The woman who poured expensive perfume on Jesus' head heard his words of appreciation: "She has done a beautiful thing to me" (Matt. 26:10).

Showing appreciation and expressing commendation motivate students to do well. Writing of the importance of applying this principle to children, Wilson said, "Often the child who has been commended will be pleased, and will want to rise to even greater heights. Usually he will be anxious to do well for the one who has commended him."[8]

7. E. L. Deci, *Intrinsic Motivation* (New York: Plenum, 1975), 141.
8. Clifford Wilson, *Jesus, the Master Teacher* (reprint, Grand Rapids: Baker, 1975), 64.

Variation: How Did Jesus Vary His Teaching?

By varying his approach and procedure in his teaching, Jesus further prompted his hearers to learn. As one educator wrote, "Variety has motivational effects. . . . People tend to pay more attention to things that are changing than to things that are unchanging."[9] Another educator, addressing this issue, stated that the principle of diversity should be engraved in every teacher's heart.[10] He added,

> In evaluating a teacher's performance, or in judging the merit of an educational approach, one of the first things I look for is diversity. Are teachers using a range of teaching approaches? Do they use visual materials as well as relying on oral and written communication? Do they alternate opportunities for independent study with group collaboration? Do they mix lectures, discussions, role plays, and simulations? Do they allow for periods of reflective analysis?[11]

Our Lord excelled in the use of teaching variety. He communicated divine truth by means of lecturing, discussions, questions, answers to questions, brief statements, conversations or dialogues, stories or parables, disputes, demonstrations, quotations, maxims, challenges, rebukes, comments, riddles, arguments, and even silence. And he often combined some of these. An example is his Olivet Discourse, in which he called attention to a visual (the temple, Matt. 24:1), made a brief, startling statement (v. 2), lectured (vv. 4–51) in response to two questions (v. 3), told two stories (parables, 25:1–30), and concluded with further lecturing (vv. 31–46).

Demonstration, lecture, and answer to student questions were methods Jesus used in the Upper Room Discourse (John 13–16). In this discourse, five of the disciples asked Jesus questions, each of which he answered before proceeding with his lecture. The questioners included John (13:25), Peter (13:36, 37), Thomas (14:5), Philip (14:8), and Judas (14:22). In addition some of the disciples were expressing among themselves their inability to understand some of what he was teaching (16:17–18), so he proceeded to explain more fully what he had been saying (16:19–28). The further teaching resulted in their admission of understanding and belief (16:31–32).

With the two believers on the road to Emmaus Jesus asked questions (Luke 24:17, 19, 26), lectured on Old Testament passages (v. 27), and

9. Wlodkowski, *Enhancing Adult Motivation to Learn*, 151.
10. Stephen D. Brookfield, *The Skillful Teacher* (San Francisco: Jossey-Bass, 1990), 69.
11. Ibid.

demonstrated who he was (vv. 30–31), with the result that the two were amazed (v. 32) and responded by sharing the news of his resurrection with the Eleven (vv. 33–35).

Lectures

Educators often disparage the lecture method, pronouncing it dead. "Yet, for having expired so frequently, its corpse displays a remarkable liveliness."[12] As Price ironically observed years ago, many have spoken against the lecture by means of lectures![13]

Jesus, however, was a masterful lecturer, using the method frequently. Table 10 in chapter 6 lists fifty subjects on which Jesus lectured.

Listening to a lecture is not the only way to learn, but it is a valid means of learning. The Gospel writers recorded many times when people listened to Jesus teach. Examples are Mark 12:37 (a large crowd); Luke 5:1 (a crowd by the Lake of Genesaret); 10:39 (Mary); 19:11 (a crowd in Jericho); and 20:45 (people in Jerusalem). Jesus often urged the people to listen to him. Chapter 4 also refers to the many times Jesus "said" or "told" information to others.

What made Jesus' lecturing so superbly memorable? Several observations provide answers to this question.

His lectures were varied. In his fifty discourses, Jesus lectured on a great variety of topics (see table 10). They range "all the way from wealth and divorce to the sabbath and missions."[14] His lectures varied in length; some were brief, others were rather long. The occasions of his lecturing also differed. He lectured in various places indoors and outdoors, and he often taught en route,[15] speaking to his disciples "on the way," as Mark and Luke put it (Mark 8:27; 9:31, 34; 10:32; Luke 16:38). Many of his lectures were occasional, that is, they were prompted by occasions. (Table 8 in chapter 5 presents twenty-two situations that led to Jesus' teaching.)

His lectures were combined with other methods. See the preceding pages for examples of this.

His lectures moved from the known to the unknown. In dealing with the Samaritan woman, Jesus started with a reference to literal water, which the woman had come to draw from the well (John 4:7–9), and then referred to the living water (vv. 10, 13–14). When an expert in the law, a scribe, approached Jesus with a question about eternal life, Jesus

12. Ibid., 71.
13. J. M. Price, *Jesus the Teacher* (Nashville: Convention, 1946), 105–6.
14. Ibid., 107.
15. Matt Friedeman, *The Master Plan of Teaching* (Wheaton, Ill.: Victor, 1990), 80.

began his response by asking the man something about the law, the area of the man's expertise (Luke 10:25–26), and then lectured, by means of a story, on the meaning of "neighbor" (vv. 29–37). Lecturing about himself as the Bread of life, Jesus first spoke of the Israelites' manna in the desert, a subject with which his audience was familiar (John 6:31–40). Reference to good and bad trees (Luke 6:43–44) provided the basis for his brief lecture about people with good and bad hearts (v. 45).

Jesus' many parables exemplify this same principle of beginning with something known to the hearers and proceeding with a truth less familiar (see chap. 16).

In his lectures, Jesus allowed for and even welcomed interruptions by comments or questions, because he eagerly longed to respond to problems raised by his students. He utilized these interruptions "again and again for the purposes of driving home his thought."[16]

For example, as Jesus was teaching in a house in Capernaum, a paralytic was lowered through the roof in front of him. He did not hesitate to deal with the man's need and to state the teachings of the law about his authority to forgive sins as well as his power to heal (Mark 2:1–12). When he learned his mother and brothers were looking for him, he used the occasion to address the subject of doing God's will (3:31–35). Once a woman interrupted his teaching by shouting, "Blessed is the mother who gave you birth and nursed you" (Luke 11:27). He responded to her interruption by a brief word about the blessing of hearing and obeying God's word (v. 28). When some of Jesus' opponents indignantly questioned why a woman wasted so much money on perfume she poured out on Jesus' feet (Mark 14:4–5), he used the occasion to lecture on the poor, his own forthcoming absence, and the significance of the woman's actions (vv. 6–9).

His lectures appealed to the various aspects of the soul. In the Sermon on the Mount, Jesus appealed to hope (Matt. 5:3–10), fears (v. 25), instinct (vv. 29–30), conscience (7:4), and reasoning (7:11).[17] His lectures approached people through their intellect, emotions, and will.

His lectures were individualized. Alfonso points out how Jesus' teaching matched the characteristics of those he taught. She deftly discusses how Jesus presented material to and dealt with eleven kinds of individuals: the insecure (an invalid, John 5:1–18), the experimenter (Peter, Matt. 14:28–33), the eager (a rich young ruler, 19:16–23), the discour-

16. Bennett Harvie Branscomb, *The Teachings of Jesus* (Nashville: Abingdon-Cokesbury, 1931), 104.

17. William Garden Blaikie, *The Public Ministry of Christ* (London: Nisbet, 1883; reprint, Minneapolis: Klock and Klock, 1984), 213.

aged (the two on the road to Emmaus, Luke 24:13–35), the humiliated (the woman caught in adultery, John 8:1–11), the masked (the Samaritan woman, John 4:1–30), the persevering searcher (Mary Magdalene, Mark 15:40–41, 47; 16:1–10; John 20:17), the unpopular and unaccepted (a man with leprosy, Matt. 8:1–4), the gifted (Nicodemus, John 3:1–12), the crafty (Zacchaeus, Luke 19:1–9), and the shy (a woman with hemorrhaging, Mark 5:25–34).[18] Alfonso also presents specific pointers for teachers today on how to deal with similar individuals in our classes, gearing our lectures to their needs and personalities.

His lectures sparkled with illustrations. Jesus' illustrations added zest to his teaching, making his lectures pleasurable to the ear.

> Jesus keenly observed common things and aptly used them to illuminate His teaching. The ubiquitous sparrow could claim the heavenly Father's love (Matt. 10:29). Splinters in eyes illustrate obstructions to spiritual discernment (Matt. 7:15); grain demonstrates the transiency of life (Matt. 6:50); and trees, the secret of true growth (Matt. 7:17, 18). Such illustrations impressed themselves on the mind more vividly than abstractions can.[19]

Table 22 lists the dozens of illustrations Jesus used from nature alone.

Table 22*
Jesus' Use of Illustrations from Nature as Recorded in Matthew

Earth, 5:5	Salt, 5:13	Sun, 5:45	Rain, 5:45
Moth, 6:19–20	Rust, 6:19–20	Birds, 6:26	Lilies, 6:28
Grass, 6:30	Sawdust, 7:3	Plank, 7:4–5	Dogs, 7:6
Pigs, 7:6	Stone, 7:9	Fish, 7:10	Snake, 7:10
Wolves, 7:15	Fruit, 7:16	Grapes, 7:16	Thornbushes, 7:16
Figs, 7:16	Thistles, 7:16	Tree, 7:17–19	Fruit, 7:16–17, 19–20
Rock, 7:24–25	Rain, 7:25, 27	Streams, 7:25, 27	Winds, 7:25, 27
Foxes, 8:20	Birds, 8:20	Wine, 9:17	Harvest, 9:37
Harvest field, 9:38	Sheep, 10:16	Wolves, 10:16	Snakes, 10:16
Doves, 10:16	Sparrows, 10:29, 31	Darkness, 10:27	Daylight, 10:27
Ground, 10:29	Hairs, 10:30	Ashes, 11:21	Skies, 11:23
Depths, 11:23	Earth, 11:25	Tree, 12:33	Fruit, 12:33
Vipers, 12:34	Huge fish, 12:40	Seed, 13:3–4, 7–8, 19, 24–27, 37–38	Birds, 13:4

*This table does not include references to nature that are part of the narrative but not part of Jesus' teaching (e.g., fish and loaves in 14:17).

18. Regina M. Alfonso, *How Jesus Taught* (New York: Alba, 1986), 15–36.
19. Donald Guthrie, "Jesus," in *A History of Religious Educators*, ed. Elmer M. Towns (Grand Rapids: Baker, 1975), 21–22.

Rocky places, 13:5, 20	Soil, 13:5, 8, 23	Sun, 13:6	Plants, 13:6–7
Root, 13:6, 21, 29	Thorns, 13:7, 22	Crop, 13:8, 23	Weeds, 13:25–27, 29–30, 36, 38, 40
Wheat, 13:25–26, 29–30	Weeds, 13:25	Harvest, 13:30, 39	Mustard seed, 13:31
Field, 13:31, 36–38, 44	Garden plants, 13:32	Tree, 13:32	Birds, 13:32
Branches, 13:32	Yeast, 13:33	Flour, 13:33	Dough, 13:33
Fire, 13:40	Sun, 13:43	Pearls, 13:45	Lake, 13:47
Fish, 13:47–48	Shore, 13:48	Bread, 14:17	Fish, 14:17
Plant, 15:13	Roots, 15:13	Stomach, 15:17	Body, 15:17
Mouth, 15:18	Heart, 15:18–19	Bread, 15:26	Dogs, 15:26
Evening, 16:2	Weather, 16:2	Sky, 16:2	Morning, 16:2
Yeast, 16:6, 11	Rock, 16:18	Earth, 16:19	Mustard seed, 17:20
Mountain, 17:20	Sea, 18:6	Sheep, 18:12–13	Hills, 18:12
Camel, 19:24	Fields, 19:29	Vineyard, 20:1–2, 4, 7–8	Fig tree, 21:19–21
Fruit, 21:19	Mountain, 21:21	Sea, 21:21	Vineyard, 21:28, 33, 39–41
Winepress, 21:33	Harvest, 21:34, 41	Crop, 21:41	Stone, 21:42, 44
Capstone, 21:42	Fruit, 21:43	Oxen, 22:4	Cattle, 22:4
Field, 22:5	Sea, 23:15	Gold, 23:16	Mint, 23:23
Dill, 23:23	Cummin, 23:23	Gnat, 23:24	Camel, 23:24
Bones, 23:27	Blood, 23:30, 35	Snakes, 23:33	Vipers, 23:33
Hen, 23:37	Chicks, 23:37	Wings, 23:37	Mountain, 24:16
Field, 24:18	Desert, 24:26	Lightning, 24:27	Carcass, 24:28
Vultures, 24:28	Sun, 24:29	Moon, 24:29	Stars, 24:29
Heavenly bodies, 24:29	Sky, 24:30	Earth, 24:30	Clouds, 24:30
Winds, 24:31	Fig tree, 24:32	Twigs, 24:32	Leaves, 24:32
Summer, 24:32	Earth, 24:35	Field, 24:40	Oil, 25:3, 9–10
Harvest, 25:26	Seed, 25:26	Sheep, 25:32–33	Goats, 25:32–33
Vine, 26:29	Sheep, 26:31	Flock, 26:31	

Because many Jews in Jesus' day engaged in farming, he often used agricultural illustrations to teach spiritual truths. Tasks such as growing crops, cultivating fruit trees, tending vineyards, and raising sheep, goats, and cattle became windows through which the master Teacher shed light on his doctrines.[20] Wild and domestic animals, birds, wild

20. The four Gospels include an amazingly large number of references by Jesus to sheep (thirty-eight) and to shepherds (eleven). He mentioned sowing twenty-eight times, reaping and harvesting twenty-nine times, and seed thirty-eight times.

and cultivated plants, natural phenomena, and domestic functions (e.g., marrying, cooking, eating, childbearing, burying) and commercial activities (e.g., selling, building, trading, tailoring, tax collecting) provided excellent sources of illustrations.

Amazingly, profound truths were taught by common means:

> What glorious truths He brought down from heaven by means of the lost sheep, the lost piece of silver, and the prodigal son! Who would have thought that a poor woman's pleasure in recovering a trifling coin could be allied to feelings that thrill the hearts of angels, and in some sense refresh the soul of God Himself? Who would have found, in the homely task of the shepherd dividing his sheep from the goats, a picture of that dread scene when small and great shall stand before the great white throne, to receive the deeds done in the body. . . . What hands but those of Christ could thus weave the homely and the sublime into the same web?[21]

As extended illustrations, Jesus' many parables expressed the truth in unforgettable vivid form. His illustrations and stories, drawn from a wide array of aspects of nature repeatedly captivated his contemporaries, thus making his lectures unequaled in impact.

Dry? Boring? Uninteresting? Not Jesus' lectures!

Imaginative? Direct? Captivating? Without question, Jesus' lectures met these criteria!

Discussions

Discussions between teachers and students furnish ample opportunity for learning. They foster interaction between the teachers and the students; broaden the students' thinking, encouraging them to explore and evaluate new ideas; enable teachers to clarify their material or to correct students' false ideas; assist teachers in knowing what the students are thinking; strengthen students' self-confidence as they express their ideas and opinions; and encourage students to change the way they think and feel about issues.[22]

On a number of occasions, Jesus engaged in discussion with his disciples or religious leaders—discussions that resulted in the learners' understanding, clarification, and change.

Conversations, discussed in the following section, are dialogues.

21. Blaikie, *The Public Ministry of Christ*, 70–71.
22. For more on these and other advantages of discussions, see Brookfield, *The Skillful Teacher*, 93–96, and William E. Cashin and Philip C. McKnight, *Improving Discussions*, Idea Paper no. 15 (Manhattan, Kan.: Center for Faculty Evaluation and Development, Kansas State University, 1986), 1.

Some authors erroneously call these discussions. Discussions also contrast with the question-and-answer method, though most if not all discussions begin with a question raised by the student or the teacher. Questions Jesus raised are discussed in chapter 14, and questions others raised and that Jesus answered are discussed in chapter 15. Often Jesus' lectures were interrupted by his hearers' questions.

The following pointers on how to lead an effective discussion are illustrated in Jesus' use of this method.

First, base discussions on an experience common to the groups or on a topic of common interest. The Lord did this when he asked, "Who do people say the Son of Man is?" (Matt. 16:13). The Twelve had been hearing people talk about Jesus, discussing his identity. When Jesus asked the disciples what they were arguing about (Mark 9:33), he began a discussion on a topic of interest to all of them. The subject of salvation for wealthy people was of interest to most Jews in that culture (Matt. 19:23), including the disciples.

Second, encourage students to contribute to the discussion. Jesus involved students by asking thought-inviting questions or making comments he was sure would induce response. He never had a lull in his discussions, because the issues he raised readily prompted participation. This is seen in his question about how people viewed his identity (Matt. 16:13), his statements about his forthcoming death and resurrection (16:21), his question on what their argument was about (Mark 9:33), his comments about salvation and the rich (Matt. 19:23–24), and his pronouncement, "I am the light of the world" (John 8:12).

Third, discuss items that are not too vague or broad and that avoid yes-or-no responses. Note Jesus' use of who and what questions in Matthew 16:13, 15 and Mark 9:33. Jesus seldom if ever asked a question for discussion that could be answered with a yes or no, for such questions do not generate discussion.

Fourth, prod student thinking toward correct answers. When the disciples answered Jesus' question about people's ideas of him, he then moved closer to the goal of his discussion by prodding them with the question, "Who do you say I am?" (Matt. 16:15). In his discussion with the Jewish leaders—certainly some "difficult" listeners—about his claim to be the light of the world (John 8:12), he kept answering their questions, moving them ahead step by step to his first point that he is God because of his existence before Abraham (8:58).

Fifth, clarify students' false concepts firmly but in a nonthreatening way. Rather than ignoring a false statement or saying outright, "That is wrong," it is preferable to ask, "How does that fit with this fact?" or "That's interesting, but have you considered this?" or "What do the rest of you think?" or to explain lovingly why the view is incorrect. When

Jesus told of his coming death and resurrection, Peter rebuked Jesus—
an amazing response to his teacher!—and said this would never happen to Jesus (Matt. 16:22). Earlier, Jesus had commended Peter for a
correct response (16:17–19), but here the Lord told Peter forthrightly
that he was wrong because he was responding from a human rather
than a divine perspective. "You do not have in mind the things of God,
but the things of men" (16:23). Then Jesus proceeded with further
teaching to the twelve disciples about sacrifice and reward in serving
him (16:24–28).

Peter's question about what reward comes to those who leave everything to follow the Master (19:27) led Jesus to answer Peter's question
(19:28) and then to speak of rewards that come to "everyone" who
leaves families and possessions to become his followers (19:29–30).

Humility must accompany service, Jesus told the Twelve, as he stood
a little child among them to illustrate his point (Mark 9:33–37). Then
John seemingly tried to change the subject: "Teacher, we saw a man
driving out demons in your name and we told him to stop, because he
was not one of us" (9:38). Jesus aptly and briefly corrected this wrong
action on their part (9:39–41) and then resumed the subject of childlike
humility by discussing three things: the enormity of inflicting spiritual
injury, the principle of the sacrifice of the lesser good for the sake of the
greater good, and the importance of maintaining saltiness in one's testimony (9:42–50).[23]

Following these five suggestions, illustrated in Jesus' instructional
ministry, can enhance the quality of teacher-led discussions and contribute to student interest and learning.

Conversations

Jesus carried on at least five dialogues with individuals, persons who
in each case were unregenerate at the beginning of the conversation.
These incidents afforded excellent opportunities for him to teach while
at the same time evangelizing.

To see the principles Jesus followed in these dialogues and to see
how Jesus varied his approach in each case, read the following verses
and write answers to the following questions.

23. Lilas D. Rixon, *How Jesus Taught* (Croydon, N.S.W.: Sydney Missionary and Bible
College, 1977), 42. The words "Have salt in yourselves" (Mark 9:50) point to the disciples'
need "to maintain allegiance to Jesus at all costs and to purge out destructive influences
(John D. Grassmick, "Mark," in *The Bible Knowledge Commentary, New Testament*, ed.
John F. Walvoord and Roy B. Zuck [Wheaton, Ill.: Victor, 1983], 148).

	How did Jesus capture his or her interest?	How did the person respond to Jesus' initial comment?	What then did Jesus say?	What was his or her response?
John 3:1–21 (Nicodemus)				
John 4:1–26 (Samaritan woman)				
Luke 7:36–47 (Simon)				
John 9:35–39 (blind man)				
Matthew 19:16–22 (rich young man)				

Now go back to the five passages and note these points: How Jesus used the element of surprise by telling the individuals things they did not expect, how Jesus used questions to draw them out or how he answered their questions (count the number of questions each one asked), how Jesus varied his approach to each individual about his or her sin, how Jesus confronted each individual, and how Jesus differed in his approach to lead them to see who he was.

In his conversations or dialogues Jesus was friendly and personable, adapted the truth to the individuals' backgrounds, spoke on their level of understanding, challenged them to think deeply of his claims, and called for a response. Because you may have non-Christians in your class, be sure to present God's plan of salvation and also pray for opportunities to speak to unsaved class attenders individually. As you do, follow the same principles Jesus used in his evangelistic-teaching dialogues: be friendly and personable, adapt the truth to the person's background, speak on his or her level, challenge the individual to think of Jesus' claims, and call for a response.

Other Methods

For discussions on how Jesus used disputes, questions, answers, maxims, and stories, see chapters 10 and 13 through 16.

Participation: How Did Jesus Involve Students?

"Learning is not a spectator sport."

So wrote two educators on college teaching.[24] They explain: "Students do not learn much just by sitting in classes listening to teachers, memorizing pre-packaged assignments, and spitting out answers. . . . They must make what they learn part of themselves."[25]

People learn by doing. By means of activities, assignments, and projects students have opportunity to reinforce what is learned in the classroom, put into practice the truths taught, internalize the concepts studied, and develop initiative and responsibility. "Principles and skills can be presented, but it is the learner's performance in activities such as outlining, problem solving, discussing, and experimenting that internalizes the learning for them."[26] As I wrote elsewhere, "The activity may be physical, mental, or emotional, but there must be activity if learning is to take place."[27] Jesus believed in the importance of student participation; this fact is evidenced by the many ways (listed chronologically) in which he involved his disciples and others in the teaching-learning process:

1. Asked the disciples to get a boat for him to sit in while teaching the people (Mark 3:9)
2. Had his disciples baptize converts (John 4:2)
3. Sent his disciples to a nearby Samaritan town to buy food (John 4:8)
4. Told the demon-possessed man of the region of the Gerasenes, whom he healed, to go tell his family what the Lord had done for him (Mark 5:19; Luke 8:19). This shows the importance of personal witnessing.
5. Sent the Twelve in groups of twos to exorcise demons, heal the sick, preach, and teach (Matt. 10:1–4; Mark 6:7–13; Luke 9:1–6; cf. Mark 3:14–15), with specific detailed instructions (Matt. 10:5–40)
6. Had them report on their ministries (Mark 6:30; Luke 9:10) and then took them away for a "rest" (Mark 6:31–32; Luke 9:10)

24. Arthur W. Chickering and Zelda F. Gamson, "Seven Principles for Good Practice in Undergraduate Education," *AAHE* [American Association of Higher Education] *Bulletin* 39 (March 1987): 5.

25. Ibid.

26. Wlodkowski, *Enhancing Adult Motivation to Learn*, 171.

27. Roy B. Zuck, *Teaching with Spiritual Power* (1963; reprint, Grand Rapids: Kregel, 1993), 161.

7. Directed the disciples to have the five thousand men (with the women and children) seated in groups, to distribute the bread and fish, and to gather what was left (Matt. 14:19–20; Mark 6:39, 41, 43; Luke 9:14–17; John 6:10, 12). He did the same with the disciples when he fed the four thousand men and their families (Matt. 15:36–37; Mark 8:6, 8).
8. Took Peter, James, and John with him to the Mount of Transfiguration (Matt. 17:1; Mark 9:2; Luke 9:28)
9. Told Peter to catch a fish and take a coin out of its mouth (Matt. 17:27)
10. Sent messengers into a Samaritan village to prepare accommodations for him (Luke 9:52). When James and John asked Jesus if they should call fire down from heaven to destroy the villagers, Jesus rebuked them. This gave them a lesson in tolerance and forgiveness.
11. Commissioned seventy-two followers in groups of twos to heal the sick and preach (Luke 10:1–17)
12. Sent two disciples to Bethphage to get a colt for him to ride (Matt. 21:1–3; Mark 11:1–3; Luke 19:29–30)
13. Sent his disciples to prepare for the Passover meal (Matt. 26:17–19; Mark 14:12–16; Luke 22:7–13)
14. Commanded his disciples to make disciples of all nations (Matt. 28:18–20), preaching the gospel everywhere (Mark 16:15)
15. Commanded Peter to feed his sheep (John 21:15–17)

Assigning the Twelve and then the seventy-two no doubt caused them to feel a mixture of emotions. Were the disciples excited over the prospect of being able to do the same things Jesus himself had been doing? Did they feel confident or fearful? Did they sense boldness or were they reticent?

Whatever their emotions, they no doubt sensed the Lord's power and authority as people responded to their message and as people were healed. When the thirty-six groups of twos returned, they were joyful about what the Lord had accomplished through them (Luke 10:17). Being so intensively involved gave these commissioned workers responsibility, a sense of belonging, and opportunity to see firsthand how the Lord could use them as they served him.

All the activities in which the Lord engaged the disciples and others enabled them to live out what they were learning from him, to put into practice the truths to which they were committed, to demonstrate their loyalty, love, and obedience to the Savior.

In light of Jesus' example of actively involving students in the learning process, teachers today do well to ask themselves, How can I involve my students in the lessons I teach? How can I give them more opportunity for participation, for learning by doing? How can I vary my teaching so that student interest is higher and student learning is greater?

Visualization: How Did Jesus Show Students What He Was Teaching?

Think of something you learned recently, a lesson that profoundly influenced you in some way. Was it something you heard? Or was it something you both heard and saw? The possibilities run high that you well remembered lessons that involved your sight as well as your hearing. We tend to forget what we hear. But when seeing accompanies our hearing, we learn more and retain it longer.

Why is this? Because vision is our dominant sense. A report published by the Xerox Corporation years ago revealed that 83 percent of what we learn comes through our sight. Hearing provides for 11 percent of what we learn, compared with extremely small percentages from the other three senses: smell, 3.5 percent; touch, 1.5 percent; and taste, 1 percent.

No wonder Jesus used visuals! Of course he had no electrically or electronically powered media. He never used a chalkboard, but he did write on the ground. He did not show a film, but he did point to objects around him.

Why are visuals effective? They make learning more enjoyable, by capturing attention. They make learning more meaningful, by bridging time and distance gaps between today and what is being studied. They make learning more lasting, by enabling students to retain facts and ideas longer.

Scanning the Gospels directs our attention to the numerous visuals Jesus employed effectively.

He pointed to the harvest to illustrate the need for evangelism (John 4:35–39).[28] How could the disciples ever forget this impressive image of the lost? As reapers, they were to harvest a crop, bringing people to himself.

He had a little boy stand beside him to visualize humility and trust in answer to the disciples' arguing about greatness (Matt. 18:2–5; Mark 9:36; Luke 9:46–48). How much more forceful for Jesus to have them see a child as he encouraged them to become like chil-

---

28. "The Samaritans in their white garments coming from the village (v. 30) may have visually suggested a wheat field ripe for harvest" (Blum, "John," 287).

dren, rather than simply verbalizing his point. Every time they saw a child, would they not recall his incisive words?

When the teachers of the law and the Pharisees tried to trap Jesus by their question about a woman caught in adultery, he wrote on the ground twice (John 8:1–8).[29] Impressed by what they saw as well as by what Jesus said (8:7), they left, convicted of their own sin and chagrined by their inability to ensnare him.

A fig tree that withered overnight at Jesus' command became a potent lesson on the power of faith in his word and on the efficacy of prayer (Mark 11:12–14, 20–24). Fig trees would thereafter no doubt cause them to think of his teaching about faith and prayer.

In another attempt to trap Jesus, the Pharisees and the Herodians asked Jesus about paying taxes to Caesar. Rather than simply voicing his answer, Jesus showed them a coin. Asking them whose inscription the coin bore, he amazed them with an answer that avoided their trap (Matt. 22:15–22; Mark 12:13–17).

Sacrifice, motives in giving, and the relative value of money were lessons burned in the hearts of the disciples as Jesus talked to them about a widow and as they saw her place all her money—only two small coins—in the temple treasury (Mark 12:41–44; Luke 21:1–4). How could they ever forget this graphic contrast between the wealthy, pompous teachers of the law (Luke 20:45–47) and the poor widow?

Leaving the temple, the disciples were impressed by the massive stones used in the temple buildings. These became a visual from which Jesus drew a lesson about the coming destruction of the city (Matt. 24:1–2; Mark 13:1–2; Luke 21:5–6).

The partaking of the bread and cup at the Lord's Supper made a lasting visual impression on the disciples (Matt. 26:17–30; Mark 14:22–26; Luke 22:14–20).

A towel and a washbasin of water were visuals Jesus used as he illustrated humility before his disciples (John 13:4–17). After his departure to heaven, they must have continued to reel under the force—even the shock—of this totally unexpected gesture on his part in washing their feet as a lowly servant. He talked about humility—and they saw him live it!

---

29. No one knows what Jesus wrote on the ground. Some have suggested he wrote the sins of the accusers; others say he wrote the sentence he spoke in verse 7; others think he wrote Exodus 23:1, "Do not spread false reports. Do not help a wicked man by being a malicious witness," or Exodus 23:7, "Do not put an innocent or honest person to death." Others say Jesus was tracing lines on the ground as he was thinking (on these views, see ibid., 347; and Raymond E. Brown, *The Gospel according to John*, Anchor Bible, 2 vols. [Garden City, N.Y.: Doubleday, 1966], 1:333–34).

Even Thomas' hand by which he touched Jesus' crucifixion wounds signals a lesson for all to believe Jesus even though they do not see him (John 20:27–29).

Jesus' many miracles were dynamic visual demonstrations to the crowds, his disciples, and the religious leaders of his power, authority, compassion, and deity. The disciples would have been strengthened in their faith and fortified in their confidence in their Lord as they watched him perform miracle after miracle.

Jesus' words transmitted significant visual images. One of the factors that made his lectures so distinct is his use of verbal illustrations. Chapters 12 and 13 develop this characteristic of Jesus' teaching in more detail.

Jesus' very life was a visual, reinforcing what he taught. The disciples were visually influenced by seeing Jesus pray (Mark 1:35–37). They saw him help people in need; they watched and listened as he silenced his accusers with clever answers; they were impressed as they saw him bless children, clear the temple, and submit to arrest. The sight of him hanging on a cross made an indelible mark on their memories and hearts, as did the empty tomb three days later!

In many ways the disciples saw Jesus as a living Visual Aid. Should they pay taxes? Should they despise tax-gatherers? Jesus did not—He ate with them and won some to his cause. Should they look down on women? Jesus did not. To him all men and women were unique individuals of inestimable value. Should they respect family life? Jesus did. Were riches all important? Jesus taught that treasure in heaven was more important, and by His Own [*sic*] example demonstrated that lesson.[30]

Were people in Jesus' day interested in what he taught? Indeed they were! They were curious, intrigued, even captivated.

How did Jesus engage such attention and demand such respect? His teaching competence is seen in his profound abilities as a motivator, his creative use of variation in teaching patterns, the way he involved his learners, and his appeal to the visual. Teachers today do well to learn from Jesus' teaching by stimulating and motivating their students, varying their methods, encouraging learners to participate, and visualizing what they verbalize.

---

30. Wilson, *Jesus the Master Teacher*, 115.

ℭWork Jt Out . . .

As you prepare the opening of your next lesson, look at the ways Jesus captured people's attention. Can you use any of these ideas to gain the interest of your class?

Think of the needs of your students and the problems they face. How well are you addressing those needs and problems in your teaching?

How can you, like Jesus, express appreciation to your learners? Are there other ideas you can use?

Evaluate your lectures, comparing them with the qualities that marked Jesus' lectures.

Make a list of sources you could turn to for illustrations and anecdotes to spark your teaching.

Look over the following list of fifty-seven teaching methods, asking yourself which ones you can use. Obviously, not all of them are equally suitable for all age levels.

Lectures	Assignments
Discussions	Research projects
Questions	Panels
Answers	Forums
Stories	Debates
Field trips	Symposiums
Outside speakers	Interviews in class
Agree-disagree sheets	Field interviews
Tests	Music
Quizzes	Student teaching
Fill-in outlines	Outreach projects
Neighbor nudging	Reading to students
Buzz groups	Choral reading
Brainstorming	Circle response

Role plays

Skits

Monologues

Pantomimes

Dramatic readings

Charades

Observations

Group reports

Individual reports

News reports

Use of workbooks

Inductive study (Scripture search)

Reaction sheets

Discussion sheets

Listening teams

Triad groups

Problem solving

Personal testimonies

Conversations

Individual tutoring

Contests

Film talkback

Dialogues

Paraphrasing

Story writing

Interviews

Programmed learning

Verse memorization

Creative writing (stories, poems, letters, music, daily journal, paraphrases)

Look at the following list of forty-two visual and audio aids, asking yourself which ones you can use in your teaching. Again, not all will be equally suitable for every age group.

Chalkboards

Flannelboards

Overhead projectors

Films

Filmstrips

Slides

Audiotapes

Videotapes

Puppets

Pictures

Posters

Cartoons

Timelines

Flat maps

Relief maps

Globes

Murals

Demonstrations

Shadow plays

Puzzles

Flashcards

Objects

Displays

Chalk drawings

Charts

Arts and crafts

Banners

Curios

Finger painting

Mosaics

Record players

Interest centers

Graphs

Clay

Mobiles	Finger plays
Bulletin boards	Sand tables
Collages	Opaque projectors
Dioramas	Magnet boards

Can you think of others?

As you plan each lesson, ask yourself two questions: What can I have the students do? What can I have the students see? Be creative!

12

How Did Jesus Use Picturesque Expressions in His Teaching?

"He dropped his watermelon!"

Anyone who has sat under the preaching or teaching ministry of Howard G. Hendricks of Dallas Theological Seminary has probably heard him make this startling statement.

In a delightfully picturesque way, the sentence immediately conveys the image of a person making such a faux pas that, like a watermelon dropped, split, and splattered, the mistake is irreversible.

"He dropped his watermelon" becomes a much more effective way of communicating the idea than the bland statement "He made a mistake," or "He'll never be able to recover from that error" or "His blunder is irrevocable."

Why is it more effective? It piques the hearer's interest. Illustrative language, or figurative speech, adds greater interest, thus engaging the person's attention immediately. It prods the listener's thinking. Colorful language prompts the audience to reflect on the meaning of the picturesque statements. The dropping of a watermelon challenges you to think, How does such a happenstance compare with a bungling mistake? Vivid speech promotes retention. Who can ever forget the image

183

of the watermelon? It imparts such a graphic picture in one's mind that it is almost impossible to forget it. Figurative speech is easily remembered for it makes indelible impressions.

Jesus used many picturesque expressions in his teaching, and he did so for the same three reasons: to capture his hearer's attention, to encourage them to reflect on what he said, and to help them remember his words. His vividly expressed teaching incorporated numerous figures of speech:

Simile
Metaphor
Hypocatastasis
Metonymy
Synecdoche
Hyperbole
Personification
Apostrophe
Euphemism
Irony
Paradox
Pun

The next chapter discusses eight other rhetorical devices Jesus used. These many figures of speech and rhetorical techniques converge to help distinguish Jesus Christ as the world's most remarkable Teacher.

Some of the most imaginative sayings and picturesque language were spoken by Jesus—words that have endured century after century and still abide today as memorable maxims and wonder-filled word pictures.

Many people today—non-Christians as well as Christians—cite some of the Savior's numerous verbal portraits. Examples include "No one can serve two masters" (Matt. 6:24); "Do not throw your pearls to pigs" (7:6); "Do to others what you would have them do to you" (7:12); "You strain out a gnat but swallow a camel" (23:24); "Can a blind man lead a blind man?" (Luke 6:39).

As Brown wrote years ago, "His familiar sayings stand to this day in the front rank of the world's greatest literature."[1]

People live and think metaphorically. They commonly compare one object to another to arrest attention. Or they make an overstatement for emphasis. Or they speak with puns to make their point more palatable. They assert contrasts, or they voice riddles, or they personify an inani-

---

1. Charles Reynolds Brown, *The Master's Influence* (Nashville: Cokesbury, 1936), 22.

mate object—all for the purpose of communication. Undeniably, as Wilder put it, "in all cultures men live by images,"[2] that is, by figurative imagery.

How else can abstract, spiritual truths be conveyed to finite minds? Jesus used concrete illustrations, commonplace objects, everyday activities, to transform his messages from heaven to his hearers. Maxims, paradoxes, humor, hyperbole, similes, personification—these and many others were his communicative tools. He relayed profound truths in easy-to-comprehend language. For example, Jesus' claim, "I am the good shepherd" (John 10:11), reveals much about his spiritual relationship to his followers. For his audience, living in an agricultural society in which many engaged in sheep-raising, this imagery would have carried a number of meaningful ideas: Jesus cares for his own, provides for them, feeds them, guides them, protects them, heals them, even dies for them. And all these profound, spiritual concepts were disclosed in simplicity and brevity.

Yet Jesus "never introduced a metaphor for the mere purpose of decorating his public addresses or gratifying a poetic fancy."[3]

Attention to Jesus' picturesque way of teaching can benefit teachers today. Using figures of speech and other rhetorical devices in our teaching can bring about the same results: latching the attention of our students, prompting them to think, and helping them remember. After all, are these not some of the very points we hope to achieve in our instruction: attention, reflection, and retention—all in order to encourage the penetration of God's truth into our students' minds and hearts? By using imaginative language, we can teach as Jesus taught.[4]

A figure of speech "is simply a word or a sentence thrown into a peculiar form, different from its original or simplest meaning or use."[5] When Jesus said, "Be on your guard against the yeast of the Pharisees and Sadducees" (Matt. 16:6), the disciples thought he was making a normal, plain statement about their bread. But when Jesus explained that he spoke figuratively, they then understood the yeast referred to the religious authorities' teaching (16:7–12). If Jesus had said in John 10:7, "I am the one in whom you are to believe in order to be saved,"

2. Amos N. Wilder, *The Language of the Gospel* (New York: Harper and Row, 1964), 127.

3. Donald Fraser, *The Metaphors of Christ* (London: Nisbet, 1885; reprint, Minneapolis: Klock and Klock, 1985), vii.

4. See Warren W. Wiersbe, *Preaching and Teaching with Imagination* (Wheaton, Ill.: Victor, 1994), for an excellent presentation on the place of imaginative figurative communication in life, the Scriptures, and preaching.

5. E. W. Bullinger, *Figures of Speech Used in the Bible: Explained and Illustrated* (London: Eyre and Spottiswoode, 1898; reprint, Grand Rapids: Baker, 1968), xv.

he would have been making a normal statement. But instead he said, "I am the gate for the sheep," and in this way he conveyed the same idea but in a more out-of-the-ordinary sense. The metaphor presented a literal truth figuratively and thus it arrests our attention, challenges us to think (in what ways is Jesus like a gate for sheep?), and is easier to recall.

Simile

A simile is a comparison of two things that are normally not alike, and that uses the word "like" or "as." In a simile "the less known is clarified by that which is better known."[6] As we read or hear similes, we are challenged to think how the two differing things are alike. Of course, the two elements are not to be considered alike in all respects. For example, when Jesus said the kingdom of heaven is like a mustard seed (Matt. 13:31), he did not mean it looks like that seed. When he said the kingdom of heaven is like yeast (13:33), he did not mean it tasted like sour dough.[7]

In studying Jesus' similes, it is helpful to note the image, the nonimage (what Jesus was referring to by the image), and the way(s) the two are similar. As an example, in Jesus' words, "I am sending you out like sheep among wolves" (Matt. 10:16), the image is "sheep among wolves," the nonimage or referent is "you," that is, the twelve disciples, and the point of similarity is that they would face danger just as sheep are in danger of losing their lives if wolves attack them. This imagery conveys Jesus' ideas more graphically than if he had said, "I am sending you on a dangerous mission."

For each of Jesus' similes in table 23, write the image, the nonimage, and the point of comparison. The first three are completed to give you examples. Note that sometimes Jesus stated the point of comparison, as in Matthew 9:36.

Jesus' similes reflect his familiarity with nature and occupations of his culture. Animate and inanimate items he referred to in his fifty similes (some of which he referred to more than once) include sheep, snakes, cloves, seed, yeast, weeds, sun, hen, lightning, wheat, light, and branch. People he mentioned were children, sower, merchant, house owner, pagans, king, "yourself," landowner, virgins, man on a journey, shepherd, youngest, servant, orphans. His similes also made compari-

---

6. Wilder, *The Language of the Gospel*, 80.
7. G. B. Caird, *The Language and Imagery of the Bible* (Philadelphia: Westminster, 1986), 145.

Table 23
Jesus' Similes

Verse	Image	Nonimage	Point of Comparison
Matthew 7:24, "Everyone who hears these words of mine and puts them into practice is *like* a wise man who built his house on the rock" (cf. Luke 6:47–48).	Building a house on a rock	Those who obey Jesus' words	Security
Matthew 7:26, "Everyone who hears these words of mine and does not put them into practice is *like* a foolish man who built his house on sand" (cf. Luke 6:49).	Building a house on sand	Those who disobey Jesus' words	Insecurity
Matthew 9:36, "They were harassed and helpless, *like* sheep without a shepherd."	Crowds	Shepherd-less	Harassed
Matthew 10:16, "I am sending you *like* sheep among wolves" (cf. Luke 10:3).			
Matthew 10:16, "Be *as* shrewd as snakes."			
Matthew 11:16, "This generation . . . is *like* children . . . calling out to others" (cf. Luke 7:31–32).			
Matthew 12:40, "*As* Jonah was three days and three nights in the belly of a huge fish, so the Son of Man will be three days and three nights in the heart of the earth" (cf. Luke 11:30).			
Matthew 13:24–25, "The kingdom of heaven is *like* a man who sowed seed in his field. But while everyone was sleeping, his enemy came and sowed weeds among the wheat."			
Matthew 13:31, "The kingdom of heaven is *like* a mustard seed" (cf. Mark 4:30–32; Luke 13:18–19).			

Verse	Image	Nonimage	Point of Comparison
Matthew 13:33, "The kingdom of heaven is *like* yeast" (cf. Luke 13:20–21).			
Matthew 13:40, "*As* the weeds are pulled up and burned in the fire, so it will be at the end of the age."			
Matthew 13:43, "Then the righteous will shine *like* the sun in the kingdom of their Father."			
Matthew 13:44, "The kingdom of heaven is *like* treasure hidden in a field."			
Matthew 13:45, "The kingdom of heaven is *like* a merchant looking for fine pearls."			
Matthew 13:47, "The kingdom of heaven is *like* a net that was let down into the lake and caught all kinds of fish."			
Matthew 13:52, "Every teacher of the law who has been instructed about the kingdom of heaven is *like* the owner of a house who brings out of his storeroom new treasures as well as old."			
Matthew 17:20, "If you have faith as small *as* a mustard seed, you can say to this mountain, 'Move from here to there,' and it will move."			
Matthew 18:3, "Unless you change and become *like* little children, you will never enter the kingdom of heaven" (cf. Mark 10:15; Luke 18:17).			
Matthew 18:4, "Whoever humbles himself *like* this child is the greatest in the kingdom of heaven."			

Verse	Image	Nonimage	Point of Comparison
Matthew 18:17, "If he refuses to listen even to the church, treat him *as* you would a pagan or a tax collector."			
Matthew 18:23, "The kingdom of heaven is *like* a king who wanted to settle accounts with his servants."			
Matthew 19:19; 22:39, "Love your neighbor *as* yourself" (cf. Mark 12:31, 33, 38; Luke 10:27).			
Matthew 20:1, "The kingdom of heaven is *like* a landowner who went out early in the morning to hire men to work in his vineyard."			
Matthew 20:28, "The Son of Man [came] . . . to give his life *as* a ransom for many" (cf. Mark 10:45).			
Matthew 22:2, "The kingdom of heaven is *like* a king who prepared a wedding banquet for his son."			
Matthew 22:30, "At the resurrection people will neither marry nor be given in marriage; they will be *like* the angels in heaven" (cf. Mark 12:25; Luke 20:35–36).			
Matthew 23:27, "You hypocrites. . . are *like* whitewashed tombs."			
Matthew 23:37, "O Jerusalem, Jerusalem . . . how often have I longed to gather your children together, *as* a hen gathers her chicks under her wings" (cf. Luke 13:34).			
Matthew 24:27, "*As* lightning that comes from the east is visible even in the west, so will be the coming of the Son of Man."			

Verse	Image	Nonimage	Point of Comparison
Matthew 24:37, "*As* it was in the days of Noah, so it will be at the coming of the Son of Man" (cf. Luke 17:26).			
Matthew 25:1, "The kingdom of heaven will be *like* ten virgins who took their lamps and went out to meet the bridegroom."			
Matthew 25:14, "It [the kingdom of heaven] will be *like* a man going on a journey, who called his servants and entrusted his property to them."			
Matthew 25:32, "He will separate the people one from another *as* a shepherd separates the sheep from the goats."			
Mark 4:15, "Some people are *like* seed along the path, where the word is sown. As soon as they hear it, Satan comes and takes away the word that was sown in them."			
Mark 4:16–17, "Others, *like* seed sown on rocky places, hear the word and at once receive it with joy. But . . . they quickly fall away."			
Mark 4:18–19, "Still others, *like* seed sown among thorns, hear the word; but the worries of this life . . . choke the word, making it unfruitful."			
Mark 4:26, "This is what the kingdom of God is *like*. A man scatters seed on the ground."			
Luke 10:18, "I saw Satan fall *like* lightning from heaven."			

Verse	Image	Nonimage	**Point of Comparison**
Luke 11:36, "If your whole body is full of light, and no part of it dark, it will be completely lighted, *as* when the light of a lamp shines on you."			
Luke 11:44, "Woe to you, because you are *like* unmarked graves, which men walk over without knowing it."			
Luke 17:6, "If you have faith *as* small as a mustard seed, you can say to this mulberry tree, 'Be up-rooted and planted in the sea,' and it will obey you."			
Luke 17:29–30, "The day Lot left Sodom, fire and sulfur rained down from heaven and destroyed them all. It will be just *like* this on the day the Son of Man is revealed."			
Luke 21:34, "Be careful, or your hearts will be weighed down . . . and that day will close on you un-expectedly *like* a trap."			
Luke 22:26, "The greatest among you should be *like* the youngest, and the one who rules *like* the one who serves."			
Luke 22:31, "Simon, Simon, Satan has asked to sift you *as* wheat."			
John 3:14, "Just *as* Moses lifted up the snake in the desert, so the Son of Man must be lifted up."			
John 12:46, "I have come into the world *as* a light."			
John 14:18, "I will not leave you *as* orphans."			
John 15:6, "If anyone does not re-main in me, he is *like* a branch that is thrown away and withers."			

sons to Jonah, Noah, Lot, and angels. Manmade objects in Jesus' similes are a house, treasure, net, ransom, tombs, lamp, graves, and trap. By employing these simple, commonplace subjects in his many similes, Jesus conveyed profound, spiritual truths. Comparing the unusual or unknown to the ordinary things of life would have quickened his listeners' thinking, making lasting impressions.

Metaphor

A metaphor is a comparison in which one thing is said to be, act like, or represent another, in which the two are unlike. In a metaphor the comparison is implicit, whereas in a simile it is explicit. In a metaphor the verb is always in the form of "to be" (is, are, was, were, have been), whereas a simile always uses the word *like* or *as*.[8] By saying "This is that," rather than "This is like that," the metaphor takes on more force. Metaphors draw attention to similarities between dissimilar things that might otherwise go unnoticed. "Metaphor is a lens; it is as though the speaker were saying, 'Look through this and see what I have seen, something you would never have noticed without the lens!'"[9]

Bringing unlike things together, saying one is to be identified with the other (e.g., "False prophets . . . are ferocious wolves," Matt. 7:15), shocks the hearer or the reader, for the comparison reveals meanings not previously considered. Aristotle wrote, "strange words simply puzzle us; ordinary words convey only what we know already; it is from metaphors that we can best get hold of something fresh."[10] "In the metaphor we have an image with a certain shock to the imagination."[11] The shock or surprise stems from the fact that the metaphors "upset conventions . . . involve tension, and . . . are implicitly revolutionary."[12] Note the similarities—and the shock effect—in Jesus' metaphors.

> Matthew 5:13, "You *are* the salt of the earth." How are believers like salt?
> Matthew 5:14, "You *are* the light of the world." How are believers like light?
> Matthew 6:22, "The eye *is* the lamp of the body" (cf. Luke 11:34). In what sense is the eye like a lamp?
> Matthew 7:15, "False prophets . . . *are* ferocious wolves." In what way(s) are false prophets like wolves?

8. Roy B. Zuck, *Basic Bible Interpretation* (Wheaton, Ill.: Victor, 1991), 148–49.
9. Caird, *The Language and Imagery of the Bible*, 152.
10. Aristotle *The Art of Rhetoric* 3.10.
11. Wilder, *The Language of the Gospel*, 80.
12. Sallie McFague, *Metaphorical Theology* (London: SCM, 1983), 17.

Matthew 13:19, "The message about the kingdom . . . *is* the seed sown." How is Jesus' message like seed?

Matthew 13:20, "[What was sown on rocky places *is*] the man who hears the word . . . and he quickly falls away." How are the seed and the man alike?

Matthew 13:22, "[What was sown among the thorns *is*] the man who hears the word, but the worries of this life . . . choke it." How do seed among thorns and a worrying person compare?

Matthew 13:37, "The one who sowed the good seed *is* the Son of Man." How is Jesus like a sower?

Matthew 13:38, "The field *is* the world." How are these alike?

Matthew 13:38, "The weeds *are* the sons of the evil one." How do these compare?

Matthew 13:38, "The enemy who sows them *is* the devil." How are these alike?

Matthew 13:38, "The harvest *is* the end of the age." Why is the end of the age likened to a harvest?

Matthew 13:38, "The harvesters *are* angels." Why are angels compared to harvesters?

Matthew 26:26, "Jesus took bread . . . [and said], 'This *is* my body'" (cf. Mark 14:22; Luke 22:19). In what way(s) is bread similar to Jesus' body?

Matthew 26:27, "He took the cup . . . [and said], . . . 'This *is* my blood of the covenant'" (cf. Mark 14:24; Luke 22:20). In what way(s) is the cup similar to Jesus' blood?

John 6:35, "I *am* the bread of life." How is Jesus like bread?

John 8:12; 9:5, "I *am* the light of the world." How does Jesus compare to light?

John 10:7, 9, "I *am* the gate for the sheep." Why did Jesus call himself a gate?

John 10:11, 14, "I *am* the good shepherd." What similarities exist between Jesus and a shepherd?

John 14:6, "I *am* the way." Why did Jesus say he is the way?

John 14:6, "I *am* . . . the truth." In what sense is Jesus the truth?

John 14:6, "I *am* . . . the life." How is Jesus the life?

John 15:1, 5, "I *am* the vine." How is Jesus like a vine?

John 15:5, "You *are* the branches." How are believers and vine branches alike?

Hypocatastasis

In this figure of speech the comparison between two normally unlike things is made by a direct naming. When Jesus referred to Herod and said, "Go tell that fox" (Luke 13:32), a hypocatastasis was used. If Jesus had used a simile, he would have said, "Herod is like a fox." If the Lord had used a metaphor, he would have affirmed, "Herod is a fox." But in a hypocatastasis he directly named Herod a "fox."

The Lord often made comparisons by calling one thing something else. He called the disciples "fishers of men" (Matt. 4:19; Mark 1:17), "workers" in the harvest (Matt. 9:37–38; Luke 10:2), "little children" (11:25; Luke 10:21), "little flock" (Luke 12:32), and "reapers" (John 4:36). John the Baptist was called a "reed" (Matt. 11:17), and a "lamb" (John 5:25). Believers are Jesus' "brothers and sisters" (Matt. 12:49), and "lambs" and "sheep" (John 21:15–16). Jesus referred to himself as a bridegroom (Matt. 9:15; Mark 2:15–20) and a light (John 12:35–36).

Serving the Lord is likened to wearing a yoke (Matt. 11:29), working for food (John 6:27), bearing a cross (Matt. 16:24; Mark 8:34; Luke 9:23),[13] and plowing (Luke 9:62).

Jesus called unbelievers "dogs" and "pigs" (Matt. 7:6), a harvest "field" (9:37–38; John 4:35), a "plant" (Matt. 15:13), and those who are "dead" (Luke 9:60). Gentiles are "dogs" (Mark 7:27), unbelieving Israelites are "lost sheep" (Matt. 10:6). Pharisees are a brood of vipers (Matt. 12:34; 23:33), their teaching is called "yeast" (Matt. 16:6; Mark 8:15), Jesus' enemies are hired hands and thieves (John 10:1, 8, 12–13), and Herod is a "fox" (Luke 13:31–32).

A minor misdemeanor is called a "speck of sawdust" and a more serious sin is a "plank" (Matt. 7:3–5). "Fire" is God's final judgment (Luke 12:49). Conduct is "fruit" (Matt. 7:16, 20), and spiritual truth is "light" (John 3:19, 21). Spiritual blessing is a "crop" (Matt. 13:23) and a "pasture" (John 10:9), and the Holy Spirit is "living water" (4:10, 11, 14; 7:38).[14] The way to heaven is a "gate" (Matt. 7:13), and burning lamps refer to spiritual alertness (Luke 12:35).

Jesus called his body a "temple" (John 2:19), his ministry, "food" (4:34), and fellowshiping with him is partaking of his flesh and blood. He called his suffering and death a "cup" (Matt. 20:22–23; 26:39; Mark 10:38; 14:36; Luke 22:42) and a "baptism" (Mark 10:38).

As with his similes and metaphors, many of Jesus' examples of hypocatastasis were from nature. Again abstract truths, clothed in concrete illustrative language, startled the hearers into reflective thought.

---

13. In the Roman Empire a convicted criminal was forced to carry his own cross to his execution, thereby publicly displaying his submission to the rule he had previously opposed. Similarly for a disciple to "take up" his "cross" meant to demonstrate his submission to the Lord against whom he had rebelled, even though it would result in suffering (Louis A. Barbieri, "Matthew," in *The Bible Knowledge Commentary, New Testament*, ed. John F. Walvoord and Roy B. Zuck [Wheaton, Ill.: Victor, 1983], 59).

14. "The Jews used the expression *living water* to denote springs, or fountains, or running streams, in opposition to dead and stagnant water" (Albert Barnes, *Barnes' Notes of the New Testament* [reprint, Grand Rapids: Kregel, 1962], 282 [italics his]). Here Jesus referred to the Holy Spirit (cf. John 7:38–39), who gives eternal life. "Jesus is speaking of the new life that He will give, a life connected with the activity of the Spirit" (Leon Morris, *The Gospel according to John*, New International Commentary on the New Testament [Grand Rapids: Eerdmans, 1971], 260).

Metonymy

In metonymy a word or phrase is substituted for another word or phrase associated with it. When Jesus referred to bringing "a sword" (Matt. 10:34), he meant not a literal sword, but what is associated with swords, namely, warfare. In addressing Korazin, Bethsaida, and Capernaum (Matt. 11:21, 23; Luke 10:13, 15), he obviously meant not the physical aspects of those cities but their inhabitants. The same is true of his reference to "every city or household" (Matt. 12:25), to Jerusalem (Matt. 22:37), and to "other towns" (Luke 4:43), by which he meant people in them.

Honoring the Lord with one's lips (Matt. 15:8) refers to one's words produced by his lips. When Jesus said, "If a house is divided against itself, that house cannot stand" (Mark 3:25), he obviously did not mean a literal house. He referred to a family living in a house.

At the Lord's Supper the "cup" of which Jesus and the Twelve drank is a metonymy, for they drank the contents of the cup, not the cup itself. This is a metonymy of association.

Synecdoche

A synecdoche is similar to a metonymy except that a synecdoche substitutes a part for the whole, or whole for the part. When Jesus spoke of "wombs that never bore" (Luke 23:29), he implied barren women, the part (wombs) suggesting the whole person.

Hyperbole

A hyperbole is an intentional exaggeration, used to add shock and emphasis to what is said. Though hyperboles are not to be taken literally, they do convey truth by overstatements, or by statements that *appear* to be impossible or unnatural. Jesus' hearers naturally understood his exaggerations as graphic means of communication, as startling words that captivated their interest in spiritual verities.

Examples of hyperbolic statements are in Matthew 5:29–30, "If your right eye causes you to sin, gouge it out and throw it away. It is better for you to lose one part of your body than for your whole body to be thrown into hell. And if your right hand causes you to sin, cut it off and throw it away. It is better for you to lose one part of your body than for your whole body to go into hell."[15] Though some people have taken these words literally, failing to see them as overstatements, and have mutilated themselves, they have not solved the problem, for one could sin with one eye or hand or even with no eyes or hands! Jesus was pointing to "the need to remove from their lives anything that might cause them to sin. There is no sin in life worth perishing over. Better to repent of that sin, even if it is as painful as tearing out an eye or tearing off a hand, and enter as a result into the kingdom of God than to cherish that sin and be thrown into hell."[16]

Announcing one's almsgiving with trumpets (Matt. 6:2), not letting one's left hand know what his right hand is doing (6:3), neglecting to remove a plank in one's eye (7:3–5), giving a son a stone instead of bread or a snake for a fish (7:9–10), acquiring the entire world (16:26), moving mountains (17:20), forgiving 490 times (18:22, a phrase that means no limit to one's attitude of forgiving), a camel going through the eye of a sewing needle (19:24; cf. Mark 10:24–25),[17] traveling over land and sea to win a single convert (23:15), straining out a gnat while swallowing a camel (23:24),[18] everyone dying by the sword if he uses the sword (26:52),[19] and hating one's parents, wife, and children (Luke 14:26; cf. Matt. 10:37),[20] are a dozen instances of Jesus' use of hyperboles, exaggerations that, like daggers, deeply penetrated the consciences of his hearers.

15. On a different occasion Jesus mentioned three body parts: hand, foot, eye (Matt. 18:8–9; Mark 9:43–47).

16. Robert H. Stein, *The Method and Message of Jesus' Teachings* (Philadelphia: Westminster, 1978), 9.

17. Jesus' point shows that though it is impossible for a large animal to pass through a small hole like a needle eye (*not* a small gate through which a camel could enter with difficulty), it is not altogether impossible for a rich person to be saved (ibid., 12).

18. Jesus did not mean the preachers of the law and Pharisees were literally doing these things (for who could swallow a camel!). He meant that while they were concerned with minute details of the law, majoring on the minors, they were neglecting more important matters, minoring on majors, like easily swallowing a camel (Zuck, *Basic Bible Interpretation*, 155). By attempting to strain out an unclean organism (Lev. 11:41), they polluted themselves by failing to avoid taking in a camel, the largest of the beasts normally found in Palestine, an animal also unclean (Lev. 11:4; Morris, *The Gospel according to Matthew*, 583).

19. This is probably a hyperbole since not *everyone* who uses a sword in battle is killed by a sword.

20. Literally hating one's closest loved ones would contradict Jesus' command to honor one's parents (Mark 7:10). Jesus was indicating that love for one's relatives should not take precedence over his love for Jesus. Human love will so pale in comparison that it will seem like hate (Stein, *The Method and Message of Jesus' Teachings*, 8–9). This command underscores the need for a person to be "willing to put God's claims before those of his father and mother" (Cecil S. Emden, "Our Lord's Impressive Rhetoric," *Church Quarterly Review* 157 [1956]: 419).

Personification

Personification is a figure of speech in which one ascribes human characteristics or actions to inanimate objects or ideas or to animals. Knowledge is ascribed to one's hands (Matt. 6:3). "Tomorrow" is treated as having the emotion of worry (6:34). Jesus spoke of the kingdom advancing like an army (11:12), of wisdom having actions (11:19), of stones crying out (Luke 19:40), of mountains being addressed as if they have ears (23:30), of Jerusalem as if it could hear (Matt. 23:37), and of the wind having a will ("the wind blows wherever it pleases," John 3:8).

Assigning aspects of human personality and action to these objects adds vividness to Jesus' remarks.

Apostrophe

The figure of speech known as apostrophe addresses an object directly as if it were an imaginary person. It differs from personification in that in an apostrophe an individual speaks directly *to* an object as if it were a person, whereas in personification someone speaks *about* an object as if it were a person. Examples from Jesus' teaching are his addressing entire cities such as Korazin, Bethsaida, Capernaum (Matt. 11:21, 23; Luke 10:13), and Jerusalem (Matt. 23:37; Luke 13:34).[21]

Euphemism

A euphemism substitutes an inoffensive or mild expression for an offensive or bold expression. Jesus used a euphemism when he told Jairus his daughter was asleep (Matt. 9:24; Mark 5:39; Luke 8:52) and when he told the disciples Lazarus was sleeping (John 11:11). Though the girl and the man were actually dead, Jesus purposefully used a milder expression.

Irony

Irony is a form of ridicule expressed as a compliment. The intended meaning thus stands as the opposite of what is said. Presenting some-

---

21. Jesus' words to Jerusalem in Matthew 23:37 and Luke 13:34 actually include four figures of speech! Addressing the city as if it were a person is personification. In addressing the city directly he used an apostrophe. In addressing the city when actually he meant the inhabitants in it, he used a metonymy. And in mentioning his desire to gather its people to him as a hen gathers her chicks, he spoke a simile.

thing unexpected, irony is like several other figures of speech that have
the element of surprise or shock.

The Pharisees and Sadducees, Jesus said, could predict the weather,
but in the area where they were expected to be experts, namely, religion,
they were unable to see the significance of Jesus' ministry (Matt. 16:2–
3). Ironically, then, they were the opposite of what one would expect.

Accused of eating with tax collectors and sinners, Jesus told the
teachers of the law who were Pharisees, "It is not the healthy who need
a doctor, but the sick. I have not come to call the righteous, but sinners"
(Mark 2:17). Irony in this statement lies in the fact that the religious
leaders *thought* themselves healthy and righteous and therefore not in
need of salvation. And yet they needed the Messiah-Savior as much as
did the tax collectors and sinners whom they despised![22] By disassoci-
ating themselves from sinners, they at the same time rejected Jesus,
their only hope of salvation. They too should have dined with Jesus and
the tax collectors!

Again the Pharisees, as religious leaders, would be expected to do
good and save life, even on the Sabbath, but by a question Jesus revealed their ironic desire to avoid Sabbath work at all costs (Mark 3:4).

Unexpectedly, and therefore ironically, in opposing Jesus, the Pharisees, who favored noninvolvement with the Romans, joined forces with
the Herodians, who encouraged submission to Rome (Mark 3:6).

Jesus spoke with a touch of irony, perhaps even sarcasm,[23] when he
said to the Pharisees, "You have a fine way of setting aside the commands of God in order to observe your own traditions!" (Mark 7:9).
"You have a fine way" sounds like a compliment, but the rest of the sentence reveals that Jesus was ridiculing them. The thought may be expressed, "How beautifully you do an ugly thing!" or "You do illegality
great justice!"[24] Jesus spoke with irony when he said, "surely no
prophet can die outside Jerusalem!" (Luke 13:33), for he knew that he,
a prophet, *would* die outside that city.

These cases are examples of verbal irony, in which the irony occurs
in what is said. Dramatic or situational irony, on the other hand, refers
to situations or actions which are the opposite of what is expected or is
appropriate. An example of dramatic irony is Jesus' story of the good
Samaritan (Luke 10:29–37). The Levite and the priest did the opposite

22. Jakob Jonsson, *Humour and Irony in the New Testament* (Leiden: Brill, 1985),
186–87.

23. Compared with irony, "sarcasm is usually heavier in tone. Being more caustic,
sarcasm is usually used to wound. It is a biting criticism. Irony, however, is a more subtle
form of ridicule" (Zuck, *Basic Bible Interpretation*, 159).

24. Jerry Camery-Hoggatt, *Irony in Mark's Gospel*, Society for New Testament Studies
Monograph Series 72 (Cambridge: Cambridge University Press, 1992), 149.

of what is expected, and the despised Samaritan did what the Jews did not expect of him.

The parable of the shrewd manager contains an ironic twist: a rich man commends his dishonest manager for acting shrewdly, and Jesus used that fact to state ironically that unbelievers "are more shrewd in dealing with their own kind" than are believers, "the people of the light" (Luke 16:8). He then applied this by telling the disciples to use "worldly wealth" for spiritual gain (16:9), and by pointing out to the Pharisees, who loved money, that no one can "serve both God and Money," like serving two masters (16:13–14).

In Jewish society people believed that wealth was a sign of divine blessing and that poverty evidenced lack of piety. Therefore Jesus' words about the rich man, who died and was tormented in hell, and the poor, sick man Lazarus, who went to "Abraham's side," no doubt stunned his listeners with dramatic irony. Similarly Jesus' parable of the Pharisee and the tax collector praying in the temple illustrates dramatic irony. In his prayer the Pharisee thanked God he was not like the tax collector, a person with a despicable occupation, and yet the tax collector was the one whom God justified (Luke 18:9–14).

One would expect a Pharisee like Nicodemus, "a member of the Jewish ruling council" (John 3:1), to be able to discern spiritual truths, but this was not the case. Jesus' query to Nicodemus therefore contains an ironic barb: "You are Israel's teacher . . . and do you not understand these things?" (3:10).

James and John asked to be placed at Jesus' right and left (Mark 10:37) without realizing that those positions would be occupied by people on crosses (15:27).[25] "In fact, the basic story lines of our Gospels are built upon extended ironies: the people of Israel reject their Messiah; God's own Son is accused of blasphemy by characters who are themselves blasphemers; people opposed to God serve as unwitting instruments in bringing God's will to pass."[26]

The subtlety of Jesus' use of irony in many of his stories and statements adds intrigue—and stunning impact—to his teaching.

Paradox

A paradox is a statement that is seemingly contradictory to normal opinion or common sense. It is not an actual contradiction; it has only the appearance of being a discrepancy.

---

25. Mark Allan Powell, *What Is Narrative Criticism?* (Minneapolis: Fortress, 1990), 31.
26. Ibid.

How arresting were the paradoxical words with which Jesus began the Sermon on the Mount. People do not normally think of the poor in spirit, the mourners, and the meek as being blessed. And yet they are the ones to whom belongs the kingdom of heaven, and who are comforted, and who will inherit the earth (Matt. 5:3–5). The disciples must have been startled to hear their Lord say, "Whoever finds his life will lose it, and whoever loses his life for my sake will find it" (10:39; Luke 9:24) and later to hear similar words: "For whoever wants to save his life will lose it, but whoever loses his life for me will find it" (Matt. 16:25; Luke 17:33; Mark 8:35; cf. John 12:25).[27]

Along a similar line the Lord told his followers that "he who is least in the kingdom of heaven is greater than John the Baptist" (Matt. 11:11). Paradoxically the "least," a believer in the Christian era, is "greater" than Jesus' own forerunner.

It seems paradoxical to say that a yoke is easy and a burden is light (Matt. 11:30), but by this paradox Jesus forced the disciples to reflect on the unique blessings inherent in following him.

To forsake one's family for Jesus' sake and receive much more in return (Matt. 19:29), to be removed from the highest position to the lowest or from the lowest to the highest (19:30; 20:16; Mark 10:31; Luke 13:30), to become great by being a servant (Matt. 20:26–27; 23:11; Mark 9:35; 10:43–44), to be humbled when exalted or to be exalted by being humble (Matt. 23:11; Luke 14:11; 18:14), to have one's possessions removed when he has little (Mark 4:25), to be without honor among one's own relatives and in his hometown (Matt. 13:57; Mark 6:4), to be the greatest by being the least (Luke 9:48), to gain one's life by losing it (John 12:25)[28]—all are baffling from a human vantage point, but they make sense from the divine perspective.

To say that prostitutes will enter God's kingdom ahead of chief priests and elders (Matt. 21:31) would have been so paradoxical it would have jolted—and embittered—the religious leaders. Also paradoxical is Jesus' observation that though rich people gave money to the temple treasury, a poor widow actually gave more because she sacrificed more (Mark 12:41–44). For Jesus to say he could raise the temple in three days when it had been under construction for forty-six years (John 2:19–20) astonished the Jews. However, this seemed a paradox to them because they failed to understand the figure of speech by which he was identifying not Herod's temple but his own body (2:21).

27. Sockman calls these people "winning losers," a paradoxical title (Ralph W. Sockman, *The Paradoxes of Jesus* [New York: Abingdon, 1936], 232–41).
28. Sockman calls this to "live by dying" (ibid., 248).

Pun

In a pun (sometimes called a *paronamasia*) similar-sounding words or the same words have different meanings. In addressing Peter (*Petros* in Greek), Jesus said the church would be built on Peter's confession, "this rock" (*petra*)—clearly a clever play on words, making Jesus' comment memorable.

Jesus' predictions of the end times included his references to famines (*loimoi*) and pestilences (*limoi*), similar-sounding words that also begin with the same letter and are therefore examples of alliteration (Luke 21:11).

Two examples of the same word having two meanings occur in Jesus' conversation with Nicodemus. In the phrase "unless [a man] is born again" (John 3:3) the Greek word *anōthen* means "again" but it also means "from above." Possibly Jesus used a double entendre, intending both meanings in the one word.

Referring to the wind, Jesus used the word *pneuma* (John 3:8) and in the same verse he spoke of *pneuma* to refer to the Holy Spirit. This was a clever pun.

The (spiritually) dead should be allowed to bury the (physically) dead, Jesus said, so that believers would be free to follow him (Matt. 8:22; Luke 9:60).

In the first half of Mark 8:35 the word *save* means to preserve physically, whereas in the second half the word speaks of spiritual fulfillment. In the same verse "lose" first means physical death and then spiritual dedication.

How about You?

Recall a picturesque statement a teacher made. Why do you remember it?

Think of a simile and a metaphor or two you could use in your next lesson.

Would a hyperbole help communicate a point in your lesson?

How might you use irony or a paradoxical statement?

After you consciously use one or more of these figures of speech in
your teaching, ask yourself, How did the students respond? How did
it help communicate the lesson content? How could I improve next
time?

"Where did this man get this wisdom....?
Isn't this the carpenter's son?"

Matthew 13:54-55;
cf. Mark 6:2b

13

How Did Jesus Use Other Rhetorical Devices in His Teaching?

The remarkable variety in Jesus' teaching appears in other rhetorical devices he employed, including humor, enigmas, maxims or aphorisms, repetition, logical reasoning, contrasts, examples and explanations, and poetry.

Humor

Humor, like irony, presents the unexpected. By stating the incongruous, the paradoxical, the preposterous, or the absurd, humor brings a smile or a laugh.

Sometimes situations are humorous. If a man meets a lady on the street, tips his hat to her, and a pigeon flies out from beneath it, that is humor of an unexpected happening. If a dog enters a classroom, the children laugh. That is situational "humor of the incongruous (putting unrelated things together)."[1]

1. *World Book Encyclopedia*, 1992 ed., s.v. "Humor," by Sarah Blacher Cohen, 9:435.

Humor, however, more often occurs in what is said, as is true in Jesus' lessons. Irony, sarcasm, hyperboles, paradoxes, and puns all have an element of humor because of the surprise of the unexpected. People smile or laugh at something humorous or they become suddenly aware of the incongruous.

Some people are surprised to think that Jesus, who came to earth on such a serious mission—to redeem sinners from sin by his sacrifice on the cross—would have laughed. However, "anyone who reads the Synoptic Gospels with a relative freedom from presuppositions might be expected to see that Christ laughed, and that he expected others to laugh, but our capability to miss this aspect of his life is phenomenal."[2]

As the world's greatest Communicator-Teacher, Jesus frequently employed humor to great advantage. A smile in appreciation of the humorous relaxes students, and a chuckle at the teacher's remarks makes his points more palatable to his learners. Jesus' humor with the disciples helps them digest his teaching, and his witty, sometimes funny responses to his critical opponents convicted and sometimes even silenced them.

However, the Lord's humor was never entertainment for entertainment's sake. He never told jokes merely to evoke hilarity. His humor was always purposeful. Nor was his humor cruel, bitter, or revengeful. He uttered humor in a pleasing, not cynical, fashion.

Seldom is humor included in lists of teacher qualifications. Yet, used rightly, it constitutes an important characteristic in effective instruction. Margo Stone, Arizona's Teacher of the Year for 1994, commented on humor in her words on effective teaching. "Good teachers," she said, "are teachers that know their field, have a sense of caring and compassion, and a sense of humor."[3]

How did Jesus exhibit humor? His hyperboles no doubt brought smiles. Who could avoid grinning at the thought of Pharisees blowing trumpets to announce their almsgiving (Matt. 6:2), or at the idea of a large piece of lumber sticking in a person's eye (7:3)? Surely words about a camel crawling through a needle eye (19:24) or a camel being swallowed by the Pharisees (23:24) elicited smiles or even laughter.

The following accounts reveal how Jesus often spoke with humor or wit.[4]

"Do you bring in a lamp to put it under a bowl or a bed?" (Mark 4:21; cf. Matt. 5:15). Placing a lamp under a bowl would suffocate a fire;

---

2. Elton Trueblood, *The Humor of Christ* (New York: Harper and Row, 1964), 15.
3. *The Arizona Republic*, 6 November 1993, 1B.
4. Wit, a kind of humor, refers to swift ease in giving apt verbal responses.

placing it under a bed would set the bed on fire. This suggestion of the ludicrous pointed up the need to be open witnesses for the Lord.[5] Just as it is foolish to think anyone would light a candle to cover it, so anyone is mistaken if he thinks "it is the purpose of Christ to gather disciples who hide themselves from the world."[6]

It is ludicrous to think anyone would throw pearls to pigs (Matt. 7:6), or give his son a stone for bread, a snake instead of a fish (7:9–10), or a scorpion for an egg (Luke 11:12), or is capable of picking grapes from thornbushes or figs from thistles (Matt. 7:16), or would build a house on sand (7:26). Yet these illustrations deliver Jesus' points with pungency.

A new patch of cloth sewn to an old garment could pull out and make the tear worse; therefore no housewife does such. And people do not pour new wine into old wineskins, because the skin would burst and the wine would spill (Matt. 9:15–17; Mark 2:21–22; Luke 5:36–39). By calling attention to such ludicrous actions that no one carried out, Jesus stressed that he was bringing in a new message, not "patching" his ministry to Pharisaic traditions.

How laughable that Jesus would say "He who has ears, let him hear" (Matt. 11:15; 13:9, 43; Mark 4:9, 23; Luke 8:8; 14:35)! After all, does not everyone have ears and does not everyone hear with his ears? Imagine the crowds smiling at Jesus' touch of humorous irony, while at the same time absorbing his point that true hearing consists of obeying.

In his conversation with the Greek woman of Syrian Phoenicia, Jesus responded to her plea for help for her demon-possessed daughter by stating that bread for children is not tossed to dogs[7] (Matt. 15:26; Mark 7:27). Though this seems like a heartless response, the Savior may have spoken with a smile on his face, for she seems to have sensed his jest. Picking up Jesus' reference to dogs, she replied that even pet dogs eat crumbs that fall from the table. In her witty answer she accepted her position as a non-Israelite ("Yes, I am a little dog"), but at the same time she indicated her desire to benefit from Jesus in at least a small way ("I would like to eat crumbs from your table"). Who could miss the delightful wit in this dialogue!

Humor can convict. It certainly put the Pharisees in their place, but without vindictiveness. For example, what wolf could actually

---

5. Trueblood, *Humor of Christ*, 18.

6. Jakob Jonsson, *Humour and Irony in the New Testament* (Leiden: Brill, 1985), 96.

7. The Greek *kynarion*, a diminutive form of *kyōn*, denotes a household pet, a "little dog," not a loose-running, scavenging street dog.

wear sheep's wool; this would be a "funny but false appearance."[8] Yet false prophets are pictured as being that deceptive (Matt. 7:15). A "blind guide," a comical idea, is no guide at all (Matt. 15:14; 23:24). And who would wash only the outside of dishes and not the inside (Luke 11:39)? It is comical, though tragic, to think of teachers of the law and Pharisees compared to whitewashed tombs (Matt. 23:27–28).

Humor, the use of the unexpected and the extreme, made Jesus' denunciations more stabbing and more unforgettable. Calling Herod a fox (a figure of speech known as a hypocatastasis, as discussed in chapter 12) may have led the disciples to chuckle as they pictured Herod as a treacherous fox (Luke 13:32).[9]

Enigmas

Good teachers, instead of always telling their learners what to know, often encourage them to think. This can be done by questions students are led to answer, problems they are encouraged to solve, enigmas they are prompted to evaluate.

Jesus sometimes spoke in obscure fashion. Was this because he was not being clear? No, it was because he voiced such statements purposely as a way of fostering learning. As you read the following puzzling sentences, think how they would have led Jesus' hearers to think, reflect, and learn.

"Let the dead bury the dead" (Matt. 8:22). This is also a pun (see chap. 12).

"I did not come to bring peace, but a sword" (Matt. 10:34).

"From the days of John the Baptist until now, the kingdom of heaven has been forcefully advancing, and forceful men lay hold of it" (Matt. 11:12).

"But I tell you, Elijah has already come, and they did not recognize him, but have done to him everything they wished" (Matt. 17:12).

"For some are eunuchs because they were born that way; others were made that way by men; others have renounced marriage because of the kingdom of heaven" (Matt. 19:12).

8. Jonsson, *Humour and Irony in the New Testament*, 187.

9. Two articles on Jesus' humor that appeared in the early years of this century are Shepherd Knapp, "Traces of Humor in the Sayings of Jesus," *Biblical World* 29 (1907): 201–7, and M. C. Hazard, "Humor in the Bible," *Biblical World* 53 (1919): 514–19.

"Wherever there is a carcass, there the vultures will gather" (Matt. 24:28).

"Whoever has will be given more; whoever does not have, even what he has will be taken from him" (Mark 4:25).

"Destroy this temple, and I will raise it again in three days" (John 2:19).

"I tell you the truth, no one can see the kingdom of God unless he is born again" (John 3:5).

"I am the living bread that came down from heaven. If anyone eats of this bread, he will live forever. . . . Then the Jews began to argue sharply among themselves, 'How can this man give us his flesh to eat?'" (John 6:51–52).

"Whoever eats my flesh and drinks my blood remains in me, and I in him" (John 6:56).

"'You will look for me, but you will not find me; and where I am, you cannot come.' The Jews said to one another, 'Where does this man intend to go that we cannot find him?'" (John 7:34–35).

"The Spirit gives life; the flesh counts for nothing" (John 7:63).

"When you are old you will stretch out your hands" (John 21:18).

Obviously, not many of Jesus' sayings were intentionally obscure. But when he did baffle his hearers, the conundrums were designed to induce thinking and thus to aid learning. Teachers today can benefit from occasionally using carefully worded remarks that perplex or confound, so long as the discussion does not leave the pupils dangling indefinitely with no resolutions or answers.

Maxims or Aphorisms

Jesus was a master at using maxims.[10] His epigrams were excellent, his aphorisms numerous and profound. The Gospels abound in his brief, pithy statements. Their power lies in their brevity and in their ability to invite the hearers to think. Their terseness make them lodge in the

10. "Maxims," "aphorisms," "epigrams," and "adages," though having some shades of difference in meaning, all refer to concise, witty statements of principles or truths. *Chreia* is another term for maxims, first used in Greek literature to refer to the philosophers' wit. For information on *chreia* see Vernon K. Robbins, "The Chreia," in *Greco-Roman Literature and the New Testament*, ed. David E. Aune (Atlanta: Scholars, 1988); *Dictionary of Jesus and the Gospels*, 1992 ed., s.v. "Chreia/Aphorism," by D. F. Watson, 104–6; and James R. Butts, "The Chreia in the Synoptic Gospels," *Biblical Theology Bulletin* 16 (October 1986): 132–38.

mind, "refusing to be forgotten, even when the mind would willingly forget" them.[11]

Aphorisms are sometimes called proverbs because of their similarities. Both are brief statements that compress or crystallize a thought in a pithy, easy-to-remember fashion. They differ, however, in that proverbs relay "collective wisdom," are "popular" in origin,[12] serving as the "voice" of a culture's traditions, whereas aphorisms or maxims "are the product of an 'individual voice,' fresh creations which express the particular way of seeing of the speaker."[13] Not every pointed statement is a proverb. Many people even today express truths in clever, compact ways but few of these comments become adages from long, accepted use by a group of people. Yet many of Jesus' aphorisms are so creative and compelling that they have become renowned around the world for centuries. A "literary proverb" is a succinct principle "expressed most frequently in a couplet of parallel lines,"[14] as in Matthew 10:24, "A student is not above his teacher, nor a servant above his master." Jesus articulated many of these.[15]

The teachers of the law in Jesus' time spoke many aphorisms,[16] but they sometimes lacked the pungent force of the Lord's words. He uttered more aphorisms than any other Bible personality, thus revealing once again his unique abilities as "a teacher who has come from God" (as Nicodemus called him, John 3:2). Scholars differ on the number of maxims Jesus spoke. Some include his beatitudes and woes, while others do not. Some include his brief commands, such as Matthew 7:1, "Do not judge, or you too will be judged," or Matthew 10:16, "Therefore be as shrewd as snakes and as innocent as doves." I do not consider these as aphorisms, though they have become adages by their long, familiar usage since Jesus spoke them. Nor should we include Jesus' words to particular individuals, such as his statement to Peter, "Unless I wash you, you have no part of me" (John 13:8), or to Thomas, "Stop doubting and believe" (20:27). Aphorisms are more universal in nature, affirming principles applicable to many persons.

Some of Jesus' aphorisms state the obvious, but they are memorable

11. William Barclay, *The Mind of Jesus* (New York: Harper and Brothers, 1961), 92.

12. Leo G. Perdue, "The Wisdom Sayings of Jesus," *Foundations and Facets Forum* 2 (September 1986): 6.

13. *Anchor Bible Dictionary*, 1992, s.v. "The Teaching of Jesus Christ," by Marcus J. Borg, 3:807; cf. John Dominic Crossan, *In Fragments: The Aphorisms of Jesus* (San Francisco: Harper and Row, 1983), 20.

14. Perdue, "The Wisdom Sayings of Jesus," 7.

15. These two-line couplets are discussed later in this chapter under "Poetry."

16. See *Pirke Aboth: Sayings of the Fathers*, ed. R. Travers Herford (New York: Shocken, 1962).

because of the fresh way the truth is stated and the way the statements are applied. The truism, "No one can serve two masters" (Matt. 6:24), was applied to the question of serving God or money. The statement, "If a blind man leads a blind man, both will fall into a pit" (Matt. 15:14),[17] was directed to the Pharisees. It pointed up the dire consequences of following those who were inept leaders because of their spiritual blindness.

Other aphorisms state the unexpected, as in Matthew 10:39: "Whoever finds his life will lose it, and whoever loses his life for my sake will find it" (cf. 16:25; Mark 8:35; Luke 9:24; 17:33; John 12:25). Aphorisms in this category pronounce surprising reversals of what is normally expected or is normally considered true.

The following verses present the Lord's aphorisms in these two categories, with thirty in each grouping.[18]

Aphorisms That State the Obvious

"If the salt loses its saltiness, how can it be made salty again?"
(Matt. 5:13; Mark 9:50; Luke 14:34)

"A city on a hill cannot be hidden" (Matt. 5:14)

"Neither do people light a lamp and put it under a bowl. Instead they put it on its stand, and it gives light to everyone in the house" (Matt. 5:15; Mark 4:21; Luke 11:33)

"The eye is the lamp of the body" (Matt. 6:22; Luke 11:34)

"No one can serve two masters" (Matt. 6:24)

"Who of you by worrying can add a single hour to his life?"
(Matt. 6:27; Luke 12:25)

"Tomorrow will worry about itself.
Each day has enough trouble of its own"
(Matt. 6:34)

"Do people pick grapes from thornbushes, or figs from thistles?"
(Matt. 7:16; Luke 6:44)

"A good tree cannot bear bad fruit" (Matt. 7:18; Luke 6:43)

---

17. Luke 6:39 words this as a question: "Can a blind man lead a blind man? Will they not both fall into a pit?" This variation from a declarative to an interrogative statement is true of several of Jesus' maxims.

18. This is less than half the number of 133 aphorisms included by Crossan (*In Fragments: The Aphorisms of Jesus*, 330–44). Many in his list are ones I exclude, as stated earlier, such as Jesus' beatitudes and commands. Still others I include are poetical statements. See the Appendix for a list of Jesus' numerous commands and directives.

"It is not the healthy who need a doctor, but the sick"
   (Matt. 9:12; Mark 2:17)

"How can the guest of the bridegroom mourn while he is with them?"
   (Matt. 9:15; Mark 2:19; Luke 5:34)

"No one sews a patch of unshrunk cloth on an old garment, for the
   patch will pull away from the garment, making the tear worse"
   (Matt. 9:16; Mark 2:21; Luke 5:36)

"Neither do men pour new wine into old wineskins.
   If they do, the skins will burst, the wine will run out
   and the wineskins will be ruined"
   (Matt. 9:17; Mark 2:22; Luke 5:37)

"The worker is worth his keep" (Matt. 10:10; cf. Luke 10:7)[19]

"A student is not above his teacher, nor a servant above his master"
   (Matt. 10:24; Luke 6:40; John 13:16; 15:20)

"Are not two sparrows sold for a penny?"
   (Matt. 10:29; cf. Luke 12:6: "Are not five sparrows sold for two
   pennies?")

"How can anyone enter a strong man's house and carry off his
   possessions unless he first ties up the strong man?"
   (Matt. 12:29; Mark 3:27;[20] Luke 11:22)

"A tree is recognized by its fruit" (Matt. 12:33; Luke 6:44)

"If a blind man leads a blind man, both will fall into a pit"
   (Matt. 15:14; Luke 6:39)

"With God all things are possible"
   (Matt. 19:26; Mark 10:27; Luke 18:27)

"Wherever there is a carcass, there the vultures will gather"
   (Matt. 24:28; Luke 17:37)

"Now learn this lesson from the fig tree: As soon as its twigs get tender and its leaves come out, you know that summer is near"
   (Matt. 24:32; Mark 13:28)

19. Luke 10:7 reads differently: "the worker deserves his wages," though the idea is
parallel. Also, this statement was spoken on different occasions: first to the Twelve (Matt.
10:10) and then to the seventy-two (Luke 10:7). Also see Matthew 23:12; Luke 14:11;
18:14.
   20. What is recorded as a question in Matthew is a statement in Mark 3:27, and a
statement in Luke 11:22. This kind of variation in Jesus' aphorisms occurs frequently.

"Now a slave has no permanent place in the family,
   but a son belongs to it forever" (John 8:36)

"Are there not twelve hours of daylight? A man who walks by day
   will not stumble, for he sees by this world's light. It is when he
   walks by night that he stumbles, for he has no light." (John 11:9–
   10)

"Unless a kernel of wheat falls to the ground and dies, it remains only
   a single seed. But if it dies, it produces many seeds."
   (John 12:24)

"The man who walks in the dark does not know where he is going"
   (John 12:35)

"A person who has had a bath needs only to wash his feet;
   his whole body is clean" (John 13:10)

"A servant does not know his master's business" (John 15:15)

"A woman giving birth to a child has pain because her time has come;
   but when her baby is born she forgets the anguish because of her
   joy that a child is born into the world" (John 16:21)

For an interesting study, read the context of each of these aphorisms
to see how Jesus applied the obvious to his hearers. For example, when
he said, "A city on a hill cannot be hidden" (Matt. 5:14), he affirmed the
important truth that his followers were to so live that others would see
their good conduct and glorify God (5:16). People should be able to
view the Christ-like behavior of believers as readily as they see a city
on a hill.

Aphorisms That State the Unexpected

"You are the salt of the earth" (Matt. 5:13)

"You are the light of the world" (Matt. 5:14)

"For where your treasure is, there your heart will be also"
   (Matt. 6:21; Luke 12:34)

"With the measure you use, it will be measured to you"
   (Matt. 7:2; Mark 4:24; Luke 6:38c)

"For I have not come to call the righteous, but sinners"
   (Matt. 9:13; Mark 2:17; Luke 5:32)

"There is nothing concealed that will not be disclosed, or hidden that
will not be made known"
(Matt. 10:26; Mark 4:22; Luke 8:17; 12:2)[21]

"And even the very hairs of your head are all numbered"
(Matt. 10:30; Luke 12:7)

"Whoever finds his life will lose it,
and whoever loses his life for my sake will find it"
(Matt. 10:39; 16:25; Mark 8:35; Luke 9:24; 17:33; John 12:25)

"Wisdom is proved right by her actions"
(Matt. 11:19; cf. Luke 7:35: "Wisdom is proved right by all her
children")

"For the Son of Man is lord of the Sabbath"
(Matt. 12:8; Mark 2:27; Luke 6:5)

"Every kingdom divided against itself will be ruined"
(Matt. 12:25a; Mark 3:24; Luke 11:17a)

"Every city or household divided against itself will not stand"
(Matt. 12:25b; Mark 3:25; Luke 11:17b)

"He who is not with me is against me,
and he who does not gather with me scatters"
(Matt. 12:30; Mark 9:40; Luke 11:23)

"Out of the overflow of the heart the mouth speaks"
(Matt. 12:34; Luke 6:45)

"Only in his home town and in his own house is a prophet without
honor" (Matt. 13:57; Mark 6:4; Luke 4:24; cf. John 4:44)

"But the things that come out of the mouth come from the heart,
and these make a man unclean"
(Matt. 15:18; Mark 7:15)

"What good will it be for a man if he gains the whole world,
yet forfeits his soul?"
(Matt. 16:26a; Mark 8:36; Luke 9:25)

"What can a man give in exchange for his soul?"
(Matt. 16:26b; Mark 8:37)

21. Some of Jesus' statements were spoken on more than one occasion, as evidenced
by this aphorism recorded in two places in Luke. The same is true of the statement in
both Matthew 10:39 and 16:25 and their parallels. This may also have been true of some
of his statements in the Sermon on the Mount.

"It is easier for a camel to go through the eye of a needle
than for a rich man to enter the kingdom of heaven"
(Matt. 19:24; Mark 10:25; Luke 18:25)

"Many who are first will be last,
and many who are last will be first"
(Matt. 19:30; Mark 10:31)

"The last will be first, and the first will be last"
(Matt. 20:16; Luke 13:30)

"Whoever wants to become great among you must be your servant,
and whoever wants to be first must be your slave"
(Matt. 20:26–27; Mark 10:43–44; Luke 22:26)

"For many are invited, but few are chosen"
(Matt. 22:14)

"For whoever exalts himself will be humbled,
and whoever humbles himself will be exalted "
(Matt 23:12; Luke 14:11; 18:14)

"For everyone who has will be given more,
and he will have an abundance—whoever does not have,
even what he has will be taken from him"
(Matt. 25:29; Luke 8:18)

"The spirit is willing, but the body is weak"
(Matt. 26:41; Mark 14:38)

"All who draw the sword will die by the sword"
(Matt. 26:52)

"Whoever can be trusted with very little can also be trusted with
much, and whoever is dishonest with very little will also be dishonest with much" (Luke 16:10)

"What is highly valued among men is detestable in God's sight"
(Luke 16:15)

"Everyone who sins is a slave to sin"
(John 8:34)

In addition to these many creative aphorisms Jesus quoted at least
four other common maxims: "Only in his hometown and in his own
house is a prophet without honor" (Matt. 13:57; Mark 6:4; Luke 4:24;
John 4:44). "Surely you will quote this proverb to me: 'Physician, heal
yourself'" (Luke 4:23). "Do you not say, 'Four months and then the har-

vest'?" (John 4:35). "Thus the saying 'One sows and another reaps' is true" (John 4:37).

As you read each of these unusual aphorisms, think how the original listeners would have been jolted by what they heard.

Repetition

Repetition, rightly used, can be an effective teaching tool by helping clinch the truth in the students' minds and hearts. Some things bear repeating!

Jesus engaged his hearers by this means also.

Nine times in Matthew he said, "Blessed are . . . " (5:3–11). "You have heard . . . but I tell you" repeatedly pointed to his authority over Pharisaic traditions (5:21–22, 27–28, 31–32, 33–34, 38–39, 43–44). "Do not worry" is stated three times in a short span (6:25, 31, 34), as are the words, "Do not be afraid" (10:26, 28, 31). Three times Jesus began clauses with the words "Anyone who" (10:37–38). Speaking of John the Baptist, three times Jesus asked, "What did you go out to see?" (11:7–9). For Jesus to ask the Pharisees "Haven't you read?" would have put them on the spot, but starting another question with those same words would have compounded their embarrassment (12:3, 5).

Five times in one chapter and three in another Jesus said, "I tell you" (18:3, 10, 18–19, 22; 26:21, 29, 34). In his denunciations of the Pharisees' hypocrisy Jesus said "Woe to you" seven times (23:13, 15–16, 23, 25, 27, 29). Imagine the sledgehammer effect of five times calling them "blind" (23:16–17, 19, 24, 26) and six times dubbing them hypocrites (23:13, 15, 23, 27, 29). First he spoke of the right eye causing a person to sin (5:29) and then he referred to the right hand causing one to sin (5:30). This reiteration added force to his point. The same tone of Jesus' words is in 10:37–38: "Anyone who loves his father or mother more than me . . ." and "Anyone who loves his son or daughter more than me. . . ."

To emphasize the difficulty many wealthy people have in sensing any need for salvation, Jesus said twice, "How hard it is for the rich to enter the kingdom of God" (Mark 10:23–24). After each of three similarly worded rhetorical questions, Jesus answered with sentences that begin with "Even 'sinners' . . ." (Luke 6:32–34). Note the repeated pattern in Luke 13:2–5: "Do you think . . .?" and "I tell you, no!"

Three times, as recorded in the Gospel of Mark, Jesus predicted his coming suffering and death, and resurrection: Mark 8:31; 9:31; 10:33–34.

In his discourse on himself as the Bread of life, the Lord repeatedly spoke of his having come "down from heaven" (John 6:33, 38, 41, 50,

51, 58). How could the Jews possibly have missed this sure affirmation of his heavenly origin and deity? In the same discourse the resurrection of believing dead is referred to four times (6:39–40, 44, 54), "believes" is mentioned three times (6:35, 40, 47), and the words "bread from heaven" were on Jesus' lips five times (6:31–33, 50, 51).

Note also Jesus' twice-repeated statements, "I am the gate" (John 10:7, 9) and "I am the good shepherd" (10:11, 14), and the fivefold repetition about his laying down his life for his sheep (10:11, 15, 17–18). Repetition also abounds in John 15 as he spoke of "fruit," "remaining," "love," and "hate."

Logical Reasoning

Teaching involves helping students to think—and to think logically and accurately. Jesus met this standard too by his careful employment of a number of reasoning processes or kinds of argument.

One of the most common forms of argumentation he used is *a fortiori*, which reasons from the lesser to the greater.[22] "The conclusion follows with even greater logical necessity than the already accepted fact or conclusion previously given."[23]

Jesus told his audience to look at the birds, which are fed by God, even though they do not farm. Based on that fact he asked, "Are you not much more valuable than they?" (Matt. 6:26; Luke 12:24), thereby implying that God would certainly care for them. Similarly, since God cares for sparrows, controlling even the timing of their death (first point), he will surely care for his disciples because they are of much greater value (second, more certain point; Matt. 10:29–30).

Since God "clothes" the grass of the field (first conclusion), how much more will he "clothe" believers (second conclusion, more certain than the first; Matt. 6:30; Luke 12:28). Parents, being "evil," give good gifts to their children (first fact), and therefore God will give gifts to his followers (second fact, more certain; Matt. 7:11; Luke 11:13).

Luke 12:25–26 records another of Jesus' *a fortiori* arguments in the Sermon on the Mount. Worrying cannot extend a person's life (a "very little thing"), and therefore worrying about food and clothing is even more needless.

"If the head of the household has been called Beelzebub, how much

22. Rabbi Hillel (30 b.c.–a.d. 9) called this form of argument *qal wahomer*, "light and heavy."
23. Robert H. Stein, *The Method and Message of Jesus' Teachings* (Philadelphia: Westminster, 1978), 20.

more the members of his household" (Matt. 10:25). Comparing himself to a household head, Jesus spoke of his being persecuted (Beelzebub being a name for Satan; cf. Matt. 12:24), and therefore his disciples, "members of his household," will certainly also be persecuted by religious and political authorities (10:17–18).

In eating bread from the tabernacle David and his companions did something specially forbidden by the law, and yet God did not rebuke them (first fact). Jesus, being much greater than David (in fact, being "the Lord of the Sabbath"), has an even greater right to pick heads of grain on the Sabbath with his disciples, without being rebuked (Matt. 12:1–8; Mark 2:23–28; Luke 6:1–8).

Another form of reasoning Jesus used is called *reductio ad absurdum*, an argument that reduces a person's view to its absurd logical outcome.

Jesus' Sermon on the Mount listeners would not have wanted to be associated with tax collectors and rogues, and yet, as Jesus argued, loving only those who loved them and greeting only their brothers places them in the same category with those sinners. Since this was an undesirable association, the hearers were introduced to the absurdity of their practice (Matt. 5:46–47).

Jesus' contemporaries were inconsistent in rejecting John the Baptist's asceticism (Matt. 11:18) while at the same time rejecting Jesus because he was gregarious (11:19). They were as self-contradictory as children first playing a dance tune on a flute and then singing a funeral dirge (11:15–17; Luke 7:31–34).

When the Pharisees and teachers of the law dared to accuse Jesus of driving out demons by the power of Beelzebub, he showed the absurdity of such a position. This would mean, he argued, that Satan would be driving out his own cohorts, thus being "divided against himself" and causing his own kingdom to fall (Matt. 12:24–26; Mark 3:22–26; Luke 11:15–18). Some of the religious leaders' own people had cast out demons, and by another question Jesus again demonstrated the absurdity of their accusation: if they said Jesus cast out demons by Satan's power, they would have to say the same thing of their "sons," that is, their own companions, some of whom were exorcists (Matt. 12:27; Luke 11:19). When Jesus added, "So, then, they will be your judges," he meant, "Your own sons will prove you wrong!" They would be able to testify to the fact that casting out demons was not a work of Satan.[24] By powerful argumentation, the Lord cleverly illustrated how absurd was their charge against him—a charge they obviously had failed to think through.

24. Leon Morris, *The Gospel according to Matthew* (Grand Rapids: Eerdmans, 1992), 316.

Even when on trial before Annas the high priest, Jesus used a reductio ad absurdum argument. When an official struck Jesus, the Lord said that if he had done something wrong, the official should tell him what it was. "But if I spoke the truth, why did you strike me?" (John 18:23). It was absurd for the official who struck Jesus on the face to accuse him of saying something wrong without specifying what it was, or to strike him if the Lord had spoken the truth. This put the man in a dilemma, in which both reactions—not saying what Jesus said wrong, and hitting Jesus—were shown up as ridiculous.

A third kind of reasoning technique Jesus employed in defending himself against his opponents was *argumentum ad hominem*, appealing to a person's feelings or prejudices, or attacking the person rather than his arguments as such. Jesus signaled the Pharisees' supposed ignorance of the law when he asked, "Haven't you read . . .?" what the Old Testament says about David (Matt. 12:3; 19:4). Such a rebuke would have chagrined his opponents, silencing their efforts to find fault in his actions or words. His many denunciations against the teachers of the law and the Pharisees were ad hominem arguments, in which he repeatedly attacked their hypocrisy (Matt. 23:13–36). Jesus unveiled the prejudice of these same religious leaders when they brought him a woman caught in adultery, and tried to trap him by their question. How clever of him to say, "If any one of you is without sin, let him be the first to throw a stone at her" (John 8:7). This put them on the defensive, thus spoiling their offensive effort against Jesus, and they all left, sullen and silenced (8:9)!

The law of the *excluded middle* is a form of reasoning in which the debater shows that only two opposites exist in a given situation. Since no middle ground is possible, one of the two positions must be accepted. "He who is not with me is against me, and he who does not gather with me scatters" (Matt. 12:30; Luke 11:23). Jesus put the chief priests and elders on the horns of a dilemma by the excluded middle: "John's baptism—where did it come from? Was it from heaven, or from men?" (Matt. 21:25; Mark 11:30; Luke 20:4). Either way they answered they would be trapped. They had attempted to trap him by asking him the source of his authority, and in quick wit he turned the tables on them by trapping them. Not wanting to make a choice (for by either answer they would indict themselves), they responded, "We don't know" (Matt. 21:25–27; Mark 11:31–33; Luke 20:5–7).

In the law of *noncontradiction* a person forces another to respond with a yes or no answer, thereby challenging the opponent to accept the person's view. "Can a blind man lead a blind man?" Jesus asked (Luke 6:39). The only possible answer is no; it cannot be contradicted. This then helped Jesus' followers see the danger of following unqualified leaders. Notice how Jesus forced his hearers to accept his points by the following questions that used the law of noncontradiction. "Suppose one of you wants to build a tower. Will he not first sit down and estimate the cost to see if he has enough money to complete it?" (Luke 14:28). "Suppose one of you has a hundred sheep and loses one of them. Does he not leave the ninety-nine in the open country and go after the lost sheep until he finds it?" (Luke 15:4). "Suppose one of you had a servant plowing or looking after the sheep. Would he say to the servant when he comes in from the field, 'Come along now and sit down to eat?' Would he not rather say, 'Prepare my supper, get yourself ready and wait on me while I eat and drink; after that you may eat and drink'? Would he thank the servant because he did what he was told to do?" (Luke 17:7–9). What was Jesus seeking to teach in each of these passages?

Jesus often gave an *analogy* to communicate a message. He reasoned from one familiar or already accepted fact so that his audience would accept another, analogous truth. As one is true, so is the other. In Jonah's time the belly of a large fish pictures Jesus' burial (Matt. 12:40; Luke 11:30), and the sudden destruction of many and the rescue of a few in the flood in Noah's day portrays a similar judgment and rescue when Jesus returns to earth (Matt. 24:37–41). The "as . . . so" pattern in analogies is also seen in John 15:9, "As the Father has loved me, so have I loved you." Jesus' love for his own stands analogous to the Father's love for him.

Do you want to try to match these reasoning techniques? Look up these six references and decide which form of logic Jesus utilized in each one.

a. A fortiori	_____ John 7:23
b. Reductio ad absurdum	_____ Mark 3:4
c. Argumentum ad hominem	_____ Matthew 12:11–12
d. Law of the excluded middle	_____ Matthew 13:40
e. Law of noncontradiction	_____ Luke 14:31
f. Analogy	_____ Matthew 23:15

(After you have done this exercise—not before!—check your answers with those at the end of the chapter.)

Contrasts

Drawing attention to an object's opposite helps highlight the characteristics of both. We speak of two people being "as different as night and day." We contrast the size of two items by likening them to a small mouse and a huge elephant. Clean and dirty, good and evil, beautiful and ugly, rich and poor, healthy and sick, hot and cold, freezing and melting, bright and dull, true and false, old and young, energetic and tired, intelligent and ignorant, whispering and shouting, sharp and dull—these are only a few of the many opposites we experience and speak of.

"In contrast each idea or person is given prominence, interest is quickened, there is a great appeal to the imagination, and therefore teaching is made more effective."[25]

Readers of the Gospels cannot help but be struck with amazement at the dozens of contrasts Jesus utilized in his teaching—opposites that made his instructions memorable.

As we noted in the section "Repetition," Jesus repeated several contrasts in his Sermon on the Mount by saying, "You have heard . . . but I tell you . . ." (Matt. 5:21–22; 27–28; 31–32; 33–34; 38–39, 43–44). Such contrasts no doubt constituted one reason the people were amazed that his teaching differed from that of the teachers of the law—a contrast they noted (Matt. 7:28–29)!

Contrasts between Jesus' followers and the hypocritical religious leaders are seen in their giving (Matt. 6:2–3), praying (6:5–6), and fasting (6:16–17). Forgiving and not forgiving (6:14–15), storing up treasure in heaven and not on earth (6:19–20), serving God and not money (6:24), being overly concerned for material needs and not trusting God to provide (6:32–33), giving bread and fish rather than a stone or a snake (7:9–10), entering heaven by the narrow gate and not the wide gate (7:13–16), and building a house on a foundation of rock and not sand (7:24–27) are among the many contrasts in Matthew 6 and 7.

The Pharisees and Sadducees' knowledge of the weather contrasts with their lack of spiritual knowledge (16:2–3). The teachers of the law and the Pharisees burden others down with details of lawkeeping but then, in contrast, do nothing to help them (23:4). Other contrasts in their conduct are seen in 23:23–24 (emphasizing the insignificant while neglecting the important matters, pictured by the opposite action of straining out a gnat but swallowing a camel), 23:25 (having clean dishes but being spiritually unclean), and 23:27 (outwardly attractive like whitewashed tombs, but inwardly repulsive). While they justify themselves before people, God knows their hearts, and what people value God does not (Luke 15:15). Good people speak good things but evil people speak evil things (Matt. 12:35). The words of the Pharisees would either acquit them, or by contrast, condemn them (12:37).

25. Claude E. Jones, *The Teaching Method of the Master* (St. Louis: Bethany, 1957), 28.

The Lord also pointed to several contrasts in his own ministry and role. Foxes and birds have lodging places, but he did not (Luke 9:58); he came not to be served, but to serve (Matt 20:28; Mark 10:45).

Contrast also dramatized the disciples' role. They were to pray because of the contrast between the small number of workers and the vast extent of the spiritual harvest (Matt. 9:37–38). What Jesus told them in secret they were to proclaim publicly (10:27). Some will acknowledge the Lord before others but others will not (10:32–33). Finding or saving one's life has consequences differing from losing one's life (10:39; 16:25). Their faith may be small, but it can effect great changes, contrasted like a mustard seed and a mountain (17:20–21). Several times Jesus differentiated between humility and greatness (18:4; 19:30; 20:16; 23:11–12).

Often contrasts showed up in Jesus' conversations. The widow's extreme sacrifice contradicted the comparatively meager sacrifice of other worshipers (Mark 12:43; Luke 21:2). Though Peter rebuked Jesus, Jesus by contrast rebuked Peter (Mark 8:32–33). The faithful and unfaithful servants suffer contrasting consequences (Matt. 25:45–46). A servant's ignorance contrasts with his master's knowledge (John 14:15). In childbirth a woman experiences great pain, but after the birth she feels great joy (15:21).

Many of Jesus' parables build on the principle of contrast: The two sons, one of whom said he would not work in the vineyard but did, and the other who said he would but did not (Matt. 21:28–32); the five foolish virgins and the five wise virgins (25:1–13); the sheep and the goats in the judgment of the Gentiles (25:33–40); the priest and the Levite who did not help an injured man and the good Samaritan who did (Luke 10:25–37); the one lost sheep in contrast to the ninety-nine other sheep (15:3–7); the one lost coin and the other nine (15:8–10); the one lost son and the elder brother (15:11–32); and the proud Pharisee in contrast to the humble, repentant tax collector (18:9–14).

What contrasts do you see in these verses, and what was Jesus teaching by means of them: Mark 2:27; Matthew 20:11, 14; John 1:5; 3:17, 18, 20–21; 8:12?

Another form of contrast is Jesus' "better" and "easier" sayings. It is better to drown than to cause a small child to sin (Matt. 18:6; Mark 9:42; Luke 17:2). It is better to be crippled or blind in one eye and go to heaven than to have both hands, feet, and eyes and go to hell (Matt. 18:8–9; Mark 9:43, 45, 47). Giving is better than receiving, Jesus said, as reported by Paul (Acts 20:35). It is easier for a camel to go through a needle's eye than for a rich person to be saved (Matt. 19:24; Mark 10:23; Luke 18:25). It is easier for heaven and earth to pass away than for any portion of the law to be lost (Luke 16:17). The points these sayings are making are these: Do not mislead little children; deal with sin in one's own life as drastically as necessary; be generous; do not trust in wealth; recognize the permanence of God's Word.

Examples and Explanations

Speaking a generalization without a specific example often leaves a student either bewildered or unchallenged. But add a tangible example and the issue comes clear. A challenging exercise would be to read the Gospels and to note all of Jesus' specific examples that follow his general assertions. These are a few examples:

General: Being angry submits a person to judgment. Specific: Do not in anger call a person "Raca," fool (Matt. 5:22).

General: Instead of retaliating against an evil person, do not resist him. Specific: "If someone strikes you on the right cheek, turn to him the other also" (5:39). Jesus suggested additional examples of this principle in 5:40–42.

General: Do not be ostentatious in your righteous acts. Specific examples: almsgiving, praying, and fasting (6:1–18).

General: Do not worry that God will not care for you. Specific examples: Birds, lilies, and grass (Matt. 6:25–31).

General: When Jesus returns to earth, unregenerate people will be taken into judgment quickly. Specific: One of two men will be working in a field, and one of two women will be grinding at a hand mill (24:30–41).

Jesus often specified reasons for his commands or actions. His explanations helped communicate his truths. This is seen in the frequent occurrence of the word *because* in Jesus' words or in the narratives explaining what Jesus did. Completing the following chart from references in Mark demonstrates the effectiveness of Jesus' explanations.

Reference	The Fact	The Explanation
Mark 1:22	The people were amazed at Jesus' teaching.	Why? Because he taught as one who had authority.
2:4		
3:9		
6:31		
6:34		
10:5		

```
10:18
12:34
13:13
13:18
13:19
13:35
```

To teach with clarity and impact, you need examples and explanations. The concrete models the abstract, while explanations help make principles intelligible and cogent.

Poetry

Jesus distinguished his teaching by the use of poetic sayings. Because of his Jewish descent and upbringing, he often cast his sayings in the form of Hebrew poetry.

Such poetry seldom possesses rhyme, as does English poetry. Instead its major characteristic is parallelism, in which lines of poetry stand in parallel relationship to each other. These may be either synonymous (or comparison), antithetical (or contrast), synthetic (or completion), or stairstep.[26] These forms add to the pleasing charm of Jesus' words. "The survival of his very words is due not only to their inherent truth, but also to their poetic beauty."[27]

In *synonymous (or comparison) parallelism* the second line repeats the thought of the first line with some of the words being different. This form, common in Old Testament poetry, was frequently on Jesus' lips. The repetition in the second line furnishes a special way of adding emphasis to the first line and yet it does so with refreshing variety. As with aphorisms, brevity is a characterizing mark of Jesus' poetry.[28]

---

26. The first three were first suggested by Robert Lowth (*Lectures on the Sacred Poetry of the Hebrews*, trans. G. Gregory [1787; reprint, Hildesheim: Olms, 1969]). C. F. Burney examined these forms in Jesus' discourses (*The Poetry of Our Lord* [Oxford: Clarendon, 1925]). Others have followed Burney in noting the poetic style of our Lord's teaching (e.g., Joachim Jeremias, *New Testament Theology* [New York: Scribner's Sons, 1971]; and Stein, *The Method and Message of Jesus' Teachings*).

27. Hermon Harrell Horne, *Jesus—Our Standard* (New York: Abingdon, 1918), 201.

28. For this reason I exclude some verses that others include in their lists of poetic parallels in the Gospels. Burney, for example, includes well over one hundred examples, and Jeremias lists 138 examples of antithetical parallelism in Matthew, Mark, and Luke. Mary Lucetta Mowry, on the other hand, finds only twenty maxims of Jesus in the Synoptics that she feels should be called poetry ("Poetry in the Synoptic Gospels and Revelation: A Study of Methods and Materials" [Ph.D. diss., Yale University, 1946]).

"Do not give dogs what is sacred;
  do not throw your pearls to pigs" (Matt. 7:6)

Note the repetition of "do not," and the parallel words *give* and *throw*, *dogs* and *pigs*, and *what is sacred* and *pearls*. This provides a nice sample of synonymous parallelism, in which some words are the same and other words are synonymous.

"A student is not above his teacher, nor a servant above his master"
  (10:24)

"There is nothing concealed that will not be disclosed,
  or hidden that will not be made known"
  (10:26; Mark 4:22; Luke 8:17; 12:2)

Sometimes not every part in the first clause has an exact parallel in the second part. In this case the parallelism is called incomplete. In Matthew 10:26 the words "there is nothing" are not repeated in any way in the second clause.

"What I tell you in the dark, speak in the daylight;
  what is whispered in your ear, proclaim from the roofs" (Matt. 10:27)

"Anyone who receives a prophet because he is a prophet
  will receive a prophet's reward,
and anyone who receives a righteous man because he is a righteous man
  will receive a righteous man's reward" (10:41)

"He who is not with me is against me,
  and he who does not gather with me scatters" (12:30; Luke 11:23)

"But blessed are your eyes because they see,
  and your ears because they hear" (Matt. 13:16)

"You build tombs for the prophets
  and decorate the graves of the righteous" (23:29)

"Which is lawful on the Sabbath: to do good or to do evil,
  to save life or to kill?" (Mark 3:4)

"If a kingdom is divided against itself,
  that kingdom cannot stand.
If a house is divided against itself,
  that house cannot stand" (3:24–25)

"What shall we say the kingdom of God is like,
   or what parable shall we use to describe it?" (4:30)

"Do you have eyes but fail to see,
   and ears but fail to hear?" (8:18)

"Can you drink the cup I drink
   or be baptized with the baptism I am baptized with?" (10:38)

"You will drink the cup I drink
   and be baptized with the baptism I am baptized with" (10:39)

"Whoever wants to become great among you must be your servant,
   and whoever wants to be first must be slave of all" (10:43–44)

"Love your enemies,
   do good to those who hate you" (Luke 6:27)

"People do not pick figs from thornbushes,
   or grapes from briers" (6:44)

"What you have said in the dark will be heard in the daylight,
   and what you have whispered in the ear in the inner rooms
     will be proclaimed from the roofs" (12:3)

"Life is more than food,
   and the body more than clothes" (12:23)

"From everyone who has been given much, much will be demanded;
   and from the one who has been entrusted with much,
     much more will be asked" (12:48)

"This brother of yours was dead and is alive again;
   he was lost and is found" (15:32)

"Why are you troubled,
   and why do doubts rise in your minds?" (24:38)

"He who comes to me will never go hungry,
   and he who believes in me will never be thirsty" (John 6:35)

"For my flesh is real food
   and my blood is real drink" (6:55)

"No servant is greater than his master,
    nor is a messenger greater than the one who sent him" (13:16)[29]

"Peace I leave with you;
    my peace I give you" (14:27a)

"Do not let your hearts be troubled
    and do not be afraid" (14:27b)

"I am returning to my Father and your Father,
    to my God and your God" (20:17)

In *antithetical (or contrast) parallelism* the second line presents a contrast to the first line. Jesus often utilized this form.[30]

"For if you forgive men when they sin against you,
    your heavenly Father will also forgive you.
But if you do not forgive men their sins,
    your Father will not forgive your sins" (Matt. 6:14–15)

"Do not store up for yourselves treasures on earth,
    where moth and rust destroy,
    and where thieves break in and steal.
But store up for yourselves treasures in heaven,
    where moth and rust do not destroy,
    and where thieves do not break in and steal" (6:19–20; Luke 12:33)

"If your eyes are good, your whole body will be full of light.
But if your eyes are bad, your whole body will be full of darkness"
    (Matt. 6:22–23; Luke 11:34)

"Either he will hate the one and love the other,
    or he will be devoted to the one and despise the other" (Matt. 6:24)

"For wide is the gate and broad is the road that leads to destruction,
    and many enter through it.
But small is the gate and narrow the road that leads to life,
    and only a few find it" (7:13–14; Luke 13:24)

"Likewise every good tree bears good fruit,
    but a bad tree bears bad fruit" (Matt. 7:17)

29. Some Bible scholars also include Matthew 5:38–39, 40–47; Mark 2:21–22; 9:43–47; and Luke 6:29–30 as verses with synonymous parallelism. However, each of these references may be a case in which Jesus cited two similar situations, using similar wording.
   30. The following examples are adopted from Burney, *The Poetry of Our Lord*, 71–81.

"A good tree cannot bear bad fruit,
   and a bad tree cannot bear good fruit" (7:18; Luke 6:43)[31]

"It is not the healthy who need a doctor, but the sick"
   (Matt. 9:12; Mark 2:12)

"Whoever acknowledges me before men,
   I will also acknowledge him before my Father in heaven.
But whoever disowns me before men,
   I will disown him before my Father in heaven"
   (Matt. 10:32–33; Luke 12:8)

"Many who are first will be last,
   and many who are last will be first" (Matt. 19:30; Mark 10:31)

"So the last will be first,
   and the first will be last" (Matt. 20:16)

"For many are invited,
   but few are chosen" (22:14)

"For whoever exalts himself will be humbled,
   and whoever humbles himself will be exalted"
   (23:12; Luke 14:11; 18:14)

"You are like whitewashed tombs, which look beautiful on the outside
   but on the inside are full of dead men's bones and everything unclean"
   (Matt. 23:27)

"On the outside you appear to people as righteous
   but on the inside you are full of hypocrisy and wickedness" (23:28)

"You give a tenth of your spices—mint, dill and cummin.
But you have neglected the more important matters of the law—
   justice, mercy and faithfulness" (23:23)

"Heaven and earth will pass away,
   but my words will never pass away" (24:35; Mark 13:31; Luke 21:33)

"For everyone who has will be given more,
   and he will have an abundance.

31. As Stein has pointed out, Matthew 7:17 and 18 are *each* examples of antithetical parallelism and also *together* they constitute an example of such parallelism (*The Method and Message of Jesus' Teachings*, 281). Unquestionably, our Lord's ability to use this poetic style goes unmatched!

Whoever does not have,
    even what he has will be taken from him"
    (Matt. 25:29; Mark 4:25; Luke 19:26)

"Then they will go away to eternal punishment,
    but the righteous to eternal life" (Matt. 25:46)

"The poor you will always have with you,
    but you will not always have me" (26:11; Mark 14:7; John 12:8)

"The spirit is willing,
    but the body is weak" (Matt. 26:41b; Mark 14:38b)

"The Sabbath was made for man,
    not man for the Sabbath" (Mark 2:27)

"You have let go of the commands of God
    and are holding on to the traditions of men" (7:8)

"He who listens to you listens to me;
    he who rejects you rejects me" (Luke 10:16a)

"However, do not rejoice that the spirits submit to you,
    but rejoice that your names are written in heaven" (10:20)

"When your eyes are good, your whole body also is full of light.
    But when they are bad, your body also is full of darkness" (11:34)

"For everyone who exalts himself will be humbled,
    and he who humbles himself will be exalted" (14:11)

"Whoever can be trusted with very little
    can also be trusted with much,
and whoever is dishonest with very little
    will also be dishonest with much" (16:10)

"If your brother sins, rebuke him,
    and if he repents, forgive him" (17:3)

"Let the little children come to me,
    and do not hinder them" (18:16)

"To everyone who has,
    more will be given,
but as for the one who has nothing,
    even what he has will be taken away" (19:26)

"Everyone who falls on that stone will be broken to pieces,
  but he on whom it falls will be crushed" (20:18)

"Daughters of Jerusalem, do not weep for me;
  weep for yourselves and for your children" (23:28)

"Flesh gives birth to flesh,
  but the Spirit gives birth to spirit" (John 3:6)

"For God did not send his Son into the world to condemn the world,
  but to save the world through him" (3:17)

"Whoever believes in him is not condemned,
  but whoever does not believe stands condemned already" (3:18)

"The one who comes from above is above all;
  the one who is from the earth belongs to the earth" (3:31)

"Everyone who drinks this water will be thirsty again,
  but whoever drinks the water I give him will never thirst" (4:13–14)

"You Samaritans worship what you do not know;
  we worship what we do know" (4:22)

"Those who have done good will rise to live,
  and those who have done evil will rise to be condemned" (5:29)

"The right time for me has not yet come;
  for you any time is right" (7:6)

"You are from below;
  I am from above" (8:23)

"Now a slave has no permanent place in the family,
  but a son belongs to it forever" (8:35)

"The thief comes only to steal and kill and destroy;
  I have come that they might have life, and have it to the full" (10:10)

"He cuts off every branch in me that bears no fruit,
  while every branch that does bear fruit he trims clean" (15:2)

"If they persecuted me, they will persecute you also.
  If they obeyed my teaching, they will obey yours also" (15:20)

"In this world you will have trouble.
   But take heart! I have overcome the world" (16:33)[32]

Synthetic (or completion) parallelism is the poetic form in which the second line completes the thought begun in the first line. The second line often gives a reason ("for," "because," "since") for what is stated in the first line; other times the second line states a consequence or result. In other verses the first line gives a condition ("if").

"Do not be like them,
   for your Father knows what you need before you ask him"
   (Matt. 6:8—reason)

"But if you do not forgive men their sins,
   your Father will not forgive your sins" (6:15—condition)

"But you are not to be called 'Rabbi,'
   for you have only one Master and you are all brothers"
   (23:8—reason)

"And do not call anyone on earth 'father,' for you have one Father,
   and he is in heaven" (23:9—reason)

"If a man of peace is there,
   your peace will rest on him" (10:6—result)

"Stay in that house, eating and drinking whatever they give you,
   for the worker deserves his wages" (10:7—reason)

"But I have a baptism to undergo,
   and how distressed I am until it is completed!" (12:50—consequence)[33]

"I did one miracle, and you are all astonished" (John 7:21—result)

"If you knew me,
   you would know my Father also" (8:19—condition)

"If you hold to my teaching,
   you are really my disciples" (8:31—condition)

"If the Son sets you free,
   you will be free indeed" (8:36—condition)

32. Other examples might be Matthew 5:19; 6:4–5; 7:24–27; and Luke 7:44b–46.
33. Luke 12:49 and 50 stand in relation to each other in synonymous parallelism, as do Matthew 23:8 and 9.

"When he lies, he speaks his native language,
  for he is a liar, and the father of lies" (8:44—reason)

A fourth kind of parallelism is *stairstep parallelism* in which the second line repeats a part of the first line in exact wording and then advances the thought. In the following examples, the identical words repeated in the two lines are italicized.

"*He who* receives you *receives me,*
  and *he who receives me* receives the one who sent me" (Matt. 10:40)

"*Whoever* welcomes one of these little children in my name *welcomes me;*
  and *whoever welcomes me* does not welcome me
    but the one who sent me" (Mark 9:37)

"*He who* rejects you *rejects me;*
  but *he who rejects me* rejects him who sent me" (Luke 10:16)

"All that the Father gives me will *come to me,*
  and whoever *comes to me* I will never drive away" (John 6:37)

"I am *the good shepherd.*
  The good shepherd lays down his life for the sheep" (10:11)

"I am going there to *prepare a place for you.*
  And if I go and *prepare a place for you,* I will come back" (14:2b–3a)

"Whoever has my commands and obeys them, *he is the one who loves me.*
  He who loves me will be loved by my Father" (14:21a)

See how well you can identify these four kinds of poetic parallelism in Jesus' sayings by looking up each of these verses and writing after the reference either "synonymous (comparison)," "antithetical (contrast)," "synthetic (completion)," or "stairstep." Two verses are in each category.

Matthew 10:39   _____
Matthew 11:30   _____
Mark 4:25   _____
Luke 6:28   _____
Luke 10:16   _____
Luke 12:40   _____
John 8:39b   _____
John 13:20   _____

A variation of this two-line parallelism is the three-line pattern (noted by Burney),[34] in which the parallel couplet is followed by a third line that explains the couplet, develops its thought, or makes a deduction from it. In the following examples of this pattern, the italicized words identify the explanatory line.

"Make a tree good and its fruit will be good,
    or make a tree bad and its fruit will be bad,
for a tree is recognized by its fruit" (Matt. 12:33; Luke 6:43–44a)

"The good man brings good things out of the good stored up in his heart,
    and the evil man brings evil things out of the evil stored up in his heart.
For out of the overflow of his heart his mouth speaks" (Luke 6:45)

"We speak of what we know,
    and we testify to what we have seen,
but still you people do not accept our testimony" (John 3:11)

"Whoever believes in him is not condemned,
    but whoever does not believe stands condemned already
because he has not believed in the name of God's one and only son" (3:18)

"Whoever believes in the Son has eternal life,
    but whoever rejects the Son will not see life,
for God's wrath remains on him" (3:36)

"You Samaritans worship what you do not know;
    we worship what we do know,
for salvation is from the Jews" (4:22)

Two other forms of parallelism are *chiasmic parallelism* and *alternating parallelism*. A chiasm is an inverted pattern in which the first and fourth elements are similar and the second and third are similar. This is signified by A, B, B′, A′. In an alternating pattern elements one and three are similar and elements two and four are similar. This is signified as A, B, A′, B′. Sometimes in a longer passage more elements are included, so that an extended chiasm is A, B, C, C′, B′, A′, or an extended alternating pattern is A, B, C, A′, B′, C′. In the following examples of the chiastic pattern in Jesus' teaching each verse is also in antithetical (contrast) parallelism.

    A "For whoever wants to save his life
        B will lose it,

---

34. Burney, *The Poetry of Our Lord*, 96–99.

     B′ but whoever loses his life for me
A′ will find it" (Matt. 16:25; Mark 8:35; Luke 9:24; 17:33)

A "But many who are first
     B will be last,
     B′ and many who are last
A′ will be first" (Matt. 19:30; Mark 10:31; cf. 20:16)

A "For whoever exalts himself
     B will be humbled,
     B′ and whoever humbles himself
A′ will be exalted" (Matt. 23:12; Luke 14:11; 18:14)

A "The Sabbath was made
     B for man,
     B′ not man
A′ for the Sabbath" (Mark 2:27)

The following verses have *alternating patterns*. Some are also in antithetical (contrast) parallelism and some are in synonymous (comparison) parallelism. Can you determine which ones are in each of these two categories?

A "How can the guests of the bridegroom fast
     B while he is with them?
A′ They cannot [fast]
     B′ so long as they have him with them" (Mark 2:19)

A "Love your enemies,
     B do good to those who hate you,
A′ bless those who curse you,
     B′ pray for those who mistreat you" (Luke 6:27–28)

A "Do not judge
     B and you will not be judged.
A′ Do not condemn,
     B′ and you will not be condemned" (6:37)

A "You are from below;
     B I am from above.
A′ You are of this world;
     B′ I am not of this world" (John 8:23)

A longer alternating pattern is in the following passage.[35]

35. T. W. Manson called attention to this pattern in *The Teachings of Jesus* (Cambridge: Cambridge University Press, 1959), 55.

A "The Queen of the South will rise at the judgment
B with the men of this generation and condemn them,
C for she came from the ends of the earth
to listen to Solomon's wisdom,
D and now one greater than Solomon is here.
A′ The men of Nineveh will stand up at the judgment
B′ with this generation and condemn it,
C′ for they repented at the preaching of Jonah,
D′ and now one greater than Jonah is here"

(Luke 11:31–32)

No doubt Jesus used these forms of poetry to aid his hearers in re-membering what he said, as well as to challenge them to act in accord with his instructions. "By placing his message in such poetic form Jesus demonstrated that his listeners were to preserve and retain his teachings in their minds as well as their hearts."[36]

Working It Out . . .

Recall a time when a teacher made humorous remarks in class that elicited laughter. How did this affect the climate of the class hour? How did it help (or hinder) the teacher's teaching?

Are there times when you can use humor in your teaching? How will you plan for it?

Have you found it helpful to use a puzzling statement to stimulate your students to think? How might you use this technique more?

Could you consider using one or more of Jesus' aphorisms in a class session? If so, which ones will you use, and how? Could you think of some maxims of your own to help underscore a point in your teaching? Could your students be encouraged to create some aphorisms of their own to summarize Bible truths?

36. Stein, *The Method and Message of Jesus' Teachings*, 32.

How can repetition be used in a session you will teach? How might repetition be overdone?

Review the forms of logical reasoning Jesus used. Might some of them be useful for you in a forthcoming lesson?

Contrasts, examples, and explanations can add impact to your teaching. Be sure to use them as you teach.

Reflect on the several forms of poetic parallelism Jesus used. What difference do you think they made in his teaching?

Answers to the exercises on pages 218 and 230:

a. A fortiori   Matthew 12:11–12
b. Reductio ad absurdum   John 7:23
c. Argumentum ad hominem   Matthew 23:15
d. Law of the excluded middle   Mark 3:4
e. Law of noncontradiction   Luke 14:31
f. Analogy   Matthew 13:40

Matthew 10:39   Antithetical
Matthew 11:30   Synonymous
Mark 4:25   Antithetical
Luke 6:28   Synonymous
Luke 10:16   Stairstep
Luke 12:40   Synthetic
John 8:39b   Synthetic
John 13:20   Stairstep

"Heaven and earth will pass away,
but my words will never pass away."

Matthew 24:35

14

How Did Jesus Use Questions in His Teaching?

Questions provide one of the most important means by which teachers can involve students of all ages in the teaching-learning process. Questions can arouse student interest and curiosity, lead students to think more clearly about a subject, stimulate discussion, help teachers ascertain what students know, obtain student opinions, guide learners to new facts or ideas, encourage students to express themselves, correct students' misconceptions, clarify issues, present proofs or arguments, and exhort students to action.

More than eighty years ago DeGarmo wrote, "In the skillful use of the question more than anything else lies the fine art of teaching; for in such use we have the guide to clear and vivid ideas, the quick spur to imagination, the stimulus to thought, the incentive to action."[1] Skillful teachers work at using questions effectively.

Not all classroom questions are as provocative as they should or can be. Reporting on the surveys of questions asked in elementary or secondary schools over several decades, Gall noted that many of the questions did not require thoughtful answers. "About 60% of teachers' questions require students to recall facts; about 20% require students to

1. Charles DeGarmo, *Interest and Education* (New York: Macmillan, 1911), 179.

think; and the remaining 20% are procedural."[2] Questions that fail to challenge students to think are "factual questions, closed questions, or rote questions, easily answered from memory without taxing other mental muscles."[3]

Research shows that the way teachers ask questions is crucial in helping students learn how to think. A study of elementary school children showed that questions asked of the teacher strongly influence other behaviors of the pupils.[4] Perhaps few Bible teachers have realized that "the way [they] ask questions can be one of the most influential parts of teaching."[5]

Questions constitute such an important role in teaching that Ashner has called the teacher a "question maker."[6] But not just any questions. They must be the right kind, the kind that promote student involvement. Indisputably Jesus was a magnificent question maker—in fact, the world's best—for he knew how to raise the right kinds of questions. Teachers can gain insight on ways to improve their use of questions by studying the ways he used the questioning method to great advantage.

The Gospels sparkle with questions Jesus asked (and with questions put to him by others, as discussed in chapter 15). Using the question-and-answer method frequently, Jesus asked clear, direct, purposeful questions that made his teaching stimulating, spirited, and soul-searching. His queries aroused interest, provoked thought, requested information, elicited response, clarified issues, applied truth, and silenced critics.

These active encounters between Teacher and student made Jesus' teaching a mutual interaction. His sessions pulsated with excitement as his questions pulled his listeners irresistibly into the teaching-learning process, tantalizing their brains and challenging their hearts. In this verbal interchange, they could not help but be intrigued, enraptured, and excited about learning what he taught.

Because of Jesus' exceptional wielding of questions for numerous purposes, no one can ever say his teaching was dull.

2. Meredith D. Gall, "The Use of Questions in Teaching," *Review of Educational Research* 40 (December 1970): 72.
   3. "Questions: Making Learners Think," *The Teaching Professor* 2 (May 1988): 1.
   4. Hilda Taba, Samuel Levine, and Freeman Elzey, *Thinking in Elementary School Children* (San Francisco: San Francisco State College, 1964), 177. For an excellent survey of additional studies on questions in relation to student behavior and achievement, see Stephen G. Fortosis, "Can Questions Make Religious Educators More Effective in the Classroom?" *Christian Education Journal* 12 (spring 1992): 86–90.
   5. R. Cunningham, "Developing Question-Asking Skills," in *Developing Teacher Competencies*, ed. James Weigand (Englewood Cliffs, N.J.: Prentice-Hall, 1971), 85.
   6. M. J. Ashner, "Asking Questions to Trigger Thinking," *NEA* [National Education Association] *Journal* 50 (1961): 44.

No monotonous monologues here!

No drawn-out, sleep-inducing, drab lectures!

No drab content delivered in dry fashion resulting in drowsing students!

His questioning kept his audiences intensely alert, for it spurred them to recall, reflect, speculate, evaluate, and meditate, while it achieved life-changing results. No wonder the master questioner was a master Teacher!

As a twelve-year-old boy, Jesus listened to teachers in the temple courts, but he also asked them questions. He was not boastfully seeking to show that he knew better then his instructors. Instead, his "unaffected questions and answers to their questions showed so many proofs of exceptional insight and lucid intelligence that the doctors marveled at it. With the Child Himself, however, there was no boasting, self-conceit, arrogance or self-exaltation."[7] His first recorded words were two questions addressed to his anxious parents who had been looking for him for several days. He replied in amazement, not reproof, with two questions: "Why is it that you sought Me? Did you not know that I must be about My Father's business?" (Luke 2:49 NKJV). Though Joseph and Mary did not comprehend the significance of his questions (2:50), his words referred to his Sonship and to his ministry of carrying out the work given him by God the Father.[8]

How Many Questions Did Jesus Ask?

Writers differ on the number of questions posed by Jesus. Joan Lyon Gibbons says the number is 110, Clarence H. Benson says "more than one hundred," and E. P. Torrance gives the number as 154. LaVerne Roy Reeser claims Jesus used more than two hundred questions, and Norman Detlav Sorensen lists 310.[9] According to my count, Jesus asked 225 *different* questions. Because a number of questions are cited

7. Norval Geldenhuys, *Commentary on the Gospel of Luke*, New International Commentary on the New Testament (Grand Rapids: Eerdmans, 1951), 127.

8. Ibid., 128.

9. Gibbons, "A Psychological Exploration of Jesus' Use of Questions as an Interpersonal Mode of Communication" (Ph.D. diss., Graduate Theological Union, Berkeley, Calif., 1979), 1133–41a; Benson, *The Christian Teacher* (Chicago: Moody, 1940), 252; Torrance, "Religious Educational Creative Thinking," in *Education and the Creative Potential* (Minneapolis: University of Minnesota, 1963), 91–99; Reeser, "Jesus' Use of the Question in His Teaching Ministry" (M.R.E. thesis, Talbot Theological Seminary, LaMirada, Calif., 1968), 1; Sorensen, "How Christ Used Questions" (Th.M. thesis, Dallas Theological Seminary, Dallas, Tex., 1953), 45.

by more than one Gospel writer, the total number *recorded* is 304 (table 24).

Table 24
Number of Jesus' Questions Recorded in Each Gospel

Matthew	90
Mark	67
Luke	96
John	<u>51</u>
Total	304

Luke recorded more questions than any of the other Gospel writers, and all fifty-one questions in the Gospel of John occur nowhere else.

The numbers in table 24 do not include questions spoken by individuals in Jesus' parables (though some commentators include them). Nor do the totals include questions Jesus said others spoke, as in Matthew 7:22.

Totals also differ depending on the Bible version used. The New International Version translates as statements some words of Jesus that are questions in other versions, such as the New King James Version and the New American Standard Bible. As an example, the New International Version renders John 6:62 as an explanation ("What if you see the Son of Man ascend to where he was before!") whereas the New King James Version and the New American Standard Bible translate it as a question. Occasionally two questions in one verse in the New King James Version (e.g., "To what shall we liken the kingdom of God? Or with what parable shall we picture it?") are one question in the New International Version (e.g., "What shall we say the kingdom of God is like, or what parable shall we use to describe it?").

Sometimes one Gospel writer recorded Jesus' words as a question and another Gospel writer wrote it as a statement. Mark 11:17, for example, reads, "And as he taught them, he said, 'Is it not written, "My house will be called a house of prayer for all nations"'?" But Matthew 21:13 and Luke 19:46 have "'It is written,' he said to them, 'My house will be called a house of prayer,' but you are making it a 'den of robbers.'" And Matthew 12:26 and Luke 11:18 record a question ("How can his kingdom stand?") and Mark 3:26 has the statement "he cannot stand."

As table 24 shows, Matthew and Luke together include almost two-thirds of Jesus' questions (186 out of 304). Also of interest is the fact that the Gospel of Luke has more questions unique to it than the other

Gospels. Table 26, at the end of this chapter, lists all 225 questions, including the individuals or groups to whom the questions were addressed, the kinds of questions, and the immediate response of the individuals questioned.

To Whom Did Jesus Address His Questions?

The master Teacher asked a remarkable number of questions. Equally remarkable is the number of groups or individuals to whom he voiced his queries. He asked his disciples (as a group) sixty-four different questions, he presented sixty-two interrogations to thirty-two individuals or small groups, he addressed fifty questions to his adversaries (as a group), and he spoke forty-nine questions to crowds.

Most of the questions to Jesus' disciples were directed to the Twelve, but five times some others were included. Other times he addressed nine, ten, or eleven of the Twelve, and on one occasion he spoke to seventy-two disciples.

Individuals or small groups included John's disciples (Matt. 9:14–15; John 1:35–38), two groups of two blind men each (Matt. 9:28; 20:32), Peter—of whom the Lord asked a total of fourteen questions!—a rich young man, the mother of James and John, James and John themselves, Peter, James, and John, a demon-possessed man of the Gerasenes, a woman with a hemorrhaging, another blind man, the father of a demon-possessed boy, the owner of a house with a large upper room, an expert in the law, Joseph and Mary, a Pharisee named Simon, someone in a crowd who asked Jesus about an inheritance, Judas, two disciples on the way to Emmaus, Mary, Nicodemus, a Samaritan woman, an invalid of thirty-eight years, Philip, a woman caught in adultery (of whom Jesus asked four questions), a healed blind man, Martha, Mary and her friends, Annas the high priest, an official, and Mary of Magdala. Of these individuals some were his disciples, some were his followers other than the Twelve, others were inquirers, some were the ones he healed, and some were acquaintances and friends. Eight of these individuals were women.

Various groups of opponents faced Jesus' questions. Understandably, some of the questions were directed to the Pharisees (sixty questions), or to Pharisees and the teachers of the law (six questions), or Pharisees and Herodians (three), or Pharisees and experts in the law (one). The chief priests and teachers of the law were addressed by seven queries, and the teachers of the law alone by three queries. "The Jews," a term used almost exclusively by John to refer to religious authorities,

particularly in Jerusalem,[10] who were hostile to Jesus, were the addressees of nine of his questions. Other adversarial groups to whom Jesus
asked questions were the Sadducees (two questions) and a synagogue
ruler with opponents (two questions). One group of enemies, to whom
Jesus addressed two questions, included Judas, with a mob of soldiers,
chief priests, and Pharisees who came to arrest Jesus (John 18:3–7).

What Kinds of Questions Did Jesus Ask?

Jesus' questions constituted powerful teaching tools. His pedagogical
arsenal was full of interrogations of various kinds that pierced the
minds and hearts of his listeners. Some truths that could have been
conveyed by discourse or declaration were more effectively communicated by means of incisive questions—questions calling for a response
either mental or verbal.

"By being drawn out from the listeners rather than by simply being
declared by Jesus, the correct answer was more convincingly and per-
manently impressed on their minds."[11] Jesus never posed questions
simply to stimulate "good discussions." An issue of extreme importance
always stood behind each question.[12] By his questions he confronted
people with matters of eternal consequence, forcing them to face their
spiritual deficiencies.

Writers differ in their classifications of Jesus' questions. Price mentions six purposes in the Lord's questioning,[13] Delnay suggests seven
purposes,[14] Habermas and Issler build on the same seven categories,[15]
Fortosis, Rixon, and Warren each mention eight (though their lists dif-

10. Raymond E. Brown, *The Gospel according to John*, Anchor Bible, 2 vols. (Garden City, N.Y.: Doubleday, 1966), 1:lxxi; Leon Morris, *The Gospel according to John*, New
International Commentary on the New Testament (Grand Rapids: Eerdmans, 1971),
130–31.

11. Robert H. Stein, *The Method and Message of Jesus' Teachings* (Philadelphia: Westminster, 1978), 23.

12. Fortosis, "Can Questioning Make Religious Educators More Effective in the
Classroom?" 94.

13. To attract attention, to secure information, to help the questioner think through
his own problems, to clarify and illustrate his teaching, to present arguments, to apply
and exhort (J. M. Price, *Jesus the Teacher* [Nashville: Sunday School Board, 1946], 111–
13).

14. To open a conversation, to prepare for instruction, to induce reflection, to pull
hearers up short, to probe for motives, to force an admission, to answer a question
(Robert G. Delnay, *Teach as He Taught* [Chicago: Moody, 1987], 73–83).

15. Ronald Habermas and Klaus Issler, *Teaching for Reconciliation* (Grand Rapids:
Baker, 1992), 366–67.

fer),[16] Wilson has twelve purposes,[17] and Reeser presents the amazing number of twenty-eight classifications (though some seem to overlap with others).[18]

I suggest these fifteen purposes, which are listed in table 26 with each question.

1. To petition for information or to recall facts
2. To promote conversation
3. To point out something contrary to fact
4. To procure assent
5. To push for an expression of faith
6. To prod for an opinion or an expression of a desire
7. To prove or to test faith or spiritual commitment
8. To promote thinking or reflection
9. To persuade critics of their errors
10. To pull person(s) up short
11. To pour out an emotion
12. To probe for motives
13. To prick the conscience
14. To pinpoint a topic
15. To press for application of the truth

To Petition for Information or to Recall Facts

When Jesus asked for information, it was not because he did not know. Being the Son of God, he is omniscient. But his questions were designed to elicit response from his hearers. For example, he asked the demon-possessed man of the Gerasenes, "What is your name?" (Mark 5:9; Luke 8:30). When a woman with a bleeding problem touched him, Jesus inquired, "Who touched my clothes?" (Mark 5:30; Luke 8:45). When feeding the five thousand, he asked his disciples, "How many loaves do you have?" (Mark 6:38), and in feeding the four thousand he asked the same question (Matt. 15:34; Mark 8:5).

Other information-seeking questions are recorded in Mark 8:23; 9:16, 21, 33; Luke 10:26; 17:17; 22:35; 24:19, 41; John 8:10; 11:34; 18:4, 7; 20:15. Only occasionally did Jesus ask individuals to recall facts. He

16. Fortosis, "Can Questioning Make Religious Educators More Effective in the Classroom?" 92–97; Lilas D. Rixon, *How Jesus Taught* (Croydon, N.S.W.: Sydney Missionary and Bible College, 1977), 32–34; David Glenn Warren, "Christ's Use of Questions and Attention-Getters," (Th.M. thesis, Dallas Theological Seminary, Dallas, Tex., 1978), 48.

17. Valerie A. Wilson, "Christ the Master Teacher," in *Introduction to Biblical Christian Education,* ed. Werner C. Graendorf (Chicago: Moody, 1981), 59.

18. Reeser, "Jesus' Use of the Question in His Teaching Ministry," 43–54.

asked the disciples, "Don't you remember the five loaves for the five thousand, and how many basketfuls you gathered?" (Matt. 16:9b; Mark 8:19). To the accusing Pharisees he responded, "Haven't you read what David did when he and his companions were hungry?" (Matt. 12:3; Mark 2:25), or "What did Moses command you?" (Mark 10:3). Of the Sadducees he asked a "Have-you-not-read" question (Matt. 22:31–32; Mark 12:26). Other recall questions are recorded in Mark 11:17; Luke 24:26; and John 11:40.

To Promote Conversation

Several of Jesus' questions opened up a conversation, thus forming a point of contact. To two of John's disciples who were following Jesus, he said, "What do you want?" (John 1:38). He began a fascinating discussion with a Samaritan woman by his request, "Will you give me a drink?" (John 4:7). He initiated a conversation with two believers on the way to Emmaus by inquiring, "What are you discussing together as you walk along?" (Luke 24:17). To the eleven disciples who were fishing after his resurrection, Jesus called out, "Friends, haven't you any fish?" (John 21:5).

To Point Out Something Contrary to Fact

Questions can help others sense truths by alerting listeners to what is not true. The query, "Who of you by worrying can add a single hour to his life?" (Matt. 6:27; cf. Luke 12:25) conveys the point more forcefully than a mere declaration such as, "No one of you by worrying can add a single hour to his life." The question causes the addressees to reflect on the answer. Similarly the questions, "Which of you, if his son asks for bread, will give him a stone? Or if he asks for a fish, will give him a snake?" (Matt. 7:9–10; cf. Luke 11:11–12), led Jesus' listeners to acknowledge that since no one would do those things to his own son, so God the Father would not neglect to give good gifts to his own (Matt. 7:11).

Referring to John the Baptist, Jesus asked the crowd, "What did you go out . . . to see? A reed swayed by the wind? . . . A man dressed in fine clothes? . . . Then what did you go out to see?" (Matt. 11:7–9). Of course they agreed that what he asked was not the case. This encouraged them to heed what he then added about John the Baptist (11:10–15).

The question, "Can you drink the cup I am going to drink?" (Matt. 20:22; cf. Mark 10:38), addressed the fact that though the disciples *thought* they could undergo what Jesus would experience, they actually were unable to do so.

Other examples of this kind of question are in Matthew 26:55; Mark 3:23; 4:21; Luke 12:51; John 8:46a; and 13:38.

To Procure Assent

By means of a question, Jesus frequently led his listeners to admit the truth of something commonly known or experienced. By giving mental assent to what was asked, they were then better prepared to agree with an assertion following the question: "Are not two sparrows sold for a penny?" (Matt. 10:29). "If any of you has a sheep and it falls into a pit on the Sabbath, will you not take hold of it and lift it out?" (12:11). "From whom do the kings of the earth collect duty and taxes—from their own sons or from others?" (17:25b). "If a man owns a hundred sheep and one of them wanders away, will he not leave the ninety-nine on the hills and go to look for the one that wandered off?" (18:12; Luke 15:4). "Can a blind man lead a blind man? Will they not both fall into a pit?" (Luke 6:39). "Did not the one who made the outside make the inside also?" (11:40).

Other examples include Mark 11:17; 12:24; Luke 14:28, 31; 15:8; 17:7–9; 18:7; 22:27; John 4:35; 8:10; 10:34; 11:9; 18:11. What points was Jesus leading up to by these assent questions? For answers, look up each reference and the succeeding verses in each context.

To Push for an Expression of Faith

On five occasions Jesus used a question to elicit a response of faith.

To two blind men: "Do you believe that I am able to do this?" (Matt. 9:28).

To the twelve disciples: "But what about you? Who do you say I am?" (Matt. 16:15; Mark 8:29; Luke 9:20).

To the blind men he healed: "Do you believe in the Son of Man?" (John 9:35).

To Martha: "I am the resurrection and the life. . . . Do you believe this?" (John 11:25–26).

To Philip: "Don't you believe that I am in the Father, and that the Father is in me?" (John 14:10).

To Prod for an Opinion or an Expression of a Desire

After telling his kingdom parables to the disciples, the Teacher asked them a question that called for a response: "Have you understood all these things?" (Matt. 13:51). He also encouraged them to respond by asking, "Who do people say the Son of Man is?" (Matt. 16:13). He encouraged two blind men near Jericho to express their desire for healing by asking, "What do you want me to do for you?" (Matt. 20:32; Mark 10:51; Luke 18:41). Other questions that prompted responses from those he questioned are recorded in Matthew 20:21a; 22:20, 42; Mark 10:36; Luke 24:19; John 5:6.

To Prove or to Test Faith or Spiritual Commitment

Jesus' question, "Where shall we buy bread for these people to eat?" (John 6:5), was directed to Philip "to test him" (v. 6), that is, to help build his faith in the Lord's ability to feed the great crowd without adequate food. To see if his disciples were committed to staying with him, Jesus asked, "You do not want to leave too, do you?" (6:67). And he tested Peter's love by his thrice-repeated query, "Do you love me?" (21:15–17).

To Promote Thinking or Reflection

Though Jesus often posed questions for the purpose of gaining verbal responses, other times he asked rhetorical questions, queries devised to stimulate mental thought and reflection. Examples abound in the Gospels. His rhetorical question, couched in metaphorical language, "If the salt loses its saltiness, how can it be made salty again?" (Matt. 5:13; Mark 9:50; Luke 14:34), provoked thought about the importance of a strong consistent witness of believers as "the salt of the earth." The two questions, "If you love those who love you, what reward will you get? Are not even the tax collectors doing that?" (Matt. 5:46; Luke 6:32), led the hearers to reflect on reasons why their love should extend to the unlovely. When Jesus chided the Pharisees with the words, "You brood of vipers, how can you who are evil say anything good?" (Matt. 12:34), this no doubt prompted them to reflect on their evil words issuing from evil hearts.

Hearing the incisive questions, "What good will it be for a man if he gains the whole world, yet forfeits his soul? Or what can a man give in exchange for his soul?" (Matt. 16:26; Mark 8:36–37; Luke 9:25), who could fail to contemplate the eternal value of spiritual matters compared with the passing fancy of worldly goods?

Jesus' strange rhetorical question, "Who is my mother, and who are my brothers?" (Matt. 12:48; Mark 3:33), would have led the crowd to wonder what he was leading up to. This brief puzzlement and reflection on their part alerted them to anticipate his answer: "Whoever does the will of my Father in heaven is my brother and sister and mother" (Matt. 12:50; Mark 3:35).

After Jesus washed his disciples' feet in his surprising act of great humility, he sat down and asked them, "Do you understand what I have done for you?" (John 13:12). This implied that something more was involved than his washing the dust from their feet, thus causing them to ponder the significance of his act. Then he answered his own question by pointing out that they were to follow his example of humble service to others (13:13–17).

Other rhetorical, thought-invoking questions in the Book of Matthew are recorded in 5:47; 6:25, 30 (Luke 12:26, 28); 9:15 (Mark 2:19; Luke 5:34); 15:17; 19:17 (Mark 10:18; Luke 18:19); Luke 2:49; 6:34; 22:27; John 3:12; 10:35–36. Think of how these questions would have induced more reflection than declarative statements.

Another way Jesus encouraged reflection was to ask, "What do you think?" Three times these words prefaced another question—to Simon (Matt. 17:25a), the disciples (18:12a), and the Pharisees (22:4–23a)—and another time those words introduced the parable of the two sons addressed to the chief priests and elders (21:28). In teaching his disciples Jesus introduced four questions with the words, "Do you think . . . ?" (Matt. 26:53; Luke 12:51; 13:2, 4).

The fact that Jesus answered several of his own questions shows he asked them in order to capture his listeners' attention. This preparation caused the answers to penetrate more deeply. Look up these references and the verses immediately following them to determine how the Lord answered his own rhetorical interrogations: Matthew 9:15 (Mark 2:19; Luke 5:34); 11:8–9; 19:17 (Mark 10:18; Luke 18:19);[19] Mark 3:33; Luke 10:15; 12:51; 13:2, 4; 22:27; John 8:43; 12:27.

To Persuade Critics of Their Errors

Sometimes Jesus replied to the critical comments or questions of his religious opponents with statements. But often he responded with questions. These were usually rhetorical questions that prompted his opponents to realize the logical inconsistency of their accusations while at the same time pricking their consciences. So powerful and gripping were his interrogative replies that six times his opponents were silenced![20]

The Pharisees were inconsistent in their logic to suggest that Jesus

19. Jesus' question, "Why do you ask me about what is good?" (Matt. 19:17), which is rendered "Why do you call me good?" in Mark 10:18 and Luke 18:19, was followed by the statement, "There is only One who is good." "This question-comment confrontation was a clever way of asking, 'By asking Me what is good, are you implying My equality with God, who is the only one who is truly good?'" (Robert Culton Singleton, "The Lord's Use of Questions in Matthew" [Th.M. thesis, Dallas Theological Seminary, 1977], 41).

20. Matthew 21:27 (Mark 11:33; Luke 20:7); 22:46; Mark 3:4; Luke 13:17; 14:4, 6.

cast out demons by satanic power (Matt. 12:27; Luke 11:19), and chief
priests and teachers of the law were inconsistent in being indignant at
children praising Jesus since the Old Testament (Ps. 8:2) speaks of children praising God (Matt. 21:16). The Sadducees' question about marriage after the resurrection was inconsistent with the Old Testament
statement in Exodus 3:6 on God as the God of the living (Matt. 22:31–
32). Jesus' questions about the Messiah's Davidic descent (Matt. 22:42–
43, 45; Mark 12:35, 37; Luke 20:41, 44) showed the inconsistency of the
Pharisees' interpretation of Psalm 110:1.

Other inconsistencies Jesus pointed out pertained to his rivals' views
on oaths (Matt. 23:17, 19), their concern about blasphemy while failing
to be concerned about a paralytic (Matt. 9:4; Mark 2:8–9), their accusing
his disciples of eating grain on the Sabbath while overlooking David's
experience (Matt. 12:3; Mark 2:25–26; Luke 6:3; cf. 1 Sam. 21:1–6), their
calling Jesus "Lord" but not obeying him (Luke 6:46), their ability to interpret the weather while not being able to understand spiritual truths
(12:56–57), and their inconsistency in caring for animals on the Sabbath but not wanting Jesus to heal humans on the Sabbath (13:15; 14:5).

In the Gospel of John the Jews (religious authorities in Jerusalem)
were shown to be inconsistent by their concern for human praise but
not for praise from God (John 5:44), their failure to believe what Moses
wrote (5:47), their having Moses' law but not keeping it (7:19), their cir-
cumcising children on the Sabbath while accusing Jesus of healing on
the Sabbath (7:23), their inability to accuse him of any sin while not believing on him (8:46), and their wanting to stone Jesus when he had performed life-restoring and life-sustaining miracles (10:32). Judas' in-
credible inconsistency stands undisguised when Jesus asked, "Judas,
are you betraying the Son of Man with a kiss?" (Luke 22:48). What
could be more incongruous than an act of betrayal accompanied by a
kiss, an act of friendship!

Of three of the six times Jesus silenced his opponents with his questions, he placed them on the horns of a dilemma. When the chief priests
and elders asked the source of his authority, he challenged them with a
question on the origin of John's baptism. If they said it was "from men,"
they feared being stoned by the people, who considered John a prophet.
But if they said John's baptism was "from God," they feared Jesus would
accuse them of not following John the Baptist. Since either answer
would pose a problem for them, they refused to respond. So Jesus said
he refused to answer *their* question (Matt. 21:12–27; Mark 11:27–33;
Luke 20:1–8).

In a synagogue one Sabbath, Jesus faced Pharisees and teachers of
the law with a dilemma on whether it is lawful on the Sabbath to save
life or destroy it (Mark 3:1–6; Luke 6:6–11). They could not answer "to

save life," for then they would have no basis for criticizing Jesus for Sabbath healings, nor could they say "to destroy life" for that would pit them against Old Testament standards.

On another occasion Jesus placed the Pharisees on similar horns of a dilemma by asking in a Pharisee's house, "Is it lawful to heal on the Sabbath or not?" (Luke 14:1–4). Answering yes would mean they could not accuse Jesus of wrongdoing, whereas saying no would suggest they were uninterested in the physical welfare of others.

By these three clever maneuvers Jesus upstaged—and silenced—his critics. And he did so solely by means of questions!

To Pull Person(s) Up Short

Delnay writes, "There comes a time in the teaching process when our disciples are on a wrong track. They are toying with a wrong doctrine, or they are getting cocky, or they are trying to go in their own strength."[21] Facing situations like these with his learners, Jesus used questions to pull them up short. Fortosis refers to these questions as those in which Jesus pointed out the students' spiritual inadequacies.[22] The hearers "may have initially sparked hostility, but truly receptive learners eventually responded with positive change."[23]

Jesus chided the disciples for their lack of faith: in the storm (Matt. 8:26; Mark 4:40; Luke 8:25), when Peter attempted to walk on the water (Matt. 14:31), when they wondered about his words on the yeast of the Pharisees and Sadduccees (Matt. 16:8), and when they were frightened at his postresurrection appearance to them (Luke 24:38). He pointed out their lack of understanding when he gave the parable of the sower (Mark 4:13), when he spoke of the yeast of his religious enemies (Matt. 16:9, 11; Mark 8:17–21), and when he responded to Philip's question about seeing God the Father (John 14:9). Lack of spiritual comprehension of Jesus' Sonship and mission was the subject he addressed in questioning his parents when they found him in the temple at the age of twelve (Luke 2:49).

Knowing that his listeners were troubled ("Does this offend you?" John 6:61) by his difficult-to-understand words on eating his flesh and drinking his blood (6:54–58), Jesus reproved their lack of spiritual insight by mentioning his ascension, an event even more difficult to comprehend: "What if you see the Son of Man ascend to where he was before!" (6:62). Their inability to understand his coming *down* as the true

21. Delnay, *Teach as He Taught*, 78.
22. Fortosis, "Can Questioning Make Religious Educators More Effective in the Classroom?" 95–96.
23. Ibid., 95.

bread from heaven would be exceeded by an even more hard-to-fathom event, namely, his going *up* to heaven.

Others who were brought up short by Jesus' questions on their spiritual shortcomings include teachers of the law ("Why do you entertain evil thoughts in your hearts?" Matt. 9:4), an inquiring rich young man ("Why do you ask me about what is good?" Matt. 19:17; Mark 10:18; Luke 18:19), a man in a crowd ("Man, who appointed me a judge or an arbiter between you?" (Luke 12:14), the Pharisees ("Why don't you judge for yourselves what is right?" 12:57), the nine thankless healed lepers (17:17–18), Nicodemus (John 3:10), the Jewish opposition ("Why is my language not clear to you? Because you are unable to hear what I say," 8:43), Annas the high priest (18:21), and Pilate (18:34). In addition, Peter, James, and John lacked physical and spiritual alertness in the garden of Gethsemane. "Could you not keep watch for one hour? . . . Are you still sleeping and resting?" (Matt. 26:40, 45; Mark 14:37, 41; Luke 22:46). Relating the use of this kind of question to teachers today, Fortosis writes, "A question may more effectively expose the problem than would accusation or innuendo. Assisting students to identify their own spiritual inadequacy is usually more effective than identifying it for them. If a teacher has gained the respect and favor of a class, a corrective question can challenge learners to change in a remarkable way."[24]

To Pour Out an Emotion

A number of Jesus' emotions—disappointment, exasperation, amazement, surprise, or anguish—were expressed in questions. At the home of Jairus, Jesus said to the people who were mourning the death of the synagogue ruler's daughter, "Why all this commotion and wailing?" (Mark 5:39). Sighing in exasperation, he asked the Pharisees why they wanted to see him perform a miracle (8:12). Coming down from the Mount of Transfiguration, he expressed disappointment and annoyance at the nine disciples' inability ("O unbelieving and perverse generation . . . how long shall I stay with you? How long shall I put up with you?" Matt. 17:17; Mark 9:19).

Aware of his coming death on the cross, Jesus acknowledged that his heart was troubled. But he asked, "What shall I say? 'Father, save me from this hour'?" (John 12:27a). Then he expressed his commitment to the purpose of his mission (12:27b–28). As Jesus hung on the cross in physical and spiritual agony, he expressed the anguish of his soul in a moving question: "My God, my God, why have you forsaken me?" (Matt. 27:46; Mark 15:34).

24. Ibid., 96.

To Probe for Motives

Questions penetrated the motives of the Pharisees and the Herodians ("Why are you trying to trap me?" Matt. 22:18; Mark 12:15), of the Jewish assailants ("Why are you trying to kill me?" John 7:19b), and of Jesus' disciples ("What were you arguing about on the road?" Mark 9:33; and "Why are you bothering this woman?" Matt. 26:10).

To Prick the Conscience

Several of the Lord's questions that we have already discussed may have pricked the conscience of the hearer(s). Additional questions serving that purpose were addressed to the Pharisees and teachers of the law: "And why do you break the command of God for the sake of your tradition?" (Matt. 15:3); "You snakes! You brood of vipers! How will you escape being condemned to hell?" (23:33).

To Pinpoint a Topic

Introducing his Olivet Discourse, Jesus asked his twelve followers, "Do you see all these things?" (Matt. 24:2). He introduced the parable of the mustard seed by the rhetorical query, "What shall we say the kingdom of God is like, or what parable shall we use to describe it?" (Mark 4:30; Luke 13:18), and the parables of the woman and the yeast by a similar question, "What shall I compare [the kingdom of God] to?" (Luke 13:20). These questions arrested the interest of his disciples, thereby securing their attention for the answers he would give.

To Press for Application of the Truth

Jesus never failed to relate his teaching to his listeners' lives. His teaching was specific, personal, and relevant, not general and abstract. One way he demonstrated this was to apply his teaching by means of questions. Remarkably, every instance in which he applied a truth by a question or helped his listeners draw a conclusion was a parable or an illustration (see table 25).

What Other Features Marked Jesus' Questions?

A number of times Jesus voiced his questions in clusters, thus adding impact and emphasis to his words. Sometimes the additional question

Table 25
Questions Jesus Used in Concluding and Applying
Parables and Illustrations

Lesson	Concluding Question	Reference	Addressees
Parable of the tenants	"Therefore when the owner of the vineyard comes, what will he do to those tenants?"	Matthew 21:40; Mark 12:9; Luke 20:15	Chief priests, elders, and teachers of the law
Illustration of faithful and wicked servants being watchful	"Who then is the faithful and wise servant, whom the master has put in charge of the servants in his household to give them their food at the proper time?" (rhetorical question)	Matthew 24:45; Luke 12:42	Twelve disciples
Illustration of the creditor and two debtors	"Now which of them will love him more?"	Luke 7:42	Simon, a Pharisee
Parable of the good Samaritan	"Which of these three do you think was a neighbor to the man who fell into the hands of robbers?"	Luke 10:36	An expert in the law
Parable of the shrewd manager	"So if you have not been trustworthy in handling worldly wealth, who will trust you with true riches? And if you have not been trustworthy with someone else's property, who will give you property of your own?"	Luke 16:11–12	Twelve disciples

or questions said the same thing as the first question in a different but parallel way; other times an additional thought was suggested.

Most of the clusters are pairs of questions, a few are a triad of queries, two have four questions each, and two clusters have five questions each.

Two-question clusters
Matthew   7:3–4 (Luke 6:41–42)
        7:9–10
        9:4–5
        11:9 (Luke 7:26)
        12:26–27 (Luke 11:18a, 19a)
        15:16–17 (Mark 7:18)
        16:26 (Mark 8:36–37)
        17:17 (Mark 9:19)
        17:25
        18:12
        21:25
        22:20 (Mark 12:16; Luke 20:24)
        22:42
        26:53–54
Mark   4:13
      4:21
Luke   2:49
      6:39
      10:26
      12:25–26
      12:56–57
      13:15–16
      13:18
      16:11–12
      18:7
      22:27
John   8:10
      8:46
      10:34–36a

Three-question clusters
Matthew 6:26b–28
Luke   17:7–9
      17:17–18
John 14:9–10

Four-question clusters
Matthew   5:46–47
              11:7–8 (Luke 7:24–25)

Five-question clusters
Matthew 16:8–11a
Mark 8:17–18

Jesus began his questions in a variety of ways. "What," "why," "do you," and "how" are the words he most often used in introducing his questions. Those question-indicators obviously would stimulate the listeners to respond in thought or word. Other introductory words are "which," "will," "who," "have you," "are you," "did," "were," "go," "do not," "was," each occurring several times. Still others, occurring only once, include "can they," "is not," "can he," "by whom," "does he," "shall I." A number of others can be seen by scanning the questions in table 25.

In his questions Jesus dealt with numerous subjects, thus again demonstrating the vast extent of his knowledge and the great variety in his teaching skills. According to Baldwin, Jesus spoke of eighty-six topics in his questions.[25]

Aliens (vs. freemen)
Ambition (presumptuous)
Anxiety
Appraisals (discerning)
Appropriation (failure in)
Arbitration (human vs. divine conciliation)
Being (perception of)
Conciliation (divine)
Coordination (of our Lord's powers)
Cost (counting of)
Desire (heart's)
Devotion (interference with)
Doubt (of our Lord's power and teaching)
Employment (the proper on the Sabbath)
Equations (spiritual)
Evil (persecution of good)
Faith (growth of)
Faith (implicit in our Lord)

25. Harry A. Baldwin, *101 Outline Studies on Questions Asked and Answered by Our Lord* (New York: Revell, 1938; reprint, Grand Rapids: Baker, 1965), 126–27.

Faith (ultimate scarcity of)
Faithfulness
Freemen (vs. aliens)
Friendship (prostitution of)
God's Son (belief on him as)
Good (persecution of by evil)
Grace (logic of God's)
Gratitude (vs. ingratitude)
Guilt (man's universal)
Identity (the Messiah's)
Identity (our Lord's)
Ingratitude (vs. gratitude)
Impatience (cause for unbelief)
Interest (our Lord's in our occupations)
Interference (sorrows)
Interfering (with each other's devotion)
John the Baptist (significance of)
Justice (God's)
Kin (true of our Lord)
Kingdom (spread and inclusiveness of)
Knowledge (Pharisees' of Scriptures)
Leadership (our Lord's)
Logic (of God's grace)
Love (tested for him)
Love (the measure of)
Mercy (God's)
Misconception (of our Lord's power and teaching)
Misjudgment (men's)
Mission (important phases of his)
Mystery (in plan of redemption)
Neighbor (true definition)
Occupation (his interest in gainful ones)
Passion (our Lord's approaching)
Patience (God's)
Perception (necessity of our Lord's)
Persecution (all-inclusive)
Persecution (persistent and unjust of our Lord)
Peter's (failure)
Power (our Lord's)
Power (doubt of our Lord's)
Power (faith in our Lord's)
Power (real source of our Lord's)
Power (our Lord's resurrection)

Powers (coordination of God-like)
Prayer (answer to)
Prayer (effectual)
Prayer (verity of)
Probity (comparative)
Procedure (faulty of disciples)
Program (our Lord's)
Prophecy (fulfillment of concerning our Lord)
Purpose (cowardly and murderous toward our Lord)
Quest (object and motive of)
Realities
Recognition (of him—interference with)
Redemption (mysterious plan of)
Sabbath (proper employment of)
Scriptures (true teaching of)
Search (God's for his own)
Sharing (his trials)
Sorrows (interference)
Source (of our Lord's power)
Teaching (our Lord's)
Time (the, to do good)
Trials (sharing our Lord's)
Truths (his knowledge of vital, spiritual)
Unbelief (cause of)
Values (real)

What Can We Learn from Jesus about the Art of Asking Questions?

Since Jesus employed the question method so extensively in his ministry, teachers today do well to emulate his example. The effective questioning of students can add sparkle, interest, curiosity, intrigue, and impact to one's teaching.

Asking questions, however, is not as simple as it may seem. "Contrary to common sense, questioning is a complex skill."[26] We should not ask "just any questions. They must be the right kind of questions and the answers accepted in a way that promotes student involvement."[27]

26. J. T. Dillon, "Research on Questioning and Discussion," *Educational Leadership* 42 (November 1984): 53.
27. Roger C. Schreffler, "The Art of Asking Questions," *Teach* 14 (summer 1973): 58.

The following suggestions, each stated both positively and negatively, stem from Christ's use of questions.

Ask questions that challenge; avoid those that give away the answers or that end in guessing. A review of Jesus' queries shows that he always spurred his listener-learners to ruminate on the issues he raised. Seldom did Jesus ask recall questions, merely asking for a recital of facts. If he did ask a "What-do-you-remember?" question, it was to lead on to interaction on an important issue. More often he challenged his students with "What-do-you-think?" questions. The disciples never had to guess at an answer, trying to discover what he had in mind. Instead, they were encouraged to think for themselves, to offer their own opinions and ideas.

Ask questions that are clear; avoid ambiguous questions. No one ever said to Jesus, "I don't know what you mean by that question. Will you reword it?" They may have puzzled over the answer, but never over the question itself. Jesus could easily submit questions on the spot, but teachers today, in order to have clear questions, do well to prepare them beforehand.

Ask questions that are specific and brief; avoid those that are too general and broad. The subjects Jesus touched on were never so broad in scope that his addressees wondered how to respond. And the queries he posed were usually brief; like a short, piercing dagger, they cut to the quick immediately.

Ask a variety of questions; avoid always asking the same kind. Jesus' scores of questions fulfilled a variety of purposes. Being in a rut was never a problem with the master Teacher!

Ask questions in an atmosphere of acceptance and respect; avoid questions that ridicule or belittle. At times, Jesus answered his critics with searching questions of reproof and correction, and other times queries pulled his hearers up short. Yet he always asked out of loving concern, never denigrating others by insult or ridicule. He expressed appreciation for his pupils' sincere attempts to respond, thus inspiring their confidence and continued efforts to learn.

Additional suggestions for asking questions with competence include these tips: When necessary, help students improve on an initially weak response. For instance, you might ask, "Can you expand on that a little more?" Or, "What do you mean by that?" Or, "Can you give an example?"[28] Encourage students to interact with each other's ideas. You might ask, "Do the rest of you agree?" "What do you think of that idea?" "Do you see any problems as well as advantages to that suggestion?" Encourage quieter students to respond to your questions by say-

28. Gall, "The Use of Questions in Teaching," 71.

ing, "Some of you haven't said much today in discussion. What do the rest of you think?" Or, "Let's hear from some of the others in class." Summarize a discussion by a phrase such as, "So far we have said that . . . ," or, "Are we agreed then on this . . . ," or, "As I see it, we have stated. . . ."

Utilizing the right questions constitutes an important part of dynamic teaching. For as DeGarmo wrote, "To question well is to teach well."[29]

What Do You Think?

In the next class you attend, jot down all the questions the teacher asks. Then analyze what kind they were and how the students responded, and evaluate whether they were good questions.

Listen for rhetorical questions in the next sermon you hear. Evaluate their effectiveness.

Do you ask questions often enough in your teaching? How might you increase your use of the question method?

As you prepare your next lesson, be sure to write out the questions you plan to ask in class. Then evaluate whether you think they are good questions. What kind of questions are they, and how do you think your students will respond?

In 1966, Norris M. Sanders, an educator, suggested seven intellectual levels of learning toward which questioning can be directed. Each level is assumed to include the cognitive skills of the levels below it: memory, translation, interpretation, application, analysis, synthesis, and evaluation (*Classroom Questions: What Kinds?* [New York: Harper and Row]). These seven levels were adapted from Benjamin S. Bloom's six levels of intellectual learning (*Taxonomy of Educational Objectives: Cognitive Domain* [New York: McKay, 1956]).

29. DeGarmo, *Interest and Education*, 179.

In asking a *memory* question, you want the student to remember, re-call, or recognize something previously learned. Helpful verbs in these questions are name, list, tell, define, identify.

In a *translation* question, the student is asked to speak an answer in a form different from that which was presented. Key verbs in these questions are paraphrase, summarize, translate, describe in your own words.

In an *interpretation* question, the student is asked to demonstrate his or her interpretation or *comprehension* of something learned. Key verbs are compare, contrast, explain, give an example, imply, in-fer.

In an *application* question, the student is challenged to *apply* learned facts or skills to a new situation. Helpful verbs are calculate, de-cide, predict, produce, solve.

An *analysis* question prods the student to *identify* parts of a problem to see how they are similar or different. Useful verbs are distin-guish, point out, select, diagram, what reasons are given, what structure is evident.

A *synthesis* question asks the student to put elements or parts to-gether to create a new plan or procedure. Verbs to use in asking and answering this kind of question are compare, create, devise, plan, reorganize, write.

An *evaluation* question, on the highest level of cognitive learning, calls for the student to judge the degree to which something meets a standard or criterion. Verbs in evaluation questions are ap-praise, assess, critique, detect fallacies, evaluate, form criteria, judge, support.

See if you can find examples of each of these levels in Jesus' teaching, especially evaluation questions.

Can you use these in your teaching? Why is an evaluation question the highest of these seven levels of learning and testing?

Table 26
Questions Jesus Asked

Questions*	References	Individual(s) or Groups Addressed	Kind of Questions[+]	Immediate Response by the One(s) Questioned
1. "If the salt loses its saltiness, how can it be made salty again?"	1–3. Matthew 5:13 (Mark 9:50; Luke 14:34)‡	Crowd at the Sermon on the Mount	8	None recorded
2. "If you love those who love you, what reward will you get?"	4–5. Matthew 5:46a (Luke 6:32)	Crowd at the Sermon on the Mount	8	None recorded
3. "Are not even the tax collectors doing that?"	6. Matthew 5:46b	Crowd at the Sermon on the Mount	4	None recorded
4. "And if you greet only your brothers, what are you doing more than others?"	7. Matthew 5:47a	Crowd at the Sermon on the Mount	8	None recorded
5. "Do not even pagans do that?"	8. Matthew 5:47b	Crowd at the Sermon on the Mount	4	None recorded
6. "Is not life more important than food, and the body more important than clothes?"	9. Matthew 6:25	Crowd at the Sermon on the Mount	4, 8	None recorded
7. "Are you not much more valuable than they?"	10. Matthew 6:26	Crowd at the Sermon on the Mount	8	None recorded
8. "Who of you by worrying can add a single hour to his life?"	11. Matthew 6:27	Crowd at the Sermon on the Mount	3	None recorded
9. "And why do you worry about clothes?"	12. Matthew 6:28	Crowd at the Sermon on the Mount	8	None recorded
10. "If that is how God clothes the grass of the field, . . . will he not much more clothe you, O you of little faith?"	13. Matthew 6:30	Crowd at the Sermon on the Mount	8	None recorded

*The numbering in this column records the number of Jesus' questions, totaling 225, and the numbering in column 2 records the occurrences of these questions in the Gospels, totaling 304.

[+]The numbers in this column correspond to the kinds of questions listed on page 241. Some questions have more than one purpose.

‡Parallel passages are given in parentheses, though the wording often differs from one Gospel to the other.

#	Question	Reference	Audience		Response
11.	"Why do you look at the speck of sawdust in your brother's eye and pay no attention to the plank in your own eye?"	14–15. Matthew 7:3 (Luke 6:41)	Crowd at the Sermon on the Mount	8	None recorded
12.	"How can you say to your brother, 'Let me take the speck out of your eye,' when all the time there is a plank in your own eye?"	16–17. Matthew 7:4 (Luke 6:42)	Crowd at the Sermon on the Mount	8, 10	None recorded
13.	"Which of you, if his son asks for bread, will give him a stone?"	18. Matthew 7:9	Crowd at the Sermon on the Mount	3	None recorded
14.	"Or if he asks for a fish, will give him a snake?"	19–20. Matthew 7:10 (Luke 11:11)	Crowd	3	None recorded
15.	"Do people pick grapes from thornbushes, or figs from thistles?"	21. Matthew 7:16	Crowd	3	None recorded
16.	"You of little faith, why are you so afraid?"	22–23. Matthew 8:26 (Mark 4:40a)	The twelve disciples	10	They were amazed and asked two questions (8:27).
17.	"Why do you entertain evil thoughts in your hearts?"	24–26. Matthew 9:4 (Mark 2:8; Luke 5:22)	Teachers of the law	9, 10	None recorded
18.	"Which is easier: to say, 'Your sins are forgiven,' or to say, 'Get up and walk'?"	27–29. Matthew 9:5 (Mark 2:9; Luke 5:23)	Teachers of the law	8	None recorded
19.	"How can the guests of the bridegroom mourn while he is with them?"	30–32. Matthew 9:15 (Mark 2:19; Luke 5:34)	John's disciples	8	None recorded
20.	"Do you believe that I am able to do this?"	33. Matthew 9:28	Two blind men	5	They responded, "Yes, Lord" (9:28).
21.	"Are not two sparrows sold for a penny?"	34. Matthew 10:29	The twelve disciples	4	None recorded
22–25.	"What did you go out into the desert to see? A reed swayed by the wind? If not, what did you go out to see? A man dressed in fine clothes?"	35–42. Matthew 11:7–8 (Luke 7:24–25)	Crowd	8, 3, 8, 3	None recorded

Questions	References	Individual(s) or Groups Addressed	Kind of Questions	Immediate Response by the One(s) Questioned
26–27. "Then what did you go out to see? A prophet?"	43–46. Matthew 11:9 (Luke 7:26)	Crowd	3, 8	None recorded
28. "To what can I compare this generation?"	47–48. Matthew 11:16 (Luke 7:31a)	Crowd	11	None recorded
29. "Haven't you read what David did when he and his companions were hungry?"	49–51. Matthew 12:3 (Mark 2:25; Luke 6:3)	Pharisees	1, 9, 10	None recorded
30. "Or haven't you read in the Law that on the Sabbath the priests in the temple desecrate the day and yet are innocent?"	52. Matthew 12:5	Pharisees	1, 9, 10	None recorded
31. "If any of you has a sheep and it falls into a pit on the Sabbath, will you not take hold of it and lift it out?"	53. Matthew 12:11	Pharisees	4	They left and plotted a way to kill Jesus (12:14).
32–33. "If Satan drives out Satan, he is divided against himself. How then can his kingdom stand? And if I drive out demons by Beelzebub, by whom do your people drive them out?"	54–57. Matthew 12:26–27 (Luke 11:18a, 19a)	Pharisees	8, 9	None recorded
34. "Or again, how can anyone enter a strong man's house and carry off his possessions unless he first ties up the strong man?"	58. Matthew 12:29	Pharisees	3, 8	None recorded
35. "You brood of vipers, how can you who are evil say anything good?"	59. Matthew 12:34	Pharisees	8	After Jesus' words to the Pharisees in Matthew 12:25–37, they and the teachers of the law asked Jesus to perform a miraculous sign (12:38).
36. "Who is my mother, and who are my brothers?"	60–61. Matthew 12:48 (Mark 3:33)	Crowd	8	None recorded

Question	Reference	Audience	No.	Response
37. "Have you understood all these things?"	62. Matthew 13:51	The twelve disciples	6	They replied, "Yes" (13:51).
38. "Why did you doubt?"	63. Matthew 14:31	Peter	10	None recorded
39. "And why do you break the command of God for the sake of your tradition?"	64. Matthew 15:3	Pharisees and teachers of the law	8, 13	None recorded
40–41. "Are you still so dull? Don't you see that whatever enters the mouth goes into the stomach and then out of the body?"	65–68. Matthew 15:16–17 (Mark 7:18)	The twelve disciples	10, 8	None recorded
42. "How many loaves do you have?"	69–70. Matthew 15:34 (Mark 8:5)	The twelve disciples	1	They replied, "Seven . . . and a few small fish" (15:34).
43. "You of little faith, why are you talking among yourselves about having no bread?"	71–72. Matthew 16:8 (Mark 8:17a)	The twelve disciples	10	None recorded
44. "Do you still not understand?"	73–74. Matthew 16:9a (Mark 8:17b)	The twelve disciples	10	None recorded
45. "Don't you remember the five loaves for the five thousand, and how many basketfuls you gathered?"	75–76. Matthew 16:9b (Mark 8:18b–19)	The twelve disciples	1, 10	None recorded
46–47. "Or the seven loaves for the four thousand, and how many basketfuls you gathered? How is it you don't understand that I was not talking to you about bread?"	77–80. Matthew 16:10–11 (Mark 8:20–21)	The twelve disciples	1, 10	After Jesus' five questions in Matthew 16:8–11, the Twelve then understood he was talking about the Pharisees' and Sadducees' teachings (16:12).
48. "Who do people say the Son of Man is?"	81–83. Matthew 16:13 (Mark 8:27; Luke 9:18)	The twelve disciples	6	They gave answers on who people thought Jesus is (16:14).
49–50. "But what about you? Who do you say I am?"	84–89. Matthew 16:15 (Mark 8:29; Luke 9:20)	The twelve disciples	5, 5	Peter answered, "You are the Christ, the Son of the living God" (16:16).

Questions	References	Individual(s) or Groups Addressed	Kind of Questions	Immediate Response by the One(s) Questioned
51. "What good will it be for a man if he gains the whole world, yet forfeits his soul?"	90–92. Matthew 16:26a (Mark 8:36; Luke 9:25)	The twelve disciples	8	None recorded
52. "Or what can a man give in exchange for his soul?"	93–94. Matthew 16:26b (Mark 8:37)	The twelve disciples	8	None recorded
53. "O unbelieving and perverse generation, . . . how long shall I stay with you?"	95–96. Matthew 17:17a (Mark 9:19a)	Nine of the twelve disciples (all except Peter, James, and John)	11	None recorded
54. "How long shall I put up with you?"	97–99. Matthew 17:17b (Mark 9:19b; Luke 9:41)	Nine of the twelve disciples (all except Peter, James, and John)	11	They asked Jesus why they were unable to drive out the demon (17:19).
55. "What do you think, Simon?"	100. Matthew 17:25a	Peter	8	None recorded
56. "From whom do the kings of the earth collect duty and taxes—from their own sons or from others?"	101. Matthew 17:25b	Peter	4	Peter answered, "From others" (17:26).
57. "What do you think?"	102. Matthew 18:12a	The twelve disciples	8	None recorded
58. "If a man owns a hundred sheep, and one of them wanders away, will he not leave the ninety-nine on the hills and go to look for the one that wandered off?"	103–104. Matthew 18:12b (Luke 15:4)	The twelve disciples	4	None recorded
59. "Haven't you read . . . that at the beginning the Creator 'made them male and female,' and said, 'For this reason a man will leave his father and mother and be united to his wife, and the two will become one flesh.'?"	105. Matthew 19:4–5	Pharisees	1, 9, 10	They asked Jesus a trick question (19:7).
60. "Why do you ask me about what is good?"	106–108. Matthew 19:17 (Mark 10:18; Luke 18:19)	A rich young man	8, 10	He asked Jesus which commandments are to be obeyed (19:18).

Question	Reference	Audience	Type	Response
61. "What is it you want?"	109–110. Matthew 20:21a (Mark 10:36)	The mother of James and John (Mark 10:36 records that James and John asked the question; apparently they did so through their mother.)	6	She answered Jesus' question (20:21b).
62. "Can you drink the cup I am going to drink?"	111–112. Matthew 20:22 (Mark 10:38)	James and John	3	They answered that they could drink his cup (20:22).
63. "What do you want me to do for you?"	113–115. Matthew 20:32; Mark 10:51; Luke 18:41	Two blind men	6	They said they wanted their sight.
64. "Have you never read, 'From the lips of children and infants you have ordained praise'?"	116. Matthew 21:16	Chief priests and teachers of the law	1, 9, 10	None recorded
65. "John's baptism —where did it come from?"	117. Matthew 21:25a	Chief priests and teachers of the law	1, 9	None recorded
66. "Was it from heaven, or from men?"	118–120. Matthew 21:25b (Mark 11:30; Luke 20:4)	Chief priests and teachers of the law	1, 9	After Jesus' two questions, they refused to answer, saying, "We don't know" (21:25c–27a).
67. "What do you think?"	121. Matthew 21:28	Chief priests and teachers of the law	8	None recorded
68. "Which of the two did what his father wanted?"	122. Matthew 21:31	Chief priests and teachers of the law	6, 8	They answered, "The first" (21:31).
69. "Therefore, when the owner of the vineyard comes, what will he do to those tenants?"	123–125. Matthew 21:40 (Mark 12:9; Luke 20:15)	Chief priests and teachers of the law	6, 8, 15	They replied that he would punish them and rent the vineyard to other tenants (21:41).

Questions	References	Individual(s) or Groups Addressed	Kind of Questions	Immediate Response by the One(s) Questioned
70. "Have you never read in the Scriptures, 'The stone the builders rejected has become the capstone; the Lord has done this, and it is marvelous in our eyes'?"	126–128. Matthew 21:42 (Mark 12:10; Luke 20:17)	Chief priests and teachers of the law	1, 8, 10	They looked for a way to arrest Jesus.
71. "You hypocrites, why are you trying to trap me?"	129–130. Matthew 22:18 (Mark 12:15b)	Pharisees and Herodians	12	They brought him a denarius as he requested (22:19).
72–73. "Whose portrait is this? And whose inscription?"	131–136. Matthew 22:20 (Mark 12:16; Luke 20:24)	Pharisees and Herodians	1, 8	They answered, "Caesar's" (22:21).
74. "Have you not read what God said to you, 'I am the God of Abraham, the God of Isaac, and the God of Jacob'?"	137–138. Matthew 22:31–32 (Mark 12:26)	Sadducees	1, 8, 9, 10	None recorded
75–76. "What do you think about the Christ? Whose son is he?"	139–140. Matthew 22:42	Pharisees	8, 6	They replied, "The son of David" (22:42).
77. "How is it then that David, speaking by the spirit, calls him 'Lord'?"	141. Matthew 22:43	Pharisees	8, 9	None recorded
78. "If then David calls him 'Lord,' how can he be his son?"	142–144. Matthew 22:45 (Mark 12:37; Luke 20:44)	Pharisees	8, 9	They could not reply, and they dared ask him no more questions (22:46).
79. "You blind fools! Which is greater: the gold, or the temple that makes the gold sacred?"	145. Matthew 23:17	Teachers of the law and Pharisees	8, 9	None recorded
80. "You blind men! Which is greater: the gift, or the altar that makes the gift sacred?"	146. Matthew 23:19	Teachers of the law and Pharisees	8, 9	None recorded
81. "You snakes! You brood of vipers! How will you escape being condemned to hell?"	147. Matthew 23:33	Teachers of the law and Pharisees	8, 13	None recorded
82. "Do you see all these things?"	148–149. Matthew 24:2 (Mark 13:2)	The twelve disciples	14	None recorded

Question	Reference	Audience		Response
83. "Who then is the faithful and wise servant, whom the master has put in charge of the servants in his household to give them food at the proper time?"	150. Matthew 24:45	The twelve disciples	8, 15	None recorded
84. "Why are you bothering this woman?"	151–152. Matthew 26:10 (Mark 14:6)	The twelve disciples	10, 12	None recorded
85. "Could you men not keep watch with me for one hour?"	153–154. Matthew 26:40 (Mark 14:37)	Peter	10	None recorded
86. "Are you still sleeping and resting?"	155–157. Matthew 26:45 (Mark 14:41; Luke 22:46)	Peter, James, and John	10	None recorded
87–88. "Do you think I cannot call on my Father, and he will at once put at my disposal more than twelve legions of angels? But how then would the Scriptures be fulfilled that say it must happen in that way?"	158–159. Matthew 26:53–54	Peter	8, 8	None recorded
89. "Am I leading a rebellion, that you have come out with swords and clubs to capture me?"	160. Matthew 26:55	Crowd who went to arrest Jesus	3	None recorded
90. "My God, my God, why have you forsaken me?"	161–162. Matthew 27:46 (Mark 15:34)	God the Father	11	None recorded
91. "Which is lawful on the Sabbath: to do good or to do evil, to save life or to kill?"	163–164. Mark 3:4 (Luke 6:9)	Pharisees	8, 9	They remained silent (3:4).
92. "How can Satan drive out Satan?"	165. Mark 3:23	Teachers of the law	3	None recorded
93–94. "Don't you understand this parable? How then will you understand any parable?"	166–167. Mark 4:13	The twelve disciples and others	10, 10	None recorded
95–96. "Do you bring in a lamp to put it under a bowl or a bed? Instead, don't you put it on its stand?"	168–169. Mark 4:21	The twelve disciples and others	3	None recorded

Questions	References	Individual(s) or Groups Addressed	Kind of Questions	Immediate Response by the One(s) Questioned
97. "What shall we say the kingdom of God is like, or what parable shall we use to describe it?"	170. Mark 4:30	The twelve disciples and others	8, 14	None recorded
98. "Do you still have no faith?"	171–172. Mark 4:40b (Luke 8:25)	The twelve disciples	7, 8	They were terrified and wondered who Jesus is (4:41).
99. "What is your name?"	173–174. Mark 5:9 (Luke 8:30)	Demon-possessed man of the region of the Gerasenes	1	He answered that the demons' names were "Legion" (5:9).
100. "Who touched my clothes?"	175–176. Mark 5:30 (Luke 8:45)	A woman with hemorrhaging	1	The disciples asked why he asked such a strange question (5:31).
101. "Why all this commotion and wailing? The child is not dead but asleep."	177. Mark 5:39	Mourners at the synagogue ruler's house	11	They laughed at Jesus (5:40).
102. "How many loaves do you have?"	178. Mark 6:38	The twelve disciples	1	They said they had five loaves and two fish (6:38).
103. "Why does this generation ask for a miraculous sign?"	179. Mark 8:12	Pharisees	11	None recorded
104–105. "Are your hearts hardened? Do you have eyes but fail to see, and ears but fail to hear?"	180–181. Mark 8:17c–18	The twelve disciples	10, 11, 13	None recorded
106. "When I broke the five loaves for the five thousand, how many basketfuls of pieces did you pick up?"	182. Mark 8:19	The twelve disciples	1	They replied, "Twelve" (8:19).
107. "Do you still not understand?"	183. Mark 8:21	The twelve disciples	10, 11	None recorded
108. "Do you see anything?"	184. Mark 8:23	A blind man	1	He said people looked like trees walking around (8:24).

Question	Reference	Audience		Response
109. "What are you arguing with them about?"	185. Mark 9:16	Crowd	1	The father of a demon-possessed boy explained the reason for the argument between the crowd and the disciples (9:17–18).
110. "How long has he been like this?"	186. Mark 9:21	The father of the demon-possessed boy	1	The father answered, "From childhood" (9:21).
111. "If you can?"	187. Mark 9:23	The father of the demon-possessed boy	7, 11	The father replied that he believed (9:24).
112. "What were you arguing about on the road?"	188. Mark 9:33	The twelve disciples	1, 12	They kept quiet (9:34).
113. "What did Moses command you?"	189. Mark 10:3	Pharisees	1, 8	They answered by referring to Deuteronomy 24:1–4 (Mark 10:4).
114. "Is it not written, 'My house will be called a house of prayer for all nations'?"	190. Mark 11:17	People in the temple courts	1, 4	The chief priests and the teachers of the law planned to kill Jesus (11:18).
115. "Are you not in error because you do not know the Scriptures or the power of God?"	191. Mark 12:24	Sadducees	4	None recorded
116. "How is it that the teachers of the law say that the Christ is the son of David?"	192–193. Mark 12:35 (Luke 20:41)	People in the temple courts	8	The crowd listened with delight (12:37).
117. "Where is my guest room, where I may eat the Passover with my disciples?"	194–195. Mark 14:14 (Luke 22:11)	Owner of a house with an upper room	1	He showed the disciples a large upper room (14:16).
118. "Are you asleep?"	196–197. Mark 14:37a (Luke 22:46)	Peter	7, 10	None recorded
119–120. "Why were you searching for me? Didn't you know I had to be in my Father's house?"	198–199. Luke 2:49	Joseph and Mary	10, 8	They did not understand his response (2:50).

Questions	References	Individual(s) or Groups Addressed	Kind of Questions	Immediate Response by the One(s) Questioned
121. "If you do good to those who are good to you, what credit is that to you?"	200. Luke 6:33	Crowd	8	None recorded
122. "And if you lend to those from whom you expect repayment, what credit is that to you?"	201. Luke 6:34	Crowd	8	None recorded
123–124. "Can a blind man lead a blind man? Will they not both fall into a pit?"	202–203. Luke 6:39	Crowd	4	None recorded
125. "Why do you call me 'Lord, Lord,' and not do what I say?"	204. Luke 6:46	Crowd	9, 10	None recorded
126. "What are they [the people of this generation] like?"	205. Luke 7:31b	Crowd	8	None recorded
127. "Neither of them had the money to pay him back, so he canceled the debts of both. Now which of them will love him more?"	206. Luke 7:42	A Pharisee named Simon	6, 15	Simon responded that the one whose larger debt was canceled would love the creditor more (7:43).
128. "Do you see this woman?"	207. Luke 7:44	A Pharisee named Simon	4, 8	None recorded
129. "And you, Capernaum, will you be lifted up to the skies?"	208. Luke 10:15	The seventy-two disciples	3, 8	None recorded
130–131. "What is written in the Law? How do you read it?"	209–210. Luke 10:26	An expert in the law	1, 6	He quoted Leviticus 19:18 (Luke 10:27).
132. "Which of these three do you think was a neighbor to the man who fell into the hands of the robbers?"	211. Luke 10:36	An expert in the law	8, 15	He answered, "The one who had mercy on him" (10:37).
133. "Did not the one who made the outside make the inside also?"	212. Luke 11:40	Pharisees	4	An expert in the law said Jesus' remarks insulted them (11:45).
134. "Are not five sparrows sold for two pennies?"	213. Luke 12:6	Crowd	4	None recorded

Question	Reference	Audience	Numbers	Response
135. "Man, who appointed me a judge or an arbiter between you?"	214. Luke 12:14	Someone in a crowd	10	None recorded
136. "Who of you by worrying can add a single hour to his life?"	215. Luke 12:25	The disciples	3	None recorded
137. "Since you cannot do this very little thing, why do you worry about the rest?"	216. Luke 12:26	The disciples	8	None recorded
138. "Who then is the faithful and wise manager, whom the master puts in charge of his servants to give them their food allowance at the proper time?"	217. Luke 12:42	Peter	8	None recorded
139. "Do you think I came to bring peace on earth?"	218. Luke 12:51	Peter	3, 8	None recorded
140. "How is it that you don't know how to interpret this present time?"	219. Luke 12:56	Crowd	9, 10	None recorded
141. "Why don't you judge for yourselves who is right?"	220. Luke 12:57	Crowd	10	None recorded
142. "Do you think that these Galileans were worse sinners than all the other Galileans because they suffered this way?"	221. Luke 13:2	Crowd	3, 8	None recorded
143. "Or those eighteen who died when the tower in Siloam fell on them—do you think they were more guilty than all the others living in Jerusalem?"	222. Luke 13:4	Crowd	8, 3	None recorded
144–145. "You hypocrites! Doesn't each of you on the Sabbath untie his ox or donkey from the stall and lead it out to give it water? Then should not this woman, a daughter of Abraham, whom Satan has kept bound for eighteen long years, be set free on the Sabbath day from what bound her?"	223–224. Luke 13:15–16	Synagogue rulers and opponents	4, 8, 9	They were humiliated, but the people were delighted (13:17).

Questions	References	Individual(s) or Groups Addressed	Kind of Questions	Immediate Response by the One(s) Questioned
146–147. "What is the kingdom of God like? What shall I compare it to?"	225–226. Luke 13:18	Disciples	8, 8	None recorded
148. "What shall I compare the kingdom of God to?"	227. Luke 13:20	Disciples	14	None recorded
149. "Is it lawful to heal on the Sabbath or not?"	228. Luke 14:3	Pharisees and teachers of the law	8, 9	They remained silent (14:4).
150. "If one of you has a son or an ox that falls into a well on the Sabbath day, will you not immediately pull him out?"	229. Luke 14:5	Pharisees and experts in the law	4, 8, 9	They said nothing (14:6).
151. "Suppose one of you wants to build a tower. Will he not first sit down and estimate the cost to see if he has enough money to complete it?"	230. Luke 14:28	Crowds	4, 8	None recorded
152. "Or suppose a king is about to go to war against another king. Will he not first sit down and consider whether he is able with ten thousand men to oppose the one coming against him with twenty thousand?"	231. Luke 14:31	Crowds	4, 8	None recorded
153. "Or suppose a woman has ten silver coins and loses one. Does she not light a lamp, sweep the house and search carefully until she finds it?"	232. Luke 15:8	Pharisees and teachers of the law	4	None recorded
154–155. "So if you have not been trustworthy in handling worldly wealth, who will trust you with true riches? And if you have not been trustworthy with someone else's property, who will give you property of your own?"	233–234. Luke 16:11–12	The twelve disciples	8, 15, 8, 15	The Pharisees, who heard this, sneered at Jesus (16:14).

Question	Reference	Audience		Response
156–158. "Suppose one of you had a servant plowing or looking after sheep. Would he say to the servant when he comes in from the field, 'Come along now and sit down to eat'? Would he not rather say, 'Prepare my supper, get yourself ready and wait on me while I eat and drink; after that you may eat and drink'? Would he thank the servant because he did what he was told to do?"	235–237. Luke 17:7–9	The twelve disciples	4, 4, 4	None recorded
159–161. "Were not all ten cleansed? Where are the other nine? Was no one found to return and give praise to God except this foreigner?"	238–240. Luke 17:17–18	The twelve disciples	1, 10, 11	None recorded
162–163. "And will not God bring about justice for his chosen ones, who cry out to him day and night? Will he keep putting them off?"	241–242. Luke 18:7	The twelve disciples	4, 8	None recorded
164. "However, when the Son of Man comes will he find faith on the earth?"	243. Luke 18:8	The twelve disciples	8	None recorded
165–166. "For who is greater, the one who is at the table or the one who serves? Is it not the one who is at the table?"	244–245. Luke 22:27	Eleven disciples (without Judas)	8, 4	None recorded
167. "When I sent you without purse, bag or sandals, did you lack anything?"	246. Luke 22:35	Eleven disciples (without Judas)	1	They answered "Nothing" (22:35).
168. "Judas, are you betraying the Son of Man with a kiss?"	247. Luke 22:48	Judas	9, 10, 11	None recorded
169. "For if men do these things when the tree is green, what will happen when it is dry?"	248. Luke 23:31	Crowd	8	None recorded

Questions	References	Individual(s) or Groups Addressed	Kind of Questions	Immediate Response by the One(s) Questioned
170. "What are you discussing together as you walk along?"	249. Luke 24:17	Two Emmaus disciples	2	They responded with amazement that he did not know what had happened in Jerusalem (24:18).
171. "What things?"	250. Luke 24:19	Two Emmaus disciples	1, 6	They said, "About Jesus of Nazareth," who was crucified and arose (24:19–24).
172. "Did not the Christ have to suffer these things and then enter his glory?"	251. Luke 24:26	Two Emmaus disciples	1	None recorded
173. "Why are you troubled, and why do doubts rise in your minds?"	252. Luke 24:38	The ten disciples (without Judas and Thomas)	10	Jesus showed them his hands and feet (24:40).
174. "Do you have anything here to eat?"	253. Luke 24:41	The ten disciples (without Judas and Thomas)	1	Jesus ate some broiled fish (24:42–43).
175. "What do you want?"	254. John 1:38	Two of John's disciples who were following Jesus	2, 6	They asked Jesus where he was staying (1:38).
176. "Dear woman, why do you involve me?"	255. John 2:4	Mary	8, 12	She told the servants to do whatever Jesus told them to do (2:5).
177. "You are Israel's teacher . . . and you do not understand these things?"	256. John 3:10	Nicodemus	10	None recorded
178. "I have spoken to you of earthly things and you do not believe; how then will you believe if I speak of heavenly things?"	257. John 3:12	Nicodemus	8	None recorded
179. "Will you give me a drink?"	258. John 4:7	Samaritan woman	2	She was surprised that he, a Jew, asked her, a Samaritan, for a drink (4:9).

#	Question	Audience		Response
180. John 4:35	"Do you not say, 'Four months more and then the harvest'?"	The twelve disciples	4	None recorded
181. John 5:6	"Do you want to get well?"	An invalid	6	The man said he had no one to help him into the pool (5:7).
182. John 5:44	"How can you believe if you accept praise from one another, yet make no effort to obtain the praise that comes from the only God?"	The Jews (Jewish leaders)	9	None recorded
183. John 5:47	"But since you do not believe what [Moses] wrote, how are you going to believe what I say?"	The Jews (Jewish leaders)	9	None recorded
184. John 6:5	"Where shall we buy bread for these people to eat?"	Philip	7	Philip responded that not enough money was available to buy food for everyone (6:7).
185. John 6:61	"Does this offend you?"	People following Jesus	10	Soon thereafter many of his followers turned back (6:66).
186. John 6:67	"You do not want to leave too, do you?"	The twelve disciples	7	Peter answered that they had no one to turn to (6:68).
187. John 6:70	"Have I not chosen you, the Twelve? Yet one of you is a devil!"	The twelve disciples	1, 4, 11	None recorded
188. John 7:19	"Has not Moses given you the law?"	People in the temple courts	4	None recorded
189. John 7:19	"Why are you trying to kill me?"	People in the temple courts	9, 12	They accused him of being demon-possessed and asked, "Who is trying to kill you?" (7:20).

Questions	References	Individual(s) or Groups Addressed	Kind of Questions	Immediate Response by the One(s) Questioned
190. "Now if a child can be circumcised on the Sabbath so that the law of Moses may not be broken, why are you angry with me for healing the whole man on the Sabbath?"	269. John 7:23	People in the temple courts	8, 9	They doubted that he is the Christ (7:25–27).
191–192. "Woman, where are they? Has no one condemned you?"	270–271. John 8:10	Woman accused of adultery	1, 8	She answered, "No one, sir" (8:11).
193. "Why is my language not clear to you?"	272. John 8:43	The Jews	10	None recorded
194. "Can any of you prove me guilty of sin?"	273. John 8:46a	The Jews	3	They said, "Aren't we right in saying that you are . . . demon-possessed?" (8:48).
195. "If I am telling the truth, why don't you believe me?"	274. John 8:46b	The Jews	8, 9	They said, "Aren't we right in saying that you are . . . demon-possessed?" (8:48).
196. "Do you believe in the Son of Man?"	275. John 9:35	The healed blind man	5	He asked who Jesus was so he could believe in him (9:36).
197. "For which of these [miracles] do you stone me?"	276. John 10:32	The Jews	9	They said they were stoning him because of blasphemy (10:33).
198–199. "Is it not written in your Law, 'I have said you are gods'? If he called them 'gods,' to whom the word of God came—and the Scripture cannot be broken—what about the one whom the Father set apart as his very own and sent into the world?"	277–278. John 10:34–36a	The Jews	4, 8	None recorded
200. "Why then do you accuse me of blasphemy because I said, 'I am God's Son'?"	279. John 10:36b	The Jews	9, 12	They tried to capture him (10:39).

No.	Scripture	Question	Audience		Response
201.	280. John 11:9	"Are there not twelve hours of daylight?"	The twelve disciples	4	None recorded
202.	281. John 11:26	"Do you believe this?"	Martha	5	She said she did believe that he is the Christ (11:27).
203.	282. John 11:34	"Where have you laid him?"	Mary and her friends	1	They said, "Come and see, Lord" (11:34).
204.	283. John 11:40	"Did I not tell you that if you believed, you would see the glory of God?"	Martha	1	None recorded
205–206.	284–285. John 12:27	"Now my heart is troubled, and what shall I say? 'Father, save me from this hour'?"	Crowd	11	A voice from heaven affirmed that the Father's name was glorified (12:28).
207.	286. John 13:12	"Do you understand what I have done for you?"	The twelve disciples	8	None recorded
208.	287. John 13:38	"Will you really lay down your life for me?"	Peter	3	None recorded
209.	288. John 14:9a	"Don't you know me, Philip, even after I have been among you such a long time?"	Philip	10	None recorded
210.	289. John 14:9b	"How can you say, 'Show us the Father'?"	Philip	10, 11	None recorded
211.	290. John 14:10	"Don't you believe that I am in the Father, and that the Father is in me?"	Philip	5	None recorded
212.	291. John 16:19	"Are you asking one another what I meant when I said, 'In a little while you will see me no more, and then after a little while you will see me'?"	The eleven disciples (without Judas)	10	None recorded
213.	292. John 18:4	"Who is it you want?"	Judas, soldiers, and some chief priests and Pharisees	1	They replied, "Jesus of Nazareth" (18:5).

Questions	References	Individual(s) or Groups Addressed	Kind of Questions	Immediate Response by the One(s) Questioned
214. "Who is it you want?"	293. John 18:7	Judas, soldiers, and some chief priests and Pharisees	1	They replied, "Jesus of Nazareth" (18:7).
215. "Shall I not drink the cup the Father has given me?"	294. John 18:11	Peter	4	None recorded
216. "Why question me?"	295. John 18:21	Annas the high priest	10	An official struck him in the face (18:22).
217. "But if I spoke the truth, why did you strike me?"	296. John 18:23	An official	9, 13	None recorded
218. "Is that your own idea, or did others talk to you about me?"	297. John 18:34	Pilate	6, 10	Pilate said it was the Jewish leaders who handed Jesus over to him (18:35).
219. "Woman . . . why are you crying?"	298. John 20:15a	Mary of Magdala	1, 6, 12	None recorded
220. "Who is it you are looking for?"	299. John 20:15b	Mary of Magdala	1	She asked him to tell her where Jesus' body was (20:15).
221. "Friends, haven't you any fish?"	300. John 21:5	The eleven disciples	2	They answered, "No" (21:5).
222. "Simon son of John, do you truly love me more than these?"	301. John 21:15	Peter	7	He said, "Yes, Lord" (21:15).
223. "Simon, son of John, do you truly love me?"	302. John 21:16	Peter	7	He said, "Yes, Lord" (21:16).
224. "Simon, son of John, do you love me?"	303. John 21:17	Peter	7	Peter was hurt and answered, "Lord, you know all things; you know that I love you" (21:17).
225. "If I want him to remain alive until I return, what is that to you?"	304. John 21:22	Peter	10	None recorded

*"You teach the way of God
in accordance with the truth."*

Matthew 22:16

15

How Did Jesus
Respond to Questions
Asked of Him?

Teaching effectiveness can be measured not only by evaluating the kinds of questions teachers ask, but also by noting the questions students ask. What kinds of questions do they ask? What kinds of questions should they be encouraged to ask? How can teachers encourage students to ask questions? How should teachers respond to student questions?

A study of questions addressed to Jesus and how he responded to them can help teachers today improve their own responses to students' verbal inquiries in class.

How many questions were addressed by individuals and groups to Jesus? Gibbons lists forty-one.[1] However, I have noted 103 separate

---

This chapter is adapted from "How Jesus Responded to Questions," in *Integrity of Heart, Skillfulness of Hands: Biblical and Leadership Studies in Honor of Donald K. Campbell*, ed. Charles H. Dyer and Roy B. Zuck (Grand Rapids: Baker, 1994).

1. Joan Lyon Gibbons, "A Psychological Exploration of Jesus' Use of Questions as an Interpersonal Mode of Communication" (Ph.D. diss., Graduate Theological Union, 1979), 1158–63. Actually her list includes forty-seven, but six of them are questions *about* Jesus addressed to others.

questions addressed to Jesus, listed in table 27 at the end of this chapter. Some questions in the New International Version are statements in other English versions, and conversely, some statements in the New International Version are questions in other versions (e.g., John 8:57 NASB).

The fact that twenty individuals and twelve groups asked Jesus questions reveals how his teaching and his presence stimulated thought and interaction. Each of the following individuals asked one question each: his mother Mary, Nathaniel, Andrew, Martha, a healed blind man, an unnamed person, Judas Iscariot, Thomas, Judas (not Judas Iscariot), a thief on the cross, and Cleopas. Those who asked more than one question include John the Baptist (two questions), Nicodemus (two), the Samaritan woman (two), the high priest (two), an expert in the law (three), a rich young man (three), demons (two questions on each of two occasions), Pilate (nine), and Peter (nine). The fact that Peter asked nine questions of Jesus points to his inquisitive, loquacious nature, and Pilate's nine questions point to his frustration in whether to condemn Jesus or free him.

Of the groups who queried Jesus, his disciples posed seventeen questions. This is not surprising since he spent an extensive amount of time with them. Other follower groups, each of whom asked one question, included Andrew and another disciple; John's disciples; Peter, James, and John; and James and John. Enemies who interrogated him were the Jews (nine questions), the Pharisees (six questions), Pharisees along with teachers of the law (two), chief priests and elders (two), Pharisees and Herodians (two). In addition crowds asked him five questions. The chief priests and teachers of the law asked him one question, as did the Sadducees.

Twelve kinds of questions were addressed to the Lord, with several questions taking on more than one characteristic.[2] The largest group of questions were *requests for information*. These total thirty-nine. The next group, a total of twenty-one, include *expressions of confusion* (or implied requests for clarification). Others were *expressions of denial* (nine), *challenge* (eight), *trickery* (seven), *expressions of anxiety* (seven), *requests for confirmation* (three), *surprise* (three), *requests for directives* (three), *expressions of rebuke* (two), and one each of *mockery* and *sarcasm*.

2. In table 27 questions 4 and 6 seem to be examples of questions containing two elements. Nathaniel's query to Jesus, "How do you know me?" (John 1:48), seems to reflect a desire for knowledge on how Jesus could have known Nathaniel before having met him and also reflects surprise. In asking Jesus how he could restore Herod's temple in three days when it had already been under construction for forty-six years, the Jews seemed to be expressing confusion as to how he could do it and also denial that it was possible.

Requests for Information

Many of the requests for information came in response to Jesus' teaching, thus demonstrating that his teaching stimulated his hearers' interest and prodded them to think about what he said and to inquire further about what he meant.

The disciples of John the Baptist asked Jesus why his followers did not fast as they and the Pharisees did (Matt. 9:14; Mark 2:18). As he diplomatically defended John, John's disciples, his own disciples, and himself, he spoke "so wisely that no breach was made between John and Himself."[3] Peter's question about whether he should forgive as many as seven times (Matt. 18:21) reveals his supposed tolerance, for the rabbis taught that forgiveness should be extended for three offenses. Twice the Jews who heard him were led to ask, "Who are you?" (John 8:25, 53). Hearing Jesus' comments about salvation after the rich young man refused to follow Jesus, Peter asked what benefit would come to those who did follow him (Matt. 19:27). After Jesus spoke of the stones of the temple being thrown down, the disciples wanted to know when it would happen (Matt. 24:3; Mark 13:4; Luke 22:9). They asked Jesus a similar question as he was teaching them just before he ascended (Acts 1:6). Jesus' comments about his betrayal led Peter to ask who would commit this act (John 13:25). When Jesus said he was going where the disciples could not go, Peter was prompted to ask where the Savior was going (John 13:36).

Expressions of Confusion

Because of their spiritual ignorance or insensitivity, those who heard Jesus did not always understand. However, they did not hesitate to express their confusion or to request an explanation or a clarification. This was true of the Jews, who asked about Jesus' remarks about destroying the temple (John 2:20), of Nicodemus, who was confused about Jesus' comments about a second birth (3:4, 9), of the Samaritan woman in her confusion about physical and "living" water (4:9, 11), of the disciples who were confused about how to secure enough bread for five thousand men (Mark 6:37; John 6:9) and four thousand men (Matt. 15:33), and of Peter, who wondered about the application of a parable (Luke 12:41). Jesus' disciples wondered who could be saved (Matt. 19:25; Mark 10:26; Luke 18:26) and about the quick withering of the fig tree (Matt. 21:20). In the Upper Room Discourse, Peter, Thomas, and

3. Lilas D. Rixon, *How Jesus Taught* (Croydon, N.S.W.: Sydney Missionary and Bible College, 1977), 37.

Judas (not Iscariot) each asked Jesus a question for clarification (John 13:37; 14:5, 22).

Expressions of Denial

Some questions addressed to Jesus were actually denials, as in the Samaritan woman's question, "Are you greater than . . . Jacob?" (John 4:12). She was presumably affirming that he was *not* greater than Jacob. The Jews' similar question, "Are you greater than our father Abraham?" (John 8:53) also was a way of their denying that he surpassed Abraham in greatness. When they inquired, "What? Are we blind too?" (John 9:40), they were obviously denying any spiritual blindness on their part.

Challenge

Questions of challenge were voiced by those who were not followers of Jesus. The Pharisees challenged Jesus by questions (Luke 6:2) on why his disciples were violating the Sabbath (Mark 2:24) and why they broke tradition by neglecting ceremonial washings (Matt. 15:2). When Jesus stated that two witnesses, himself and his Father, supported his testimony, the Pharisees challenged him to show them who his Father was. They asked, "Where is your father?" (John 8:19). They hoped to discredit his second witness by his inability to show them the One who they thought was his earthly father.

The question, "By what authority are you doing these things?" (Matt. 21:23; Mark 11:28; Luke 20:2), asked of Jesus by the chief priests and elders, challenged him to declare the basis of the authority by which he taught and ministered.

When Jesus was on trial before Caiaphas the high priest, the Lord refused to answer two accusers. Disturbed, the priest stood up and asked, "Are you not going to answer?" (Matt. 26:62; Mark 14:60). This was a challenge for Jesus to respond. Standing before Pilate, Jesus refused to answer some of his questions also. His silence frustrated Pilate, so that he challenged Jesus: "Do you refuse to speak to me? Don't you realize I have power either to free you or to crucify you?" (John 19:10). One of the two criminals crucified with Jesus challenged him by asking, "Aren't you the Christ? Save yourself and us!" (Luke 23:39).

Trickery

Some interrogations directed to the Lord were efforts to trick him by forcing him to take one of two views, either of which would pose a problem for him. By the question, "Is it lawful to heal on the Sabbath?"

(Matt. 12:10), the Pharisees hoped to place Jesus in a dilemma. If he responded that it was lawful to heal on the Sabbath, they could then accuse him of violating the Mosaic law by working on the Sabbath. If he said it was unlawful, then he would be unable to restore the man's withered hand. When the teachers of the law and the Pharisees asked Jesus if a woman caught in adultery should be stoned, they were trying to trap him (John 8:1–6). For if he said no, he would be contradicting an Old Testament commandment. But if he favored her stoning, he might jeopardize his popularity with the people.

Two questions about the law and divorce were voiced by Pharisees in Matthew 19:3, 7 (cf. Mark 10:2). With both questions they hoped to force Jesus to take one of two positions, either of which would mean some people would agree with him and others would disagree. The two questions about paying taxes to Caesar (Matt. 22:17; Mark 12:14–15; Luke 20:22), asked by the Pharisees and the Herodians together, were again designed to trick Jesus. If he denied the need to pay taxes, he would be stating disloyalty to Caesar and would be offending the Herodians. If he affirmed the need to pay taxes, he would seemingly be siding with the Romans against Israel, which would offend the Pharisees and would deny his own right to kingship. Their intent was "evil," as Matthew noted (22:18).

Another group, the Sadducees, also tried to trick Jesus by asking which of several brothers in the resurrection would be the husband of a woman who had married each of them (Matt. 22:28; Mark 12:23; Luke 20:33). The Sadducees, who denied the resurrection, hoped to present a question Jesus could not answer successfully. An expert in the law then tried to trap him with a question debated among Jewish authorities: "Which is the greatest commandment in the Law?" (Matt. 22:36). They hoped that his answer would demean whichever commandments were not cited, so that they could accuse him of denigrating much of the law.

Expressions of Anxiety

Questions expressing anxiety were voiced by Jesus' mother when he was twelve years of age (Luke 2:48), by demons when Jesus approached demoniacs (Matt. 8:29; Mark 1:24; 5:7; Luke 4:34; 8:28), and by the disciples, when they feared they would drown (Mark 4:38).

Requests for Confirmation

Four times the Jews, enemies of Jesus, asked him to confirm what he was doing. On two occasions, with three questions, they requested a confirming miraculous sign (John 2:18; 6:30 [two questions]) so they could believe, and once they harshly accused him of being a demon-possessed Samaritan and asked him to confirm the truth of their accusation (8:48).

Surprise

Surprise was expressed in the questions presented by Nathaniel (John 1:48), by Peter in the upper room (John 13:6), and by Cleopas on the Emmaus road (Luke 24:18).

When Jesus approached Peter to wash his feet, Peter responded in surprise: "Lord, are you going to wash my feet?" (John 13:6). Apparently Peter felt this was inappropriate for Jesus. In Greek, Peter's sentence stresses the words *you* and *my*—"Lord, are *you* going to wash *my* feet?"—thereby expressing surprise.

Requests for Directives

Three times Jesus' disciples asked him for a directive on what to do. James and John wanted to know if he desired them to call down fire from heaven to destroy the Samaritan village where people had rejected him (Luke 9:52–54). One wonders how they thought they had the power to perform such a miracle. A similar inquiry in the face of opposition was made by his disciples when Jesus was being arrested: "Lord, should we strike with our swords?" (Luke 22:49). The other request for a directive from the Lord was their question about where they should prepare to share the Passover (Matt. 26:17; Mark 14:12; Luke 22:9).

Expressions of Rebuke

Martha expressed a question of rebuke when she asked Jesus if he was concerned that Mary had left her to do all the housework herself (Luke 10:40). Another question of rebuke was stated by the chief priests and teachers of the law when children were praising Jesus in the temple area: "Do you hear what these children are saying?" (Matt. 21:16). These religious leaders seemed to have been accusing the children of their disturbing words and rebuking Jesus for not chiding the children.

Mockery and Sarcasm

Mockery is seen in the Jews' question, "Who hit you?" when people slapped Jesus on the face at his trial (Matt 26:68). Sarcasm may have been present in Pilate's response to him, "Am I a Jew?" (John 18:35).

Jesus began his questions in an interesting variety of ways (see chap. 14). The same holds true of his questioners. They most often asked "what," "how," "are you," "who," "why," and "where" questions. Other inquiries voiced less often begin with "do you," "don't," "is it," "which," "are we," "when," along with a few others.

The subjects addressed by these interrogators total sixty-three, according to Baldwin.[4]

Accusation (against our Lord)
Adultery
Authority (our Lord's)
Authority (our Lord's over unclean spirits)
Authority (our Lord's source of)
Baptizing (propriety of)
Betrayal of our Lord
Bread of life (our Lord)
Christ (deity)
Christ (identity)
Christ (kingship)
Christ (messiahship)
Christ (origin)
Christ (knowledge)
Christ (power of)
Claims (our Lord's, of deity)
Commandment (greatest)
Companionship (our Lord's)
Conduct (seeming infraction of)
Deity (our Lord's)
Deity (accusation against)
Divorce
Duty (Mary's supposed neglect of)
Fasting (need of)
Food (for five thousand)
Forgiveness
Freedom (spiritual)
Identity (our Lord's)
Identity (source of our Lord's)
Judgment (on Samaritans)
Kingdom of God (the coming of)
Kingship (our Lord's)
Knowledge (our Lord's)
Knowledge (source of our Lord's)

4. Harry A. Baldwin, *101 Outline Studies on Questions Asked and Answered by Our Lord* (New York: Revell, 1938; reprint, Grand Rapids: Baker, 1965), 126.

Knowledge (his, of God)
Life (attainment of Christian)
Life (attainment of eternal)
Life (John's span of)
Life (mystery of twice-born)
Lifting up
Marriage (relationship after resurrection)
Messiahship
Mission (meaning of Christ's)
Mystery (of twice-born life)
Origin (our Lord's)
Parables (use of)
Passover (place of)
Power (our Lord's superhuman)
Power (our Lord's)
Preferments
Saved (number of)
Saved (who will be)
Scribes ("Elijah" teaching of)
Son of man
Subjects (many undisclosed)
Suffering (mystery of)
Teaching ("Elijah" of scribes)
Teachings (Samaritans vs. Jews)
Temple (destruction of)
Tribute
Truth (appropriation of)
Twice-born life (mystery of)
Washing feet (propriety of)

When teachers today are presenting challenging content, they can expect students to respond with requests for further information. Other responses may reflect confusion or the desire for clarification. Still other responses may occasionally be those of surprise, requests for a directive, requests for confirmation, or expressions of anxiety. Occasionally students may challenge what a teacher is presenting. Sometimes a student may deny what is being taught. Some kinds of questions, however, may be considered unique to Jesus and his ministry. These would include questions expressing trickery, rebuke, self-justification, mockery, and sarcasm.

As teachers become aware of the kinds of questions they may expect from their students, they can be better prepared for their teaching tasks. In addition they should seek to teach in such a way that students will be encouraged to ask for further information and for points of clarification.

Jesus' Answers to Questions

The Lord Jesus responded to questions in a great variety of ways. He was always eager to respond, never refusing to interact with his inquirers except when addressed by Caiaphas (Matt. 26:62), the Jews on one occasion (26:68), Pilate (27:13; John 18:38; 19:9—Jesus answered some of Pilate's questions but not others), and the thief on the cross (Luke 23:39). Also Herod plied Jesus "with many questions," but "Jesus gave him no answer" (Luke 23:9). As Barnard wrote,

> Very striking are those instances where the silence of Jesus was more eloquent than words could have been. It was useless to attempt any answer to the charges of witnesses brought against Him before judges who had procured their false evidence (Mk 14⁶¹ =Mt 26⁶³), or to similar charges before Pilate (Mk 15⁵ = Mt 27¹⁴) and Herod (Lk 23⁹); it was useless to discuss with such a man as Pilate the nature of truth (Jn 18³⁸), or His heavenly mission (Jn 19⁹). Only when such questions are asked in a right spirit is it worth answering them. When Pilate asked Him (Mk 15² = Mt 27¹¹ = Lk 23³, cf. Jn 18⁵⁷) whether He was "the King of the Jews," He gave an ambiguous answer—"Thou sayest": it was a title He himself had not claimed, and which belonged to Him only in a sense that Pilate could not understand. But Christ did not hesitate, in spite of the obvious danger, to give direct answers to questions concerning His own claims (Mk 14⁶² = Mt 26⁶⁴, cf. Lk 22⁷⁰).⁵

Jesus answered patiently, directly, and without demeaning people.⁶ "He was never at a loss what to say nor how to say it."⁷ Nor was he ever taken unawares; he was always in command of the situation, never dodging a question or bungling an answer.⁸

Jesus gave explanations in response to questions by John the Baptist; Nicodemus; John's disciples; his own disciples; Peter, James, and John; the crowd; the Jews; Martha; the Pharisees; a rich young man; Peter; the Pharisees and the Herodians; the Sadducees; and an expert in the law.

Many times Jesus responded to a question with a question of his own. This is true of his reply to the first recorded question addressed to

---

5. *Dictionary of Christ and the Gospels*, 1909 ed., s.v., "Questions and Answers," by P. M. Barnard, 462.

6. Robert G. Delnay, *Teach as He Taught* (Chicago: Moody, 1987), 34.

7. Richard Montague, "The Dialecting Method of Jesus," *Bibliotheca Sacra* 41 (July–September 1884): 551.

8. B. A. Hinsdale, *Jesus as a Teacher* (St. Louis: Christian, 1895), 141.

him. When his mother asked why he had stayed behind in the temple, twelve-year-old Jesus answered her with two questions: "Why were you searching for me? Didn't you know I had to be in my Father's house?" (Luke 2:49). His parents, though, did not understand what he meant.[9] He also voiced questions to Nicodemus (John 3:10, 12), John's disciples (Matt. 9:15), the Pharisees (Matt. 12:11; 19:4), the disciples in the storm (Mark 4:40), the disciples with the five thousand (Mark 6:38) and the four thousand to be fed (Matt. 15:34), Peter (John 6:70; Luke 12:42; John 21:22), an expert in the law who asked what he must do to inherit eternal life (Luke 10:26), the rich young man (Matt. 19:17), the chief priests and teachers of the law (Matt. 21:16), the chief priest and elders (Matt. 21:25), Pilate (John 18:34), and Cleopas (Luke 24:19). These counterquestions prompted his interrogators to think through the answers to their own questions or to ask further questions.

Sometimes, however, Jesus' answers were in questions his interrogators could not answer. The dynamic effect of his words is seen in the response of the Pharisees when Jesus spoke to them about his Davidic ancestry: "No one could say a word in reply, and from that day on no one dared to ask him any more questions" (Matt. 22:46). His opponents, after months of vicious and subtle forays at his integrity, were stopped in their tracks—defeated and silenced in their repeated efforts to silence the Lord Jesus!

When individuals requested information, Jesus always gave the facts they needed. This is seen in his responses to Andrew's question about where Jesus was staying (John 1:38), Nathaniel's question about how Jesus knew him (John 1:48), Peter's question about how many times to forgive (Matt. 18:21), the healed blind man's question about who Jesus was (John 9:36), the rich young man's question about which commandment to obey and what he still lacked (Matt. 19:18, 20), his disciples' questions about the sign of his coming (Matt. 24:3; Mark 13:4; Luke 21:7), their question about where to make preparations for the Passover (Matt 26:17; Mark 14:12; Luke 22:9), and their questions about who would betray him (Matt. 26:22, 25; John 13:25).

Some questions, however, Jesus evaded or answered indirectly. When the Pharisees asked, "Where is your father?" (John 8:19), he answered by stating, "You do not know me or my Father." After Jesus spoke of his return, when some would be taken with him and others would be left, his disciples asked, "Where, Lord?" (Luke 17:37), that is, "Where will they be taken?" Jesus replied somewhat enigmatically, "Where there is a dead body, there the vultures will gather." The idea in that response seems to be that much as a dead body results in vultures

9. See comments on Jesus' answers in chapter 14.

gathering around it, so dead people will be confined to judgment if they are not ready for the Lord's return. One is as certain as the other.

When the crowd asked Jesus about his statements that the Son of man would be lifted up (John 12:34), he did not answer their question. Instead he encouraged them to "trust in the light" (v. 36). He pressed on to their real need. Without telling specifically how he could wither a fig tree so quickly (Matt. 21:20), Jesus told the disciples that by exercising faith great things can be accomplished (v. 22).

Jesus cleverly avoided answering the question the chief priests and elders asked about his source of authority (Matt. 21:23) by asking *them* about the source of John the Baptist's authority (vv. 24–27). When Peter expressed surprise that Jesus was about to wash his feet (John 13:6), Jesus explained that later Peter would realize the significance of what he was about to do (13:7). Nor did Jesus answer Peter's question about where he was going (v. 36). When Pilate queried, "Are you the king of the Jews?" (18:33), Jesus did not answer the question but instead asked if that was Pilate's own idea (v. 34). And when Pilate responded, "Am I a Jew?" (18:35), Jesus did not answer that question either. He replied, "My kingdom is not of this world" (v. 36).

To Thomas's direct question, "How can we know the way?" (John 14:5), that is, the place where Jesus was going, the Lord answered him directly with an affirmation: "I am the way, the truth and the life" (v. 6). And when Judas (not Judas Iscariot) asked for a reason why Jesus said he would show himself to them and not to the world (v. 22), Jesus responded indirectly. Instead of giving a reason, he emphasized that individuals who love him will be obedient to him (vv. 23–24), implying that the world does not love or obey him.

Sometimes Jesus' response to questions was in the form of a rebuke. This is true of his response to demons (Matt. 8:32; Mark 1:25; 5:8; Luke 4:35), to the disciples in the storm (Mark 4:40), to James and John, who asked about calling down fire from heaven (Luke 9:55), to the crowd who accused him of being demon-possessed (John 7:20), when he asked them why they were angry for his healing on the Sabbath (7:23), to the chief priests and teachers of the law who asked him if he heard what the children were saying when they were praising him (Matt. 21:16), and when he asked if they had never read Psalm 8:2. He rebuked the Pharisees and the Herodians by calling them hypocrites when they asked about taxes to Caesar (Matt. 22:18). The Lord also rebuked Peter (John 21:22) when the apostle asked about John.

A few times Jesus corrected the false teaching of his questioners. He pointed out to the Pharisees that Moses permitted divorce but did not command it as they had said (Matt. 19:7–8; Mark 10:4). The Sadducees' denial of the resurrection was corrected by Jesus' response to their query about marriage in the resurrected life (Matt. 22:29–32; Mark 12:24–27; Luke 20:34–38). On trial before Pilate, Jesus corrected Pilate's false assumption that he had power to release or crucify Jesus (John 19:10–11).

Occasionally Jesus found it necessary to give negative answers to his inquirers' questions. When the Jews asked him if he was a demon-possessed Samaritan, he simply replied, "I am not possessed by a demon" (John 8:48–49). Then he used that occasion to point out the difference between those who do not honor him and those who keep his word (vv. 49–50). When Peter asked, "Why can't I follow you now?" and affirmed, "I will lay down my life for you" (13:37), Jesus negated his supposed readiness for martyrdom by asking, "Will you really lay down your life for me?" (v. 38). At his ascension, when the disciples wanted to know if he would restore the kingdom to Israel then (Acts 1:6), Jesus told them they were not privileged to know the time (v. 7). He then proceeded to disclose a truth of greater importance to them at that time, namely, the fact that they would receive spiritual power from the Holy Spirit on the day of Pentecost (v. 8).

Questions from his audiences also gave Jesus opportunity to teach in parables. He did this on at least four occasions. When John's disciples wondered why Jesus' disciples did not fast (Matt. 9:14; Mark 2:18), he spoke in parabolic statements about old garments and new cloth and old wineskins and new wine (Matt. 9:16–17; Mark 2:19–22). Jesus' parable of the unmerciful servant (Matt. 18:23–35) followed Peter's question about the number of times one should forgive others (v. 22). The well-known parable of the good Samaritan (Luke 10:30–36) was given in response to the question of the expert in the law, "Who is my neighbor?" (v. 29). Sometimes Jesus went beyond the question asked and taught additional truths. For example, each question of the crowd in the synagogue at Capernaum (John 6:25, 28, 30) enabled the master Teacher to give further teaching.

Jesus' replies to questions included affirmations of truth. "How much more valuable is a man than a sheep!" (Matt. 12:12) was his reply to the Pharisees' question about healing on the Sabbath. In response to Pilate's question to Jesus, "Am I a Jew?" Jesus affirmed, "My kingdom is not of this world" (John 18:35). And in response to Peter's query, "What then will there be for us?" (Matt. 19:27) the Lord said, "Many who are first will be last, and many who are last will be first" (v. 30).

Queries addressed to Jesus gave him opportunity to challenge his interrogators to action. When the crowd asked when Jesus had arrived at Capernaum (John 6:25), he ignored the question and used the occasion to challenge them to "work . . . for food that endures to eternal life" (v. 27), rather than follow him for the sake of material food. When the disciples asked, "Who is the greatest in the kingdom of heaven?" (Matt. 18:1), he challenged them to be humble, becoming like little children (v. 3). A rich young man who asked, "What do I still lack?" (Matt. 19:20) was challenged to sell his possessions and to follow Jesus (v. 21). When the crowd asked about Jesus being lifted up as the Son of man (John 12:34), he challenged the people to trust in him the Light (v. 36).

Fifteen responses of the questioners to Jesus' answers included additional questions. These were asked by Nicodemus (John 3:9), the Samaritan woman (4:11), Jesus' disciples (Mark 4:41), the crowd at Capernaum (John 6:28, 30), the Jews (8:53), the Pharisees (Matt. 19:7), the rich young man (Matt. 19:18, 20), Peter (John 13:25, 36–37), Judas (Matt. 26:25), Caiaphas (Mark 14:61), and Pilate (John 18:35; 19:10).

Jesus even answered unspoken questions! As the omniscient Son of God, he knew what others were thinking or talking about, and so he addressed their questions and concerns. This is seen in Matthew 9:4 (cf. Mark 2:8; Luke 5:21); 12:25; 16:8 (cf. Mark 8:17); 17:25; 22:18 (cf. Mark 12:15); 26:10; Luke 7:39–40; and John 6:42.

"We are left with a sense of wonder at the infinite variety, delicacy and vigour of our Lord's way with inquirers. There is no pattern, no set of rules—always the fresh response to the unique situation."[10]

What Can We Learn from Jesus about the Art of Responding to Questions?

A number of implications for teachers today can be drawn from this study of the scores of questions addressed to Jesus and how he responded to them.

1. Be open to students' questions and give them thoughtful, appropriate answers. Jesus never called any questions foolish or unnecessary.
2. Teach in such a way that students are stimulated to think about the content and to ask questions about the material communicated. As Jesus taught, his listeners were prompted to respond.
3. Recognize the variety of kinds of questions students may ask. Students may want additional information; they may desire clarification; they may even express anxiety or surprise.
4. Respond to student questions with attentiveness and give ap-

10. David H. C. Read, "The Mind of Christ; IX. His Way with Inquirers," *Expository Times* 63 (October 1951): 40.

propriate answers with explanations and clarifications. Some questions, however, may call for indirect answers or for correction of false concepts, for additional questions, for additional teaching (by way of truths or illustrations of truths), or for challenges to action.

5. Respond to all questions with respect, even those that are irrelevant or that challenge your views. Jesus used such queries to give additional insights, without embarrassing the students.

As Fortosis wrote, "When students are posing questions freely in the classroom, it is usually a very positive sign. It suggests that there is a relaxed atmosphere and an accepting attitude on the part of the instructor. It also suggests that students are motivated to learn more about the subject matter."[11]

Students' questions and teachers' responses to them comprise a highly significant element in the teaching-learning classroom. Teachers do well to learn from Jesus how to stimulate and respond to questions.

How Do You Respond?

Think of questions students asked in recent class sessions. What kinds of questions were they? Or have someone write down questions asked in a class and give you the list afterward to analyze.

Think of the ways you responded to those questions. How could you improve your responses?

Ask yourself, Am I teaching in such a way that I am stimulating students to ask questions?

As you prepare each class session, write out questions you anticipate students will ask. This is a helpful part of lesson preparation!

---

11. Stephen G. Fortosis, "Can Questioning Make Religious Educators More Effective in the Classroom?" *Christian Education Journal* 12 (spring 1992): 100.

Table 27
Questions Addressed to Jesus and His Responses

Reference*	Person(s) Who Asked	Question	Kind of Question or Problem	Place	Jesus' Answer	Kind of Answer by Jesus	Immediate Responses of the Questioner(s)
1. Luke 2:48	Mary, Jesus' mother	"Son, why have you treated us like this?"	Anxiety	Temple in Jerusalem among the teachers	"Why were you searching for me? . . . Didn't you know I had to be in my Father's house?"	Explanation	Mary and Joseph did not understand his response.
2. Matthew 3:14	John the Baptist	"I need to be baptized by you, and do you come to me?"	Expression of confusion	Jordan River	"It is proper for us to do this to fulfill all righteousness."	Explanation	John consented to baptize Jesus.
3. John 1:38	Andrew and another disciple	"Rabbi, where are you staying?"	Request for information	Bethany beyond the Jordan River	"Come, and you will see" (v. 39).	Information	They went with him.
4. John 1:48	Nathanael	"How do you know me?"	Request for information, and surprise	Galilee	"I saw you while you were still under the fig tree before Philip called you."	Information	Nathanael said Jesus was the Son of God and the King of Israel.
5. John 2:18	Jews	"What miraculous sign can you show us to prove your authority to do all this?"	Request for confirmation	Temple in Jerusalem	"Destroy this temple and I will raise it again in three days."	Enigmatic statement	They misunderstood what he was referring to.
6. John 2:20	Jews	"It has taken forty-six years to build this temple, and you are going to raise it in three days?"	Expression of confusion, and denial	Temple in Jerusalem	None (apparently he left them confused)	None	None recorded

*These references are listed in chronological order. The references in parentheses are parallel passages, though the wording often differs from one Gospel to another.

Reference	Person(s) Who Asked	Question	Kind of Question or Problem	Place	Jesus' Answer	Kind of Answer by Jesus	Immediate Responses of the Questioner(s)
7. John 3:4	Nicodemus	"How can a man be born when he is old?"	Expression of confusion	With Jesus at night	Jesus explained that he was speaking of spiritual rebirth.	Explanation	Nicodemus asked a second question, again reflecting confusion.
8. John 3:9	Nicodemus	"How can this be?"	Expression of confusion	With Jesus at night	Jesus expanded on the way of salvation.	Two questions (vv. 10, 12) and further explanation	None recorded
9. John 4:9	Samaritan woman	"How can you ask me for a drink?"	Expression of confusion	Samaria	Jesus explained that if she knew who he was, she would have received "living water."	Explanation	She asked a second question, again reflecting confusion.
10–11. John 4:11–12	Samaritan woman	"Where can you get this living water? Are you greater than . . . Jacob?"	Expression of confusion; denial	Samaria	Jesus explained the meaning of living water.	Explanation	She requested the water.
12–13. Mark 1:24 (Luke 4:34)	Demon	"What do you want with us, Jesus of Nazareth? Have you come to destroy us?"	Anxiety	Capernaum	"Be quiet!"	Rebuke	The demon departed.

Reference	Asked by	Question/Statement	Type	Location	Jesus' Response	Form of Response	Result
14. Matthew 9:14 (Mark 2:18)	John's disciples	"Why do we and the Pharisees fast, but your disciples do not fast?"	Request for information	Capernaum	Jesus said that a bridegroom's attendants "cannot mourn as long as the bridegroom is with them, can they?" Then he said they will fast later, and he spoke parabolically of old garments and wineskins.	A question, an explanation, and parables	None recorded
15. Mark 2:24 (Luke 6:2)	Pharisees	"Look, why are they doing what is unlawful on the Sabbath?"	Challenge	Galilee	Jesus answered with a question and a quotation, and said, "The Sabbath was made for man, not man for the Sabbath."	A question, a quotation, and an explanation	None recorded
16. Matthew 12:10	Pharisees	"Is it lawful to heal on the Sabbath?"	Trickery	Galilean synagogue	Jesus asked if on the Sabbath they would lift a sheep out of a pit, and then said man is more valuable than sheep.	A question (by an illustration) and a statement of a truth	Pharisees discussed how to kill him.
17. Matthew 11:3 (Luke 7:20)	John the Baptist	"Are you the one who was to come, or should we expect someone else?"	Expression of confusion	Galilee	Jesus referred to his miracles.	Presentation of evidence by which John's disciples could draw a conclusion	None recorded
18. Matthew 13:10	Jesus' disciples	"Why do you speak to the people in parables?"	Expression of confusion	In a boat by the shore of the Sea of Galilee	Jesus explained that parables enabled believers to comprehend further and further blinded unbelievers.	Explanation	None recorded

Reference	Person(s) Who Asked	Question	Kind of Question or Problem	Place	Jesus' Answer	Kind of Answer by Jesus	Immediate Responses of the Questioner(s)
19. Mark 4:38	Jesus' disciples	"Teacher, don't you care if we drown?"	Anxiety	In a boat on the Sea of Galilee	Jesus calmed the storm and then rebuked them by asking, "Why are you so afraid? Do you still have no faith?"	Two questions of rebuke	Fear and confusion expressed by the question, "Who is this?"
20–21. Matthew 8:29 (Mark 5:7; Luke 8:28)	Demons	"What do you want with us, Son of God? . . . Have you come here to torture us before the appointed time?"	Anxiety	Gerasa	Jesus exorcised the demons.	None	The demons went out of the man and into pigs.
22. Mark 6:37	Jesus' disciples	"Are we to go and spend that much on bread and give it to them to eat?"	Expression of confusion	Bethsaida	"How many loaves do you have? . . . Go and see."	A question and a directive	The disciples found five loaves and two fish.
23. John 6:9	Andrew	"Here is a boy with five small barley loaves and two small fish, but how far will they go among so many?"	Expression of confusion	Bethsaida	Jesus ignored the question and told the disciples to have the people sit down.	Evasion of the question, and a directive	The disciples obeyed.
24. John 6:25	Crowd	"Rabbi, when did you get here?"	Request for information	Capernaum	Jesus ignored the question and then encouraged them to do work of eternal significance.	Evasion of the question, and a challenge	They asked him another question.
25. John 6:28	Crowd	"What must we do to do the works God requires?"	Request for information	Capernaum	"The work of God is to do this: to believe in the one he has sent."	Explanation	They asked him a third question.

Reference	Who	Question/Statement	Type	Location	Jesus' Response	Response Type	Result
26–27. John 6:30	Crowd	"What miraculous sign then will you give that we may see it and believe you? What will you do?"	Request for confirmation	Capernaum	Jesus spoke of himself as the "true bread from heaven," a sign already given by God the Father.	Explanation	They requested the true bread.
28. John 6:68	Peter	"Lord, to whom shall we go? You have the words of eternal life."	Request for information	Capernaum	Jesus asked, "Have I not chosen you, the Twelve? Yet one of you is a devil."	A question that evaded Peter's question	None recorded
29. Matthew 15:2 (Mark 7:5)	Pharisees and teachers of the law	"Why do your disciples break the tradition of the elders?"	Challenge	Gennesaret	Jesus asked, "And why do you break the command of God for the sake of your tradition?"	A question, a quotation, and denunciation	None recorded
30. Matthew 15:12	Jesus' disciples	"Do you know that the Pharisees were offended when they heard this?"	Request for information	Gennesaret	Jesus said that plants not planted by God will be pulled up and that the Pharisees should be left alone because they are blind guides.	Explanation by an illustration	Peter asked Jesus to explain the parable.
31. Matthew 15:33 (Mark 8:4)	Jesus' disciples	"Where would we get enough bread in this remote place to feed such a crowd?"	Expression of confusion	By the Sea of Galilee	Jesus asked, "How many loaves do you have?"	A question	They commented that they had seven loaves of bread and a few small fish.
32. Matthew 17:10 (Mark 9:11)	Peter, James, and John	"Why then do the teachers of the law say that Elijah must come first?"	Expression of confusion	Mount of Transfiguration	Jesus explained that "Elijah has already come."	Explanation	They understood that he was referring to John the Baptist.

Reference	Person(s) Who Asked	Question	Kind of Question or Problem	Place	Jesus' Answer	Kind of Answer by Jesus	Immediate Responses of the Questioner(s)
33. Matthew 17:19 (Mark 9:28)	Jesus' disciples	"Why couldn't we drive it [a demon] out?"	Expression of confusion	Near the Mount of Transfiguration	"Because you have so little faith."	Explanation	None recorded
34. Matthew 18:1	Jesus' disciples	"Who is the greatest in the kingdom of heaven?"	Request for information	Capernaum	Placing a child among them, Jesus talked about humility and not causing children to sin.	Explanation and challenge by an illustration	None recorded
35–36. Matthew 18:21	Peter	"Lord, how many times shall I forgive my brother when he sins against me? Up to seven times?"	Request for information	Capernaum	Jesus said 490 times and then told the parable of the unmerciful servant.	Information and a parable	None recorded
37. Luke 9:54	James and John	"Lord, do you want us to call fire down from heaven to destroy them?"	Request for a directive	A Samaritan village	Jesus turned and rebuked them.	Rebuke	None recorded
38. John 7:20	Crowd	"You are demon-possessed. Who is trying to kill you?"	Denial	Temple courts in Jerusalem	"Why are you angry with me for healing . . . on the Sabbath?"	Explanation and a rebuke by a question	Some doubted that he was the Christ.
39. John 8:5	Teachers of the law and Pharisees	"In the Law Moses commanded us to stone such women. Now what do you say?"	Trickery	Temple courts in Jerusalem	Jesus did not answer the question, but wrote on the ground.	Evasion of the question and a rebuke	They left, trapped by their own trap.
40. John 8:19	Pharisees	"Where is your father?"	Challenge	Temple courts in Jerusalem	"You do not know me or my Father."	Evasion of the question	None recorded

Ref	Asker	Question	Type of question	Location	Jesus' response	Type of response	Result
41. John 8:25	Jews	"Who are you?"	Request for information	Temple courts in Jerusalem	"Just what I have been claiming all along."	Evasion of the question	They did not understand.
42. John 8:33	Jews	"How can you say that we shall be set free?"	Denial	Temple courts in Jerusalem	"Everyone who sins is a slave to sin."	Explanation	They protested, "Abraham is our father."
43. John 8:48	Jews	"Aren't we right in saying that you are a Samaritan and demon-possessed?"	Request for confirmation	Temple courts in Jerusalem	"I am not possessed by a demon."	Denial	They affirmed, "Now we know that you are demon-possessed," and they asked two other questions.
44–45. John 8:53	Jews	"Are you greater than our father Abraham? ... Who do you think you are?"	Denial; request for information	Temple courts in Jerusalem	"My Father...glorifies me.... Abraham [saw] my day and was glad."	Explanation	They could not believe he was older than Abraham.
46. Luke 10:25	An expert in the law	"Teacher,... what must I do to inherit eternal life?"	Request for information	Judea	"What is written in the Law?... How do you read it?"	Two questions	The man quoted Leviticus 19:18.
47. Luke 10:29	An expert in the law	"And who is my neighbor?"	Request for information	Judea	Jesus gave the parable of the good Samaritan.	A parable to illustrate who is one's neighbor	None recorded
48. Luke 10:40	Martha	"Lord, don't you care that my sister has left me to do the work by myself?"	Rebuke	Bethany	Jesus said Mary had chosen what is better.	Explanation	None recorded
49. Luke 12:41	Peter	"Lord, are you telling this parable to us, or to everyone?"	Expression of confusion	Judea	"Who then is the faithful and wise manager?"	A question and information about a wise manager and his servants	None recorded

Reference	Person(s) Who Asked	Question	Kind of Question or Problem	Place	Jesus' Answer	Kind of Answer by Jesus	Immediate Responses of the Questioner(s)
50. John 9:2	Jesus' disciples	"Rabbi, who sinned, this man or his parents, that he was born blind?"	Request for information	Jerusalem	Jesus said, "Neither," and then gave the reason for the man's blindness.	Explanation	None recorded
51. John 9:36	Healed blind man	"Who is he, sir?"	Request for information	Jerusalem	"You have now seen him."	Information	The man believed and worshiped Jesus.
52–53. John 9:40	Pharisees	"What? Are we blind too?"	Surprise; denial	Judea	"If you were blind, you would not be guilty of sin; but now that you claim you can see, your guilt remains."	Enigmatic statement and rebuke	None recorded
54. John 10:24	Jews	"How long will you keep us in suspense? If you are the Christ, tell us plainly."	Request for information	Jerusalem	"I did tell you, but you do not believe. . . . I and the Father are one."	Explanation	The Jews picked up stones to stone him.
55. Luke 13:23	Someone	"Lord, are only a few people going to be saved?"	Request for information	Perea	Jesus gave an affirmative answer by speaking of few entering a narrow door.	Explanation by an illustration	None recorded
56. John 11:8	Jesus' disciples	"Rabbi, . . . a short while ago the Jews tried to stone you, and yet you are going back there?"	Anxiety	Perea	Jesus said, "Are there not twelve hours of daylight?" Then he said Lazarus was sleeping.	A question and an explanation	They were confused.
57. Luke 17:37	Jesus' disciples	"Where, Lord?"	Request for information	Between Samaria and Galilee	"Where there is a dead body, there the vultures will gather."	Indirect answer by an enigmatic statement	None recorded

Reference	Who Asked	Question	Type	Location	Jesus' Response	Response Type	Reaction
58. Matthew 19:3 (Mark 10:2)	Pharisees	"Is it lawful for a man to divorce his wife for any and every reason?"	Trickery	Perea	Jesus asked, "Haven't you read . . . ?" and quoted Genesis 1:27 and 2:24 and affirmed the permanency of marriage.	A question and an explanation	They asked him another question.
59. Matthew 19:7	Pharisees	"Why then, . . . did Moses command that a man give his wife a certificate of divorce and send her away?"	Trickery	Perea	Jesus corrected them about Moses and again affirmed the permanence of marriage.	Correction and explanation	The disciples responded with a statement expressing confusion.
60. Matthew 19:16 (Mark 10:17; Luke 18:18)	A rich young man	"Teacher, what good thing must I do to get eternal life?"	Request for information	Perea	"Why do you ask me what is good? . . . Obey the commandments."	Information	The man asked which commandments he should obey.
61. Matthew 19:18	A rich young man	"Which ones?"	Request for information	Perea	Jesus stated six commandments	Information	The man asked what he still lacked.
62. Matthew 19:20	A rich young man	"What do I still lack?"	Request for information	Perea	"Sell your possessions . . . follow me."	Information and challenge	The man went away sad.
63. Matthew 19:25 (Mark 10:26; Luke 18:26)	Jesus' disciples	"Who then can be saved?"	Expression of confusion	Perea	"With God all things are possible."	Explanation	Peter asked a question.
64. Matthew 19:27	Peter	"We have left everything to follow you. What then will there be for us?"	Request for information	Perea	"You who have followed me will also sit on twelve thrones . . . Many who are last will be first."	Explanation and the parable of the vineyard workers	None recorded
65. Matthew 21:16	Chief priests and teachers of the law	"Do you hear what these children are saying?"	Rebuke	Temple in Jerusalem	Jesus said "Yes" and then asked if they had ever read Psalm 8:2.	Affirmation and a question in the form of a rebuke	Jesus left them.

Reference	Person(s) Who Asked	Question	Kind of Question or Problem	Place	Jesus' Answer	Kind of Answer by Jesus	Immediate Responses of the Questioner(s)
66-67. John 12:34	Crowd	"How can you say, 'The Son of Man must be lifted up'? Who is this 'Son of Man'?"	Denial; request for information	Jerusalem	Jesus encouraged them to "trust in the light."	Evasion of the question in the form of a challenge	Jesus left them.
68. Matthew 21:20	Jesus' disciples	"How did the fig tree wither so quickly?"	Expression of confusion	Between Bethany and Jerusalem	Jesus said that by faith great things can be done.	Evasion of the question by an explanation	None recorded
69-70. Matthew 21:23 (Mark 11:28; Luke 20:2)	Chief priests and elders	"By what authority are you doing these things? . . . And who gave you this authority?"	Challenge; denial	Temple courts in Jerusalem	Jesus asked them about the origin of John's baptism.	Evasion of the question by asking a question that put them on the horns of a dilemma.	They admitted they could not answer his questions.
71-72. Matthew 22:17 (Mark 12:14-15; Luke 20:22)	Pharisees and Herodians	"Tell us then, what is your opinion? Is it right to pay taxes to Caesar or not?"	Request for information; trickery	Jerusalem	Jesus rebuked them ("You hypocrites"), asked why they were trying to trap him, and then answered their question by referring to a coin.	Rebuke, a question, and an explanation by using an object	They were angered and left.
73. Matthew 22:28 (Mark 12:23; Luke 20:33)	Sadducees	"Now then at the resurrection, whose wife will she be of the seven, since all of them were married to her?"	Trickery	Jerusalem	Jesus explained that in the resurrection people will not marry and then he corrected their denial of the resurrection.	Explanation and correction	None recorded
74. Matthew 22:36 (Mark 12:28)	An expert in the law	"Teacher, which is the greatest commandment in the Law?"	Trickery	Jerusalem	Jesus quoted Deuteronomy 6:5 and Leviticus 19:18.	Explanation	None recorded

Reference	Speaker	Quote	Type	Location	Jesus' Statement	Category	Result
75–76. Matthew 24:3 (Mark 13:4; Luke 21:7)	Jesus' disciples	"When will this happen, and what will be the sign of your coming and of the end of the age?"	Request for information	Mount of Olives	Jesus gave his lengthy Olivet Discourse.	Information	None recorded
77. Matthew 26:17 (Mark 14:12; Luke 22:9)	Jesus' disciples	"Where do you want us to make preparations for you to eat the Passover?"	Request for a directive	Jerusalem	Jesus told them to go to the city and find a large upper room.	Information	They did as he said.
78. John 13:6	Peter	"Lord, are you going to wash my feet?"	Expression of surprise	Jerusalem	"You do not realize now what I am doing, but later you will understand."	Evasion of the question by an explanation	Peter said Jesus would never wash his feet.
79. Matthew 26:22	Jesus' disciples	"Surely not I, Lord?"	Expression of confusion	Jerusalem	"The one who has dipped his hand into the bowl with me will betray me."	Information	Peter asked a question.
80. John 13:25	Peter	"Lord, who is it?"	Request for information	Jerusalem	"It is the one to whom I will give this piece of bread."	Information	Judas asked a question.
81. Matthew 26:25	Judas	"Surely not I, Rabbi?"	Denial	Jerusalem	"Yes, it is you."	Information	Judas left the upper room.
82. John 13:36	Peter	"Lord, where are you going?"	Request for information	Jerusalem	"Where I am going, you cannot follow now, but you will follow later."	Evasion of the question by an explanation	Peter asked another question.
83. John 13:37	Peter	"Lord, why can't I follow you now? I will lay down my life for you."	Expression of confusion	Jerusalem	"Will you really lay down you life for me? . . . Before the rooster crows, you will disown me three times."	Denial by asking a question	None recorded

Reference	Person(s) Who Asked	Question	Kind of Question or Problem	Place	Jesus' Answer	Kind of Answer by Jesus	Immediate Responses of the Questioner(s)
84. John 14:5	Thomas	"Lord, we don't know where you are going, so how can we know the way?"	Expression of confusion	Jerusalem	"I am the way and the truth and the life."	Indirect answer by an affirmation	None recorded
85. John 14:22	Judas (not Judas Iscariot)	"But, Lord, why do you intend to show yourself to us and not to the world?"	Expression of confusion	Jerusalem	Jesus explained that those who love him obey him.	Indirect answer by an affirmation	None recorded
86. Luke 22:49	Jesus' disciples	"Lord, should we strike with our swords?"	Request for a directive	Mount of Olives	Before Jesus answered, Peter cut off the ear of the high priest's slave, Malchus. Then Jesus healed the man's ear, and told Peter to stop.	Directive	None recorded
87–88. Matthew 26:62 (Mark 14:60)	Caiaphas, the high priest	"Are you not going to answer? What is this testimony these men are bringing against you?"	Challenge; request for information	High priest's courtyard in Jerusalem	Jesus remained silent.	Silence	The high priest asked another question.
89. Mark 14:61 (Luke 22:70)	High priest	"Are you the Christ, the Son of the Blessed One?"	Request for information	High priest's courtyard in Jerusalem	"I am."	Affirmation	The high priest accused Jesus of blasphemy.
90. Matthew 26:68 (Luke 22:64)	Jews	"Who hit you?"	Mockery	High priest's courtyard in Jerusalem	None recorded	Silence	None recorded

Reference	Speaker	Question/Statement	Type of question	Location	Jesus's response	Type of response	Result
91. John 18:33	Pilate	"Are you the king of the Jews?"	Request for information	Pilate's hall	"Is that your own idea or did others talk to you about me?"	Evasion of the question by asking another question	Pilate asked another question.
92–93. John 18:35	Pilate	"Am I a Jew? . . . What is it you have done?"	Sarcasm; request for information	Pilate's hall	"My kingdom is not of this world."	Evasion of the question by stating a truth	Pilate answered his own questions by stating, "You are a king, then."
94. Matthew 27:11 (Luke 23:3)	Pilate	"Are you the king of the Jews?"	Request for information	Pilate's hall	"Yes, it is as you say."	Affirmation	None recorded
95. John 18:38	Pilate	"What is truth?"	Request for information	Pilate's hall	None recorded	None recorded	Pilate told the people he found no fault in Jesus.
96. Matthew 27:13	Pilate	"Don't you hear the testimony they are bringing against you?"	Request for information	Pilate's hall	Jesus did not answer.	Silence	Pilate was greatly amazed.
97. John 19:9	Pilate	"Where do you come from?"	Request for information	Pilate's hall	Jesus did not answer.	Silence	Pilate asked another question.
98–99. John 19:10	Pilate	"Do you refuse to speak to me? . . . Don't you realize I have power either to free you or to crucify you?"	Challenge	Pilate's hall	"You would have no power over me if it were not given to you from above."	Correction	Pilate tried to set Jesus free.
100. Luke 23:39	Thief on the cross	"Aren't you the Christ? Save yourself and us!"	Challenge	Golgotha	None	Silence	The other thief answered the first thief.

Reference	Person(s) Who Asked	Question	Kind of Question or Problem	Place	Jesus' Answer	Kind of Answer by Jesus	Immediate Responses of the Questioner(s)
101. Luke 24:18	Cleopas	"Are you only a visitor to Jerusalem and do not know the things that have happened there in these days?"	Expression of surprise	Emmaus road	"What things?"	Question	They answered that they were referring to Jesus.
102. John 21:21	Peter	"Lord, what about him?"	Request for information	Near the Sea of Tiberias	"What is that to you?"	Rebuke in the form of a question	None recorded
103. Acts 1:6	Jesus' disciples	"Lord, are you at this time going to restore the kingdom to Israel?"	Request for information	Jerusalem	Jesus answered that they were not to know the times or dates.	Denial	None recorded

16

How Did Jesus Use Stories in His Teaching?

The police force marched up the hill through the forest, looking for his farm. Finding it, they knocked on his door, barged in, and yelled, "Hans, you are under arrest!"

Frightened, his wife cried, "Arrest? What for?" In a rough voice the leader of the group barked, "For preaching against the views of the state church, and for refusing to obey the officials' order to stop your preaching!"

The policeman yanked Hans's arms behind his back and tied him up, not in ropes but in chains. He didn't resist as they led him out of the house, threw him up on a horse, and took him away, while his wife and children looked on helplessly with tear-filled eyes and broken hearts.

For almost two years Hans lay in a dark, damp prison. He was given only water and bread made from a poor kind of wheat usually fed to cows and horses.

Twenty months later Hans heard good news. He and several of his preacher-prisonmates were being released. But the bad news was that they were being taken away from their country to another nation.

Do you know who this man was? He was your great-great-great-great-great-great-great-great-great grandfather, Hans Zaugg. This is the true story of how he was treated because he was preaching the Bible and was faithful to the Lord.

Do you know when and where this happened? He was taken prisoner on January 31, 1659, more than three hundred years ago, from his beautiful farm in Signau, Switzerland. We have a wonderful heritage, don't we?

305

In 1992 I told this story to two of my grandchildren, Jason and Jennifer, then ages nine and six. I wanted them to know of their ancestor's faithfulness to the Lord in hard times.

Their reaction? They were enthralled.

The reason? Children love stories, both true and fictional. And so do adults. Weeks later when I asked Jason and Jennifer about this story, they remembered almost all the details.

This story illustrates two points about all stories: People love them, and stories convey principles in memorable form. Telling my grandchildren this story was far more effective than if I had merely pronounced the precept, "You should always live for the Lord even if it means you suffer." They grasped that truth not by an abstract statement, but by means of a story.

Think of the most recent sermon you heard in church, over the radio, or on television. Or recall the most recent class lecture you listened to.

How much of it do you remember? Probably, like almost everyone, you can recollect only a small portion. The outline? Perhaps. All the details? Not likely. The stories or illustrations? Most probably!

Inject a story into a verbal presentation, and your audience perks up. The mind awakens, brain cells become attentive.

Tell a story to children and watch their attention span lengthen, their eyes sparkle with interest. Why? Because stories are about people—people who face what we face, undergo what we experience, feel as we feel, do what we do.

Telling stories—putting principles and precepts into skin and bones, truths and ideas into real or imaginary people and situations—excels as a means of communication. An abstraction may hold some interest, but embody it in a story and it becomes clear, understandable, and compelling.

Jesus knew this. That is why one-fourth of his recorded words are narratives—true-to-life, could-have-happened stories we call parables.

In fact, the Gospel writers recorded thirty-nine stories Jesus told. And two thousand years later, a number of them are known even by people who do not call themselves Christians: the parables of the good Samaritan, the prodigal son, and of the sower, to name a few. Many people "speak of burying one's 'talent' (Matt. 25:25), 'counting the cost' (Luke 14:28), being a 'good Samaritan' (Luke 10:29–37), etc., frequently without realizing that in so doing they are in fact quoting from the parables of Jesus."[1]

1. Robert H. Stein, *An Introduction to the Parables of Jesus* (Philadelphia: Westminster, 1981), 15.

People loved—and remembered—Jesus' stories because they were realistic and because they each made a point, a strong, easy-to-grasp principle understandably relevant to them. Jesus' ability to tell the right story, some long and some short, at the appropriate moment demonstrates his remarkable teaching skill, his unusual ability as a master Storyteller.

Do you want to improve as a teacher? Then tell stories or illustrations as the Lord did—thereby teaching as Jesus taught!

Parables in the Gospels

Telling short stories was Jesus' favorite method of instruction; "it stands out more prominently in his teaching than any other"[2] means. As Mark wrote, "He taught them [the crowd] many things by parables" (4:2). He also taught his disciples by parables and addressed his enemies by stories. "No other teacher of whom we have read used parables so freely and so effectively."[3]

People in Jesus' day would have been familiar with this technique, for the rabbis often taught in parables. Hundreds of parables are scattered throughout the rabbinical writings known as the Talmud and the Midrash.[4] According to one source, about "two thousand rabbinic parables have been collected."[5] But since these were told by many Jewish authorities, Jesus still remains as the world's most reputable narrator of short stories.

The word *parable* transliterates the Greek *parabolē,* which consists of the two words *para* (beside or alongside) and *ballein* (to throw). So a parable is a story that places one truth beside another to clarify or emphasize a point. An unknown, unclear, or abstract idea is explained by being placed verbally along with something already known, clear, or concrete. The Greek philosopher Aristotle (384–322 B.C.) wrote that a parable is a "juxtaposition, setting one thing by the side of another for the purpose of comparison or illustration."[6]

Parabolē occurs fifty times in the New Testament, all of them being

2. J. M. Price, *Jesus the Teacher* (Nashville: Sunday School Board, 1946), 99.
3. C. B. Eavey, *Principles of Teaching for Christian Teachers* (reprint, Grand Rapids: Zondervan, 1968), 245.
4. A. E. Baker, *The Teaching of Jesus for Daily Life* (London: Eyre and Spottiswoode, 1933), 7.
5. *Dictionary of Jesus and the Gospels,* 1992 ed., s.v. "Parables," by K. R. Snodgrass, 593.
6. Aristotle *Rhetoric* 2.20.2.

in the synoptic Gospels except for two instances in Hebrews.[7] Matthew includes the word seventeen times, Mark used it thirteen times, and it occurs eighteen times in Luke. The word does not occur in the Gospel of John. Like its companion Hebrew word *māšāl* in the Old Testament, *parabolē* carries meanings that are broader than the English word. Some of the forty-eight occurrences of *parabolē* refer to maxims or aphorisms. For example, Mark wrote that Jesus spoke "in parables" and then wrote that he said, "How can Satan drive out Satan?" (3:23). After the Lord told a crowd, "Nothing outside a man can make him 'unclean' by going into him" (7:15), the disciples "asked him about this parable" (7:17).

Similarly when Jesus said, "If a blind man leads a blind man, both will fall into a pit," Peter asked that he explain the *parabolē* to them (Matt. 15:14–15; cf. Luke 6:39). The New International Version translates *parabolē* by "proverb" in Luke 4:23, "Surely you will quote this proverb to me, 'Physician, heal yourself!'" Another example of a brief saying being called a *parabolē* is Luke 21:29–30, "He told them this parable: 'Look at the fig tree and all the trees. When they sprout leaves, you can see for yourselves and know that summer is near.'" Even a brief admonition is called a *parabolē*: "When he noticed how the guests [at a Pharisee's house for dinner] picked the places of honor at the table, he told them this parable: 'When someone invites you to a wedding feast, do not take the place of honor, for a person more distinguished than you may have been invited'" (Luke 14:7–8). Jesus placed this fact about the wedding alongside the principle, "For everyone who exalts himself will be humbled, and he who humbles himself will be exalted" (14:11).

Writers differ on the number of parables Jesus told, partly because some lists include his maxims. For example, Bruce discussed thirty-three parables and listed eight "parable-germs,"[8] whereas Scroggie lists fifty-one parables and then adds another twenty "parabolic illustrations."[9] Rixon presents a list of sixty-three parables,[10] and Stein's list includes forty-nine parables, followed by twenty-six "possible parables."[11] Borg referred to Jesus' thirty parables, adding, "This is a

7. Hebrews 9:9 used *parabolē* in referring to Old Testament tabernacle regulations as a "symbol" (NASB) or "illustration" (NIV) pointing ahead to "the new order" under Jesus Christ, and Hebrews 11:9 includes *parabolē* in an adverbial prepositional phrase translated "figuratively speaking."

8. A. B. Bruce, *The Parabolic Teaching of Christ* (London: Hodder & Stoughton, 1895; reprint, Minneapolis: Klock and Klock, 1980), xvii–xviii.

9. W. Graham Scroggie, *A Guide to the Gospels* (London: Pickering and Inglis, 1948), 549–51.

10. Lilas D. Rixon, *How Jesus Taught* (Croydon, N.S.W.: Sydney Missionary and Bible College, 1977), 57–58.

11. Stein, *An Introduction to the Parables of Jesus*, 22–26.

remarkably large number, given the relatively small compass of Jesus' teaching."[12] In this chapter, however, I am including the parables the Lord gave as stories—short stories with a brief storyline or plot.

Table 28
Jesus' Parables

1. The Two Houses — Matthew 7:24–27 (Luke 6:47–49)
2. The New Cloth — Matthew 9:16 (Mark 2:21; Luke 5:36)
3. The New Wineskins — Matthew 9:17 (Mark 2:22; Luke 5:37–39)
4. The Rude Children — Matthew 11:16–19 (Luke 7:31–35)
5. The Sower — Matthew 13:5–8 (Mark 4:3–8; Luke 8:4–8, 11–15)
6. The Weeds — Matthew 13:24–30
7. The Mustard Seed — Matthew 13:31–32 (Mark 4:30–32; Luke 13:18–19)
8. The Yeast — Matthew 13:33 (Luke 13:20–21)
9. The Hidden Treasure — Matthew 13:44
10. The Pearl of Great Price — Matthew 13:45–46
11. The Fishing Net — Matthew 13:47–50
12. The House Owner — Matthew 13:52
13. The Unforgiving Servant — Matthew 18:23–35
14. The Vineyard Workers — Matthew 20:1–16
15. The Two Sons — Matthew 21:28–32
16. The Wicked Vinegrowers — Matthew 21:33–44 (Mark 12:1–11; Luke 20:9–18)
17. The Wedding Banquet — Matthew 22:1–14
18. The Fig Tree — Matthew 24:32–35 (Mark 13:28–31; Luke 21:29–33)
19. The Two Servants — Matthew 24:45–51 (Luke 12:42–48)
20. The Ten Virgins — Matthew 25:1–13
21. The Talents — Matthew 25:14–30
22. The Seed Growing Secretly — Mark 4:26–29

12. *Anchor Bible Dictionary,* 1992, s.v. "The Teaching of Jesus Christ," by Marcus J. Borg, 3:807. Also Richard Chenevix Trench discussed thirty parables (*Notes on the Parables of Our Lord* [New York: Appleton, 1847]), and more recently Bernard Brandon Scott considered thirty-one parables (*Hear Then the Parables* [Minneapolis: Fortress, 1989]).

23. The Doorkeeper	Mark 13:34–37 (Luke 12:35–40)
24. The Two Debtors	Luke 7:41–43
25. The Good Samaritan	Luke 10:25–37
26. The Friend at Midnight	Luke 11:5–8
27. The Rich Fool	Luke 12:16–21
28. The Wise and Foolish Servants	Luke 12:42–48
29. The Barren Fig Tree	Luke 13:6–9
30. The Great Banquet	Luke 14:15–24
31. The Unfinished Tower and the King at War	Luke 14:28–33
32. The Lost Sheep	Matthew 18:12–14 (Luke 15:3–7)
33. The Lost Coin	Luke 15:8–10
34. The Prodigal Son	Luke 15:11–32
35. The Shrewd Manager	Luke 16:1–9
36. The Servant's Reward	Luke 17:7–10
37. The Unjust Judge	Luke 18:1–8
38. The Pharisee and the Tax Collector	Luke 18:9–14
39. The Minas	Luke 19:11–27

As table 28 shows, eleven of the parables are recorded only in Matthew, one is unique to Mark (4:26–29), and the Gospel of Luke has fifteen parables that occur only in that book. Six parables are all in three Gospels, Matthew and Luke share six parables, and Mark and Luke have only one parable in common. Since Mark presented Jesus as a Person of action, it is not surprising that Mark records only eight parables.

Why Are Parables Interesting?

What is the value of teaching by means of parables or stories? Several answers may be given. First, people enjoy hearing about other people. The immense popularity of television talk shows that feature people demonstrates this fact. Also, biographies, fictional books, magazines, and tabloids that feature people illustrate the point that people have interest in people. Almost all of Jesus' parables relate in some way to people.

Second, parables have intrigue because of the challenge of analogies. "The parable . . . presents [a] challenge to discover the meaning (it is a kind of puzzle one wants to solve)."[13] As an implied comparison, a parable challenges the hearer or reader to decipher the point being made. "The comparison is not always obvious; but once it is grasped by the hearer it sheds fresh light on the subject under discussion."[14]

Third, people enjoy learning abstract truths and ideas by means of concrete examples. "Truth made concrete in characters who live before the hearer is much easier to understand than if presented in any other form."[15]

Fourth, in stories, listeners by their imagination can vicariously identify with others' situations. The audience empathizes with the needs of those in the story, is caught up in the plot conflicts, and feels the emotions of the stories' characters.

Jesus' stories conveyed truths vividly, thereby making lasting impressions on those who heard him. Who could forget the danger of selfish greed after hearing Jesus tell the parable of the rich fool (Luke 12:15–21)? Reading the parable of the good Samaritan readily leads people to know the meaning of true neighborliness (Luke 10:30–37). Jesus' conclusion that those who exalt themselves will be humbled (and vice versa) packed great force because it followed immediately after his story to the Pharisee and the tax collector (Luke 18:9–14). Those who heard the Lord give the parable of the friend at midnight followed by Jesus' well-known words about asking, seeking, and knocking (Luke 11:5–13) could not help be impressed by God the Father's willingness to answer the prayers of his own.

> Christ could have said, "You should be persistent in your prayer life," a statement that His hearers would probably have shrugged off and quickly forgotten. Instead He told them of a widow who kept begging an unjust judge to help her, until the judge finally decided to answer her petitions to stop her complaining. Christ then taught the lesson of the parable: if an unjust judge who cares nothing about a widow can be swayed by persistent begging, how much more will a loving heavenly Father answer those who consistently pray to Him.[16]

People naturally remember stories longer than they remember cold facts.

13. Herman Harrell Horne, *Jesus the Master Teacher* (1922; reprint, Grand Rapids: Kregel, 1964), 80.

14. Madeleine Boucher, *The Mysterious Parable* (Washington, D.C.: Catholic Biblical Association of America, 1977), 25.

15. Eavey, *Principles of Teaching for Christian Teachers*, 245.

16. Henry A. Virkler, *Hermeneutics* (Grand Rapids: Baker, 1981), 163.

Why Did Jesus Teach in Parables?

Jesus related stories in order to help people comprehend spiritual truths. As verbal pictures, his parables illumined heavenly concepts. In Mark 4:9, 23–24 he challenged the people to hear his teaching, that is, to comprehend it: "He who has ears to hear, let him hear." "If anyone has ears, let him hear. Consider carefully what you hear." And he taught parables "as much as they could understand" (4:33). When Jesus told the parable of the sower and the seeds, the disciples inquired, "Why do you speak to the people in parables?" (Matt. 13:10). His reply showed one of his reasons for parabolic teaching: "The knowledge of the secrets of the kingdom of heaven has been given to you" (13:11).

Why then did Jesus quote Isaiah 6:9–10 in Mark 4:11–12? "But to those on the outside everything is said in parables, so that, 'they may be ever seeing but never perceiving, and ever hearing but never understanding; otherwise they might turn and be forgiven!'" Matthew 13:13–17 and Luke 8:9–10 record this same idea. Does this purpose to conceal truth contradict Jesus' stated purpose to reveal truth?

Both purposes are true of Jesus' parables of the secrets of the kingdom: to reveal and to conceal. A clue to the seeming conflict in purpose shows up in the parable of the sower itself. The result of the sowing depends not on the seed itself but on the kind of soil.[17] The teachers of the law had accused Jesus of being demon-possessed (Matt. 12:24; Mark 3:22), thereby revealing their rejection of him and the kingdom he offered and showing the hardened condition of their hearts. Like soil unresponsive to seed, their calloused hearts prevented their receiving certain truths given in parables. "The knowledge of the secrets of the kingdom of heaven has been given to you, *but not to them*" (Matt. 13:11, italics added). Jesus' quotation of Isaiah 6:9–10 showed the true nature of "those on the outside" (Mark 4:11).[18] They heard but did not perceive what they heard. Therefore because their minds were closed to the King and his kingdom, the meaning of the parables of the secrets of the kingdom were closed to them too. By concealing the truth from those hardened to it, Jesus was following his own advice not to give what is holy to dogs or pearls to pigs (Matt. 7:6).

According to Matthew 13:13 the *reason* Jesus spoke in parables is the prior hardening of the unbelievers' hearts ("Therefore I speak to them in parables because [Greek *hoti*] while hearing they do not hear, nor do they understand," NASB). However, according to Mark 4:11–12 the hard-

17. T. W. Manson, *The Teaching of Jesus* (Cambridge: Cambridge University Press, 1955), 77.
18. Ibid., 80.

ening is the *result* of the parables ("But to those on the outside everything is said in parables so that [Greek *hina*] they may be . . . ever hearing but never understanding"). In Matthew the hardening seems to have preceded the parables, whereas in Mark it followed the parables. In Matthew the parables were the result, whereas in Mark they were the cause. The Jewish leaders had already rejected the King and what he taught (Matt. 12:24), thereby rendering themselves incapable of receiving truth about the secrets of the kingdom (13:11). And, as Mark put it, the parables of the kingdom would further harden them against the truth. "The same sun that melts the ice also hardens the clay."[19]

In these parables of the secrets of the kingdom it was as if the Lord were saying to the Jewish leaders, "Reject the King, and you also reject the kingdom. But here is what will take place while the rejected King is in heaven and the kingdom is postponed. But since you rejected the simple announcement of the kingdom, you will not be able to understand this additional truth. In fact the parables will only further encrust your unreceptive hearts."[20]

But to those with hearts receptive to the truth, Jesus was saying, in effect, "The establishing of my kingdom rule on earth has been postponed because of the nation's rejection of me as her King. But here are new truths ('secrets'), facts not previously revealed, about what will occur while you await the kingdom to be established.[21] By understanding the parable of the sower and the soils, you show that you are spiritually qualified to understand the other parables. 'Whoever has will be given more, and he will have an abundance' (Matt. 13:12). Just as seed produces more seed, so your hearts, like good soil, will be open to more truth."[22]

---

19. Warren W. Wiersbe, *Meet Yourself in the Parables* (Wheaton, Ill.: Victor, 1979), 11.

20. "The use of parables on this occasion was a penalty for judicial blindness on those who will not see" (A. T. Robertson, *Word Pictures in the New Testament*, 6 vols. [Nashville: Broadman, 1930], 4:296). By not perceiving that Jesus was the Son of God, they would find the parables of the "kingdom secrets" "to be as enigmatic as the miracles and the man himself" (Harold Songer, "Jesus' Use of Parables: Matthew 13," *Review and Expositor* 59 [October 1962]: 493).

21. The Greek *mysterion* refers not to something mysterious or eerie but to spiritual truths previously unrevealed by God and therefore unknown by man but now revealed by the Lord. These new facts presented in Matthew 13 include different responses to the Lord with most people rejecting his message (the sower), people with false profession of faith existing along with people of genuine faith (the wheat and the weeds), initial insignificance and great growth (the mustard seed and the yeast), great value and sacrifice (the hidden treasure and the pearl), and future judgment (the net).

22. Jesus was "instructing His disciples regarding a hitherto unrevealed period of time prior to the establishment of the kingdom," the present span of time "in which the millennial kingdom is being postponed" (Stanley D. Toussaint, *Behold the King: A Study of Matthew* [Portland, Ore.: Multnomah, 1980], 171–72; also see 172–79).

The inability of those with hearts unresponsive to comprehend Jesus' parabolic teaching seems limited to these "kingdom-secrets" parables, for his enemies readily understood other parables. Later Matthew wrote, "When the chief priests and the Pharisees heard Jesus' parables, they knew he was talking about them" (21:45; cf. Mark 12:12; Luke 20:19). Jesus' statements in Matthew 13:11–13; Mark 4:10–12; and Luke 8:9–10 "should not be taken as the general reason that Christ taught in parables. This answer was given in answer to the question, 'Why do you speak to *them* . . . ?' not 'Why do you teach in general?' This is evident as most of Jesus' parables were not freighted with concealed meaning."[23]

Matthew 13 is a turning point not only in Jesus' method of presentation but also in the content of his teaching. Several facts point to this change. First, he no longer spoke about the nearness of the kingdom, as he had done previously (Matt. 3:2; 4:17; 10:7). Rather than being "near" by its being offered personally by the King, the kingdom, he said, will appear later in association with his second coming (Matt. 24–25; 26:11). Second, after Matthew 13 Jesus did not preach "the good news of the kingdom" (4:23; 9:35). Third, not until the national rejection of the King and his presentation of new information about the kingdom did Jesus speak of his sufferings on the cross (16:21). Fourth, after Matthew 13 Jesus spoke of the establishing of the church (16:18), and he stated that the kingdom was being taken from that generation in Israel (21:28–22:14) and would be given to a future generation who will respond to the Messiah and over whom he will establish his millennial reign (21:43).[24]

Clearly, then, Jesus' parables served to shed light on spiritual truths (except for the kingdom parables hidden from those who renounced him and his kingdom offer). They constituted a striking and often-used form of teaching. Through his short stories Jesus did not entertain; he educated. Each parable awakened his listeners' conscience rather than amused their minds.

Jesus also used parables to disarm his opponents. Parables became powerful tools to silence his religious enemies and to show up the fallacies of their thinking. Each parable in those situations was "a weapon of controversy."[25] In light of the chief priests' and elders' two questions about Jesus' authority (Matt. 21:23), the Lord "put them in their place"

23. Francis Herbert Roberts, "The Teaching Methods of Jesus" (Th.M. thesis, Dallas Theological Seminary, 1955), 17.

24. These four points are taken from Mark R. Saucy, "The Kingdom-of-God Sayings in Matthew," *Bibliotheca Sacra* 151 (April–June 1994): 203–5.

25. Arthur Temple Cadoux, *The Parables of Jesus, Their Art and Use* (New York: Macmillan, 1931), 13.

by a trilogy of parables: the two sons (21:28–32), wicked vinegrowers (21:33–46), and the wedding banquet (22:1–14). Hearing the first two parables, the chief priests and Pharisees "knew he was talking about them" (21:45). Jesus also disarmed Simon the Pharisee's complaint by his story of the two debtors (Luke 7:41–43). The Lord gave another trilogy of parables (the lost sheep, coin, and son, Luke 15:3–32) to his adversaries (the Pharisees and the teachers of the law) when they complained that he was eating with sinners (vv. 1–2). And the story of the Pharisee and tax collector praying in the temple plainly showed up their sin of arrogance (18:9–14).

What Made Jesus' Stories So Intriguing?

Jesus' parables have appeal for many reasons.

They were *concise*. A story need not be long to be interesting and effective. These "masterpieces of literature"[26] told by the Lord ranged from one verse (e.g., Matt. 9:16, 17; 13:33, 44, 52) to twenty-two verses (Luke 15:11–32), with the average being six verses (see table 28). Remarkably, the well-known parable of the good Samaritan is only six verses long (Luke 10:30–35) with 166 words in English (NIV) but only 105 words in the Greek (though the surrounding conversation between Jesus and the expert in the law takes another seven verses). Jesus got his points across quickly and incisively.

Jesus' parables dealt with *common, everyday elements* known in first-century Palestine. Elements of nature he referred to include rock, rain, winds, sand, streams, wine, wineskins, seed, birds, rocky places, soil, sun, plants, root, thorns, crop, fields, weeds, wheat, heads of wheat, harvest, mustard seed, garden plants, trees, branches, plants, lake, fish, vineyard, fruit, oxen, cattle, fig tree, twigs, leaves, summer, oil, ground, night, day, grain, stalk, head, kernel, donkey, sheep, open country, pigs, pods, calf, and goat.

Manmade items include house, foundation, patch of old garment, clothing, path, barn, flour, dough, treasure, net, baskets, storeroom, talents, prison, denarius, marketplace, wall, winepress, city, lamps, jars, door, property, sickle, clothes, inn, silver coins, loaves of bread, streets, alleys, roads, country lanes, tower, robe, sandals, temple, minas, and cities.

Humans Jesus referred to include the following: sower, enemy, servants, harvesters, woman, fisherman, owner of a house, king, master,

26. Clifford A. Wilson, *Jesus the Master Teacher* (Grand Rapids: Baker, 1974), 92.

wife, children, landowner, hired vineyard workers, foreman, father, vineyard owner, sons, farmers, tenants, wedding guests, attendants, drunkards, virgins, bridegroom, bankers, moneylender, priest, Levite, Samaritan, innkeeper, friend, rich man, banquet guests, poor people, crippled people, blind, lame, shepherd, father of the prodigal son, brother of the prodigal son, shrewd manager, debtors, judge, widow, Pharisee, tax collector, robbers, evildoers, adulterers, man of noble birth.

This list reveals the master Teacher's astounding ability to use commonly known items and people in his stories. His audiences could readily identify with those objects and individuals—items of commerce and farming, domestic and social items and events, architecture and agriculture, people in religious and civil occupations, people of varying qualities.

"The parables of Jesus glow with life in all its kaleidoscopic vividness."[27] A woman baking, a farmer sowing, fishermen casting their nets, a shepherd looking for a lost sheep, a king going on a journey— these disclose the true-to-life situations of which he spoke, thus enhancing their believability.

A third feature making Jesus' parables dramatic is their *suspense*. Readers are held in suspense wondering how the merciful master will treat his unmerciful servant (Matt. 18:21–35). What will happen to the seeds that fall on various kinds of soil (13:5–8), or what will happen to the landowner's tenants who killed his servants and his son (21:33–46)? When the prodigal son returns home, will he be welcomed or rejected (Luke 15:11–32)? What will the king do when he returns home and hears that one of his servants stored rather than invested the money he received (19:11–27)? Suspense helped captivate his listeners so that they heard his stories to the end. No lulling to sleep here!

Plot *conflicts* characterize many of the Lord's stories. The unmerciful servant was in conflict with his debtors from whom he demanded payment, and then was in conflict with his master (Matt. 18:23–35). The men who worked in the vineyard all day voiced conflict with the landowner who paid other workers the same amount (Matt. 20:1–16). Tenants of a vineyard were in conflict with servants the landowner sent to collect grapes (21:33–46). Other examples include the wise virgins who refused to give oil to the foolish virgins (25:1–13), the persistent man in conflict with his friend who had already gone to bed (Luke 11:5–8), the conflict between the fig tree owner and his vineyard keeper (13:6–9), the conflict between the prodigal son and his father and between the prodi-

27. Hillyer Hawthorne Stratton, *A Guide to the Parables of Jesus* (Grand Rapids: Eerdmans, 1959), 26.

gal son and his older brother (15:11–32), and the persistent widow and the judge (18:1–8).

A fifth feature is the element of *surprise,* unexpected turns or reversals. We are surprised to read of a man refusing to cancel a small debt when he himself had been forgiven a large debt (Matt. 18:23–35). It is surprising to hear of workers being paid the same amount regardless of how long they worked (20:1–16), and of tenants of a vineyard beating and killing their landowner's servants and son (21:33–46). It is surprising that a man would hide money in the ground rather than invest it (25:14–30), that a hated Samaritan showed more compassion to an injured Jew than did religious leaders (Luke 10:25–37), that a manager of an estate would beat his master's servants (12:42–48), that a farmer would want to cut down his fig tree (13:6–9), or that people would want to be excused from attending a banquet (14:15–24). Why should a bad son be given a banquet and not the older son (15:11–32), or a dishonest manager be commended for his shrewdness (16:1–9)? Why would a judge be unjust (18:1–8), or a tax collector be justified rather than a Pharisee (18:10–14)?

Another element adding intrigue to the parables is the sometimes startling *departure from normal procedure.*[28] It is unlikely that anyone in Jesus' day would owe a ten-thousand-talent debt, equal to several million dollars in today's currency (Matt. 18:23–35).[29] It is unusual for guests invited to a large banquet to give lame excuses for not attending (Luke 14:15–24). It was abnormal for a tax collector to be humble before God in his prayer of repentance (Luke 18:10–14), and a man would not normally sell everything he had to buy a field (Matt. 13:44).[30]

Several parables include the literary feature of so-called *end stress,* in which the last element of a parable is the most important.[31] In the parable of the sower, the good soil is mentioned last. In other parables the last person to be sent to the vineyard was the landowner's son, the last traveler in the story of the good Samaritan was the only kind one, those who were invited last to the banquet accepted the invitation, and the last servant, who did not invest his mina, was judged harshly.

---

28. G. B. Caird, *The Language and Imagery of the Bible* (Philadelphia: Westminster, 1980), 164.

29. Stein observes that the annual income of Herod the Great was nine hundred talents (Stein, *An Introduction ot the Parables of Jesus*, 40).

30. For more on these unusual circumstances in the parables see Norman A. Huffman, "Atypical Features in the Parables of Jesus," *Journal of Biblical Literature* 97 (1978): 207–20.

31. Leland Ryken, *How to Read the Bible as Literature* (Grand Rapids: Zondervan, 1984), 142.

Direct conversation is another parabolic feature. In several parables Jesus cited the words spoken by the characters. Related to this is soliloquy, in which a character in the story talks to himself, so that the hearers and readers know what he is thinking. This is seen in the words of a wicked servant (Matt. 24:48), of a rich fool (Luke 12:17–19), the prodigal son (15:17–19), the shrewd manager (16:3–4), and the unjust judge (18:5).

As in all good stories, Jesus' parables include denouement, or *resolution* of a problem or plot conflict. Sometimes the stories are tragic, that is, they have unhappy endings. Note these endings in reference to the unforgiving servant (Matt. 18:34), the wicked vinegrowers (21:41), the wedding banquet (22:13), the unfaithful servant (24:50–51), the foolish virgins (25:10–12), the lazy servant (25:27–28), the rich fool (Luke 12:20), the foolish servant (12:47–48), and the unwise servant (19:22–26).

Stories with comic, that is, happy endings, include the good Samaritan (Luke 10:25–37), the friend at midnight (11:8), the people invited to a great banquet (14:23–24), the lost sheep, coin, and son (15:5, 9, 22–24), the widow who pleaded with the judge (18:5), and the repentant tax collector (18:14).

A tenth feature rendering Jesus' stories appealing is *characterization,* which "refers to the way a narrator brings characters to life in a narrative."[32] Sometimes Jesus described the characters (e.g., the five foolish and five wise virgins, Matt. 25:2; the shrewd, dishonest manager, Luke 16:8; the judge who neither feared God nor cared about people and was unjust, 18:2, 6), whereas more often the master Storyteller presented characterization by the individuals' actions or words. The speech of the children identifies them as rude though the Lord does not call them that (Luke 7:31–35). The Samaritan who cared for the injured stranger was good, though Jesus never used that word of him; the man's actions revealed his character (10:25–37). The shepherd going after his sheep, the woman looking for her coin, and the father welcoming home his wayward son all reveal joy in their discoveries (Luke 15). The actions and words of the Pharisees and the tax collector convey their proud and humble spirits, respectively (18:9–14).

Contrasts stand out prominently in the parables. Table 29 lists these contrasts. A number of times two persons of similar character are contrasted to a single character (e.g., two servants invested their mina, in contrast to one servant who did not; a merciful creditor is seen in contrast to two debtors who were unable to pay; and the good Samaritan differs from the other two passersby).

---

32. John R. Donahue, *The Gospel in Parable* (Philadelphia: Fortress, 1988), 23.

Table 29
Contrasts in the Parables*

House built on a rock	House built on sand
New cloth	Old garment
New wine	Old wineskins
Seed on good soil	Seed on poor soil
Sower sowed wheat	Enemy sowed tares
Small mustard seed	Huge tree
Small amount of leaven	Huge amount of meal
Treasure, and pearl	All one's possessions of less value
Good fish	Bad fish
A servant forgiven a huge debt	He refused to forgive another a small debt
Vineyard workers worked all day for a denarius	Other workers worked one hour for the same wage
A son refused to work but later did	A son promised to work but didn't
Those invited to a wedding feast refused to attend	Those compelled to attend a wedding feast attended
Faithful servant	Evil servant
Five foolish virgins	Five wise virgins
Two servants invested their mina	One servant did not invest his one mina
Creditor	Two debtors unable to pay
Priest and Levite passed by the wounded man	Good Samaritan cared for the wounded man
Friend at midnight	Sleeping friend
Rich man acquiring more wealth	Rich man losing his soul
Fig tree owner anxious to cut down the tree	Vineyard-keeper anxious to wait one more year
Prodigal son whose return was celebrated	Older brother who was not celebrated

*Roy B. Zuck, *Basic Bible Interpretation* (Wheaton, Ill.: Victor, 1991), 200.

Many parables have *three characters or groups,* a feature sometimes called the rule of three. A king, a forgiven servant, and an unforgiven servant are seen in Matthew 18:23–35. A landowner's workers hired during the day, and workers hired at the eleventh hour are noted in Matthew 20:1–16. Triads in other parables include these:

Man, first son, second son (Matt. 21:28–32)

Landowner, tenants, son (Matt. 21:33–36)

King, those who refused to go to the wedding banquet, and those who did come (Matt. 22:1–14)

Master, wise servant, wicked servant (Matt. 24:45–51)

Bridegroom, five wise virgins, five foolish virgins (Matt. 25:1–13)

Master, servants who invested their money, servant who did not invest (Matt. 25:14–30)

Moneylender, debtor owing a large debt, debtor owing a small debt (Luke 7:41–43)

Injured Jew, uncaring religious leaders, compassionate Samaritan (Luke 10:25–37)

Man who is asked to help, guest who asked for help, the friend in need (Luke 11:5–8)

Guests invited to a great banquet with three excuses (Luke 14:15–24)

Shepherd, ninety-nine sheep, one lost sheep (Luke 15:4–7)

Father, prodigal son, older brother (Luke 15:11–32)

Judge, widow, her opponent (Luke 18:1–8)

Jesus' short stories also are fascinating because of the wide *variety of topics* he discussed. The parables may be grouped under five headings: God's reign, God's character, God's disciples, God's enemies, and God's judgment. They discuss facts about the kingdom and the interim between Jesus' two advents, responsibilities and obligations of those who would follow him, attitudes of those who oppose the Lord, and the Lord's coming judgment on those who reject him. "These illustrative stories tell us how God is working in human circumstances, what our response to that work should be—with repentance a dominant theme—and especially who God is. . . . The picture of God dominates the parables; they can be called theology pure and proper."[33] Table 30 illustrates how the parables can be grouped under these five headings.

In the parables Christ compared himself to a sower (Matt. 13:5–8), a merchant (13:44), a creditor (18:23–35), a landowner (20:1–16; 21:33–46), a master (24:45–51), a bridegroom (25:1–13), a host (Luke 14:15–24), a shepherd (15:3–7), a father (15:11–32), a judge (18:1–8), and a nobleman (19:11–27).

Of interest is the fact that eleven of the Lord's parables pertain to money: the hidden treasure (Matt. 13:44), the pearl of great price (13:45–46), the unforgiving servant (18:23–35), the vineyard workers

33. David Allan Hubbard, *Parables Jesus Told* (Downers Grove, Ill.: InterVarsity, 1981), 7–8.

Table 30
Five Topics Addressed in Jesus' Parables

God's Reign*	Matthew 9:16, 17; 13:24–30, 31–32, 33, 44, 45–46, 47–50, 52
God's Character	
Sovereignty	Matthew 20:1–16
Compassion	Matthew 21:28–32; 22:1–14; Luke 14:15–24; 15:3–7, 8–10, 11–32; 18:1–8, 9–14
Forgiveness	Luke 7:41–43
Sacrifice	Matthew 13:44, 45
God's Disciples	
Reception of the Word	Matthew 13:5–8; Luke 18:9–14
Obedience	Matthew 7:24–27
Forgiveness	Matthew 18:23–35
Diligence	Matthew 25:14–30
Compassion	Luke 10:25–37
Prayerfulness	Luke 11:5–8; 18:1–8
Service	Luke 14:28–33; 17:7–10; 19:11–27
Watchfulness	Matthew 24:45–51; 25:1–13; Mark 13:34–37
God's Enemies	
Rejection of the Word	Matthew 13:5–8; 21:33–46; Luke 7:31–35
Materialism and greed	Luke 12:16–21; 16:1–9
Pride	Luke 18:9–14
God's Judgment	Matthew 13:24–30, 47–50; 21:33–46; Mark 4:26–29; Luke 13:6–9

*For information on how all the parables refer in some way to the kingdom of God, see Zuck, *Basic Bible Interpretation,* 204, 208–11.

(20:1–16), the talents (25:14–30), the two debtors (Luke 7:41–43), the good Samaritan (10:25–37), the rich fool (12:16–21), the shrewd manager (16:1–9), the Pharisee and the tax collector (18:9–14), and the minas (19:11–27).[34]

34. For other groupings of parables see Zuck, *Basic Bible Interpretation,* 205–8. Also see Claus Westerman, *The Parables of Jesus in the Light of the Old Testament,* trans. and ed. Friedemann W. Golka and Alastair H. B. Logan (Philadelphia: Fortress, 1990), 184–201.

How Did Jesus Use Parables to Encourage Thinking?

The thirteen colorful features of Jesus' parables, discussed on the preceding pages, certainly challenged his hearers to think. In addition two other aspects of his stories summoned his audiences to consider the import of his words. One was the way he introduced his stories, and the other was the way he concluded them.

Several times Jesus broached his parabolic discourses with questions, prodding his listeners to anticipate and consider his stories.

"To what can I compare this generation?" (Matt. 11:16; cf. Luke 7:31)
"What shall we say the kingdom of God is like, or what parable shall we use to describe it?" (Mark 4:30; cf. Luke 13:18)
"Again he asked, 'What shall I compare the kingdom of God to?'" (Luke 13:20)
"What do you think?" (Matt. 21:28)
"Who then is the faithful and wise manager?" (Luke 12:42)
"Who then is the faithful and wise servant . . . ?" (Matt. 24:45)

Other times Jesus introduced a parable with a statement and then asked a rhetorical question to prompt listeners to think further before he gave the parable itself.

Statement: "So you also must be ready" (Matt. 24:44). Question: "Who then is the faithful and wise servant?" (v. 45). Parable: The two servants (vv. 45–51).
Statement: "Suppose one of you wants to build a tower" (Luke 14:28a). Question: "Will he not first sit down and estimate the cost . . . ?" (v. 28b). Parable: The unfinished tower (vv. 28–30).
Statement: "Or suppose a king is about to go to war" (Luke 14:31). Question: "Will he not first . . . consider whether he is able . . . ?" (v. 31b). Parable: The king at war (vv. 31–32).
Statement: "Suppose one of you has a hundred sheep and loses one of them" (Luke 15:4a). Question: "Does he not leave the ninety-nine . . . and go after the lost sheep . . . ?" (v. 4b). Parable: The lost sheep (vv. 4–7).
Statement: "Or suppose a woman has ten silver coins and loses one" (Luke 15:8a). Question: "Does she not . . . search carefully until she finds it?" (v. 8b). Parable: The lost coin (vv. 8–9).
Statement: "Suppose one of you had a servant plowing or looking after the sheep" (Luke 17:7a). Question: "Would he say to the servant . . . 'Come along now and sit down to eat?' Would he not

rather say, 'Prepare my supper . . . '? Would he thank the servant
. . . ?" (vv. 7b–9). Parable: The servant's reward (vv. 7–10).

So the conclusions of Jesus' parables often confirmed his points either by questions or statements, though other times he implied the application, leaving it up to his hearers to surmise his teaching.

In at least fourteen parables, Jesus spelled out the application. At the
end of the parable of the good Samaritan, Jesus asked the experts in the
law, "Which of these three do you think was a neighbor to the man who
fell into the hands of robbers?" (Luke 10:36), thereby forcing the legal
expert to respond to his own question about his neighbor (v. 29). The
story of the persistent friend at midnight is applied (Luke 11:5–8) by the
admonition, "Ask and it will be given you; seek and you will find; knock
and the door will be opened to you" (v. 9), which is followed by several
more verses on the Lord's response to prayer (vv. 10–13).

Following the parable of the rich man, who felt his wealth guaran-
teed a life of ease, Jesus said, "This is how it will be with anyone who
stores up things for himself but is not rich toward God" (Luke 12:21).
Jesus' point was that spiritual wealth exceeds material wealth in value.
Jesus spoke of the unfinished tower and the king at war and then spoke
of the need for would-be disciples to count the cost: "In the same way,
any of you who does not give up everything he has cannot be my disciple" (Luke 14:33). When Jesus gave the parable of the unforgiving servant, he concluded, "This is how my heavenly Father will treat each of
you unless you forgive your brother from your heart" (Matt. 18:35).
After presenting the parable of the vineyard workers who worked various lengths of time but were paid the same (Matt. 20:1–15), Jesus summarized his earlier statements about reward for serving him (19:29–30)
by the brief assertion, "So the last will be first, and the first will be last"
(20:16). The disciples were left to consider how this related to them.

Jesus applied the parable of the shrewd manager by stating, "No servant can serve two masters" (Luke 16:13). Speaking of the servant's reward, the Lord said, "So you also, when you have done everything you
were told to do, should say, 'We are unworthy servants; we have only
done our duty'" (Luke 17:10). The parable of the Pharisee and the tax collector was applied by the principle, "For everyone who exalts himself will
be humbled, and he who humbles himself will be exalted" (Luke 18:14).

Jesus related the parable of the wicked vinegrowers to his opponents
by quoting Psalm 118:22–23 and then stating that the kingdom of God
would be taken away from them (Matt. 21:42–43). Speaking of a king
inviting people who refused to go his son's wedding banquet, Jesus applied the story to the subject of spiritual receptivity: "For many are invited, but few are chosen" (22:14). The purpose of the parable of the ten

virgins was stated in his exhortation, "Therefore keep watch, because you do not know the day or the hour" (25:13). Matthew 25:29, "For everyone who has will be given more. . . . Whoever does not have, even what he has will be taken from him" concluded Jesus' parable of the talents (in 25:14–28). But this cryptic statement no doubt left the disciples pondering its spiritual implications. After telling Simon the Pharisee about two debtors, Jesus constrained Simon to apply the parable to himself by asking, "Now which of them will love him more?" (Luke 7:42). He did a similar thing with the chief priests and elders in telling them the parable of the two sons. He asked, "Which of the two did what his father wanted?" (Matt. 21:31). Having to admit that the son who changed his mind and worked in the vineyard pleased his father, they left themselves open for his arrow of application: Tax collectors and prostitutes, like the first son, would enter the kingdom of God, but that the religious leaders would not. Without stating it explicitly, he was showing them the need for repentance.

These parables that concluded with applications prove that entertaining his audiences was not Jesus' purpose in storytelling. Each parable had a point, explicit or implicit, calling for decisions, appealing for action, inviting spiritual change. To make a judgment about him, to repent or to forgive, to be warned or comforted, to renounce pride or greed, to persist in prayer and obedience, to be compassionate and watchful, to acknowledge God's sovereignty and plans—these are some of the Lord's parabolic purposes.

Sometimes the master Storyteller stated an exhortation or truth-principle first, following it up with a parable. For example, after encouraging his disciples to "keep watch" because they did not know when the Lord will return (Matt. 24:42), he cited the parable of the two servants (24:45–51). Similarly, after the command, "Be on guard! Be alert! You do not know when that time will come" (Mark 13:33), the Lord related the parable of the doorkeeper (13:34–37).

Parables without a spelled-out application include the barren fig tree (Luke 13:6–9). The farmer's plan to cut it down, followed by his agreeing to wait a year, illustrates Jesus' call to his hearers to repent (vv. 2–5). While Jesus did not spell out the application of the parable of the talents (Matt 25:14–30), the lesson inheres in the story itself: be faithful in serving the Lord Jesus while he is away.

What Situations Prompted Jesus to Tell His Stories?

Jesus did not tell stories simply to awaken a drowsy audience or to amuse himself. He fitted them to various situations as they arose.

He recounted some parables *in answer to questions.*

John the Baptist's disciples asked why Jesus' disciples did not fast (Matt. 9:14). In answer the Lord told the two brief parables of the new cloth (v. 16) and the new wineskins.

When Peter asked how many times he should forgive someone who wronged him (Matt. 18:21), Jesus told the parable of the unmerciful servant (vv. 22–35) to show the need for a magnanimous heart of forgiveness.

The parable of the two sons, one who obeyed his father and one who did not (Matt. 21:28–32), followed the question the chief priests and elders raised about the source of Jesus' authority (v. 23). Refusing to answer that question by putting them on the horns of a dilemma with a question of his own, Jesus turned the tables on them by denouncing, by means of the parable, their refusal to repent.

The rich young man's questions, "Teacher, what must I do to get eternal life?" (Luke 10:25) and "Who is my neighbor?" (v. 29), led the Lord to narrate the fascinating story of the kind Samaritan (vv. 30–35).

He delivered parables *in answer to requests.*

One of the disciples asked Jesus to teach them to pray (Luke 11:1). After presenting a model prayer (vv. 2–4), he cited the brief but graphic parable of the friend at midnight (vv. 5–8).

When an anonymous person in a crowd asked the Teacher to order his brother to divide the inheritance with him (Luke 12:13), Jesus, sensing the man's anxiety about material things, told the story of the rich fool (vv. 16–21). Such an alarming situation—the rich man's life being taken the very night he gloated in his wealth—would have jolted the inquirer to consider refocusing his priorities.

Jesus voiced some parables *in response to complaints.*

While Jesus was eating dinner with Simon, a Pharisee, a sinful woman poured perfume on his feet in demonstration of her repentant heart (Luke 7:36–39). Simon complained to himself that if Jesus was really a prophet he would know this woman was a sinner (v. 39) and would deport her. Knowing the man's thoughts, the Lord related the parable of the two debtors to teach that she would love the Lord deeply because her many sins would be forgiven (vv. 40–50).

A few times Jesus told parables not in response to a question, a request, or a complaint voiced by someone, but *to illustrate his own stated purpose.*

To show his disciples "that they should always pray and not give up" (Luke 18:1), he told of the unjust judge (vv. 2–8).

The parable of the Pharisee and the tax collector praying in the temple (Luke 18:10–14) chided "those who were confident of their own righteousness and looked down on everybody else" (v. 9).

To correct the crowds' view "that the kingdom of God was going to appear at once" (Luke 19:11), Jesus sketched the parable of the minas (vv. 12–27). This parable also was aimed at his enemies who did not want him to be king, evidenced by the content of the story which included a nobleman going away to be appointed king and his subjects hating him and not wanting him to be king (vv. 12–14), but who were killed because of their defiance (v. 27).

A few parables were told *to apply truth to situations that arose.*

Concluding his Sermon on the Mount, Jesus urged people to put his words into practice by referring to a man building a house on a rock and another on sand (Matt. 7:24–26).

The parable about the rude children (Luke 7: 31–35) followed the situation in which the religious authorities were rejecting Jesus' words (vv. 29–30), and the parable drew a comparison between those authorities and children acting rudely toward others.

The seven parables of the secrets of the kingdom of heaven (Matt. 13) were told because of the nation's rejection of the King and his kingdom.

The parable of the great banquet (Luke 14:16–24) was to correct a statement by a Pharisee, "Blessed is the man who will eat at the feast in the kingdom of God" (v. 15).

Storytelling Today

Because Jesus' short stories were so superbly effective in communicating and applying truths, he used them often, and with a variety of individuals and groups.[35] Teachers today should follow his example, for both children and adults enjoy stories and can learn from them. Here are some tips on how to tell stories, based on ways Jesus told them.

1. Tell stories your students can understand.
2. Arouse interest quickly at the beginning of the story.
3. Keep them short. Stories need not be long to be effective.
4. Include suspense, surprise, end stress, conversation, resolution, and characterization in your stories.
5. Include a question, exhortation, or statement as a means of challenging the students to think and to apply the story.

35. For an interesting study, look up each of the parables (see table 27) and write down to whom Jesus addressed the stories and how the individuals or groups responded. For five suggestions on how to interpret parables, see my *Basic Bible Interpretation*, 211–12.

6. Give attention to gestures, visuals, and voice variation in your stories. Sometimes, with stories for children, use puppets, pictures, or flannelgraph figures. Or have the children act out a story.

Go for It!

Analyze your teaching. How often do you use stories? Have they been effective? Why or why not? How can you enhance your teaching by more stories?

Review the characteristics that made Jesus' stories effective. Do your stories include those elements?

Review the situations that prompted Jesus to tell stories. Can you tell stories in similar situations—in answer to questions, requests, or complaints, to illustrate certain truths, to apply truth to situations that arise?

In preparing to tell a story, practice it aloud, including the six ideas suggested under the section "Storytelling Today."

*"Therefore everyone
who hears these words of mine
and puts them into practice
is like a wise man
who built his house on the rock."*

Matthew 7:24

Epilogue

Can you teach as Jesus taught?
Yes! If you . . .

Recognize the high privilege of teaching others the truths of God, encouraging them to love the Lord and grow in him.
Study the Scriptures, to know them thoroughly.
Seek to cultivate the qualities that contribute to successful teaching.
Communicate the Word with clarity, excitement, and commitment.
Model God's truth consistently.
Develop personal interest in your students and communicate that loving concern to them.
Encourage your students to think.
Relate your teaching to students' needs.
Engage your students in a variety of learning methods, and utilize various audio and visual aids.
Seek to add colorful expressions to your teaching.
Ask your students a variety of questions.
Tell captivating stories that illustrate your teaching.

We can never teach *exactly* as Jesus Christ taught, for he is God. But we can prayerfully seek to follow his example as the greatest Communicator-Educator-Teacher the world has ever known.

In this way we can be *teaching as Jesus taught!*

Appendix

Jesus' 481 Commands

Matthew (162 commands)

"Away from me, Satan!" (4:10)

"Come, follow me" (4:19)

"Rejoice and be glad, because great is your reward in heaven" (5:12)

"Let your light shine before men, that they may see your good deeds and praise your Father in heaven" (5:16)

"Leave your gift there in front of the altar. First go and be reconciled to your brother; then come and offer your gift" (5:24)

"Settle matters quickly with your adversary who is taking you to court. Do it while you are with him on the way" (5:25)

"If your right eye causes you to sin, gouge it out and throw it away" (5:29)

"And if your right hand causes you to sin, cut if off and throw it away" (5:30)

"Do not swear at all" (5:34)

"And do not swear by your head" (5:36)

"Simply let your 'Yes' be 'Yes' and your 'No,' 'No'" (5:37)

"Do not resist an evil person" (5:39a)

"If someone strikes you on the right cheek, turn to him the other also" (5:39b)

"And if someone wants to sue you and take your tunic, let him have your cloak as well" (5:40)

"If someone forces you to go one mile, go with him two miles" (5:41)

"Give to the one who asks you, and do not turn away from the one who wants to borrow from you" (5:42)

"Love your enemies and pray for those who persecute you" (5:44)

"Be perfect, therefore, as your heavenly Father is perfect" (5:48)

"Be careful not to do your 'acts of righteousness' before men, to be seen by them" (6:1)

"So when you give to the needy, do not announce it with trumpets, as the hypocrites do in the synagogues and on the streets, to be honored by men" (6:2)

"But when you give to the needy, do not let your left hand know what your right hand is doing, so that your giving may be in secret" (6:3–4a)

"But when you pray, do not be like the hypocrites" (6:5)

"But when you pray, go into your room, close the door and pray to your Father, who is unseen" (6:6)

"And when you pray, do not keep on babbling like pagans" (6:7)

"Do not be like them, for your Father knows what you need before you ask him" (6:8)

"When you fast, do not look somber as the hypocrites do, for they disfigure their faces to show men they are fasting" (6:16)

"But when you fast, put oil on your head and wash your face" (6:17)

"Do not store up for yourselves treasures on earth, where moth and rust destroy, and where thieves break in and steal" (6:19)

"But store up for yourselves treasures in heaven, where moth and rust do not destroy, and where thieves do not break in and steal" (6:20)

"Therefore I tell you, do not worry about your life" (6:25)

"Look at the birds of the air; they do not sow or reap or store away in barns, and yet your heavenly Father feeds them" (6:26)

"See how the lilies of the field grow" (6:28)

"So do not worry, saying, 'What shall we eat?' or 'What shall we drink?' or 'What shall we wear?'" (6:31)

"But seek first his kingdom and his righteousness" (6:33)

"Therefore do not worry about tomorrow" (6:34)

"Do not judge, or you too will be judged" (7:1)

"You hypocrite, first take the plank out of your own eye" (7:5)

"Do not give dogs what is sacred" (7:6)

"Do not throw your pearls to pigs" (7:6)

"Ask and it will be given to you" (7:7)

"Seek and you will find" (7:7)

"Knock and the door will be opened to you" (7:7)

"In everything, do to others what you would have them do to you, for this sums up the Law and the Prophets" (7:12)

"Enter through the narrow gate" (7:13)

"Watch out for false prophets" (7:15)

"Be clean!" (8:3)

"See that you don't tell anyone" (8:4)

"But go, show yourself to the priest and offer the gift Moses commanded, as a testimony to them" (8:4)

"Go! It will be done just as you believed it would" (8:13)

"Follow me, and let the dead bury their own dead" (8:22)

"Go!" (8:32)

"Take heart, son; your sins are forgiven" (9:2)

"Get up, take your mat and go home" (9:6)

"Follow me" (9:9)

"Go and learn what this means" (9:13)

"Take heart," daughter, he said, "your faith has healed you"" (9:22)

"Go away. The girl is not dead but asleep" (9:24)

"See that no one knows about this" (9:30)

"Do not go among the Gentiles or enter any town of the Samaritans" (10:5)

"Go rather to the lost sheep of Israel" (10:6)

"As you go, preach this message: 'The kingdom of heaven is near'" (10:7)

"Heal the sick, raise the dead, cleanse those who have leprosy, drive out demons" (10:8)

"Do not take along any gold or silver or copper in your belts; take no bag for the journey, or extra tunic, or sandals or a staff" (10:10)

"Whatever town or village you enter, search for some worthy person there and stay at his house until you leave" (10:11)

"As you enter the home, give it your greeting" (10:12)

"If the home is deserving, let your peace rest on it; if it is not, let your peace return to you" (10:13)

"If anyone will not welcome you or listen to your words, shake the dust off your feet when you leave that home or town" (10:14)

"Therefore be as shrewd as snakes and as innocent as doves" (10:16)

"But when they arrest you, do not worry about what to say or how to say it" (10:19)

"When you are persecuted in one place, flee to another" (10:23)

"So do not be afraid of them" (10:26)

"What I tell you in the dark, speak in the daylight" (10:27)

"What is whispered in your ear, proclaim from the roofs" (10:27)

"Do not be afraid of those who kill the body but cannot kill the soul. Rather, be afraid of the One who can destroy both body and soul in hell" (10:28)

"Do not suppose that I have come to bring peace to the earth" (10:34)

"Go back and report to John what you hear and see" (11:4)

"He who has ears, let him hear" (11:15)

"Come to me, all you who are weary and burdened, and I will give you rest" (11:28)

"Take my yoke upon you and learn from me" (11:29)

"Listen then to what the parable of the sower means" (13:18)

"You give them something to eat" (14:15)

"Bring them here to me" (14:18)

"Take courage! It is I. Don't be afraid" (14:27)

"Come" (14:29)

"Listen and understand" (15:10)

"Be on your guard against the yeast of the Pharisees and Sadducees" (16:6, 11b)

"Get behind me, Satan" (16:23)

"Get up," he said. "Don't be afraid"" (17:7)

"Don't tell anyone what you have seen" (17:9)

"Bring the boy here to me" (17:17)

"If your brother sins against you, go and show him his fault, just between the two of you" (18:15)

"Let the little children come to me, and do not hinder them, for the kingdom of heaven belongs to such as these" (19:14)

"Go sell your possessions and give to the poor. . . . Then come, follow me" (19:21)

"Go to the village ahead of you" (21:2)

"Untie them [a donkey and her colt] and bring them to me " (21:2)

"Listen to another parable" (21:33)

"Show me the coin used for paying the tax" (22:19)

"Give to Caesar what is Caesar's, and to God what is God's" (22:21)

"Love the Lord your God with all your heart and with all your soul and with all your mind" (22:37)

"So you must obey them [the teachers of the law and the Pharisees] and do everything they tell you. But do not do what they do, for they do not practice what they preach" (23:3)

"And do not call anyone on earth 'father,' for you have one Father, and he is in heaven" (23:9)

"Watch out that no one deceives you" (24:4)

"Pray that your flight will not take place in winter or on the Sabbath" (24:20)

"So if anyone tells you, 'There he is, out in the desert', do not go out; or 'Here he is, in the inner room,' do not believe it" (24:26)

"Now learn this lesson from the fig tree" (24:32)

"Therefore keep watch" (24:42)

"But understand this" (24:43)

"Therefore keep watch because you do not know the day or the hour" (25:13)

"Go into the city to a certain man" (26:18)

"Take and eat, this is my body" (26:26)

"Sit here while I go over there and pray" (26:36)

"Stay here and keep watch with me" (26:38)

"Watch and pray so that you will not fall into temptation" (26:41)

"Rise, let us go!" (26:46)

"Friend, do what you came for" (26:50)

"Put your sword back in its place" (26:52)

"Do not be afraid" (28:10)

"Go and tell my brothers to go to Galilee" (28:10)

"Therefore go and make disciples of all nations, baptizing them in the name of the Father and of the Son and of the Holy Spirit, and teaching them to obey everything I have commanded you" (28:19–20)

Mark (93 commands)

"Repent and believe the good news" (1:15)

"Come, follow me" (1:17)

"Be quiet! . . . Come out of him" (1:25)

"Be clean!" (1:41)

"See that you don't tell this to anyone. But go, show yourself to the priest and offer the sacrifices that Moses commanded for your cleansing" (1:44)

"I tell you, get up, take your mat and go home" (2:11)

"Follow me" (2:14)

"Stand up in front of everyone" (3:3)

"Listen! A farmer went out to sow his seed" (4:3)

"If anyone has ears to hear, let him hear" (4:23)

"Consider carefully what you hear" (4:24)

"He . . . said to the waves, 'Quiet! Be still!'" (4:39)

"Come out of this man, you evil spirit" (5:8)

"Go home to your family and tell them how much the Lord has done for you" (5:19)

"Go in peace and be freed from your suffering" (5:34)

"Don't be afraid; just believe" (5:36)

"Little girl, I say to you, get up!" (5:41)

"Take nothing for the journey except a staff" (6:8)

"Wear sandals but not an extra tunic" (6:9)

"Shake the dust off your feet when you leave" (6:11)

"Come with me by yourselves to a quiet place and get some rest" (6:31)

"You give them something to eat" (6:37)

"How many loaves do you have? . . . Go and see" (6:38)

"Take courage! It is I. Don't be afraid" (6:50)

"Listen to me, everyone, and understand this" (7:14)

"Be opened!" (7:34)

"Be careful. . . . Watch out for the yeast of the Pharisees and that of Herod" (8:15)

"Don't go into the village" (8:26)

"Get behind me, Satan!" (8:33)

"You deaf and dumb spirit. . . . I command you, come out of him and never enter him again" (9:25)

"Have salt in yourselves, and be at peace with each other" (9:50)

"Let the little children come to me, and do not hinder them" (10:14)

"Go, sell everything you have and give to the poor. . . . Then come, follow me" (10:21)

"Go . . . your faith has healed you" (10:52)

"Go to the village ahead of you . . . untie [a colt] and bring it here" (11:2)

"Have faith in God" (11:22)

"Whatever you ask for in prayer, believe that you have received it" (11:24)

"And when you stand praying, if you hold anything against anyone, forgive him" (11:25)

"John's baptism—was it from heaven, or from men? Tell me!" (11:30)

"Bring me a denarius and let me look at it" (12:15)

"Give to Caesar what is Caesar's and to God what is God's" (12:17)

"Watch out that no one deceives you" (13:5)

"Do not be alarmed" (13:7)

"You must be on your guard" (13:9)

"Do not worry beforehand what to say. Just say whatever is given you at the time" (13:11)

"Pray that this will not take place in winter" (13:18)

"At that time if anyone says to you, 'Look, here is the Christ!' or 'Look, there he is!' do not believe it" (13:21)

"So be on your guard" (13:23)

"Now learn this lesson from the fig tree" (13:28)

"Be on guard! Be alert!" (13:33)

"Therefore keep watch" (13:35)

"Do not let him find you sleeping" (13:36)

"I say to everyone, 'Watch!'" (13:37)

"Leave her alone" (14:6)

"Go into the city, and a man carrying a jar of water will meet you. Follow him" (14:13)

"Say to the owner of the house he enters . . ." (14:14)

"Make preparations for us there" (14:15)

"Take it; this is my body" (14:22)

"Stay here and keep watch" (14:34)

"Watch and pray so that you will not fall into temptation" (14:38)

"Rise! Let us go!" (14:42)

Luke (159 commands)

"Be quiet! . . . Come out of him!" (4:35)

"Put out into deep water, and let down the nets for a catch" (5:4)

"Don't be afraid" (5:10)

"Be clean!" (5:13)

"Don't tell anyone, but go, show yourself to the priest and offer the sacrifices that Moses commanded for your cleansing" (5:14)

"Get up, take your mat and go home" (5:24)

"Follow me" (5:27)

"Get up and stand in front of everyone" (6:8)

"Stretch out your hand" (6:10)

"Rejoice in that day and leap for joy, because great is your reward in heaven" (6:23)

"Love your enemies, do good to those who hate you" (6:27)

"Bless those who curse you, pray for those who mistreat you" (6:28)

"If someone strikes you on one cheek, turn to him the other also" (6:29)

"If someone takes your cloak, do not stop him from taking your tunic" (6:29)

"Give to everyone who asks you, and if anyone takes what belongs to you, do not demand it back" (6:30)

"Do to others as you would have them do to you" (6:31)

"Love your enemies, do good to them, and lend to them without expecting to get anything back" (6:35)

"Be merciful, just as your Father is merciful" (6:36)

"Do not judge, and you will not be judged. Forgive, and you will be forgiven" (6:37)

"Give, and it will be given you" (6:38)

"First take the plank out of your eye" (6:42)

"Don't cry" (7:13)

"Young man, I say to you, get up!" (7:14)

"Go back and report to John what you have seen and heard" (7:22)

"Your faith has saved you; go in peace" (7:50)

"He who has ears to hear, let him hear" (8:8)

"Therefore consider carefully how you listen" (8:18)

"Return home and tell how much God has done for you" (8:39)

"Daughter, your faith has healed you. Go in peace" (8:48)

"Don't be afraid" (8:50)

"Stop wailing. . . . She is not dead but asleep" (8:52)

"My child, get up!" (8:54)

"Take nothing for the journey" (9:3)

"Whatever house you enter, stay there until you leave that town" (9:4)

"If people do not welcome you, shake the dust off your feet when you leave their town" (9:5)

"You give them something to eat" (9:13)

"Have them sit down in groups of about fifty each" (9:14)

"Listen carefully to what I am about to tell you: The Son of Man is going to be betrayed into the hands of men" (9:44)

"Do not stop him . . . for whoever is not against you is for you" (9:50)

"Ask the Lord of the harvest, therefore, to send out workers into his harvest field" (10:2)

"Go! I am sending you out like lambs among wolves" (10:3)

"Do not take a purse or bag or sandals; and do not greet anyone on the road" (10:4)

"When you enter a house, first say, 'Peace to this house'" (10:7)

"Stay in that house . . . do not move around from house to house" (10:7)

"Eat what is set before you" (10:8)

"Heal the sick who are there and tell them, 'The kingdom of God is near you'" (10:9)

"Go into its streets and say, 'Even the dust . . . we wipe off against you'" (10:10–11)

"Do not rejoice that the spirits submit to you, but rejoice that your names are written in heaven" (10:20)

"Do this and you will live" (10:28)

"Go and do likewise" (10:37)

"Ask and it will be given you; seek and you will find; knock and the door will be opened to you" (11:9)

"See to it, then, that the light within you is not darkness" (11:35)

"Give what is inside the dish to the poor" (11:41)

"Be on your guard against the yeast of the Pharisees, which is hypocrisy" (12:1)

"Do not be afraid of those who kill the body" (12:4)

"Fear him who, after the killing of the body, has power to throw you into hell. Yes, I tell you, fear him" (12:5)

"Don't be afraid; you are worth more than many sparrows" (12:7)

"Do not worry about how you will defend yourselves or what you will say" (12:11)

"Watch out! Be on your guard against all kinds of greed" (12:15)

"Do not worry about your life" (12:22)

"Consider the ravens" (12:24)

"Consider how the lilies grow" (12:27)

"And do not set your heart on what you will eat or drink; do not worry about it" (12:29)

"But seek his kingdom" (12:31)

"Do not be afraid, little flock" (12:32)

"Sell your possessions and give to the poor" (12:33)

"Provide purses for yourselves that will not wear out" (12:33)

"Be dressed ready for service and keep your lamps burning" (12:35)

"As you are going with your adversary to the magistrate, try hard to be reconciled to him on the way" (12:58)

"Make every effort to enter through the narrow door" (13:24)

"Go tell that fox, 'I will drive out demons and heal people today and tomorrow'" (13:32)

"When someone invites you to a wedding feast, do not take the place of honor" (14:8)

"But when you are invited, take the lowest place" (14:10)

"When you give a luncheon or dinner, do not invite your friends . . . invite the poor, the crippled, the lame, the blind" (14:12–13)

"Use worldly wealth to gain friends for yourselves" (16:9)

"So watch yourselves. If your brother sins, rebuke him, and if he repents, forgive him. If he sins against you seven times a day, and seven times comes back to you and says, 'I repent,' forgive him" (17:3–4)

"So you . . . should say, 'We are unworthy servants; we have only done our duty'" (17:10)

"Go, show yourselves to the priests" (17:14)

"Rise and go; your faith has made you well" (17:19)

"Listen to what the unjust judge says" (18:6)

"Let the little children come to me, and do not hinder them" (18:16)

"Sell everything you have and give it to the poor. . . . Then come, follow me" (18:22)

"Receive your sight; your faith has healed you" (18:42)

"Zacchaeus, come down immediately" (19:5)

"Go to the village ahead of you. . . . Untie it [a colt] and bring it here. If anyone asks you, 'Why are you untying it?' tell him, 'The Lord needs it'" (19:30–31)

"Tell me, John's baptism—was it from heaven, or from men?" (20:3)

"Show me a denarius" (20:24)

"Then give to Caesar what is Caesar's, and to God what is God's" (20:25)

"Beware of the teachers of the law" (20:46)

"Watch out that you are not deceived" (21:8)

"Do not follow them" (21:8)

"When you hear of wars and revolutions, do not be frightened" (21:9)

"But make up your mind not to worry beforehand how you will defend yourselves" (21:14)

"Stand up and lift up your heads" (21:28)

"Be careful, or your hearts will be weighed down with dissipation, drunkenness and the anxieties of life" (21:34)

"Be always on the watch, and pray that you may be able to escape all that is about to happen" (21:36)

"Go and make preparation for us to eat the Passover" (22:8)

"Follow him to the house that he enters, and say to the owner of the house, 'The Teacher asks: Where is the guest room . . . ?'" (22:10–11)

"Make preparations there" (22:12)

"Take this and divide it among you" (22:17)

"Do this in remembrance of me" (22:19)

"Strengthen your brothers" (22:32)

"But now if you have a purse, take it, and also a bag; and if you don't have a sword, sell your cloak and buy one" (22:36)

"Get up and pray so that you will not fall into temptation" (22:46)

"No more of this!" (22:51)

"Daughters of Jerusalem, do not weep for me; weep for yourselves and for your children" (23:28)

"Look at my hands and my feet. It is I myself! Touch me and see" (24:39)

John (67 commands)

"Come . . . and you will see" (1:39)

"Finding Philip, he said to him, 'Follow me'" (1:43)

"Fill the jars with water" (2:7)

"Now draw some out and take it to the master of the banquet" (2:8)

"To those who sold doves he said, 'Get these out of here!'" (2:16)

"Destroy this temple, and I will raise it again in three days" (2:19)

"Go, call your husband and come back" (4:16)

"Get up! Pick up your mat and walk" (5:8)

"Stop sinning or something worse may happen to you" (5:14)

"Do not be amazed at this" (5:28)

"Have the people sit down" (6:10)

"Gather the pieces that are left over. Let nothing be wasted" (6:12)

"It is I; don't be afraid" (6:20)

"Do not work for food that spoils, but for food that endures to eternal life" (6:27)

"Stop grumbling among yourselves" (6:43)

"You go to the Feast. I am not yet going up to this Feast" (7:8)

"Go now and leave your life of sin" (8:11)

"Go . . . wash in the pool of Siloam" (9:7)

"Do not believe me unless I do what my Father does" (10:37)

"Believe the miracles, that you may know and understand that the Father is in me, and I in the Father" (10:38)

"Take away the stone" (11:39)

"Lazarus, come out!" (11:43)

"Take off the grave clothes and let him go" (11:44)

"Leave her alone. . . . It was meant that she should save this perfume for the day of my burial" (12:7)

"Walk while you have the light, before darkness overtakes you" (12:35)

"Put your trust in the light while you have it" (12:36)

"What you are about to do, do quickly" (13:27)

"Love one another" (13:34)

"Do not let your hearts be troubled. Trust in God; trust also in me" (14:1)

"Do not let your hearts be troubled and do not be afraid" (14:27)

"Ask whatever you wish, and it will be given you" (15:7)

"Now remain in my love" (15:9)

"Love each other as I have loved you" (15:12)

"If the world hates you, keep in mind that it hated me first" (15:18)

"Ask and you will receive, and your joy will be complete" (16:24)

"If you are looking for me, then let these men go" (18:8)

"Put your sword away!" (18:11)

"Why question me? Ask those who heard me" (18:21)

"Do not hold on to me, for I have not yet returned to the Father. Go instead to my brothers and tell them, 'I am returning to my Father and your Father, to my God and your God'" (20:17)

"Receive the Holy Spirit" (20:22)

"Put your finger here; see my hands. Reach out your hand and put it into my side. Stop doubting and believe" (20:27)

"Throw your net on the right side of the boat" (21:6)

"Bring some of the fish you have just caught" (21:10)

"Come and have breakfast" (21:12)

"Feed my lambs" (21:15)

"Take care of my sheep" (21:16)

"Feed my sheep" (21:17)

"Follow me!" (21:19)

Subject Index

Scripture Index